HARPER'S NEW TESTAMENT COMMENTARIES

GENERAL EDITOR: HENRY CHADWICK, D.D.

THE ACTS OF THE APOSTLES

A COMMENTARY ON

THE ACTS OF THE APOSTLES

C. S. C. WILLIAMS

HENDRICKSON
PUBLISHERS
PEABODY, MASSACHUSETTS 01961-3473

A COMMENTARY ON THE ACTS OF THE APOSTLES

Copyright © 1964 by A. & C. Black Ltd.

Hendrickson Publishers, Inc. edition

ISBN: 0-913573-56-6

reprinted by arrangement with
A. & C. Black (Publishers) Limited

First printing — February, 1988

Printed in the United States of America

CONTENTS

BIBLIOGRAPHY AND ABBREVIATIONS

(A) General

A.J.T., *American Journal of Theology.*

B.A., *Biblical Archaeologist.*

B.A.H., H. J. Cadbury, *The Book of Acts in History*, 1955.

B.A.S.O.R., *Bulletin of the American Society of Oriental Research.*

B.C., *The Beginnings of Christianity*; see below under Commentaries.

B.D.B., F. Brown, S. R. Driver, and C. A. Briggs, *Hebrew and English Lexicon of the Old Testament.*

B.J.R.L., *Bulletin of the John Rylands Library.*

B. of B.C., *Bulletin of the Bezan Club.*

B. S. Easton, *Purpose; The Purpose of Acts*, 1936.

C.D.A., C. C. Torrey, *The Composition and Date of Acts*, H.T.S. i, 1916.

C.I.G., *Corpus Inscriptionum Graecarum.*

C.I.L., *Corpus Inscriptionum Latinarum.*

C.Q.R., *Church Quarterly Review.*

Credibility, F. H. Chase, *The Credibility of the Acts of the Apostles*, 1902.

Coniect. Neot., *Coniectanea Neotestamentica.*

D.A.C., Hastings' *Dictionary of the Apostolic Church.*

D.A.S.G., A. Harnack, *Date of Acts and the Synoptic Gospels*, tr. J. R. Wilkinson, 1911.

Dibelius, *Studies; Studies in the Acts of the Apostles*, tr. M. Ling, 1956, from *Aufsätze zur Apostelgeschichte*, 1951.

D.P.C., C. C. Torrey, *Documents of the Primitive Church*, n.d.

D.T.C., *Dictionnaire de Théologie Catholique.*

Dupont, *Problèmes; Les Problèmes du livre des Actes d'après les travaux récents, Analecta Lovanensia Biblica et Orientalia*, II, 17, 1950.

E.R.E., *Encyclopaedia of Religion and Ethics*, ed. J. Hastings.

E.T., *Expository Times.*

E.T.L., *Ephemerides Theologicae Lovanienses.*

Exp., *Expositor.*

Goodspeed, *N.S.N.T.P.*; E. J. Goodspeed, *New Solutions to New Testament Problems*, 1927.

H.A.H.L., G. A. Smith, *Historical Atlas of the Holy Land.*

H.D.B., Hastings' *Dictionary of the Bible.*

H.T.R., *Harvard Theological Review.*

BIBLIOGRAPHY AND ABBREVIATIONS

H.T.S., *Harvard Theological Studies*.

I. (L. or S.) N.T., *Introduction to the (Literature or Study of the) New Testament*.

J.B.L., *Journal of Biblical Literature*.

J.E.H., *Journal of Ecclesiastical History*.

J.R., *Journal of Religion*.

J.R.S., *Journal of Roman Studies*.

J.T.S., *Journal of Theological Studies*.

Knox, *Acts*; W. L. Knox, *The Acts of the Apostles*, 1948.

— *Gentiles*, W. L. Knox, *St. Paul and the Church of the Gentiles*, 1939.

— *Jerusalem*; W. L. Knox, *St. Paul and the Church of Jerusalem*, 1925.

— *S.H.E.P.C.*; W. L. Knox, *Some Hellenistic Elements in Primitive Christianity*, 1942.

L.A.E., A. Deissmann, *Light from the Ancient East*, 1927.

Mél. Goguel, *Aux sources de la tradition chrétienne, Mélanges offerts à M. Maurice Goguel*, 1950.

M.M., *V.G.T.*, Moulton and Milligan, *Vocabulary of the Greek Testament*.

Ramsay, *P.T.R.C.; St. Paul the Traveller and Roman Citizen*, 1905.

R.B., *Revue biblique*.

R.H.Ph.R., *Revue d'Histoire et de Philosophie religieuses*.

R.H.R., *Revue d'Histoire des Religions*.

R.Sc.R., *Revue des Sciences religieuses*.

R.S.V., *Revised Standard Version*.

T.L.Z., *Theologische Literaturzeitung*.

T.R., *Theologische Rundschau*.

T.W.D.B., *Theological Word Book of the Bible*, ed. A. Richardson, 1950.

T.W.N.T., *Theologisches Wörterbuch zum Neuen Testament*, ed. G. Kittel.

V.T., *Vetus Testamentum*.

Williams, *Alterations*; C. S. C. Williams, *Alterations to the Text of the Synoptic Gospels and Acts*, 1951.

Z.N.T.W., *Zeitschrift für die neutestamentliche Wissenschaft*.

(B) Particular

Adams, J. Q., *Paul at Athens, E.T.* 32, 1920–1, 376 f.

Amann, É., *D.T.C.* xiv. 2130–40 (on Simon the Magian).

Bacon, B. W., *The Chronological Scheme of Acts, H.T.R.* 14, 1921, 137 ff.

THE ACTS OF THE APOSTLES

Bacon, B. W., *Stephen's speech, Biblical and Semitic Studies*, Yale Bicentenary Publication, 1901, 213-76.

— *Some Western Variants in the Text of Acts*, H.T.R. 21, 1928, 113-45 (puts xii. 1-23 before ix. 32-xi. 18).

— *Peter's Triumph at Antioch*, J.R. 9, 1929, 204-23.

— *More philological criticisms of Acts*, A.J.T., 1908, 1-23.

Barnikol, E., *Theologisches Jahrbuch*, 9, 1941, 88 f. (on Acts i. 28).

Barton, G. A., J.T.S. xxxvi, 1935, 357-73 (on Torrey's theory).

Beare, F. W., *The sequence of events in Acts ix-xv*, J.B.L. 62, 1943, 295-306.

Benoit, P., *Mél. Goguel*, 1-10 (on summaries in Acts).

Bickerman, E. J., *The Name of Christians*, H.T.R. 42, 1949, 109-24.

Black, M., *An Aramaic Approach to the Gospels and Acts*, 1946, 2nd ed. 1954.

Blaisdell, J. A., *The authorship of the we-sections*, H.T.R. 13, 1920, 136-58.

Brownlee, W. H., *The Dead Sea Manual of Discipline, Bulletin of the American Society of Oriental Research, Suppl. Studies*, 10-12, 1951.

— *B.A.S.O.R.* 132, Dec., 1953, 8 ff. (on a suffering Messiah).

Bruce, F. F., *The Speeches in the Acts of the Apostles*, 1942.

Burch, V., E.T. 30, 1918-19, 521 f. (on iii. 16 and viii. 10).

Burkitt, F. C., J.T.S. xx, 1919, 320-9.

— *The Gospel History and its Transmission*, 1906, 105-10.

Buzy, D., R.B. 45, 1936, 66-71 (on xviii. 5).

— *Épître aux Galates*, 1948.

Cadbury, H. J., see above, under *B.A.H.*

— and Lake, K., *Beginnings of Christianity*, iv, Commentary.

— *Luke, translator or author?* A.J.T. 24, 1920, 436-55.

— J.B.L. 59, 1940, 70 f. (on the speeches).

— *The Style and Literary Method of Luke*, H.T.S. 6, 1919-20.

— *The Making of Luke-Acts*, 1927.

— *The Odour of the Spirit*, J.B.L. 47, 1928, 237-56.

Calder, W. M., E.T. 37, 1925-6, 528 (on xiv. 12).

— *Adoption and Inheritance in Galatia*, J.T.S. xxxi, 1929-30, 371-4.

Causse, A., R.H.Ph.R., xviii, 1938, 377-414; xx, 1940, 120-41.

Cerfaux, L., *La Composition de la première partie du livre des Actes*, E.T.L. 13, 1936, 667-91.

— *Mél. Goguel*, 43-51 (on scriptural citations).

— *Studi e Testi*, 121, 1946, 107-46 (on ch. xv in the light of ancient literature).

— *La Communauté apostolique*, 1943, 2nd ed. 1951.

— *Le Supernomen dans le livre des Actes*, E.T.L. 15, 1938, 74-80.

Chambers, C. D., J.T.S. xxiv, 1922/3, 183 ff. (cf. W. F. Howard, *ibid.* 403 f.).

BIBLIOGRAPHY AND ABBREVIATIONS

Clark, A. C., *The Acts of the Apostles*, 1933.

Clarke, W. K. L., *The Acts . . . in recent criticism, Theology*, 4, 1922, 69-80 and 314-22.

— *Theology*, 6, 1923, 100 f. (on ix. 5).

— *Theology*, 30, 1935, 230-2 (on Matthias' election).

— *J.T.S.* xv, 1914, 599 f. (on Acts xvi and the Testament of Joseph viii).

Conybeare, F. C., *Two notes on Acts, Z.N.T.W.* 20, 1921, 36-42.

Cotter, W. E. P., *E.T.* 39, 1927-8, 235 (on Paul and the Eucharist).

Couchoud, P. L. and Stahl, R., *Les Deux Auteurs des Actes, R.H.R.* 97, 1928, 6-52.

Creed, J. M., *The Text and Interpretation of Acts*, i, 1-2, *J.T.S.* xxxv, 1934, 176-82.

Cullmann, O., *Peter, disciple-apostle-martyr*, tr. F. V. Filson, 1953.

— *R.H.Ph.R.* 10, 1930, 294-300 (on 1 Clement and the deaths of Peter and Paul).

Cunliffe-Jones, H., *Congregational Quarterly*, 27, 1949, 116-21 (on Ananias and Sapphira).

Cutten, G. B., *Speaking with Tongues*, 1928.

d'Alès, A., *Recherches de Science religieuse*, 24, 1934, 199 f. (on v. 3).

Davies, J. G., *Pentecost and Glossolalia, J.T.S.*, n.s. iii, 1952, 229-31,

Dewar, L., *The Problem of Pentecost, Theology*, 9, 1924, 249-59.

Dibelius, M., *Studies*, see above.

— *A Fresh Approach to the New Testament and Early Christian Literature*, 1936.

de Zwaan, J., *Was the Book of Acts a posthumous edition? H.T.R.* 17, 1924, 95-153.

Dillistone, F. W., *E.T.* 46, 1934-5, 380 (on x. 10).

Dodd, C. H., *According to the Scriptures*, 1952.

— *The Apostolic Preaching and its Developments*, 1936.

— *Studies in Honour of, The Background of the New Testament and its Eschatology*, ed. W. D. Davies and D. Daube, 1956.

Dupont, J., see *Problèmes* above.

— *Notes sur les Actes . . . R.B.*, 1955, 45-59.

— *Recherches de Science religieuse*, 35, 1948, 522 ff. on xiii. 33.

— *E.T.L.* 29, 1953, 289-327 (on O.T. citations).

Edwards, H. E., *Theology*, 16, 1928, 248-52 (on Pentecost).

Ehrhardt, A., *The Apostolic Succession in the first two centuries*, 1953.

— *Jewish and Christian Ordination, J.E.H.* 5, 1954, 125 ff.

Eltester, W., *T.L.Z.* 79, 1954, 202-27.

Enslin, M. S., *J.B.L.* 52, 1933, 230-8 (on B.C. i-v).

Fotheringham, D. R., *E.T.* 45, 1933-4, 430 (on xi. 20).

Frey, J. B., *Biblica* 12, 1931, 129-56 (on Judaism at Rome).

Fridrichsen, A., *Coniect. Neot.* 3, 1938, 13-16 (on xxvi. 28).

Fridrichsen, A., *The Apostle and His message*, 1947.

Gapp, K. S., *The Universal Famine under Claudius*, H.T.R. 28, 1935, 258-65 (on xi. 27-30).

Giet, S., *R.S.R.* 25, 1951, 264-9 (on xi. 27-30, xii. 24 f).

— *Recherches de Science religieuse*, xxxix, 1951, 203-20 (Who was Symon? ch. xv).

Glynne, W., *Psychology and Glossolalia*, C.Q.R. 106, 1928, 281-300.

Goguel, M., *Introduction au Nouveau Testament*, iii, 1922.

— *La Naissance du christianisme*, 1946, tr. H. C. Snape, 1954.

— *Les Premiers Temps de l'Église*, 1949.

— *R.H.Ph.R.* 3, 1923, 138-44 (on Acts xv).

— ditto 12, 1932, 321-23 (on xviii. 9-11).

— ditto 13, 1933, 197-241 (on Jesus and the Church).

— *R.H.R.* 106, 1932, 381-430 and 490-524 (on eschatology).

Goodspeed, E. J., *Expositor*, 58, 1919, 387-91 (on date of Acts).

— *The Origin of Acts*, J.B.L. 39, 1920, 83-101.

Grant, W. M., *The Ideals of the Early Church*, 1923.

Hanson, R. C. P., *Theology*, L, 1947, 142-5 (on Stephen's Speech).

Harnack, A. von, see *D.A.S.G.* above.

— *Luke the Physician*, 1907, trans. J. R. Wilkinson.

— *The Acts of the Apostles*, 1909, ditto.

Harris, J. R., *Four Lectures on the Western Text*, 1894.

— *Testimonies* (with V. Burch), 1916, 1920.

— *A lacuna in the Text of Acts*, E.T. 36, 1924-5, 173-5 (on ii. 32).

Hatch, W. H. P., *H.T.R.* 21, 1928, 141-59 (on Apostles).

Herber, J., *R.H.R.* 129, 1945, 45 ff. (on the death of Judas).

Holmes, B. T., *J.B.L.* 54, 1935, 63-72 (on Luke's description of John Mark and on the meaning of 'minister').

Hunkin, J. W., *J.T.S.* xxvii, 1925-6, 272-83 (on Acts xv. 28).

Hunter, A. M., *Interpreting the N.T.*, 1951, 105 ff.

Jackson, F. J. Foakes, *Peter, Prince of Apostles*, 1927.

— *J.B.L.* 49, 1930, 283-6 (on Stephen's speech).

— *H.T.R.* 10, 352-61.

Johnson, S. E., *The Dead Sea Manual of Discipline and the Jerusalem Church of Acts*, Z.A.T.W. lxvi, 1954, 106-20.

— *Paul and the Manual of Discipline*, H.T.R. xlviii, 1955, 157-65.

Kellett, E. E., *E.T.* 34, 1922-3, 188 f. (on xiii. 42).

— ibid., 563 f. (on xxvi. 28).

Kenyon, Sir F. G., *The Western Text of the Gospels and Acts*, 1938.

— *The Chester Beatty Biblical Papyri*, Fasc. II, 1933.

Kilpatrick, G. D., *J.T.S.* xlvi, 1945, 136-45 (on vii. 52).

Kirk, K. E., *C.Q.R.* 116, 1933, 291-7 (on B.C. iv and v).

Kl.,n, A. F. J., *A Survey of the Researches into the Western Text of the Gospels and Acts*, 1949.

BIBLIOGRAPHY AND ABBREVIATIONS

Knox, A. D., *J.T.S.* xxv, 1923–4, 289 (on the death of Judas).

Knox, J., *Marcion and the New Testament*, 1942.

Knox, W. L., see *Jerusalem* and *Gentiles*, etc., above.

Kümmel, W. G., *Theologische Rundschau*, xviii, 1950.

Lake, K. and Cadbury, H. J., see *B.C.* iv, under Commentaries.

Lake, K., *The Theology of Acts*, *A.J.T.* 19, 1915, 489-508.

— *Landmarks in the History of Early Christianity*, 1920.

Lampe, G. W. H., *The Seal of the Spirit*, 1951.

Larrañaga, V., *L'Ascension de Notre-Seigneur dans le N.T.*, 1938.

Lattey, C., *E.T.* 36, 1924-5, 381 (on xix. 16 cf. H. G. Machen, *ibid.* 477).

Lauterbach, J. Z., *The Jewish Encyclopaedia*, ix, 428-30 (on ordination).

Leclerq, A., *Dictionnaire d'Archéologie Chrétienne*, xv (1) 1950, 1459-1463 (on Simon the Magian).

Lietzmann, H., in *Amicitiae Corolla* (essays in honour of J. R. Harris, on Acts xv. 20, 29) 1933, 203-11.

Lightfoot, J. B., *St. Paul's Epistle to the Galatians*, 10th ed., 1890.

Linton, O., *The Third Aspect, Studia Theologica*, 1950, 79-95 (on the relation of chs. ix and xv to Gal. i-ii.).

Logan, I., *E.T.* 39, 1927-8, 428 (on xv. 20, 29).

Lohmeyer, E., *Galiläa und Jerusalem*, 1936 (for the doctrine of the Son of Man, followed by R. H. Lightfoot, *Locality and Doctrine in the Gospels*, 1938).

— *Gottesknecht und Davidssohn*, 1945.

Lösch, S., *Der Kämmerer der Königin Kandace, Theologische Quartalschrift*, 111, 1930, 477-516 (on viii. 27).

Lyonnet, S., *Verbum Domini*, 24, 1944, 64-75 (on glossolalia).

— *Biblica*, 35, 1954, 485 ff. (on the 'Righteous one' etc.).

McCasland, S. V., *The Cult Story of the Early Church*, *J.R.* 8, 1928, 247-60.

McConnachie, J., *E.T.* 36, 1924–5, 90 (Simon the tanner a netmender?).

McDonald, W. A., *Archaeology and St. Paul's journeys in Greek lands*, *B.A.* 3, 1940, 18-24; 4, 1941, 1-10; 5, 1942, 36-48 cf. M. M. Parvis, *ibid.*, 8, 1945, 62-80.

McIntyre, D. M., *The earliest witnesses to the Gospel story*, *E.T.* 33, 1921–2, 309-12.

McNeile, A. H., *New Testament Teaching in the Light of St. Paul's*, 1923.

— *Introduction to the Study of the N.T.*, 2nd ed. 1953.

— *St. Paul, His Life, Letters and Christian Doctrine*, 1920.

Manson, T. W., *B.J.R.L.* xxiv, 1940, 59-80.

Martin, I. J., *J.B.L.* 63, 1944, 123-30 (on glossolalia).

Menoud, P. H., *Society of New Testament Studies*, ii, 1951, 19-32 (on the Western text and theology).

Menoud, P. H., *Mél. Goguel*, 146-52 (on Ananias and Sapphira).

Meyer, Ed., *Ursprung und Anfänge des Christentums*, 1921-3.

Moffatt, J., *Exp.* 8, v, 17, 1919, 229-40 and 271-4.

Molland, E., *Studia Theologica*, ix, 1955, 1-39 (on Acts xv, 20, 29).

Montgomery, J. A., *J.B.L.* 52, 1933, 261 (on Acts xv).

Moore, G. F., *Christianity in the first Century of the C.E.*, 1927-30.

Morrill, R. J., *Theology*, 24, 1932, 281 (on glossolalia).

Mosbech, H., *Apostolos in the N.T.*, *Studia Theologica*, ii, 1948, 166-200.

Moule, C. F. D., *E.T.* lxv, 1954, 220 f.

— *An Idiom Book of N.T. Greek*, 1953.

Moule, H. W., *E.T.* li, 1940, 396.

Munck, J., *Israel and the Gentiles in the N.T.*, *J.T.S.* n.s. ii, 1951, 3-16.

— *Mél. Goguel*, 153-70 (on Acts xx. 17-38).

Mundle, W., *Z.N.T.W.* 20, 1921, 133-47 (on Stephen's speech).

Nairne, A., *J.T.S.* xi, 1910, 560 (on xii. 25).

— *J.T.S.* xxi, 1919-20, 171 (on xxvi. 28).

Nineham, D. E. (ed.), *Studies in the Gospels*, 1955.

Nock, A. D., *Early Gentile Christianity and its Gentile Background* in *Essays on the Trinity and Incarnation*, ed. A. E. J. Rawlinson, 1928, 51-156.

— *St. Paul*, 1938.

— *Gnomon*, 25, 1953, 497-506 (on Dibelius' views).

Norden, E., *Agnostos Theos*, 1913.

North, R., *The Damascus of Qumran Geography*, *Palestine Exploration Quarterly*, 87th year, 1955, 34-48.

Pallis, A., *Notes on St. Luke and the Acts*, 1928.

Pennell, T. J., *E.T.* 44, 1932-3, 476 (on xiii. 13; cf. R. Hughes, *ibid.* 45, 1933-4, 44 f.).

Parvis, M. M., see under McDonald.

— and Wikgren, A. P., *New Testament Manuscript Studies*, 1950.

Pirot, L., *Actes*, *Suppl.*, *Dictionnaire de la Bible*, i, 1926, 42-86.

Plooij, D., *The Apostolic Decree and its Problems*, *Exp.* 49, 8, 25, 1923, 81-100 and 223-38.

Pohlenz, M., *Paulus und die Stoa*, *Z.N.T.W.* 42, 1949, 69-104.

Porter, J. R., *J.T.S.* xlvii, 1946, 169-74.

Price, S. H., *The authorship of Luke-Acts*, *E.T.* 55, 1943-4, 194.

Rackham, R. B., see under Commentaries.

— *J.T.S.* i, 1900, 76 ff.

Ramsay, Sir W. M., *The Church in the Roman Empire*, 4th ed. 1895.

— *The Cities of St. Paul*, 1907.

— *Luke the Physician*, 1908.

— *The Bearing of Recent Discovery on the Trustworthiness of the N.T.*, 1915.

BIBLIOGRAPHY AND ABBREVIATIONS

Ramsay, Sir W. M., see *P.T.R.C.* above.
— *Exp.* 5, 7, vii, 1909, 172 ff. (on authorities used in i-xii).
— *The Intermixture of Races in Asia Minor, Proceedings of the British Academy*, vii, 1915–16, 359-422.
Rengstorf, K. H., *Apostleship*, from T.W.N.T., tr. by J. R. Coates, 1952.
Renié, J., *L'Enseignement doctrinal des Actes, Nouvelle Revue théologique*, 62, 1935, 268-77.
— *R.B.* 55, 1948, 43-53 (on the election of Matthias).
— *Revue apologétique*, 61, 1935, 2, 24-37.
Riddle, D. W., *J.B.L.* 59, 169-80 (on Cephas-Peter).
Roberts, J. E., *Exp.* 49, 8, 26, 1923, 376-82 (on the Eutychus story).
Roberts, R., *E.T.* 48, 1936–7, 438-441 (on xx. 35).
Robinson, D. F., *J.B.L.* 53, 1944, 169-72 (on xi. 27 ff.).
Ropes, J. H., see *B.C.* iii.
Rowley, H. H., *Hebrew Union College Annual*, xv, 1940, 313-34.
Russell, H. G., *H.T.R.* xlviii, 1956, 167 ff. (Was Acts before Luke?).
Sahlin, H., *Der Messias und das Gottesvolk*, 1945.
Sanders, H. A., *H.T.R.* 20, 1927, 1-20 (on the Michigan papyrus).
Schmid, W., *Philologus*, 95, 1942, 79-120 (on xvii).
Schmidt, K. L., *The Church*, from T.W.N.T., trans. J. R. Coates, 1950.
Schütz, R., *Apostel und Jünger*, 1921.
Sharp, D. E., *E.T.* 44, 1932–3, 528 (on xiv. 3).
Shepherd, M. H., in *Munera Studiosa*, 1946, 90-105.
Simcox, G. A., *J.T.S.* 2, 1901, 586-90 (on xii. 25).
Simon, M., *J.E.H.* 2, 1951, 127-42 (on Stephen's speech and the Temple).
Simpson, E. K., *Vettius Valens, The Evangelical Quarterly*, ii, 1930, 389 ff.
Smith, James, of Jordanhill, *The Voyage and Shipwreck of St. Paul*, 4th ed., 1880.
Snaith, N. H., *E.T.* 43, 1931–2, 379 f. (on Pentecost).
Snape, H. C., *H.T.R.* 47, 1954, 1-14 (on the views of Goguel and Brandon).
Sparks, H. F. D., *J.T.S.* n.s. i, 1950, 16–28 (on 'Semitisms').
Stanton, V. H., *The Gospels as Historical Documents*, Pt. 88. ch. iv, 1909.
Streeter, B. H., *The Four Gospels*, 1924.
— *The Primitive Church*, 1929.
— *Cambridge Ancient History*, xi, 1936, 253-93.
Swain, J. W., *H.T.R.* 37, 1944, 341-9 (on v. 34-9).
Taylor, B. E., *E.T.* 57, 1945–6, 222 (on xix. 14).
Taylor, R. O. P., *E.T.* 40, 1928–9, 300-3 (on Pentecost).
— *What was Barnabas? C.Q.R.* 136, 1943, 59-79.

Taylor, R. O. P., *E.T.* 54, 1942–3, 136-8 (on John Mark).

Taylor, V., *The Names of Jesus*, 1953.

Tenney, M. C., *A N.T. Survey*, 1954.

Thackeray, H. St. J., *Josephus, the Man and the Historian*, 1929.

Thieme, K., *Le Plan des Actes, Dieu vivant*, 26, 128 ff.

Thompson, Sir Herbert, *The Coptic Version . . .*, 1932.

Thomson, W. S., *E.T.* 38, 1926–7, 284-6 (on Pentecost).

Thorne, E. A., *C.Q.R.* 121, 1935–6, 109-117 (on the earlier missionary journeys).

Thornton, L. S., *The Common Life in the Body of Christ*, 1941.

— *The Choice of Matthias, J.T.S.* 46, 1945, 51-9.

Tonneau, R., *R.B.* 38, 1929, 5-34 and 321-63.

Torrey, C. C., see *C.D.A.* and *D.P.C.* above.

— *Fact and Fancy concerning Acts, A.J.T.* 23, 1919, 61-86.

— *The 'rest' in Acts v. 13, E.T.* 46, 1934–5, 428 f.

Turner, C. H., *Theology*, 20, 1930, 41-4 (on Acts xv).

— *The Chronology of the N.T., H.D.B.* i, 403-25.

— *The Study of the N.T.*, 1883 and 1920.

Weinstock, S., *The Geographical Catalogue of Acts ii. 9-11, Journal of Roman Studies*, xxxviii, 1948, 43-6.

Weiss, J., *The History of Primitive Christianity*, tr. F. C. Grant, 1937.

Wendt, H. H., *Z.N.T.W.* 24, 1925, 293-305.

Wensinck, A. J., *B. of B.C.* xii, 1937, 11-48 (on Semitisms in the Bezan text, D).

Wikenhauser, A., *Biblica*, 29, 1948, 100-111 (on double-dreams).

— *Die Apostelgeschichte und ihr Geschichtswert*, 1921.

Wilder, A. N., *Variant traditions of the Resurrection in Acts, J.B.L.* 62, 1943, 307-18.

Williams, R. R., *Authority in the Apostolic Age*, 1950.

Willinck, M. D. R., *Theology*, 14, 1927, 237-9 (on the Ascension).

Wilson, M., *The Origin and aim of the Acts . . .* 1912.

Windisch, H., *Z.N.T.W.* 31, 1932, 1-23 (on ix. 22 ff.).

Young, G. M., *J.T.S.* n.s. i, 1950, 156 (on i. 8).

Zuntz, G., *A textual criticism of some passages of Acts, Classica et Mediaevalia*, 3, 1940, 20-46.

(C) Commentaries

B.C., *The Beginnings of Christianity*, Pt. i, vols. i-v, (esp. iv, The Commentary by K. Lake and H. J. Cadbury), ed. by Lake and F. J. Foakes Jackson, 1920–33.

Blunt, A. W. F., 1923 (Clarendon B.).

Browne, L. E., 1925 (Indian Church Com.).

BIBLIOGRAPHY AND ABBREVIATIONS

Bruce, F. F., 1951 (Tyndale Press), cited below as 'Bruce'.

Camerlynck, A., and van der Heeren, A., *Commentarius in Actus Apostolorum*, 7th ed., 1923.

Findlay, J. A., 1934 (S.C.M.).

Furneaux, W. M., 1912.

Jackson, F. J. Foakes, 1931 (Moffatt Com.).

Jacquier, E., 1926.

Knowling, R. J., 1900 (Expositors Greek Test.).

Loisy, A., 1920.

Macgregor, G. H. C., 1954 (The Interpreter's Bible, ix).

Page, T. E., 1886.

Rackham, R. B., 1902 (Westminster Com.).

Wendt, H. H., 1913 (Meyer).

Weiss, B., 1893.

Wikenhauser, A., 1938.

NOTE TO SECOND EDITION

Among recent literature on Acts attention may be drawn to the revised edition of E. Haenchen's Commentary (1957), the Short Commentary by G. W. H. Lampe (*Peake's Commentary*, 1962) and the following books and articles:

Bultmann, R., in *New Testament Essays in memory of T. W. Manson*, 1959 (on sources).

Cadbury, H. J., in *The Background of the N.T. and its Eschatology* (*in honour of C. H. Dodd*), 1956 (Acts and eschatology).

Dupont, J., *Les Sources du livre des Actes*, 1960 (E.T. 1964).

— *Le Discours de Milet* (*Actes* 20, 18-36), 1962.

Ehrhardt, A., *Studia Theologica*, xii, 1958, 45-79 (construction and purpose).

Haenchen, E., *Zeitschrift für Theologie und Kirche*, lviii, 1961, 329-66 (we-passages).

— in *Festschrift für J. Jeremias*, 1960 (source-criticism of Acts xv).

Ogilvie, R. M., *J.T.S.* n.s. ix, 1958, 308-14 (Phoenix, Acts xxvii. 12).

O'Neill, J. C., *The Theology of Acts in its historical setting*, 1961.

Rengstorf, K. H., *Studia Theologica*, xv, 1961, 35-67 (the choice of Matthias).

Strecker, G., *Z.N.T.W.* liii, 1962, 67-77 (Acts xi. 27-30).

Van Unnik, W. C., *Novum Testamentum* iv, 1960, 26-59 (the purpose).

Wilckens, U., *Die Missionsreden der Apostelgeschichte*, 1960.

THE ACTS OF THE APOSTLES

The following books and articles, published since 1963, should be noted:

Commentaries by H. Conzelmann, Die Apostelgeschichte (1963), and by R. P. C. Hanson, New Clarendon Bible (1967).

Barnes, T. D., *J.T.S.* n.s. xx (1969), 407-419 (Paul before the Areopagus).

Epp, E. J. *The theological tendency of Codex Bezae Cantabrigiensis in Acts* (1966); thereon see R. P. C. Hanson's review in *New Testament Studies* xiv (1968), 282-286.

Studies in Luke Acts: Essays presented in honor of Paul Schubert, edited by L. E. Keck and J. L. Martyn (1966).

Sherwin-White, A. N. *Roman Society and Roman Law in the New Testament* (1963).

Simon, M., *B.J.R.L.* lii, 2 (1970), 437-460 (the Apostolic Decree, Acts xv. 23-29).

Van Unnik, W. C. in *Mullus: Festschrift Theodor Klauser* (1964), 366-373 (on Acts xvi. 20 f.).

Wilcox, M., *The Semitisms of Acts* (1965).

INTRODUCTION

1. EXTERNAL EVIDENCE FOR THE AUTHORSHIP OF ACTS

IT is not to be expected that Luke's name should be given in the book of Acts, either in the narrative or still less in the title according to the earliest manuscripts. Yet the evidence in favour of Luke being the author is fairly strong:

(a) The anti-Marcionite prologue to Luke. This has been dated either before or after the writings of St. Irenaeus (*fl.* A.D. 180). After speaking of the author of the third Gospel as Luke, a Syrian of Antioch, a doctor by profession who had been a disciple of the apostles and had accompanied Paul until the latter's martyrdom, it tells us that Luke served the Lord without distraction, unmarried, childless, and that he fell asleep at the age of eighty-four in Boeotia, full of Holy Spirit. The prologue writer ends: 'And indeed afterwards the same Luke wrote the Acts of the Apostles while, later, John the Apostle, one of the Twelve, wrote the Apocalypse in the Isle of Patmos and, after that, the Gospel'. Cf. A. H. McNeile, *An Introduction to the Study of the New Testament*, 2nd ed., 1953, 26, 29, 286 f.; cf. the sixth or seventh century Coptic inscription in a chapel on Mount Assiut in Egypt: 'As for Luke the physician, he was a disciple of the Apostles till he followed Paul. He lived eighty-four years. He wrote this gospel being in Achaia. Then he wrote Acts.' (G. Lefebvre, *Egypte chrétienne*, x. i, 1909, cited by Goguel, *I.N.T.* iii. 372.)

A searching examination, however, of the Anti-Marcionite Prologues was made by R. G. Heard, *J.T.S.*, N.S., vi, 1955, 1-16. He concluded that the prologue to Luke, designed as we have it to serve as a prologue to a copy of Luke circulating separately, contains a phrase drawn from Irenaeus, and dates from the third or early fourth century. 'Its first paragraph, which may represent an earlier form of the Prologue, contains valuable information about Luke and is an important witness to the truth of the tradition on his authorship of the third

gospel. The Prologue is not specifically anti-Marcionite. . . .'
On pp. 7-9 he gave the Greek text and translation of the whole
Prologue with textual and other notes.

(b) The fragmentary *Muratorian Canon* probably dates back
to *c.* A.D. 180–200 and may be due to Hippolytus himself, giving
the list of canonical books accepted by the Church in Rome at
that time. Lines 2 to 8 discuss Luke's authorship of the third
Gospel; lines 34 ff. add: 'But the Acts of all the Apostles were
written in one volume. Luke compiled for the "most excellent
Theophilus" what things were done in detail in his presence, as
he plainly shows by omitting both the death of Peter and also
the departure of Paul from the city when he departed for Spain.'

(c) St. Irenaeus (*Adv. Haer.* iii. 14, 1) *c.* A.D. 180 makes it
clear that he too thought that Luke wrote Acts.

(d) Writers between *c.* 200 and 230, such as Clement of
Alexandria (*Strom.* v. 12) and Tertullian (*Adv. Marcion.* iv. 2)
and Origen (*apud* Eusebius, *H.E.* vi. 25, etc.) show that Luke's
authorship was well established in their day.

(e) Earlier than any of these writers stands St. Ignatius of
Antioch, *fl. c.* A.D. 110. As W. L. Knox pointed out (*Acts*, 2,
n. 1 and 40 f.), Ignatius is steeped in a New Testament of
which Acts is part. 'The book [of Acts], if not "Holy Scripture",
was a Christian classic well before A.D. 117.' Also, as Knox
shows, Ignatius knew the Pastoral Epistles, especially 2 Tim.;
and the Pastoral writer, probably not St. Paul himself, drew his
knowledge of Paul's career in 2 Tim. iii. 11 from Acts. 'We have
to imagine,' writes Knox, 'a compiler who is interested enough
in Paul to write his life, yet does not know his Epistles [or at
least his extant ones] since he has never read Galatians. Yet he
is early enough for his works to be accepted by the author of
2 Timothy, which again is early enough for Ignatius to be
familiar with it and to treat it as Scripture, while Ignatius was
martyred before A.D. 117. Yet again he is not early enough to
have access to any authentic record of Paul's travels or Paul's
theology.' Knox thinks that Luke was this compiler.

(f) The author of the 'Gospel of Truth' seems to have been
acquainted with the book of Acts. If the author of this Gnostic
work was indeed Valentinus, he may well witness to the
recognition of Acts at Rome *c.* 140–150 as authoritative. See

INTRODUCTION

W. C. van Unnik in *The Jung Codex*, ed. F. L. Cross, 1955, 122.

(g) M. Dibelius (*Studies in the Acts of the Apostles*, 1956, 104 and elsewhere) is content to argue that as both Luke's books were addressed to Theophilus, their authorship must have been known as soon as the books were known, probably as 'Luke's Acts of Jesus' and 'Luke's Acts of Paul'. But was the authorship of the work, e.g., addressed to Diognetus known?

2. INTERNAL EVIDENCE OF THE NEW TESTAMENT

(a) Of Paul's companions mentioned in his epistles and in Acts, Luke is most probably the one who wrote Acts or part of it. In certain sections of Acts the first person plural is found, viz. xvi. 9-18, xx. 5-15 (16-end?), xxi. 1-18, xxvii. 1-xxviii. 16. As we may exclude those mentioned by name in Acts, Silas (xvi. 19), Timothy (xvi. 1), Sopater (xx. 4), Aristarchus (xix. 29), Secundus (xx. 4), Gaius (*ibid.*), Tychicus and Trophimus (*ibid.*), we must expect a companion of Paul mentioned by him to have been the author of at least the 'we-sections'. In the 'captivity epistles', which were probably written from Rome, not Ephesus (with the possible exception of Philippians), Aristarchus, Mark, and Jesus Justus are mentioned (Col. iv. 10 f.), but as 'men of the circumcision' or Jewish Christians, and it is usually argued that Acts must have been written by a Gentile Christian to judge from his interests. Epaphras (Col. iv. 12) is mentioned, but as a Colossian and probably the founder of the Church at Colossae (Col. i. 7, Alexandrian reading); Acts shows no particular interest in the Church in the Lycus Valley. Demas (Col. iv. 14, Philemon 24) had been a companion of Paul, but if 2 Tim. iv. 10 is a genuine fragment, at least of a Pauline letter, he deserted Paul, 'having loved this present world'. Admittedly this same verse mentions Crescens and Titus and the next verse has 'Luke alone is with me', cf. Col. iv. 14, 'Luke the beloved physician'. Of these, Titus might seem to have a good claim to consideration. It is striking that he is never mentioned in Acts, but often by Paul and in the warmest terms. To account for the silence of Acts it has been suggested that he should be identified with Titus or Titius Justus, Acts xviii. 7, or with Silas himself.

3

THE ACTS OF THE APOSTLES

Alternatively, he may have been Luke's brother, and if Luke
was the author of Acts, Luke may have suppressed his own and
Titus' name from modesty.

This line of argument, however, is not altogether convincing,
as it leaves loopholes which grow wider if A. H. McNeile's
suggestion is adopted that the author of Acts was not a Gentile
but a 'Hellenist' in the sense of a Greek-speaking Jew (*New
Testament Teaching in the Light of St. Paul*, 1923, 132). If the
point is pressed that Luke's name was not prominent in the
Church of Apostolic days, and that unless he wrote Acts there
is no reason apparent why the Church should have fastened the
authorship on him rather than on Titus, for instance, the reply
can be made, as by H. J. Cadbury, that the book is not by Luke
but that the Church examined the references to Paul's companions in the New Testament and picked on Luke as the most
likely, at some time during the second century.

(b) If the widely attested variant of the Western text of xi. 28
is right, it was known at least as early as the second century that
the author of Acts was connected with Antioch, cf. Eus. *H.E.*
iii. iv. 7, and the Anti-Marcionite prologue, p. 1 (a) above. Those
scholars, like T. W. Manson, who believe that this Western
variant and the tradition of Luke's Antiochene origin are independent of one another take the tradition to be correct; if so,
Luke was a member of the church in Antioch before meeting
St. Paul and he had already come under the influence of the
leaders of the Palestinian church. On this view xi. 28 must be
added to the list of we-sections.

(c) Luke is called 'the beloved physician' (Col. iv. 14). Acts,
like the Third Gospel, shows an interest in things medical.
There was no technical medical vocabulary in Paul's day, and
it was a mistake for Hobart to describe some four hundred
terms in Luke-Acts as 'medical'; for any educated Greek-
speaking person could have used most of them. Harnack
accepted many of Hobart's conclusions, but H. J. Cadbury rejected the theory entirely, pointing out that a large number of
these terms occur in the LXX and that on the same showing a
writer like Lucian could be proved to be a doctor!

The author of Acts, however, evinces at least a medical
interest, as in the contexts where he used *iaomai*, 'I heal'; ix. 34,

4

x. 38, xxviii. 8, cf. Luke v. 17, vi. 17, 19, vii. 7, viii. 47, ix. 2, 11,
42, xiv. 4, xvii. 15, xxii. 51, cf. *therapeuo*, 'I cure', Acts iv. 14,
v. 16, viii. 7, xvii. 25, xxviii. 9, cf. Luke iv. 23, 40, v. 15, vi. 7,
18, vii. 21, viii. 2, 43, ix. 1, 6, x. 9, xiii. 14, xiv. 3, compare the
references to such things as the 'mist', Acts xiii. 11; 'feet and
ankles', iii. 7, 'to fasten on' in the sense of 'to bite' (of a snake),
xxviii. 3, 'scales' or 'flakes', ix. 18, 'to swell up', xxviii. 6, 'to
be afflicted' (with an unclean spirit), v. 16; cf. the note on 'to
be hungry', x. 10.

3. Was the Author of the We-sections the Author also of the rest of Acts and of the Third Gospel?

1. There are four main theories with regard to these sections:
    (a) The traditional view is that the diarist and the compiler of
Acts are one and the same person, whose conscious use of the
first person plural indicates that he was present with Paul at
least from Troas to Philippi, from Philippi to Miletus, from
Miletus to Jerusalem and from Caesarea to Rome and perhaps
on other occasions too where 'we' is not used.
    (b) Another view is that the diarist filled up the intervening
portions of narrative and that his record was used by a different
person, the compiler of Acts.
    (c) A third view is that the diarist wrote only the we-sections
and that he is different from the writer who added the intervening portions of Acts xvi-end, while a final editor later combined the second part of Acts thus formed with the first.
    (d) The fourth view is that the diarist wrote only the we-
sections and that someone else compiled the intervening parts
of xvi-end as well as i-xv.
    Of these theories (b) and (c) are the weakest. It is possible to
eliminate (b) because there is no convincing reason for asserting
that the compiler of xvi-end was different from the author of
i-xv. Similarly, (c) can be rejected as highly improbable as there
is no convincing reason for postulating the hand of a third
person. The choice lies between (a) and (d); cf. McNeile,
I.S.N.T. 106 f.
    There are twenty-one words and phrases in the New Testa-
ment found only in the we-sections and in the rest of Acts; and

there are sixteen words and phrases peculiar to the we-sections and to the third Gospel, ten of which occur also in the remainder of Acts, some several times; also, not counting words and phrases characteristic of Luke, there are words and phrases, twenty-eight in all, 'found in the we-sections and also used predominantly, though not exclusively, in the rest of Acts or Luke or either of them' (Sir John Hawkins, *Horae Synopticae*, 1899, 152 f.). A consideration of the vocabulary characteristic of the third Gospel shows that it is 'utterly improbable that the language of the original writer of the we-sections should have chanced to have so very many more correspondences with the language of the subsequent compiler than with that of Matthew or Mark' (*ibid.* 150). Compare Harnack, *Luke the Physician*, ii. 26-120. Again, as Luke in using Mark's Gospel allowed the style of the latter to shine through, as it were, in his own work and as the style and vocabulary of the we-sections are more characteristic of Luke than are his passages parallel to Mark, it is extremely probable that the compiler of Luke-Acts was revising and incorporating portions not of another person's diary but his own. These arguments are important; V. H. Stanton rightly took writers like Windisch (*B.C.* ii. 298 ff.) to task for neglecting them (*J.T.S.* xxiv, 1923, 374-81). Cadbury minimized the stylistic and linguistic arguments, in working out his theory that the theory of Luke's authorship of Acts was due to a guess made in the second century.

2. Despite the arguments of Harnack and Hawkins, an attempt was made by A. C. Clark (*Acts*, 393-408) to maintain that the author of Acts was not the author of the Third Gospel, chiefly on the ground of numerous differences in the use of particles, prepositions, conjunctions, and other small parts of speech and of variations in the use of common words and the choice between synonyms. But Clark's failure to weigh words instead of counting them was shown by Knox (*Acts*, 2-15, 100-9). Clark did not allow enough for Luke's sources 'shining through' his own more polished work in the Gospel and for the inevitable frequency of such a phrase as 'Son of Man' there, which is used only once in Acts. Incidentally, it is often assumed that Luke's vocabulary is a very rich one; this assumption is invalid, despite H. J. Cadbury (*H.T.S.* vi, 1919–20); 'of ver-

nacular writers of narrative in "free" Greek, St. Luke employs the smallest vocabulary' (C. D. Chambers, *J.T.S.* xxv, 1923-4, 160 ff.). It is all the more striking that this 'limited' vocabulary of Acts should be shared so much by the author of the third Gospel.

3. A theory like that of Loisy (*Acts*) that a diary of Luke was used by a later compiler of Acts involves the supposition that the we-sections of Acts were a source which the editor revised completely without altering the first to the third person plural. E. Norden (*Agnostos Theos*, 1913, 313 ff.) sought to adduce 'parallels' to the adoption by another writer of the first person plural by a previous author and Goguel (*I.N.T.* iii. 164 ff.) supports his references to Cicero, *ad Att.* v. 20 and *ad Fam.* xv. 4, and his contention that magistrates, army leaders, provincial governors, and travellers giving account of events or expeditions under their aegis used the first or third person whether they had been personally present or not. But on examination these and other 'parallels' are far from close. 'I know of only one possible parallel for the emphatic use of a questionable "we" in consecutive narrative outside literature which is palpably fictional' (A. D. Nock, *Gnomon*, 25, 1953, 503).

It is therefore extremely probable that the author of the we-sections wrote the rest of Acts and the Third Gospel.

It should be noted that Dibelius (*op. cit.* 73 ff., 197 ff.) prefers to speak of an 'Itinerary' which is different from and larger than the usual amount of 'we-sections'. The latter, however, may have included parts of the former even though 'we' is not used and Dibelius' arguments are somewhat subjective.

4. Did Luke use Sources?

1. (a) It can be argued that as Luke used Mark's Gospel and probably other sources in compiling the third Gospel, so he used sources also in compiling the first half of Acts, i-xv, and, quite apart from the we-sections, perhaps on occasions in compiling the second half; also that it is probable that the study of Luke's use of Mark throws light on the way in which he used sources in Acts (cf. H. J. Cadbury, *H.T.S.* vi). For instance, while Luke does not alter the general picture presented by

Mark's Gospel, he shortens the Marcan material considerably and omits usually the Marcan notes of time; he refines Mark's somewhat uncouth Greek often and he makes alterations *ad reverentiam* where Marcan expressions would jar on the religious susceptibilities of his readers or where they would welcome a more classical Greek style. Any argument, however, based on a comparison between the only long speech in Mark attributed to Jesus, Mark xiii, and Luke xxi must be used cautiously in view of the tendency now to suppose that Luke xxi rests on independent oral tradition rather than on Mark. However, if Mark's Gospel did not exist, it would be impossible to reconstruct it accurately from Luke's (or even from Luke's and Matthew's); so any reconstruction of the sources behind Acts must be tentative.

(b) Sources may be said to be indicated by, and in some measure to account for, roughnesses, gaps, and discrepancies in the narrative of Acts (cf. Harnack, *Acts*, 203-29) unless these were due to Luke's lack of a final revision of his work, of which there are indications in both parts of Acts.

(c) Some of the many attempts to analyse the sources of Acts may be seen in Moffatt's *I.L.N.T.* 286-9, cf. Goguel, *op. cit.* 51-72. Following on Harnack's lines, it can be maintained that most of Acts i-xv is connected with Jerusalem, except xiii and xiv, which refer to Antioch, and possibly xv. 1-35 also. xii. 20-25 serve as an introduction to a Jerusalem-Antiochean source. xiii. 1 presupposes xi. 27-30 with its account of the prophets at Antioch, so that xi. 27-xv. 35, except for xii. 1-19, is to be connected with Antioch. Working back, xi. 27 picks up xi. 19-26 which in turn presuppose viii. 1 and 4 and are connected also with vi. 1-8, the central interest of which appears to be Antioch, though Luke is convinced that Jerusalem is the mother-church. Of the remainder of Acts i-xv, i-v are closely and the rest loosely connected with Jerusalem; ix. 1-30 is a 'passage concerning the conversion of St. Paul interpolated from a separate source', cf. xxii. 3-16, xxvi. 9-18; ix. 19-30 may be a continuation of the Jerusalem-Antiochean tradition; and though Jerusalem is the centre, Caesarea is the immediate place of interest in the narratives about Peter and Philip in viii. 5-40, ix. 31-xi. 18 and xii. 1-24 which may be attributed to a

'Jerusalem-Caesarean or Petro-Philippine source'. i-v differ from the rest in outlook, theology, and style as well as in their presentation of the main actors, according to Harnack; he connected ii. and v. 17-42 closely together, the omission of which in his opinion would leave a smooth narrative in iii. 1-26, iv. 1-33, 35-v. 11, 12-16 (Jerusalem A source); these sections not only serve as an introduction to the early life of the Church but also contain peculiar expressions such as 'Servant of God' or 'Son of God' (*pais* is ambiguous); in comparison ii and v. 17-42 (Jerusalem B) are inferior, disjointed, and inclusive of 'doublets' parallel to sections in the Jerusalem A source. For instance, Harnack thought that there is an inferior account of the outpouring of the Holy Spirit at Pentecost in ii, while iv has the more original story. Harnack found the miraculous distasteful to his religious and philosophical outlook and thought that the Pentecost story was 'the beginning of a legend'. As for i, the early part including the account of the Ascension he took to be 'probably the latest tradition' in Acts and to have been inserted by Luke on the authority of a legend of very advanced development. He could not decide about the place to which the latter half of i should be assigned (*Acts*, 188 n.). To summarize his conclusions: apart from i, ii belongs to Recension B which as compared with A is 'worthless'; iii. 1-v. 16, A, derived probably from Philip or one of his daughters; v. 17-42, continuation of B; vi. 1-viii. 4, Jerusalem-Antiochean source (with interpolated references to St. Paul) of high historical value, derived possibly from Silas; viii. 5-40, A continued; ix. 1-30, story of Paul's conversion from a separate source; ix. 31-xi. 18, A source; xi. 19-30 Jerusalem-Antiochean source; xii. 1-23, A source; xii. 25-xv. 35, Jerusalem-Antiochean source.

(d) With such a division one may compare and contrast the results of L. Cerfaux's work, *E.T.L.* 13, 1936, 667 ff. (contrast Kümmel, *T.R.*, N.F., xviii, 1950, 1-53). Cerfaux ascribes i. 1-14 to traditional Galilean material, i. 15-ii. 40 to C¹ (Caesarean group); ii. 41-v. 40, Descriptive documents (D); v. 41-viii. 1a, E², Hellenistic dossier; viii. 1b-40, C² (Gr. Caesarean) except for viii. 14-25, the work of a redactor; ix. 1-30, C³; ix. 31-xi. 18, C⁴, except xi. 1-18, the work of a redactor; xi. 19-30, E¹, another Hellenistic dossier; xii, 1-23, 'X, Mark, C⁵'. His D group consists, he thinks, of a coherent collection with well-marked traits; the C groups are not homogeneous, C¹ being a written source, C² notes collected by Luke, C³ oral tradition, C⁴ a document, C⁵ oral and E being very composite, supplementing C.

(e) C. C. Torrey (*C.D.A.*), however, maintained that Acts i-xv is the translation of a single Aramaic document; he based his argument mainly on supposed Aramaisms or on mistranslations into Greek from the supposed Aramaic original. It is ndeed possible that Luke knew Aramaic if he lived in Antioch (cf. Dibelius, *Z.N.T.W.* 12 (1911), 342; Loisy, *Luke*, 63; Sahlin, 28; Moffatt, *I.L.N.T.* 267). Some of Torrey's points seem convincing, especially those in the early speeches in Acts. But other Aramaic scholars assess the evidence differently. Some, like de Zwaan (*B.C.* ii, 50 ff.) and Dodd (*A.P.* 35) allow only Acts i. 1 (apart from its opening clause) to v. 16 and ix. 31-xi. 18 to have had an Aramaic origin, not counting the speeches. These may not have had a real connexion with their present context and they often betray Aramaisms of thought if not of written composition. Of these two sections Knox (*Acts*, 18 f.) would allow that for the former at least Torrey established his case. It is possible, however, that the presence of citations from the LXX, not from the Aramaic or the Hebrew, point even in these sections to the original being Greek (cf. A. W. Argyle, *J.T.S.*, N.S., iv, 1953, 213 ff.) unless, as happened so often with Biblical citations in the Fathers, the quotations were altered by the Greek 'reviser' into the form with which he was most familiar, here into the form of the LXX text (cf. Metzger, *E.T.* lxv, 1954, 125).

2. (a) 'It has been said that in the early decades of the present century splitting the Acts into sources was almost as popular a pastime with the critics, as splitting the atom is nowadays with the scientists. And to tell the plain truth, the scientists have been much more successful than the critics' (A. M. Hunter, *I.N.T.* 110). The tendency to reject Torrey's arguments as well as to deny the necessity to look for sources, apart from a minimum, can be noticed in H. F. D. Sparks' article (*J.T.S.*, N.S., i, 1950, 16 ff.) where Torrey's arguments are countered and where Luke's use of 'Septuagintalisms' is rightly stressed.

INTRODUCTION

If Luke in writing the Third Gospel was not an innovator and inevitably used sources, Sparks says, 'there is nothing whatever to suggest that anyone else before him had ever thought of writing "Acts", and, if not, it is probable through sheer force of circumstances that he was dependent for his information on what he could learn by word of mouth'. Sparks points out that F. H. Chase, after starting with a presumption in favour of the theory of Luke's use of sources, came ultimately to the conclusion that the evidence was against written sources of any kind (*Credibility*, 15 f.). Similarly, W. L. Knox (*Acts*, 39) sums up his discussion of the sources of Acts by suggesting that 'apart from the speeches, representing a more or less fixed pattern of preaching, which may have been reduced to writing, we have no written sources with the possible exception of chapters i-v inclusive, but excluding most of the speeches'. Again, Foakes Jackson can say, 'We should constantly remember that source-criticism in the New Testament is largely guess-work (*Acts*, xv).

(b) With the growth of the influence of the Form-critical school, many are willing to recognize that, despite the many exaggerations of that school, it is not unreasonable to hold that the distinction between written and oral sources used in the early Church is a false one, if the latter became so fixed and stereotyped in preaching, teaching, and arguing that they amounted almost to written documents (cf. McNeile, *I.S.N.T.*, 2nd ed., ch. iii, and S. E. Johnson, *Anglican Theological Review*, xxi, 1939, 22-31). Yet it is doubtful whether the stories in Acts were ever so fixed during the oral stage of transmission before being written down by St. Luke as were the stories in the Gospels about our Lord. It may well be that Luke's sources were persons like St. Paul, St. Barnabas, Silas, Philip and his daughters, and John Mark (cf. Luke i. 1-4) and that Luke wove together these oral traditions so skilfully that it is impossible now to tell what his sources were. As Kümmel has argued, the fact that Luke's record of the primitive community contains teaching or traits that are undoubtedly ancient is no proof that the author used a written source as opposed to an oral one.

(c) Some of the 'doublets' previously supposed to point to two different written sources may have another explanation. The two arrests of the apostles in iv and v may be due to legal procedure as J. Jeremias has argued (*Z.N.T.W.* xxxvi, 1937, 205-221), according to which legal warning (ch. iv) had to be given before legal action (ch. v) could be taken. Again, a 'doublet' may be due to Luke's partiality for two typical events of a similar nature.

(d) F. C. Burkitt suggested that Acts i-xv was a Lucan revision of Mark's document which included originally not only Mark's Gospel but also the 'Lost Ending' of Mark and his account of the primitive church, but there is no evidence for this theory, which would, in effect, reduce Luke's sources to one person for Acts i-xv (contrast (b) above).

(e) H. Sahlin suggested that Luke-Acts appeared in three stages. (1) A written account of the work of Jesus and of the early Church, the first part of which was in Hebrew and underlies Luke i. 5-iii. 7a, the second part, Luke iii. 7b-Acts xv, being in Aramaic (cf. Torrey, 1 (e) above); the author was a Jewish-Christian, perhaps at Antioch, writing *c.* A.D. 50. (2) A Greek Christian, wanting to defend Paul on trial, probably Luke himself, revised and adapted this earlier work, adding Luke i. 1-4 and also a narrative of Paul's activities as well as many intervening paragraphs. (3) Luke-Acts thus formed was split in two, by adding an end to the third Gospel and an introduction to Acts, which may account for some of the textual difficulties of these two passages. Contrast Cadbury (*B.C.* v. 337): 'It has been pointed out that as they stand Luke and Acts are volumes of almost identical length, which suggests that the original author divided his material to fit a uniform (and standard) length of book roll and planned them as they are.'

(f) The present writer (*E.T.* lxiv, 1953, 283 ff.) suggested that Luke composed an early draft of Gospel material which he sent to Theophilus as his 'first treatise'; this was not necessarily 'Proto-Luke' as B. H. Streeter and V. Taylor have defined that document. Then Luke may have composed Acts after obtaining a copy of Mark's Gospel, some of the phrases of which are echoed in Acts but not repeated in the 'parallels' to Mark in the third Gospel. Then, on the basis of Mark's chronology, he revised the 'early draft', thus producing the third Gospel as we have it, intending perhaps to revise Acts later but being prevented from doing so. 'On this view Luke consciously or not assimilated some of the actions of the apostles in Acts to those of Jesus but carefully omitted from his Gospel later all such allusions.' This theory leaves open the question whether in compiling Acts Luke used other written sources besides Mark's Gospel rather than oral sources.

Note.—Since the above paragraph was written, H. G. Russell ('Which was the first, Luke or Acts?', *H.T.R.* xlviii, 1956, 167 ff.) has drawn attention to the importance of this suggestion, and he seems willing to adopt it. He points out that Luke, like other writers, may well have added his prologues last, after the rest of the work was complete.

In any event, an ancient work was liable to pass through several stages before it reached the public; the best account of these stages is now to be found in R. Devreesse's *Introduction à l'étude des manuscrits grecs*, 1954, 76-9, who describes 'le commerce d'amitié' by which a book reached the public.

5. THE DATE OF ACTS

(1) Whereas many Roman Catholic scholars, being bound by the decision of the papal commission that Acts was written by St. Luke *c*. A.D. 62, plead for an early date, others, both Anglican and Protestant, have inclined usually in favour of a later date between 70 and 85 or even 90, e.g. M. Goguel, who favours a date *c*. 80–90. There are exceptions to this rule, however. C. C. Torrey, who has dated all four Gospels much earlier than most scholars do, no doubt in the interests of his Aramaic theory, pleads for a date for Acts *c*. 64 (*C.D.A.*). 'It is a conjecture which is more than merely plausible, that during the two years (xxiv. 27) of Paul's imprisonment at Caesarea, Luke was collecting, examining and translating the materials for his Gospel.' He dates the Third Gospel *c*. A.D. 60 and Acts four years later; 'with the date 50 for I Acts (i.e. i-xv), 60 for the Gospel and 64 for II Acts we have a wonderfully suitable and convincing series', he wrote (*A.J.T.* xxiii, 1919, 193). Another exception is Dr. T. W. Manson (*B.J.R.L.* xxviii, 1944, 382-403), who argues that Luke wrote to defend Christians who were implicated, at least according to popular opinion, to a greater or lesser degree in the Jewish war, *c*. 66–70. While the Christian Church is the

true heir of Judaism, she is distinct from it. This thesis would lose much of its point after A.D. 70. Another and much earlier exception was R. B. Rackham (*J.T.S.* i, 1900, 76-87, cf. his commentary on Acts, l-lv), who argued for an early date for Acts because: (a) Paul's martyrdom is not mentioned in Acts; (b) silence about the Fall of Jerusalem in A.D. 70 is hard to explain if Acts was written after that date; (c) an apologia for Paul and for Christianity before A.D. 70 was needed and supplied by Luke; (d) Luke did not use a collection of Paul's letters. Certainly, the later in the first century Acts is dated, the harder this fact is to explain, unless we accept Goodspeed's view that the *auctor ad Ephesios* was the first to collect Paul's letters at all, which he did, prefacing them with Ephesians.

(2) To these points the critics may reply: (a) that Luke had traced the spread of Christianity from Jerusalem to Rome and was not concerned in Acts to relate Paul's death, for whom there remained 'only the trivial business of dying' (Dibelius) or else that Luke planned—not necessarily finished—yet a third volume; (b) that Luke wrote Luke xxi. 20 with the Fall of Jerusalem in mind because it had happened and that Acts was written after the third Gospel; (c) that an apologia for Christianity was needed after A.D. 70 as well as before it, for instance during the alleged persecution of Domitian, who ruled from A.D. 81-96; (d) that a companion of Paul, even if he knew none of his extant letters, would not have been guilty of the grave discrepancies said to exist between Paul's letters and Acts; this point is stressed by those who deny the Lucan authorship; (e) that while the theology of Acts and the historical and archaeological details are entirely consistent with a first-century date for Acts, there is no need to postulate that it was written before A.D. 70; (f) that, as some assert, Luke may have been familiar with the *Antiquities* of Josephus which was not published before A.D. 93 and that therefore Acts was written after that date.

(3) The present writer (art. cit.) has challenged the assumption that Acts was written after the third Gospel (in its early form), and as C. H. Dodd has shown, there is nothing in Luke xxi that Luke could not have derived from the Septuagintal prophecies of the future Fall of Jerusalem (*J.R.S.* xxxvii, 1947,

46-54), cf. Rackham, art. cit., 87 n. The *terminus a quo* for Acts need not be any longer the date of the Lucan Gospel. Some of the other points mentioned in (2) above remain to be discussed, but if an answer to them is found to be more or less convincing, then a date for Acts *c.* 66–70 would be a possible one; if an answer cannot be found that is convincing, the date *c.* 80–85 is more probable. For if Acts was not written before the Neronian persecution and Paul's death either occurred or was known in the writer's locality to have occurred, one must allow time for Christian emotions roused by these events to become stable. Unless dependence on Josephus is postulated, which would mean that Acts was written *c.* 93–100, then a date soon after 64 or else *c.* 85 can be maintained.

The strength of the case for dating Acts before the Fall of Jerusalem is obvious. If that disaster had occurred when Luke wrote, it is almost incomprehensible why he does not refer to it or to the desolation of Jerusalem and the Temple. But the possibility must be allowed that Luke may have written Acts before A.D. 70 and put it on one side after that date, when so much of Acts would have appeared beside the point. The 'publication' of Acts may have been postponed for many years after its composition.

6. THE PURPOSE AND THE CONCLUSION OF ACTS

A. (1) According to B. S. Easton (*The Purpose of Acts*, 1936), Luke addressed a wider audience than Theophilus alone. Christianity is a *religio licita*, i.e. a religion to which the state has given official recognition, since its recognition of Judaism. Any local Jewish community could claim the privileges allowed to Judaism by Rome (Juster, *Les Juifs dans l'empire romain*, i. 246, 422), so why should not any local Christian community? For Christians are the true Jews; as followers of the 'Way' they had a centralized Jewish authority established in Jerusalem. Corresponding to the high priests and elders of the Jews there stand the apostles and elders of the Church in the early period, and James and the elders later. Christianity is part of Judaism in the eyes of all with a right to speak (Acts i-iii).

(2) W. G. Kümmel (*op. cit.*) criticized this view because it

does not go far enough. Not only did Luke write to show that Christianity is politically respectable but Luke also had in mind a strong missionary purpose, to help to build up the Christian communities and to edify catechumens.

(3) Some scholars, like J. I. Still, have argued that Acts was written as a defence of Paul while he awaited trial and that the 'most excellent Theophilus' was not necessarily a Christian but a magistrate due to hear the case when it came up; cf. D. Plooij (*Exp.* viii. 8, 1914, 516). 'The emphasis . . . with which St. Luke makes his appeal to Roman justice implies . . . that the book was written as information for some Roman official (or more of them) whose influence in the process of Paul was of eminent importance.' (One may compare and contrast Streeter's suggestion that 'Theophilus', the God-fearing proselyte, was Flavius Clemens (*The Four Gospels*, 539).)

(4) One theory which is no longer held, except perhaps with one modern exception, is that of the Tübingen school of F. C. Baur and his followers more than a century ago. 'In accordance with the Hegelian watchword that all which happens is determined by the sequence, thesis, antithesis, synthesis, the Tübingen school constructed two periods; the first was one of embittered conflict between Paul and the Judaisers, who were at one with the original apostles; and the second was a period of conciliation which gradually made itself effective and marked the transition from Christianity to Catholicism' (*B.C.* ii. 299). History, as Streeter showed (*op. cit.* 543 ff.), cannot be forced into the Hegelian mould. We need not assume that Acts was written with an eirenic purpose to gloss over the past 'embittered conflict' between Paul and the Twelve.

The one exception mentioned above is Dr. S. G. F. Brandon, who makes a violent contrast between the narrow 'Judaistic' Gospel which was nationalistic in outlook but adoptionist in its Christology and 'Paulinism' which, he says, derived its doctrine of the Incarnation from the needs of Gentile hearers rather than from the historic facts of Jesus' life and which offered to them a Saviour after the manner of a mystery cult! He suggests that the Jewish Christians escaped in A.D. 70 not only to Pella, as tradition says, but also to Alexandria, where he thinks Judaistic Christianity was set up until the adherents of Paul arrived and overthrew it, establishing in its place a world-religion. His book, *The Fall of Jerusalem and the Christian Church*, suspects not only all the New Testament records but also the apostles themselves of tendentiousness and unscrupulous dealing at every turn. To turn to a corrective, Sir Idris Bell has shown in *Cults and Creeds in Graeco-Roman Egypt* (1953) how little evidence there is for the existence of Christians in Egypt during the first two centuries A.D.; even his remark (p. 80), 'The presence of a Christian heresy [Gnosticism at Alexandria] implies that of a Christian orthodoxy' must be modified by adding 'but an orthodoxy prevalent perhaps outside Egypt'. To suggest, as Brandon does, a relation between Paulinism and the Mystery cults is to raise a bogy that was laid more than a generation ago by A. D. Nock (*Essays on the Trinity and Incarnation*, ed. A. E. J. Rawlinson, 1928, 51-156; cf. the latter's Appended Note vi in his *The New Testament Doctrine of the Christ*, 1926; and N. P. Williams' essay on the Sacraments in *Essays Catholic and Critical*, ed. E. G. Selwyn, 1927, 367-423).

(5) According to Dibelius (= *Aufsätze* (Studies), reviewed by A. D. Nock, *Gnomon*, 25, 1953, 497 ff., to whom this paragraph is indebted), Luke's purpose was theological, but not in the sense that the Tübingen school supposed. He wrote to show 'what the Christian belief is and what effects it has' (*Studies*, 102). Luke's emphasis is on the typical rather than the isolated event. It was God, not man, according to Luke, who controlled the spread of the good news and it is God or His Spirit who issues commands. This theocratic outlook affected the methods of Luke's composition, giving prominence to certain episodes like that of Cornelius' conversion or the decision of the Council of Acts xv or the vision of the man of Macedonia. There was no question of Paul arranging his route on a map spread before him. Luke's purpose is seen even in the Speeches in Acts (see below) and in the generalizing summaries or *Sammelberichte* which cement the episodes together; the Acts of God are done through the apostles. Luke refrained from giving personal sketches of the apostles, though this would have been in line with an ancient historian's practice. He addressed cultivated folk on the theme of what God had done and he relied on Theophilus to disseminate the work even among non-Christians.

Though Luke may have intended to write a third volume, the end of the present one is on a happy note of triumph (cf. the end of the Third Gospel) when the apostle is left preaching at Rome, though Paul's death, foreshadowed at Miletus, xx. 28 ff., and at Caesarea, xxi. 10 ff., was known to the readers, Dibelius thinks, and could be assumed by them.

B. *The Conclusion of Acts*. Dibelius' view of the close of Acts is not the only one, and many other theories have been put forward, cf. *B.C.* iv. 349 f.

(i) 'The only really easy explanation of the "abrupt" ending,' wrote D. Plooij, 'is that Acts has been written just on the point of time where it ends, viz., at the beginning of the trial of Paul' (*Exp.* viii. 8, 1914, 514); cf. A. Harnack, 'The narrative had caught up with the events' (*D.A.S.G.* 90-125). If, as the present writer suggested (cf. 5 (3) above), Luke wrote Acts before his final draft of the Third Gospel, it is possible that Luke feared that Paul would not see his disciples in the East again, cf. xx. 25, 38, but he did not know *c.* A.D. 66 what Paul's fate was. This seems more likely than the view that Luke's source ceased at Paul's stay in Rome or that Luke, knowing Paul's death, did not relate it because he had not witnessed any more than Acts records. Contrast, however, the words of Professor E. J. Goodspeed, 'That our Acts was produced before the death of Paul is quite out of the question in view of the farewell chapters xx and xxi. . . . The death of Paul as I read the Acts is not even recent. It is long past and Paul has become a hallowed memory so that his last will and testament to the Ephesian elders . . . is freighted with the authority of one whose greatness has been vindicated by the passing years. His figure has grown to heroic proportions. . . . All this brings us to the late 80's or 90's' (*N.S.N.T.P.* 86 f.).

(ii) Another view is that the original ending, now lost, went on to narrate Paul's death, but has been mutilated to allow for further travels by Paul undertaken in the East (cf. the Pastoral letters) and for a second imprisonment at Rome; cf. Pfister's suggestion summarized in *B.C.* v. 336 f.

(iii) Another view is that a third volume was planned but not necessarily finished by Luke. This, it could be said, would explain why Theophilus is not mentioned at the end of the second volume (Acts) where we should normally, though not invariably, expect a mention of the person addressed in the Prologue (to the Gospel). It would relate Paul's end.

(iv) In *B.C.* v, note 26, it is argued that at the end of two years Paul's imprisonment would have ended because during the first eighteen months of it no Jewish accusers had come to take legal action against him. Because the prosecutors defaulted, Paul was automatically set free. While this was favourable to Paul, it was 'disappointing to Luke from the point of view of Christian apologetic'. But would it have been so disappointing? Like Gallio's treatment of Paul, it would have shown that Rome was quite impartial towards him. The present writer is not convinced that even if more definite proof were forthcoming that after two years' imprisonment, a prisoner whose accusers did not appear was freed, Luke would not have recorded this release had he known it.

7. DID LUKE USE JOSEPHUS' 'ANTIQUITIES'?

If the author of Acts used the *Antiquities*, which was written *c.* A.D. 93, then Acts could not have appeared till almost the end of the first century and St. Luke could hardly be the author unless he was a young man in St. Paul's day and lived to a very great age (cf. (1) (a) above).

A fair statement of the case for Luke's dependence on Josephus is to be found in F. C. Burkitt's *The Gospel History and its Transmission*, 1911, 105-10; he says: 'If he had read the *Antiquities*, and I cannot help drawing this inference, we must date the composition of Acts later than A.D. 94' (p. 108).

(a) The most crucial passage, the 'only one that need be taken seriously' (T. W. Manson) is *Ant.* xx. 5, 1 where Josephus records that while Fadus, who became procurator after Herod's death in A.D. 44 was in office, a sorcerer called Theudas persuaded a multitude 'to take their possessions and to follow him to the river Jordan'. Theudas claimed as a prophet to be able to divide the river and to make a way across it. Fadus' cavalry attacked the insurgents, killed many and captured Theudas, who was beheaded. If Luke is dependent on Josephus here, he is guilty of an anachronism, for he has attributed to Gamaliel, speaking before A.D. 36, a reference to events occurring after A.D. 44, and Luke is guilty of worse, for he goes on, after mention of Theudas, to refer to Judas; but Josephus, in the section following that outlined above, refers to the *sons of* Judas, who were executed under Alexander, the next procurator. If Luke had read Josephus, he was wrong in imagining that Judas followed Theudas. Now it is known that Josephus used sources, like the history of Nicolaus of Damascus, and the most casual comparison of Josephus' own works where they refer to the same events shows that Josephus was wildly inaccurate, especially about figures (compare his *Vita* with the *Jewish War* or the latter with parts of the *Antiquities*). Josephus or one of his Greek scribes that he employed may have used a source referring to Theudas and to Judas' sons, which was similar to a source used by Luke.

It is possible that another insurgent with a name like Theudas e.g. Theodorus, rose and fell before Judas of Galilee (J. B. Lightfoot, Smith's *Dict. of Bible*, i. 40), or it is possible that Luke, if he wrote Acts *c.* A.D. 80–85, heard Josephus lecture in Rome before the latter published his *Antiquities* (B. H. Streeter) and that Luke's notes, taken hurriedly, became the source of his mistake, or again it is possible that we should translate the opening words of v. 36 as 'before these days' or 'in the recent past' and those of v. 37 not 'after him', but 'my next example is' (T. W. Manson, *B.J.R.L.* 28, 1944, 400 n.). However, since it is difficult to see how any normal person on reading the passage in Josephus could arrive at Acts v. 36 f. or could leave out mention of Fadus as procurator, it is best to postulate a common source that mentioned Judas and Theudas together, though they lived some fifty years apart. In any case, Luke's narrative seems the more sober, for he speaks of four hundred followers of Theudas while Josephus tells of the 'majority of the people' following him, though he tells too of five hundred cavalry being enough to defeat the insurgents. The theory that the name of Theudas has been interpolated into Acts from Josephus (Hilgenfeld) or from Acts into Josephus (Blass) is a desperate resource of criticism. (See Dibelius, *Studies*, 186 ff.)

(b) In Acts xxi. 38 the tribune asks Paul, Art thou not the Egyptian who before these days revolted and led out four

thousand men of the Sicarii into the desert? To some critics
this reads like Josephus, *B.J.* ii. 13, 3, where he describes the
Sicarii and then goes on in the next paragraph to talk of false
prophets who led men into the desert and whom Felix destroyed; then in the following paragraph Josephus tells of the
Egyptian who led thirty thousand men out of the desert, many
of whom the Romans killed. Here again, details, like the direction taken by the insurgents, differ; Luke's 4000 compares
favourably with Josephus' 30,000. 'The number of rebels grows
in tradition more often than it decreases, and Luke's figure is
surely the more probable' (*B.C.* ii. 357). It is too often forgotten
that Josephus' *Jewish War* appeared first in an Aramaic form,
no longer extant, and it is possible that Luke knew that. More
probably, however, he gives a separate account from a similar
source.

(c) In Acts xii. 21 ff. Luke describes the death of Herod
Agrippa. His account differs from that of Josephus, *Ant.* xix.
8, 2, who describes it as a divine retribution for failing to rebuke
the flatterers at Caesarea when he appeared before them in a
shining silver robe and was hailed as divine. Josephus does not
refer to the conflict with the Tyrians and Sidonians, as Luke
does; and Luke does not mention the omen of the owl sitting on
a rope, as Josephus does, which Herod took to presage death.
Elsewhere (*ibid.* xvii. 6, 5) Josephus describes the death of
Herod the Great as caused by worms; but this form of death
was commonly attributed to tyrants, cf. 2 Macc. ix. 5 ff. of
Antiochus Epiphanes.

(d) Reference should be made here also to Luke iii. 1 where
Lysanias, tetrarch of Abilene is mentioned. Some have thought
that here Luke depended on Josephus (*ibid.* xv. 10, 1; xx. v, cf.
B.J. i. 20, 4) and that Luke was mistaken in thinking that
Lysanias lived early in the first century before Abila was ceded
to Agrippa II. But the existence of two men of this name can
be inferred from *C.I.G.* 4523 and 4521. As J. M. Creed wrote
on this passage in his commentary on Luke (309): '. . . Luke's
reference to Lysanias, being probably correct, does not suggest
the hypothesis of a mistaken inference from Josephus and does
not support the conjecture that Luke knew Josephus. On the
contrary, this is one of the several cases in which Luke draws

upon sources of information independent of Josephus'; contrast
B.C. ii. 357: 'It is clear that an inaccurate knowledge of
Josephus would adequately account for the error in Luke'.

If a student will read the *Antiquities*, xviii-xx, asking himself
how much the Evangelist would have drawn on those books, if
he had read them, he will probably conclude that the theory of
Luke's dependence on Josephus is flimsy. It is incredible that
Luke 'should have bestowed so much time on a book which
gave him so little information, and enquired so minutely, only
to fall into such errors as the mention of Theudas and Judas of
Galilee. . . . Most of the persons he mentions were of public
notoriety and so familiar to everybody that it was not necessary
to read an historical work to discover them' (Foakes Jackson,
Acts, xiv f.). M. Goguel (*I.N.T.* 117 ff.) rightly rejects the
extreme views of Krenkel (*Josephus und Lukas*, 1894) and he
himself concludes that Luke's work was not dependent on that
of Josephus.

8. ARE THE DISCREPANCIES BETWEEN ACTS AND THE PAULINE
   EPISTLES SO GRAVE THAT THE CONCLUSION IS IRRESISTIBLE
   THAT A COMPANION OF PAUL COULD NOT HAVE WRITTEN
   ACTS?

In approaching this problem one has to remember that the
author of Acts has applied to his canvas broad sweeps and not
minute strokes of his brush, and that, though Luke may have
collected some of his material before meeting Paul, the latter's
epistles are more nearly contemporaneous with the events and
have a greater claim to be treated as historical: also that when
Luke met Paul, he did not come to know him so intimately as
we are apt to assume, and that Paul probably looked forward to
the future 'to the mark of the goal' and not very much to the
past, except to his unforgettable experience on the Damascus
road, with the result that Luke's account of Paul's life in the
narrative before the we-sections open, xvi. 1, was gleaned from
others than Paul himself and probably written when Paul· was
absent (or dead?). There is no need to assume that a companion
of Paul must have known a collection of the epistles, though he
may have known some no longer extant, still less that he was

influenced much by Pauline doctrine which few in the first century could grasp. (Harnack said that Marcion was the first to understand St. Paul and that he misunderstood him.) It may well be that Luke was a Greek-speaking Jew who had long been familiar with the Septuagint and with the Jewish-Christian teaching derived ultimately from Christians in Jerusalem and that he was not a Greek converted shortly before meeting Paul.

In his essay, 'The Case against the Tradition', *B.C.* ii. 298 ff., H. Windisch made the most of the alleged discrepancies and C. W. Emmet, *ibid.* 265 ff., made the least, 'The Case for the Tradition'.

(i) If Luke was a companion of Paul and the author of Acts, why did he not mention Paul's visit to Arabia, the region around Damascus, Gal. i. 17? Acts ix. 19 f. omits all reference to it. A sufficient answer is that it was not part of Luke's purpose to record all the minor details of Paul's movements, even if he knew them.

(ii) In Galatians i-ii Paul stresses his independence of the apostles at Jerusalem. In speaking of the first visit that he paid to Jerusalem after his conversion, he maintains that he did not go there at once but to Arabia and then to Antioch. Only after three years did he visit Jerusalem, Gal. i. 18-24. This was a private visit to meet Peter, with whom he spent a fortnight, seeing also James only but not visiting the churches of Judaea (as opposed perhaps to Christians inside Jerusalem). In Acts ix. 26 ff. Luke, writing on the assumption that the Christian Church went out from Jerusalem to the ends of the earth, relates how Paul was received by the apostles, thanks to Barnabas, and how he preached and argued with the Hellenists. The basis of Luke's account may have been a casual allusion of Paul to his having met 'the apostles' and having preached at various houses in Jerusalem.

(iii) Acts stresses far more than Paul's letters that Paul took the Gospel first to Jews, then to Gentiles. Luke seems to have thought that normally Paul's message was first welcomed, then rejected by the Jews, who forced him to turn to the Gentiles, cf. xiii. 46, xviii. 6, xxviii. 25 f. This alleged discrepancy is not serious. Paul's most fruitful field lay among the Hellenists and the adherents to the Synagogue, by converting whom he roused the wrath of the Jews; though the 'apostle to the Gentiles', he longed for the conversion of his fellow-Jews (Rom. ix), and so far from leaving them alone he became to the Jews as a Jew that he might win Jews (1 Cor. ix. 20). Similarly some have wondered if Paul could indeed have taken on himself a 'Nazirite' vow, xxi. 23 ff., paying the expenses of other Jewish Christians who were completing their vows. Yet though he knew that the Law was inferior and temporary and not binding on Gentile-Christians, he himself was a 'Pharisee of the Pharisees' and probably dressed as such in Jerusalem and was willing to become 'all things to all men that he might save some'.

(iv) In Acts xvii. 15, xviii. 5 the details of the movements of Silas and Timothy differ from those implied in 1 Thess. iii. 1-6; but cf. (i) above; those movements were unimportant to Luke as he recorded the spread of the Gospel from Jerusalem to Rome.

(v) The account in Acts xviii. 18-xix. 22 is very condensed and does not refer to the hostility and suffering which Paul faced according to 1 Cor. iv. 9-13, xv. 32, 2 Cor. i. 8, iv. 8-12. Various reasons have been given for the condensation of Luke's account, cf. notes on xviii. 18. Why should a companion of Paul minimize his sufferings? Was it to stress the tolerance of the civic authorities at Ephesus towards Christianity? Or was it that Luke was not present on this occasion and that Paul did not normally boast of his infirmities except to prove his apostolic status?

(vi) The most difficult problem is raised by the account in Acts xv of the Council meeting in relation to Galatians ii. In Acts i-xv at least three if not four (cf. xii. 25) visits of Paul to Jerusalem after his conversion are mentioned, ix. 26-30, xi. 27-30 (the famine-visit), and xv (the Council visit). But in Galatians only two such visits are recorded, Gal. i. 18-24 and ii. 1-10. Though Paul was stressing his independence of the Jerusalem church, his solemn oath that he was not lying and his proximity in time to the events must weigh the scales in favour of Galatians, if there is any doubt, unless we take the view that an excited protagonist in the debate, such as Paul, would be more liable to error than a sober historian writing later. The problem is not so much to equate the first visit mentioned in Acts ix. 26-30, with the first visit mentioned in Galatians, i. 18-24, as to equate the second visit mentioned in Acts, xi. 30 (cf. xii. 25, which despite the better attested textual evidence should be taken to mean that the mission of Barnabas and Saul to Jerusalem was completed, cf. McNeile, *op. cit.* 118 n.), with that of Gal. ii. 1-10, the second visit mentioned in the epistle; or whether we are to equate the latter with the Council visit of Acts xv. In the main, three views have been widely held: (a) the visit of Gal. ii is that of Acts xv; (b) the visit of Gal. ii is that of Acts xi; (c) the visit of Gal. ii is recorded twice by Luke in xi and xv, both being different accounts of the same visit, a view advocated by Weizsäcker, McGiffert, Schwartz (*B.C.* v. 195 ff.), and latterly by K. Lake. To these should be added at least two other possible views: (d) neither Acts xi nor xv refers to the visit of Gal. ii, Acts being unhistorical on this point; (e) an imaginative reconstruction of the events must be made from Acts xi and xv on the basis of Paul's words.

(a) The visit of Gal. ii is that of Acts xv. J. B. Lightfoot's arguments have been taken up by many continental scholars especially, e.g. J. L. Leuba (*New Testament Pattern*, 1953, 72 f.), who argues that the same persons appear in each account, the Jerusalem church as a whole (Acts xv. 4, 22, Gal. ii. 2) and in particular Peter and James (Acts xv. 7, 13, Gal. ii. 9) and on the other hand Paul and Barnabas (Acts xv. 2, 12, Gal. ii. 9) who are to return later to Antioch (Acts xv. 30, Gal. ii. 11). Secondly, the primary object of the meeting appears the same in both accounts: to discuss whether Gentile Christians should be circumcised as the Pharisees demanded (Acts xv. 5, Gal. ii. 4). Thirdly, in both accounts the solution seems the same; circumcision was not to be required of Gentile Christians (Acts xv. 6 ff., 28, Gal. ii. 5-6) to whom Paul's mission was recognized (Acts xv. 12, Gal. ii. 2).

On this view Paul did not mention the visit of Acts xi, as he was thinking not so much of the journeys made to Jerusalem as of conversations held with the chief apostles. If anyone had said to him after reading Galatians, 'What about the famine-visit?' Paul could have scored a good debating point, 'The apostles had left, of course' (cf. K. E. Kirk, *C.Q.R.* 116, 1933, 291-7): besides, Luke makes it clear that the apostles handed their gifts over to the 'elders' not the 'apostles' (xi. 30). On this view, then, a private agreement between Paul and the 'pillars' of the Church was regularized later at a fuller meeting. A subsidiary point was that the similarity between Romans and Galatians is so strong that they must have been written about the same time. Alternatively, the account of Acts xi. 27-30 with its mention of Paul may be inaccurate. Streeter (*The Four Gospels*, 557 n.) suggested that Barnabas took someone, not Paul, with him and that Luke assumed that the latter was the former's companion wrongly.

(b) The visit of Gal. ii is that of Acts xi. There are weaknesses in Leuba's arguments; e.g. mention of John is absent in Acts. Galatians was written in a white-hot passion, Romans in a calmer, reflective mood about the same subject, and so with reference to the same Old Testament figures and citations. Sir W. Ramsay and others have felt so acutely the difficulty of Paul's neglect of the famine-visit that they identify it, not that of xv, with that of Gal. ii. (*P.T.R.C.* 55 ff., cf. C. W. Emmet, *B.C.* ii. 277 ff.)

In Gal. ii. 2 Paul says that he went up 'by revelation', cf. the prophecy of Agabus, Acts xi. 27. It is possible on this view that Galatians was written on the eve of the Council visit before the Council of Acts xv met or its decrees were passed. W. L. Knox argued (*Acts*, 49) that on this assumption we find a clear historical development. Peter was compelled by the Cornelius incident to recognize the possibility of baptizing uncircumcised Gentiles; during the famine-visit he with James and John agreed to let Paul preach to Gentiles. But at Antioch Peter wavered under pressure from Jewish-Christian extremists so that he refused to eat any more with Gentile-Christians. Paul protested in vain. The decision of the church in Antioch to send out a mission to Gentiles followed. This brought about a crisis. Paul's success in the Galatian churches led Jewish converts to demand the circumcision of all converts; the question was referred to a council at Jerusalem. In any event, 'Luke's credit as a writer need not depend so completely on a reconciliation of Acts xv and Gal. ii as is sometimes supposed. If we assume that the account of the Council existed as an independent document possessed by one of the great Churches and representing the events of Gal. ii in this way, it is quite possible that Luke, if he came across it, might have inserted it bodily into his narrative' (*ibid.* 41). It seems probable that if Paul wrote Galatians after the Council meeting he would have mentioned the decrees and the letter, Acts xv. 23-9. For these would have been a complete answer to the Judaizers' points. These arguments appear decisive to F. Amiot (*S. Paul, Épître aux Galates,* 1946, 32).

At the same time there are scholars like Jacquier, Burton, and Askwith who accept Ramsay's arguments that the epistle was addressed to 'south Galatia', to churches in Pisidian Antioch, Lystra and Derbe, not to north Galatia, to places like Ancyra, Pessinus, and Tavium, and who equate the visit of Acts xv with that of Gal. ii (as Nock, D. Round, and Amiot do not) and who date Galatians after the Council meeting not, as Ramsay did, from Syrian Antioch before Paul started on the 'third missionary journey' but earlier, shortly after 2 Corinthians was written and before Romans (Askwith, *The Epistle to the Galatians,* 1899, 99-132). On such a view, the reason why Paul did not apparently communicate the decisions of the Council to his converts was that the farther he went from Palestine the more he was willing to argue about food laws, as in 1 Cor. viii and Rom. xiv, from first principles not on the authority of the Jerusalem church.

(c) The visit of Gal. ii is recorded in both Acts xi and xv. This theory falls into line with that of the use of written sources (see 4 above); two written sources, one perhaps emanating from Jerusalem, the other from Antioch, are both reproduced in Acts (K. Lake's later theory, citing Schwartz, *B.C.* v. 195-212). On this hypothesis the interview between Paul and the chief apostles mentioned in Gal. ii must be put either earlier or later than the first missionary journey of Acts xiii-xiv, and most critics who adopt this theory would place it earlier. The Council meeting is therefore dated at about the time of the events of Acts xi. But a variant of this theory is gaining popularity, that Acts xv results from the combination of two sources, one of them referring to the meeting of Acts xi and the other to a different event, cf. Dupont, *Problèmes,* 63-4. On either view it would be difficult to maintain that Acts was written before A.D. 80 or that Luke was a careful historian.

(d) To reject the historicity of Acts altogether and to deny that xi and xv correspond in any way to Gal. ii is the drastic solution of Sahlin, who takes xi. 27-30 to be void of any historical basis while the insertion of Paul's name into xv is fraudulent. 'Luke' was, on this view, not a scrupulous editor. But it may seem arbitrary to reject Luke's historicity on this point if one is compelled to accept his careful attention to historical detail on others.

(e) Among several imaginative reconstructions that can be made on the basis of Galatians, two may be mentioned: (1) The article by a former pupil, the Rev. J. R. Porter, *J.T.S.* xlvii, 1946, 169-74, who finds in xi. 27-30 and in xi. 1-18 a doublet of xv. His conclusion is that Paul's second visit to Jerusalem preceded his first missionary journey although he had already done considerable missionary work among Gentiles in Syria and Cilicia, Gal. i. 22, ii. 2. His visit coincided with the opening of the dispute on table-fellowship between Jewish- and Gentile-Christians which Peter's own behaviour had brought to a head. The author of Acts, besides duplicating his account of Paul's visit has also duplicated Peter's defence in xi and xv. This accounts for the highly suspicious presence of Peter and Paul in the account of xv. The result of the discussion on table-fellowship was that Gentile-Christians need not observe Jewish food-laws. Porter suggests that after Peter had fled to Antioch, John Mark returned to Jerusalem from the first missionary journey suspecting that Paul and Barnabas intended to undertake a great mission to the Gentiles; James and his party decided to assert the Jewish character of the church over the Gentile-Christians of the Antioch area. 'Certain from James, among whom was John Mark, brought a decree allowing table-fellowship *on Jewish terms*, to Antioch. The Gentile-Christians refused to obey; Peter broke off intercourse with them at meals, as did Barnabas on his return, thus arousing the wrath of Paul. Barnabas signalised his complete adherence to the party of James by sailing away with John Mark to Cyprus.' Even if one agrees with Dupont that this reconstruction allows too much for fancy, it is possible that the dispute over table-fellowship and that over circumcision were originally distinct and that Luke has conflated them.

(2) In the *B.J.R.L.* 24, 1940, 59-80, Dr. T. W. Manson thinks that the whole account in Gal. ii seems to imply a private conference between leaders of the Church at Jerusalem and Antioch conducted in a friendly spirit and ending in an amicable and sensible allocation of missionary tasks. This does not seem to resemble what is described either in Acts xi or xv nor does the visit described in Gal. ii fit the circumstances which occasioned either of the visits described in Acts. The visit is to be placed on the eve of the first missionary journey, which is to be dated *c.* A.D. 47 or 48. It was followed by the Antioch incident and the rebuke to Peter. 'The essence of the matter is that the Council was ostensibly concerned to deal with the question of the circumcision of Gentile Christians, and that it ended by issuing regulations about the common table of Jewish and Gentile Christians.' The decrees [xv. 20, 29] are the answer to the questions raised in Gal. ii. 11-14; they are not, and cannot be, the answer to the issue raised in Acts xv. 1. The decrees or better 'working compromise' settled the problem of table-fellowship. Then the years passed and the situation was changed. Jewish-Christian opponents appear in Philippians and Corinthians and Paul's apostolic authority is questioned. The compromise was made the basis for further Jewish-Christian demands, viz. to keep the Jewish calendar, cf. Gal. iv. 8-11, vi. 11-13. Hence Galatians, which is not on this view the earliest extant Pauline letter. The demand to circumcise Gentile converts, Acts xv. 1, 5, may have been made at a later time than the Council.

Other articles which deserve mention are those of Dibelius (*T.L.* 2, 72, 1947, 4, 193-8, cf. *Studies*, 97 ff.), who denies the historicity of Acts xv: everything which Luke records of the Council is his doctrinal development, intended to stress that the call of the Gentiles came from God, not men. Galatians is the only authoritative source: of F. W. Beare, *J.B.L.* lxii, 1943, 295-306, cf. D. F. Robinson, *ibid.* lxiii, 1944, 169-72, where the historicity of the visit of Acts ix is denied while that of xi. 27-30 is identified with that of ix. 26-30 and Gal. i. 18-24. Enough has been said to show that the historicity of ix-xv, especially of xv, is seriously questioned and that many theories are possible without any one being convincing. The present writer is inclined to accept the view of W. L. Knox and F. Amiot given above; but it would be safer perhaps to suspend judgement on this last, sixth point. On the other five points, however, there seems no good reason to withold a verdict that the alleged discrepancies between the Pauline epistles and Acts are not so grave as to compel the decision that Acts could not have been written by a companion of Paul. One finds that any attitude to the sixth point is affected by an estimate of the historicity of the local conditions depicted in Acts, the officials, and the places mentioned.

9. LOCAL KNOWLEDGE SHOWN IN ACTS

It is well known that Sir William Ramsay began his study of Acts and his famous archaeological explorations with a prejudice in favour of a second-century date for the work, but his conclusions forced him to accept a first-century date and made him an ardent champion of Luke's authorship. As even Schmiedel admitted, there are many points in Acts of real historical value, corroborated by external evidence and showing the general trustworthiness of the author. He distinguishes correctly between senatorial and imperial provinces, the former being governed by a Proconsul on behalf of the Senate, the latter by a Propraetor representing the Emperor. Luke makes no mistake over these terms and this is all the more impressive as the status of a province was liable to change with the times; in peace it would be governed by a Proconsul, in times of disturbance by a Propraetor. When Luke refers in xiii. 7 to Sergius Paulus, Proconsul of Cyprus, and in xviii. 12 to Gallio, Proconsul of Achaia, he was dealing with provinces whose administration had changed. In xxviii. 7 he calls Publius the 'first man', *protos*, or '*Primus*'; this title is not found in extant literature but is known from inscriptions found at Malta. Similarly the magistrates at Philippi are rightly called Praetors in xvi. 20, while those at Thessalonica are politarchs in xvii. 6, a title confirmed by many inscriptions. Luke also shows accurate knowledge of persons holding high office in Paul's lifetime and he places them in their historical setting, e.g. Herod Agrippa I, Agrippa II, Felix, and Festus. Again, he gives the correct geographical colouring for Lystra, Neapolis, Philippi (which is rightly called a 'colony'), Thessalonica, Beroea, Achaia, and Athens and Corinth.

The student is referred not only to Ramsay's works but also to W. A. McDonald, *The Biblical Archaeologist*, iii, 1940, 18-24; iv, 1941, 1-10; v, 1942, 36-48; and to M. M. Parvis, *ibid.* viii, 1945, 62-80; also to the notes below on the 'universal' famine, xi. 28, with K. S. Gapp's article, and on the edict of Claudius, xviii. 2, and on the town-clerk or scribe of the *demos*, xix. 31, 35; and for the 'priests of Zeus', xiv. 12, to the admittedly third century A.D. inscriptions that mention them, from which the existence of such priests earlier may be inferred.

10. The Apostolic Decree of Acts xv, 20, 29, cf. xxi. 25

A. (1) According to the non-Western text of the 'decree', a translation would run, 'Therefore my judgement is that we should not trouble those of the Gentiles who turn to God, but should write to them to abstain from the pollutions of idols and from unchastity (*porneia*) and from what is strangled and from blood'. (2) The Western text omits 'and from what is strangled', adding after v. 20 the negative form of the Golden Rule, 'let them not do to others what they would not have done to themselves'. (3) The Chester Beatty Papyrus, P. 45, and some other evidence from the Ethiopic and a few Latin vulgate mss. omit, 'and from unchastity'. (See the present writer's *Alterations* ... 72-75.)

After a long and tedious debate, scholars are coming to the conclusion that the Western form (2) is not original. Dupont (*Problèmes*, 70) says that the text of the decree at least seems settled and it is a long time since Harnack defended the Western text here. Among the reasons for this conclusion are: (a) the negative form of the Golden Rule seems an obvious interpolation possibly from a Jewish source, cf. Tobit, iv. 15 and Hillel's 'What to thyself is hateful to thy neighbour thou shalt not do' (*T.B. Shabbath*, 31a) or possibly from Tatian's Diatessaron (R. H. Connolly, *J.T.S.* xxxv, 1934, 351-7, cf. O. E.

Evans, *E.T.* lxiii, 1951, 31 f.); (b) the motive of the Western scribe was apparently to give a moral law against idolatry, fornication, and bloodshed and not a ritual rule about food tabus, viz. things sacrificed to idols, blood-drinking, and partaking of things strangled [from which the blood had not been drained away], which the Alexandrian text gives. 'Fornication' may mean not so much 'unchastity' in general as marriage within the forbidden degrees in the Levitical sense; though it is far from being a complete moral law, the Western form of the Decree would correspond to the 'Noachian commands', forbidding idolatry, fornication, and murder, binding on all the sons of Noah (cf. *B.C.* v. 208); the W-text as a moral law would easily displace an earlier food-law; the reverse is almost unthinkable; (c) the verb, 'to abstain from' suggests a food-law rather than a moral one. It is rather absurd to suppose that the apostles solemnly passed a Decree based on 'abstinence from' murder and fornication; 'abstention' from these should have been no 'burden' (cf. xv. 28). In fact they asked the Gentile Christians in eating alongside Jewish Christians to abstain from foods forbidden to the latter or to Jews, so that the latter might not feel embarrassed by the presence of a 'sinner'. These ritual rules were the minimum necessary for social intercourse, for instance, at an Agape or common meal.

The omission in P. 45, etc., of 'and fornication' probably is due to a scribe noticing the incompatibility of a prohibition of immorality among some food tabus. It cannot be treated as the original from which both the Alexandrian and Western forms have been derived, but rather as a compromise between them.

B. Granting that the text of the Decree is settled, there remains the question whether Luke has placed it correctly where he does. Many scholars are inclined to separate the Decree from the Council meeting altogether because the Decree in its original form was a food law unrelated to the problem of circumcision mentioned in xv. 1-5, and because Paul says nothing about the Decree in Galatians (though this is explained on the view of Knox and Amiot that Paul wrote Galatians before the Council meeting) and because according to xxi. 25 Paul did not yet know the terms of the Decree, unless this verse is taken to mean that he was reminded of it and the words 'as you very well know' are to be supplied and because Paul did not quote the Decree later in writing to the Corinthians when he deals with the question of eating meats offered to idols (1 Cor. viii), unless we account for this silence by supposing that he wanted to argue the matter *de novo*.

It is possible that if Luke's narrative is not historical, he may have imposed the problem of circumcising Gentile converts on to the problem of food tabus and he may have placed the solution of the one on top of the other, whereas the two were originally distinct though closely connected problems.

11. THE CHRONOLOGY OF THE EVENTS NARRATED IN ACTS

A. (1) The student is referred to the excellent articles on this subject (i) by C. H. Turner in *H.D.B.* i. 415-24 and (ii) by K. Lake, *B.C.* v. n. xxxiv. As the latter says (173) with reference to the exact fixing of the few definite data that we possess, 'none can be established quite exactly and only in the case of the death of Herod, the Proconsulate of Gallio and—I should be inclined to add—the appointment of Festus, can it be said that the margin of possible error is not great. This is not very much to work upon; there is consequently considerable strain on the dead-reckoning from event to event, and different investigators estimate differently the probable lapse of time. That this difference is, after all, not extreme may be shown by the following selection of typical events in tabular form.' He then prints the following:

	Petavius	Wieseler	Harnack	Turner	Zahn	Lightfoot	Weber	Plooij	Lake
The Crucifixion	31	30	29 or 30	29	30	(30)	—	29	29–30
Paul's conversion	33	40	30	35	35	34	31	30–1	32
Famine relief	41	45	(44)	46	44	45	46–7	45–6	} 46
Apostolic Council	49	50	47	49	52	51	50	48	
Corinth	50	52	48	50	52	52	50	50	49
Last visit to Jerusalem	53	58	54	56	58	58	55	57	55
Appointment of Festus	56	60	56	56	60	60	55	59	55

3

(2) With Lake's table we may list the dates given by more recent writers:

	Bacon	Cadoux	McNeile	Amiot	Bruce	Tenney
The Crucifixion	29	—	—	30	30	29
Paul's conversion	33	35	39	32–3	c. 33	—
Famine relief	c. 44	47–8	46	45–6	c. 46	—
Apostolic Council	48	49	49	49	c. 49	48–9
Corinth	50	50	50	—	50–2	50–2
Last visit to Jerusalem	55	57	57	—	57	—
Appointment of Festus	c. 57	c. 57	—	—	c. 59	57–60

We note that Lake is able to compress the Famine relief visit and the Apostolic Council; and to put the events before Paul's arrival in Corinth and the appointment of Festus within fewer years than others do because he recognizes the possibility that the Famine relief visit was followed by a single long journey through Asia Minor, Macedonia, and Achaia, unbroken by any return to Antioch (art. cit. 473 f.).

The tendency in recent years to accept a date *c.* 50 for Paul's arrival in Corinth is due to the discovery since Turner wrote of the value of the Gallio inscription, cf. Lake, 460 ff., from which (and from other inscriptions) it is seen that Gallio's Proconsulship included probably the year 52, though it is not known if he became Proconsul in 51 or 52 nor how long he remained in that office. Acts xviii. 12 refers to his entry upon that office probably in July 52 or possibly 51, cf. A. H. McNeile, *St. Paul*, xiii-xix.

B.   C. H. Turner (art. cit. 421) spoke of the 'picture, cut up, as it were, into six panels, each labelled with a general summary of progress: (i) the first period begins with i. 1 and leads to a general summary in vi. 7; (ii) the second period with vi. 8 leading to ix. 31; (iii) the third with ix. 32 leading to xii. 24; (iv) the fourth with xii. 25 leading to xvi. 5; (v) the fifth with xvi. 6 leading to xix. 20; (vi) the last with xix. 31 leading to xxviii. 31.

This theory was developed by C. J. Cadoux (*J.B.L.* 56, 1937, 177 ff.), who inserted seven 'rubrics' into his full chronological list, ii. 47b, vi. 7, ix. 31, xii. 24, xvi. 5, xix. 20, xxviii. 31 with the following seven dates against each in turn, A.D. 30, 35, 40, 45, 50, 55, 60. The suggestion is that Luke divided up his material chronologically and inserted a 'rubric' to correspond to each quinquennium. This theory seemed to some almost too good to be true and it met with criticism from B. W. Bacon (*H.T.R.* 14, 1921, 137-166), who says, for instance, that xxviii. 31 is not a true 'rubric' and from J. de Zwaan (*ibid.* xvii, 1924, esp. 100-6) according to whom the summaries should be called 'stops'. These are not keystones in Luke's edifice, which resembles a pyramid, the broad Palestinian basis in i. 1-xi. 18 rising to the structure of the Antioch church, xi. 19-xv. 35, and up to the apex in Paul's work, xv. 36-end, with a third volume planned to follow, even if it was never executed.

Criticism of Turner's view, at least, also came from Jacquier (*Actes*, introd., ch. v), according to whom there are at least eight 'panels', ii. 47 and xi. 21 to be added to Turner's summaries, if the theory holds water at all; cf. also the criticism made by F. W. Beare, *J.B.L.* 62, 1943, 295-306 (esp. 302 ff.): there are 'summaries' placed apparently at random in the Third Gospel, Luke i. 80, ii. 40, 52, iv. 14 and 37. A fuller list of 'summaries' is given by P. Benoit (*Mél. Goguel*, 1, n. 1) in his study of ii. 42-7, iv. 32-5, and v. 12-16, cf. H. J. Cadbury, *B.C.* v. n. xxx.

On the whole, Cadbury's cautious conclusion seems to be justified: 'The historical value of the summaries is . . . open to question. The inherent difficulty of generalizing judgements and memories, the obviously late and derivative character of the descriptions distilled out of the specific scenes, the natural tendency to exaggerate the growth and influence of Christianity, and the editorial demands which made these summaries necessary—all these factors justify a reasonable doubt about their contents. On the other hand, we are really not sure how much additional data Luke and his predecessors may have had beyond the specific items they have passed down to us. Certain items are mentioned with a definiteness and brevity that imply that his knowledge or his sources were more complete. In that case the summaries may rest on more information than we ourselves now have access to. They can be judged, if at all, only each for itself' (art. cit. 402). Cf. Lake's conclusion (*B.C.* v. 484) that we are dealing with selected episodes, not a continuous history.

12. THE SPEECHES AND THE THEOLOGY OF ACTS

It is usually agreed that the speeches in Acts provide a main clue to Luke's understanding of Christian theology. Different assumptions may be made about them, however. Are they Luke's compositions? Do they reflect accurately the tradition of the common teaching of early mission preachers? Do they represent the words used by Peter, Stephen, and Paul? Yet the fact cannot be denied that Luke incorporated the speeches in Acts, presumably to show his readers what the Christian faith was.

A radical view that they are Luke's compositions, has been maintained. It is argued that Luke, writing shortly if at all before A.D. 90, inserted speeches into his narrative to give it variety or to give his view of history with the veil drawn back and the hand of God revealed. It is assumed that Luke followed the Greek historians, especially Thucydides, and the exact words of the latter are treated as though they implied that an ancient historian started with a *tabula rasa* and allowed himself free composition. But Thucydides did not mean this when he wrote (*Hist.* I. 22), 'As for the speeches which were made by different men either when they were about to begin the war or when they were already engaged therein, it has been difficult to recall the words actually spoken with strict accuracy, both for me about what I myself heard and for those who from various other sources have brought me reports. So the speeches are given in the language in which, as it seemed to me, the several speakers would express, on the subjects under consideration, the sentiments most befitting the occasion, though at the same time I have adhered as closely as possible to the general sense of what was actually said.' Thucydidean scholars have debated this passage at length, and especially the meaning of 'general sense' (*xumpasa gnomē*). It is sometimes forgotten that these scholars differ widely among themselves (cf. H. Patzer, *Das Problem der Geschichtsschreibung des Thukydides* . . . 1937, esp. pp. 44 ff.). While Grossinsky would say that Thucydides is claiming for the reporting of speeches a considerable degree of subjectivity (*Das Program des Thukydides*), Pohlenz would assert that the contrast here is with Herodotus whose speeches were composed on the Epic model and were entirely free composi‑ tions without any relation to actually delivered speeches; on this view Thucydides was not claiming a freedom for himself but referring for the first time to the imposition of an objective bond by which he felt himself bound in the sphere of the *logoi* as well as the *erga*, the parallelism between which is significant as it sets the *logoi* in a new light; instead of being mere artistic embellishments of the historical narrative, they become objects of historical research (*Thukydidesstudien*, 1919–20). Few would go as far as Gomme in maintaining that there is no problem and that Thucydides tells us that he is going to report speeches as nearly as he can, though of course in his own words. While some speeches are more generalized than others, we can regard them, he maintains, on the whole as authentic, giving us fairly closely an idea of what was said (*Essays in Greek History and Literature*). So far as one can sum up the findings of the majority of students of Thucydides, it is that in this famous passage he meant that he inserted speeches which seemed appropriate for a given speaker in a given situation, telling us what the speakers should have said in the light of their actions and characters and sometimes at least on the basis of what Thucydides or his sources remembered. (For the views on Thucydides I am indebted to my colleague, Mr. A. R. W. Harrison.)

Dibelius (*Studies*, 141) admits that the words of Thucydides have been variously interpreted and that the whole question of the relation in ancient historiography of subjective judgement to objective reproduction is a vexed one, cf. Gärtner, *The Areopagus Speech and Natural Revelation*, 13 ff. It is true that no ancient historian quoted verbatim, and to do so would have been against his stylistic canons. Tacitus in his *Annals* (xi. 24, cf. *C.I.L.* xiii. 1) purports to give a speech of the Emperor Claudius to the Senate; it differs widely from the inscription of the original which is extant and which Tacitus must have known. At the same time Dibelius (*op. cit.* 142 ff.) goes too far in his assessment of the ancient conventions. After dealing briefly with the methods and aims of Thucydides, Dionysius of Halicarnassus, Xenophon, Dio of Prusa, and Tacitus and Sallust (the two latter in the Latin tradition), he sums up: 'This survey was merely intended to show concerning historical writing in ancient times that, where it contains speeches, it follows certain conventions. What seems to the author his most important obligation is not what seems to us the most important one, that of establishing what speech was actually made; to him, it is rather that of introducing speeches into the structure in a way which will be relevant to his purpose. Even if he can remember, discover, or read somewhere the text of the speech which was made, the author will not feel obliged to make use of it. At most he will, use it in composing the great or small pattern of the speech with which he provides his account. This pattern will, however, either enliven the whole, if direct speech takes the place of a prosaic report or it will serve as an artistic device to help to achieve the author's aims. In any case, the tradition of ancient historical writing teaches us that even the interpreter of historical speeches of such a kind must first ask what is the function of the speeches as a whole.' (*Op. cit.* 144 f.) It seems that Dibelius' dating of Acts *c.* 90 and his Form-critical treatment of the book as simply a literary-theological document, in no sense 'historical' as that word is normally understood, have led him to underestimate an ancient historian's desire to include, so far as possible, in the speeches recorded the 'general sense' of what was said or would have been said on each occasion, so far as Luke or his informants remembered.

Gärtner also takes Dibelius to task for failing to mention the influence upon Luke of the Old Testament and Jewish tradition. In this respect H. J. Cadbury in his article on the speeches in Acts, *B.C.* v. 402-7, failed also. Gärtner suggests that in the Jewish tradition the view of history which is presented is stamped by the belief in God's intervention, punishment, restitution, and help, *op. cit.* 22. Cf. Ps. lxxviii; history is as God uses it.

Again, when Dibelius divides the speeches in Acts into two groups, (a) those that can be understood from ancient historiography and (b) missionary sermons, and when he puts Paul's speech at Athens with Stephen's in the former group, as though they had nothing in common with the latter, he is classifying his material subjectively, as Form-critics tend to do with their material, cf. McNeile, *Introduction to the Study of the New*

Testament, 2nd ed., 52 f.; Dibelius has to admit that there are many differences between his former group and 'parallel' Greek and Latin speeches. Yet he can reach the following conclusion about Paul's speech at Athens: 'It is because Athens, which is not intrinsically important in the history of Paul's mission, is the centre of Hellenistic piety and Greek wisdom, that this city is chosen by Luke as the setting for a speech in which the Christian apostle employs Greek ideas. All questions as to whether Paul made such a speech, and whether he made it at Athens, must be waived if we are to understand Luke. He is not concerned with portraying an event which happened once in history, and which had no particular success; he is concerned with a typical exposition, which is in that sense historical, and perhaps more real in his own day than in the apostle's time. He follows the Greek tradition of historical writing in antiquity in that he freely fixes the occasion of the speech and fashions its content himself' (*Studies*, 154 f.).

Paul's speeches at Lystra and Athens are the only two in Acts in which Gentiles are addressed, who have not had the *praeparatio evangelica* of Judaism. But their doctrine of God is based on that of Hellenistic Judaism (Knox, *Acts*, 69 f.). Gärtner, in his full-length study of the Areopagus speech, has shown that the speech at Athens, the more important of the two, has its roots in the soil of the Jewish and Old Testament revelation of God, and not, as Dibelius and others have assumed, in the 'Natural Theology' of Stoicism (*op. cit.*, 167 ff.). According to Dibelius the Areopagus speech is a Hellenistic one about recognizing God and doing so philosophically, the arguments employed being nearer to those of second-century apologists than to those of Paul's epistles! Gärtner denies this and refutes it in detail. Knox too would agree with Gärtner to the extent of saying (i) that the Jews of the Dispersion commonly equated the God of the pagan philosopher with the God revealed in the Old Testament, (ii) that in Rom. i. 20 (which Dibelius would contrast with Acts xvii) Paul shows himself familiar with the Jewish line of argument borrowed from good Gentile philosophers that God is one and holy and that as God has revealed Himself to the Jews, theirs was the true religion. Dibelius does not allow enough for the probability that Jewish anthologies of

THE ACTS OF THE APOSTLES

Gentile philosophic arguments were known to Paul from circles
of the Jewish Dispersion. It must be added that Paul seems to
have used increasingly in his later epistles, e.g. 2 Cor., language
which would appeal to the Gentile-Christian reader but which
had a Jewish substratum of thought. If Gärtner's analysis of the
content of phrases used in the Areopagus speech is correct, the
same phenomenon is found there. (See his book, 145-169.) The
findings, then, of Dibelius and of Gärtner about his speech are
diametrically opposed: (a) Dibelius thinks that the philosophical
basis of the speech is to be maintained and that by a process of
literary criticism one can allot different parts of the speech to
different sources. The speech, therefore, loses its homogeneity.
(1) Idolatry is criticized and the plea is made to abolish poly-
theism. (2) Any points of contact in cultus or theology are noted.
Acts xvii. 26-8 come in parenthetically, having no contact with
the Bible. Vs. 29 strikes a polemical note and vss. 30 f. end with
a kerygma. (b) Gärtner preserves the unity of the speech, which,
he maintains, correlates man's worship of God with his knowledge of God. The criticism of idolatry, which is the main
motive, rests on a true conception of God in so far as this can
be attained by His self-revelation to men. Paul at Athens adopts
a 'pessimistic' view of man's grasp of this knowledge, as in
Rom. i, where all are seen as sinners. In Acts xvii all men are
seen to be in ignorance, which leads to Christ's saving act. Thus
both Rom. i and Acts xvii agree, and they provide clues to the
nature of the missionary preaching to the Gentiles. 'Both texts
can be said to be an exposition of that God Whom men should
have known but Whom they have made into the "Unknown
God". Left to himself, man falls into ignorance of God, and
this leads to idolatry. The purpose of the missionary preaching
as exemplified in Acts xvii is not to reinstate the natural knowledge of God by enlightening the misapprehensions of man's
nous, but to show the uselessness and the vanity in the Gentiles'
conception of God and the worship of God. This is followed by
a proclamation of the salvation in Christ' (op. cit. 169). Of these
two treatments of the Areopagus speech, that of Gärtner, who
preserves the homogeneity of the speech, is preferable.

Dibelius admits that his second group of speeches, including
the missionary sermons, have no counterpart in the Greek

tradition. Luke reproduced the pattern of sermons in the Church, not simply because he thought that they would serve as models for preachers c. A.D. 90, but because a pattern of apostolic preaching had evolved (a kerygma); cf. C. H. Dodd, *The Apostolic Preaching and its Developments*, 1936; T. F. Glasson, *Hibbert Journal*, 1953, 1 ff.; Bo Reicke in *A Root of the Vine*, ed. A. Fridrichsen, 1953.

The pattern would be somewhat as follows:

(a) All that has been foretold about the Messiah 'according to the Scriptures' has come to pass (cf. C. H. Dodd, *According to the Scriptures*); the Jews on hearing the apostles would 'search the Scriptures . . . to see if these things (said of Christ) were so, Acts xvii. 11, cf. ii. 14, iii. 13, 24, ix. 22. The old Dispensation culminated in John the Baptist, who heralded the new one; he stands at the beginning of the pattern of the kerygma, cf. x. 36 ff., xiii. 17 ff. (And now he that is least in the Kingdom of God is greater than he, Luke vii. 28, because the new Order has begun with Christ.)

(b) The saving acts of God in sending His Son to do good are briefly recited, these reaching their climax in the story of the Passion and Resurrection, cf. ii. 14 ff., iii. 13 ff., iv. 10 ff., v. 30 ff., x. 36 ff. This is the heart of the Gospel preaching. The details of His preaching and teaching are omitted, as in the later Creeds.

(c) Apostolic witness supports these facts as true, ii. 32, iii. 15, v. 32, x. 39, 41, xiii. 31, xxvi. 16, 22 (Glasson, art. cit.).

(d) Jesus is Lord and Christ, raised to God's right hand; He is the donor of the Holy Spirit, ii. 17 f., 33, 36; iii. 13, v. 31 f., x. 36. The Resurrection is the final proof that God raised His Son as Lord and Christ, ii. 32 ff., cf. Rom. i. 4 and the Holy Spirit is the first pledge and instalment of the new Order, 2 Cor. i. 22, v. 5; Acts ii. 17 ff.

(e) Despite Glasson (art. cit.) the normal pattern of the kerygma probably included a warning of the future Advent and Judgement. 'The death and resurrection of Jesus were in themselves eschatological events, and part of the process through which the Kingdom of God was to come. But after the Ascension men await the second Advent of Jesus' (Gärtner, *op. cit.* 31).

41

(f) The message 'Repent and be baptised' recurs, ii. 38, iii. 19, v. 31, x. 43, xiii. 38 f., xvii. 30, xxvi. 18, 20.

The Pauline Epistles corroborate the theory that such was the pattern of apostolic preaching, cf. Dodd, *The Apostolic Preaching* and his chart at the end of his book, cf. 1 Thess. i. 9 f., 1 Cor. xv. 3 f., Rom. i. 1-4, viii. 34, xiv. 9. Gärtner sums up Paul's kerygma thus: 'Jesus was born of the seed of David, Rom. i. 3; died, was buried, but rose again on the third day, 1 Cor. xv. 3 f. There are eye-witnesses to these events, 1 Cor. xv. 5 f. All these things have happened according to the Scriptures, 1 Cor. xv. 3 f. He is now exalted over all things as Lord over the living and the dead, Phil. ii. 9 f.; and shall come again as Judge and Saviour, 1 Thess. i. 9 f. Repent ye, for Christ died for our sins, 1 Cor. xv. 3. This message is for all, including the Gentiles, Rom. i. and xv. 8 ff. We can therefore venture to state that the sermon type found in the Acts exemplifies the apostolic message as promulgated by Peter and Paul' (*op. cit.* 32-3).

Gärtner in a footnote (p. 33) criticizes Dibelius rightly for placing too little confidence in the genuine lines of thought of the speeches, as though their 'form' were wholly subordinated to the main tendency of Acts to present a theological document to readers *c.* A.D. 90. So Gärtner refuses wisely to judge Luke's treatment of the missionary preaching as unhistorical: 'On the contrary,' he says, 'his samples of the apostolic message must reflect the preaching manner of Peter and Paul, even if only in general outline. Indubitably, those who had heard and were acquainted with the apostles must have been great in number; and they, living at the time of the "publishing" of Acts, could verify Luke's facts. Nor can we disregard Luke's own words for the apostolic sermons as presented by him, "The word of God" or "of the Lord", xiii. 44.'

Professor Nineham (*Studies in the Gospels*, 229 ff.) has attacked Dr. Dodd's thesis as it was presented in the *Expository Times*, June 1932, and in his *Apostolic Preaching*. Nineham asks, 'Does not this line of argument prove either too little or too much? On the one hand if the speeches in the early part of Acts reflect genuine historical reminiscences of what was said by the apostles, then they can afford no evidence for the existence of a formal outline account of the ministry; for it can hardly be supposed that the original apostles were dependent on any such traditional outline; they had their own memories. If on the other hand (and this seems more probable to many scholars) these speeches were produced by the author of Acts as a general survey of the sort of thing likely to have been said, after the Thucydidean model, then the outline of the ministry contained in them can have no independent evidential value; for it may have been derived by St. Luke from St. Mark's Gospel, which we know him to have had before him.' Comment on this need only be brief: (1) The Jewish method of teaching was to make pupils learn by rote and the apostles and their 'ministers' no doubt followed this method so that very soon a 'pattern' of preaching which the apostles might have used consciously or not would have been likely to arise. (Cf. Mishna, *Aboth*, ii. 8.) It is equally probable that a pattern of the general outline of the ministry of Jesus would be remembered. (2) Such an outline may be in the main historical, despite the Form-critics, cf. F. C. Burkitt, *Jesus Christ*, 1932, so that the apostles would follow it inevitably in narrating the saving acts of God done through Christ. (3) The 'pattern' of the kerygma can be discerned in the Fourth Gospel and 1 John and in the Epistle to the Hebrews as well as in the speeches in Acts. Are all these writers to be dismissed as dependent on Mark? (4) The reference to the Thucydidean model is too vague. It is unlikely that Thucydides started with a *tabula rasa* for his speeches, cf. the discussion above.

One speech above all stands out in Acts, the speech of Stephen, vii. 2-53. See the note prefacing the translation of this speech. In view of all the research done on this subject it is surprising to find that Dibelius, as late as 1944 ('The Speeches in Acts and Ancient Historiography', *Studies*, 167 ff.), says 'The irrelevance of most of this speech has for long been the real problem of exegesis. It is indeed impossible to find a connexion between the account of the history of Israel to the time of Moses (vii. 2-19) and the accusation against Stephen: nor is any accusation against the Jews, which would furnish the historical foundation for the attack at the end of the speech, found at all in this section.' He takes the speech to have been inserted by Luke into the story of the martyrdom of Stephen, which Luke had already at his disposal. He assumes that here, as in the missionary speeches, the didactic element prevails and that the content of the speech 'paves the way for the separating of the Christians from the Jewish community'. So far as there is truth in this last point, the question might be asked how soon Church and synagogue separated. Dr. Selwyn maintains that the rupture was seen to be complete some years before A.D. 70, when James the Just was put to death by the Jews c. 62; 'The work of the second Annas must have seemed to seal for ever the severance of the two religions' (*The First Epistle of St. Peter*, 58); this would involve dating Acts vii or its source c. 64–70, not c. A.D. 90.

The Christology expressed in Stephen's closing words, 'I see the heavens opened and the Son of Man standing on the right hand of God' may be due simply to Mark xiv. 62; a copy of Mark probably lay before Luke as he wrote Acts where the death of Stephen is narrated in a way which recalls Mark's rather than Luke's Passion narrative. It is a well-known fact that only Acts vii. 56 has the phrase 'Son of Man' outside the Gospels or attributes it to any other lips than those of Jesus. It may be that Stephen was aware of the Lord's utterance at His trial and that the phrase in Acts vii. 56 is an accurate record of his echo of the Lord's words or it may be that the account of Stephen's death was coloured by interpolations from the Passion story (or vice versa): but the detail in Stephen's vision of the Son of Man standing at God's right hand, as opposed to His session in Mark, suggests that here Luke has preserved an ancient Christological tradition, a Son of Man Christology, which is reproduced in Rom. v. 12 ff., 1 Cor. xv. 20-22; cf. Eph. i. 10 where the second Adam is contrasted with the first, though the phrase 'Son of Man' is avoided because it would be meaningless to a non-Semitic reader.

Finally, the early speeches in Acts are to be considered. On any view of the date of Acts, these speeches are the most remote in time from the date when the author wrote. The problem is whether he was 'consciously archaeologising' or reproducing early written or oral sources.

(a) Acts ii. 14-36 may have been penned earlier by Luke than Luke xxii. 22, cf. 4 (f) above. When the Israelites killed Jesus, God raised Him up as the prophets had foretold. Apostolic witness testified to the Davidic Messiahship of Christ, cf. Ps.

INTRODUCTION

cx. 1. God has made Jesus the Crucified both Lord and Christ. Men therefore are to repent and be baptized to receive remission of sins and the gift of the Holy Spirit. This is a reproduction of the primitive kerygma; cf. above.

(b) iii. 13-26. Peter is again the speaker. The God of Abraham, Isaac, and Jacob has glorified His servant Jesus, when He had been delivered up to and denied before Pilate and though Pilate had decided to release Him. The Holy and Righteous One (cf. xxii. 14 and the 'Teacher of Righteousness' of the Qumran Scrolls) was rejected in favour of a murderer. The Pioneer or Captain, cf. v. 31, Heb. ii. 10, xii. 2, of Life (or Salvation) was killed but God raised Him. The apostles bore witness to this. Healings in His name are publicly performed. The long-promised Suffering Messiah has come, iii. 18. So men are to repent that 'times of refreshing' may come; there is no Jewish phrase of this kind for the consummation and it may refer rather to the respite before the actual end. The fore-appointed Messiah Jesus will be sent, though heaven must receive Him until the time of the 'restoration' or 'establishment' of all things predicted; this good news is confirmed by the prophets, especially Deut. xviii. 15, cf. Lev. xxiii. 29. God will indeed 'raise up' (*anastēsei*) 'a prophet like unto' Moses to whom every Israelite will hearken, cf. Luke ix. 35 (the voice at the Transfiguration) and the blessing upon obedience to the voice (Gen. xxii. 18 of Abraham) is earned, cf. Gal. iii. 6, by the people of the new covenant. Primitive traits appear here, especially in the conception of the *pais*, servant or son, the 'pioneer' and the implicit belief that the sending of the Messiah is delayed presumably till all have repented.

(c) iv. 8-12. The healing described has been wrought by the 'name' of Jesus Messiah, iv. 10. The rulers of the people and elders crucified Him, but God raised (*ēgeiren*) Him from the dead. Thus the ancient prophecy of the Stone is fulfilled, Ps. cxviii. 22, cf. 1 Pet. ii. 7; did Luke xx. 17 pick up this text again later? In no other than Jesus does salvation exist, nor is there any other name under heaven wherein we must be saved.

(d) iv. 24 ff. (The prayer.) Jesus is God's holy *pais* Whom He anointed; God is the sovereign Lord (*Despotēs* (cf. Luke ii. 29)) and Jesus is the Lord's Servant. When Herod, Pilate, the

45

Gentiles, and Israel are gathered against Christ, Ps. ii. 2 is given its fulfilment.

(e) v. 29 ff. (The second appearance before the Sanhedrin.) The God of the patriarchs raised (*ēgeiren*) Jesus from the dead when He had been slain by Jews hanging Him on a 'tree', (*xulon*), cf. Deut. xxi. 23, cf. Acts x. 39, xiii. 29, Gal. iii. 13, Rev. xxii. 2 where *xulon* is used of the Cross. God exalted (*hupsosen*) Him to be Pioneer and Saviour ... to give repentance to Israel and remission of sins. The apostles witnessed to these sayings (or events) and also the Holy Spirit (the Alexandrian text omits the relative here probably by accident), which God gave to the obedient.

(f) viii. 31-5 (the Ethiopian Eunuch and Philip) is in dramatic rather than speech form, but makes the Servant Christology explicit.

(g) x. 34 ff. (Peter's speech in Cornelius' house.) A reference to the sending of the divine and healing word (Ps. cvii. 20) and to the beatitude for preachers of peace (Isa. lii. 7) may be picked up later in Luke ii. 14, xix. 38. Jesus Messiah is Lord of all. It is known what happened throughout all Judaea beginning from Galilee after John's baptism. That word (or event) consisted in Jesus of Nazareth, anointed by God with Holy Spirit and power (which may be picked up later in Luke i. 35), Who went about doing good and healing those oppressed by the devil, God being with Him. The apostles witnessed to what He did in Judaea and Jerusalem. Him they slew, hanging Him on a 'tree' (see above). God raised (*ēgeiren*) Him on the third day and made Him manifest to the people and to chosen witnesses who ate and drank with Him after the Resurrection (which may be picked up later in Luke xxiv. 30 and Acts i. 4). The apostles were commanded to preach that He is ordained by God to be judge of living and dead (cf. the close of the speech at Athens, xvii. 30 f.).

(h) xiii. 16b ff. (Paul at Antioch.) A brief history of the patriarchs includes a reference to Paul's eponymous ancestor, Saul, also of the tribe of Benjamin. According to the promises made to David God has given Israel a Saviour, Jesus of the seed of David (a point which may be taken up later in Luke ii. 11); John the Baptist had preached His coming when he had proclaimed a baptism of repentance (cf. Luke iii. 3) to all the people of Israel, xiii. 24. John had denied that he was himself the Christ, a point taken up perhaps later in Luke iii. 15 f. and not by the other Synoptic evangelists. In condemning Christ and demanding His death the Jews fulfilled the prophecies. They took Him down from the 'tree' (*xulon*), xiii. 29, and laid Him in a tomb. (Luke omits any reference here to Joseph of Arimathea, a member of the Sanhedrin, as though his part in Jesus' burial belonged to the Jews; in Luke xxiii. 51 (later?) Luke alone emphasizes that Arimathea was a city of the Jews.) God raised (*ēgeiren*) Him from the dead and He was seen for many days by those who came up with Him from Galilee to Jerusalem, cf. Acts i. 1-5 and contrast Luke xxiv. 50 ff. Ps. ii. 7 is fulfilled, xiii. 33, a text which is used (later?) of the Baptism not the Resurrection of Jesus, Luke iii. 22. The Septuagint text of Isa. lv. 3 is allusively cited in Rabbinic fashion in the light of a quotation from Ps. xvi. 10, which was already used as a proof-text by Peter earlier, ii. 27. Because David had died and saw corruption, the promise of incorruption remained, for Jesus, through Whom remission of sins is proclaimed, xiii. 38. For the ambiguity in vs. 39, see Notes. Luke introduced, no doubt consciously, the Pauline word for 'justified' or 'set right with God'; the same word is used (later?) in Luke xviii. 14 in the Parable of the Pharisee and the Publican, which expresses what Paul had meant in his donnish fashion by Justification by Faith.

Each of the early speeches of Peter and Paul reflects the ideas of the primitive kerygma, but they are often found to have an individual flavour in keeping with the speaker. Many of the points may have been developed (later in the Third Gospel?) by Luke from what he knew that the speakers said or from what he knew that they would, as early missionaries, have said. Where Luke's account can be tested, it shows great restraint. For instance, though the word Saviour is used of God in the O.T. it is not applied freely to Jesus by Luke or by Paul; Luke uses it in v. 31 and xiii. 23 (cf. Luke ii. 11, Matt. i. 21, John iv. 42) and Paul in Phil. iii. 20 cf. Eph. v. 23. On the other hand, the authors of the Catholic and Pastoral Epistles use it frequently, seven times of God and ten times of Jesus. It may be, as V. Taylor has said (*The Names of Jesus*, 107), that the use of this name in Greek religion and above all in Caesar worship restricted and delayed its currency in the primitive tradition. It is highly improbable that any Christian writing as late as A.D. 90 would have observed these restrictions.

For any contrast between the early speeches of Paul and his speech to the elders of Ephesus at Miletus, see notes on xx. 18 ff.

As Knox says (*Acts*, 77 f.) : 'It is not until the conversion of Paul that we get anything which corresponds to the later and more developed Christology of the Pauline Epistles. . . . Here it seems we have a striking testimony to Luke's fidelity to his sources and to their reliability.' While all are agreed that Luke would not have subscribed to any modern doctrine of development of Christology in the early Church, his language in the early speeches reflects what appears to have been primitive teaching. (For the opposite point of view see the very able presentation of Dibelius' thesis by Mr. C. F. Evans, *J.T.S.*, N.S., vii, 1956, 25-41.)

No better summing-up can be given than that of J. H. Bernard, 'The Historical Value of Acts', in *The Criticism of the New Testament*, 1902, where he says that the language used in the speeches, at least of Peter, is quite clearly primitive and entirely consonant to what the probabilities of a case would suggest; that the Christology bases itself consistently on the fulfilment of prophecy, Jesus being the Christ who was to come, as was demonstrated by His resurrection. 'Christ' was still used as a title rather than as a personal name. The phrase 'Servant of God' used of him is found nowhere else in the N.T. and goes back to the prophecies of deutero-Isaiah. All this is totally unlike Pauline language, though it is entirely harmonious with it in substance. The Christianity is a Judaic one. Similarly the Church organization is incomplete and primitive, Christianity being conceived of as a reformed Judaism. Use is still made, 'thankfully and habitually', of Temple and synagogue worship. There has been no break with Judaism, such as came at a later date.

13. THE TEXT OF ACTS

The problems presented by the text of Acts are many, difficult, and complicated. It is impossible sometimes to decide whether to follow the reading supported by the Alexandrian group of MSS. headed by B, Vaticanus (B ℵ A C Ψ 81 33 104 and P45) or that supported by the 'Western' group headed by D, Codex Bezae (D h P29 P38 P48 Syr.Harc.mg. Cyprian and Augustine) should be preferred.

The text of B has been set out in full by J. H. Ropes, *B.C.* iii, 1926, with the text of D on the other side. Ropes usually favoured the B-type of text. A. C. Clark (*The Acts of the Apostles*, 1933), on the other hand, championed the 'Western' text of which he took the B-type of text to be an abbreviation. In their commentary on Acts, *B.C.* iv, 1933, K. Lake and H. J. Cadbury favoured the B-type of text less than Ropes but far more than Clark. It is now a commonplace of criticism that each variant has to be considered on its own merits; a textual type cannot be accepted *in toto*. It is also a commonplace that 'Western' is a misnomer to describe one type; for the 'Western' or D-type of text was widespread in the second century and papyri of this type have been discovered in Egypt. It is also generally agreed that Luke could not have been the author of both recensions (cf. the present writer's *Alterations to the Text*, 54 f.), as Blass argued. On the whole, the probability is that the 'Western' text is a second-century recension, which sometimes preserves a good reading lost in the other main textual type and that the Alexandrian text is a careful product of Alexandrian scholarship somewhat nearer to the original than the 'Western' text is, and yet not to be identified with the original, if only because the original seems to have been left in a rather unfinished state, which the Alexandrian scribes trimmed and polished. The present writer (*op. cit.* 56 ff.) has followed Lagrange in detecting certain tendencies in the 'Western' text, both pietistic and explanatory. Whatever may be the origin of the 'Western' text of the Gospels, which is marked by omissions rather than by additions, that of the text of Acts, which is characterized by additions, may have been the result of a 'publication' of the text in the first half of the second century; this may have incorporated harmonizing details and 'gossip' to attract the lay reader becoming familiar with the Apocryphal Gospels. For there seems to be a 'hard core' of 'Western' readings in Acts, to which additions were made later from time to time; these additions are not so well attested textually.

Since Ropes' monumental study of the text of Acts appeared in 1933, research has continued; cf. A. F. J. Klijn, *A Survey of the Researches into the Western Text of the Gospels and Acts*, 1949. The possibility of the influence of a translation upon the text of D has not been overlooked. In 1931 D. Plooij (*Bulletin of the Bezan Club*, ix) had maintained that the Greek of D was influenced by the 'common text' but was derived mainly from the Old Latin Acts, represented in the text of *d* and *h*, which in turn depended on a Syriac version paraphrased by Tatian (as did also the Old Syriac Acts) and that in its turn depended on an early second-century Greek text into which Pauline tradition and local knowledge had infiltrated. The influence of the Latin translation, *d*, on the Greek side, D, must always be borne in mind, indeed, but the possibility of other Semitic influence than that of a Syriac translation is also to be noted. In 1941 C. C. Torrey (*Documents of the Primitive Church*) maintained that the 'Western' text was simply a new Semitic version of the Four Gospels and Acts, the work of a Jewish Christian. The latter took the Greek text current in his day and rendered it into Aramaic for other Jewish Christians to use, who were more familiar with Aramaic than with Greek. This fairly faithful Aramaic rendering included 'improvements' and additions. Later, this Aramaic translation was put back into Greek; hence the 'Western' text. He illustrates this theory (p. 145) by suggesting that in Acts iii. 14 the Aramaic editor rendered the Greek for 'you denied' by the Aramaic *kdbtun*, 'you denied, declared false', correctly; this was wrongly copied, *kbdtun*, which was taken as a Hebraism, and rendered into Greek by a word meaning 'you oppressed', found in D and the Latin translation of Irenaeus. Compare his instances on the same page from Acts ii. 30 and xii. 5, on p. 146 from xiv. 27 and xviii. 4 and on p. 147 from xvi. 12.

Torrey's previous view that Acts i. 1b-xv. 35 was originally an Aramaic written document (*The Composition and Date of Acts*, 1916) has been criticized by other Semitic scholars, notably Dr. H. F. D. Sparks, *J.T.S.*, N.S., i, 1950, 16-28. It remains to be seen whether Torrey's later view can stand up to the criticism of Dr. M. Black, *An Aramaic Approach to the Gospels and Acts*, 1954 (2nd ed.).

Some noteworthy 'Western' readings in Acts include: i. 2, 'on which day he chose the apostles through Holy Spirit and commanded them to preach the gospel'; i. 5, 'which you are about to receive not many days hence until Pentecost'; iv. 18, 'when they had agreed to the judgement, they (called them and) warned them'; v. 15, add 'for they were healed of all sickness which each of them had'; v. 39, 'leave these men alone and let them go without polluting your hands; for if this power be of human will, its force will be destroyed, but if this power be of the will of God, you cannot destroy it, neither you, nor kings nor tyrants. Therefore refrain from these men, lest you be found fighting against God'; vi. 10, add 'because they were refuted by him with all boldness. Not being able therefore to withstand the truth'; viii. 24, add 'he did not cease from much wailing'; viii. 37, add 'and Philip said to him, If thou believest with all thine heart, it is possible; and he answered and said, I believe that Jesus Christ is the Son of God'; viii. 39, 'Holy Spirit fell on the eunuch but an angel of the Lord seized Philip from him'; ix. 7 f., 'seeing no man when he was speaking but he said to them, Raise me from the ground. And when they raised him . . .'; x. 25, 'And as Peter drew nigh to Caesarea one of the servants ran on and announced that he was come. And Cornelius leapt forth and met him'; xi. 1 f., 'And it became known to the apostles and to the brethren who were in Judaea that the Gentiles also had received the word of God. Now Peter after much time wanted to go to Jerusalem, and calling the brethren and having strengthened them (he departed), speaking much throughout the country, teaching them; who also met them and announced to them the grace of God. But the brethren of the circumcision disputed with him'; xi. 28, 'and there was much rejoicing, and when we had conversed together, one of them, by name Agabus . . .'; xii. 10, 'and going out they descended the seven steps' (see my *Alterations*, 62 f.); xii. 23, 'and coming down from the throne he became eaten with worms while he was yet alive and so he gave up the ghost'; xiv. 2, 'But the chiefs of the synagogues of the Jews and the rulers of the synagogue (or 'of the Iconians') raised persecution for them against the saints and made the minds of the Gentiles ill-disposed towards the brethren. But the Lord soon gave peace'; xiv. 4, 'others with the apostles, cleaving to them for the sake of the word of God. And the Jews with the Gentiles raised persecution again a second time and they stoned them and turned them out of the city'; xiv. 6, 'Lystra and Derbe and the whole neighbourhood and they were preaching there and the whole multitude was moved by the teaching. And Paul and Barnabas were staying in Lystra'; xv. 2, 'And some who came down from Jerusalem were teaching the brethren, Unless you are circumcised and walk in the custom of Moses, you cannot be saved. And when no small strife and discussion arose between them and Paul and Barnabas, for Paul affirmed and said that the converts should stay as they were, those who had come from Jerusalem ordered Paul and Barnabas themselves and certain others to go up to the apostles and elders at Jerusalem to be judged before them concerning this question'; xv. 5, 'But those who had ordered them to go up to the elders arose and said that they must circumcise them, and command them to observe the law of Moses'; xv. 20 and 29, see §10 above; xvi. 35, 'And when it was day, the magistrates came together into the market-place, and remembering the earthquake which had occurred they were afraid and they sent the police, saying, Let those men go whom you took yesterday'; xviii. 21, 'I must at all costs keep the coming feastday in Jerusalem, I will return to you, God willing . . .'; xviii. 27, 'And some Corinthians staying in Ephesus heard him and asked him to cross over with them to their own country. And when he agreed, the Ephesians wrote to the disciples in Corinth to receive the man; who while he stayed in Achaia greatly helped the churches'; xix. 1, 'But though Paul wished to go according to his own plan to Jerusalem, the Holy Spirit told him to return to Asia'; xix. 9, 'in the hall of one Tyrannus, from the fifth hour till the tenth' (see my *Alterations*, 63 f.); xix. 14, 'Among whom also the sons of one Sceva, a priest, wanted to do the same; they had a custom of exorcizing such men; and going in to the demon-possessed they began to call upon him the Name . . .'; xxi. 16 f., 'And these brought us to those with whom we should lodge, and coming to a certain village we were with a certain Mnason, a man of Cyprus. And going out thence we came to Jerusalem'; xxi. 25, 'But concerning the Gentiles who have believed, they have nothing to say to thee, for we sent a despatch judging that they were to observe nothing of such a kind but to keep themselves . . .'; xxiv. 6 f., 'whom also we seized and wished to judge according to our law but Lysias the chiliarch came and with great violence took him out of our hands, ordering his accusers to come to thee'; cf. my *Alterations*, 70 f.; xxv. 24 f., 'both in Jerusalem and here, that I should deliver him for punishment without defence. But I could not deliver him because of the commands which we have from the emperor. But if anyone wished to accuse him, I told him to follow me to Caesarea where he was being guarded. When they came, they cried out that he should be taken away from life. But when I heard both sides, I perceived that on no ground was he liable to death. But when I said, Dost thou wish to be judged with them in Jerusalem, he appealed to Caesar'; xxvii. 1, 'Thus therefore the governor decided that he should be sent to Caesar. And on the morrow he summoned a certain centurion by name Julius (of the cohort Augusta) and he delivered to him Paul with the other prisoners'; xxviii. 16, 'The centurion delivered the prisoners to the stratopedarch but he allowed Paul to remain by himself outside the camp'; xxviii. 31, 'that this is Jesus the Son of God, through whom the whole world is about to be judged'.

In the following pages the MSS. cited particularly are the Alexandrian B, Vaticanus, fourth century and א, Sinaiticus, fourth century. Also to this group belongs P⁴⁵, Chester Beatty, third century. The chief 'Western' MSS. cited are D, the Bezan text, fifth-sixth century, and *h*, codex Floriacensis, sixth century. For full information see J. H. Ropes, *B.C.* iii.

THE ACTS OF THE APOSTLES

i-viii. 1a

THE EARLY SCENES AT JERUSALEM

i. 1-5

(1) I wrote the first book, Theophilus, about everything which Jesus began to do and to teach, (2) until the day when having given commands through the Holy Spirit to the apostles whom He had chosen He was taken up; (3) to whom also He presented Himself alive after His passion by many proofs, for forty days being seen by them and telling them what concerns the kingdom of God, (4) and sharing common meals with them He commanded them not to depart from Jerusalem, but to await the pro--mise of the Father, which (He said) you heard from Me, (5) for John baptized with water but you will be baptized after a few days with Holy Spirit.

(1) **First** may mean 'former', as usually in St. Luke; see Introduction, 4 (f) for the suggestion that Acts was written before the Third Gospel but after an early draft of the latter. **Theophilus**, lit. a 'God-fearer'; see Introduction, 6 (3); the title **most excellent** ascribed to him in the prologue to Luke may imply that he had equestrian status. (2) The 'Western' text avoids the difficulty of the Greek original more nearly reproduced by the Alexandrian text (see J. M. Creed, *J.T.S.* xxxv, 1934, 176-182). Acts has been called the Gospel of the Holy Spirit. **Apostles**; see Appendix 1. Acts alone refers to an interval of **forty days** between Christ's Resurrection and Ascension; Luke may have corrected his (earlier?) account in Luke xxiv. 51 intentionally, unless the D-text there is right to omit a reference to the Ascension. (3) The appearances of the risen Christ to His

54

disciples, with the evidence for the tomb being empty on Easter
morning and with the miraculous change in the outlook of the
disciples since Good Friday, make the Resurrection a well-
attested fact, and if a fact the most important one, of history;
cf. 1 Cor. xv. 5-7 for a list of His appearances. (Contrast R.
Bultmann, 'New Testament and Mythology' in *Kerygma and
Myth*, ed. H. W. Bartsch, Eng. Trans., 1953, 1-44.) The kingdom of God, His rule or sway, ideally universal but in practice
obeyed only by the true Israelite, had come with Jesus the King
Messiah, though its full consummation lies in the future; cf.
Mark i. 15. (4) For **sharing a common meal** cf. C. R. Bowen,
Z.N.T.W. xiii, 1912, 259. The disciples were not to keep depart-
ing, perhaps to Bethany, still less Galilee. (5) For the contrast
between John Baptist's water baptism and Christ's (water
and) Spirit baptism, cf. xi. 16, Mark i. 8, Matt. iii. 11, Luke
iii. 16, John i. 33. The curious order of words, literally 'not
after many days' may be an Aramaism (Torrey and Burney)
or possibly a Latinism (Blass).

i. 6-11. THE ASCENSION

**(6) So then when they had come together, they asked
Him, 'Lord, dost Thou at this time restore the kingdom to
Israel?' (7) But He said to them, 'It is not for you to know
the times or seasons which the Father has fixed by His
own authority. (8) But you will receive power, when the
Holy Spirit has come upon you, and you will be my witnesses both in Jerusalem and in all Judaea and Samaria
and unto the end of the earth.' (9) And when He had said
these words, while they looked He was lifted up, and a
cloud took Him away from their eyes. (10) And as they
were gazing into heaven, while He went, behold, two
men stood by them in white clothes, (11) who also said,
'Men of Galilee, why do you stand looking into the
heaven? This Jesus, who was taken up from you into the
heaven, will come in the same way as you saw Him
going into the heaven.'**

(6 ff.) For the Ascension, see A. M. Ramsey's article in Richardson's *T.W.B.B.* 22 f. (6) The hardness of the disciples' hearts is apparent here as in Mark's Gospel; they awaited a material kingdom, for the Spirit was not yet poured out on them to give them a more enlightened conception of it. (7) The phrasing may be due to Luke's knowledge of Mark xiii. 32, the 'times or seasons' referring not to the date of the future kingdom's arrival so much as to 'stages' to be passed before it can come; cf. 2 Thess. ii. It may be unusual to think of God as having 'authority' as here, yet cf. Luke xii. 5, Jude 25. (8) The power of the Holy Spirit is conceived almost physically by Luke; cf. his visual imagery of the dove at our Lord's baptism, Luke iii. 22.

Luke's purpose was to trace the spread of the Gospel from 'Jerusalem . . . to the end of the earth', cf. Rom. xv. 19. Luke omits Galilee, though Matt. iv. 15 f., John ii. 11, and Acts x. 37 attest that Galilee was the place of origin of the kerygma or preaching; Luke may have been influenced to adopt this view by Jewish Christians and perhaps, in particular, as Causse has suggested, by the doctrine that the New Age would begin according to the prophets and psalmists at Jerusalem when all Israel would be represented at a great feast (*R.H.Ph.R.* xviii, 1938, 377-414 and xx, 1940, 120-41). The apostolic witness was an element in the apostolic pattern of preaching and it should be included in Dr. C. H. Dodd's outline of the 'kerygma' (cf. T. F. Glasson, *Hibbert Journal*, 51, 1953, 129 f.); cf. Isa. xliii. 10. (9) The cloud was the visible token of God's presence, cf. Exod. xxxiii. 7-11, Luke i. 35, Mark ix. 7. (10) **Gazing** translates a favourite word of Luke, cf. iii. 4, 12, xii. 30, used by him ten times out of twelve N.T. occurrences. The **white clothes** denoted semi-divine beings, cf. Enoch lxii. 15 f. ('garments of glory') and Mark ix. 3, especially those associated with the 'last days'. (11) If Jesus was glorified at His resurrection, then the Ascension meant to His disciples that 'the series of appearances to them was ending, that Jesus was entering upon a new mode of existence and activity, and that He was not only raised from death, but exalted into the glory of God . . .' (Ramsey, art. cit.). The Ascension, cf. Acts ii. 33, iii. 21, 1 Pet. iii. 22, 1 Thess. iv. 14-16, Eph. i. 20, iv. 10, Col. iii. 1, 1 Tim. iii. 16, Heb. iv. 14,

ix. 24 and R, the old Baptismal Creed of Rome, was part of the Christian faith from the earliest times; cf. Luke xxiv. 51 (B-text).

i. 12-14. THE UPPER ROOM

(12) Then they returned to Jerusalem from the mount called 'olive-grove', which is near Jerusalem, a sabbath day's journey distant. (13) And when they had entered, they went up to the upper room where they were lodging, both Peter and John and James and Andrew, Philip and Thomas, Bartholomew and Matthew, James the son of Alphaeus, and Simon the zealot, and Judas the son of James. (14) These all adhered firmly with one accord to the prayer, with the women and Mary, the mother of Jesus, and with His brothers.

(12) The Mount of Olives was the scene of the Lord's victory, cf. Zech. xiv. 4, and probably the site of the *logion* of Mark xi. 20 ff. **A sabbath day's journey** would be reckoned by Rabbis to be not more than 2000 cubits. (13) The **upper room** is possibly the one where the Last Supper had been held; it may have been in the house of Mark's mother, cf. xii. 12, which was a natural centre for the apostles apparently, though if Mark made a mistake (which is doubtful) about the date of the Last Supper in relation to the Passover, this second possibility should be rejected. The names of the apostles (see Appendix 1) from Peter to James the son of Alphaeus occur also in Mark iii. 16 ff., Matt. ii. 2 f., and Luke vi. 14 ff.; Simon the zealot, here as in Luke vi. 15, is identified with Simon the Canaanean (Aram. *qan'ana*) of Mark iii. 18, Matt. x. 4. The Zealots were the extreme nationalist party who may have acquired this name *c*. A.D. 66, perhaps as the result of being the followers of John of Gischala (K. Lake, *H.T.R.* 10, 1917, 57-63); there is no need to assume with S. G. F. Brandon (*op. cit.* 104 ff.) that Jesus sympathized with their aims. The nationalist tendency had long existed in Palestine. Yet the adjective here may mean simply 'zealous' in a general sense. (14) **The**

prayer denotes a liturgical form of prayer based probably on that of Temple or synagogue worship. Mary, Jesus' mother, is mentioned here for the last time in the New Testament, cf. John xix. 27, and His brothers (the word means 'kinsmen' in the Adler papyri) who had not believed in Him during His ministry (John vii. 5) were now members of the Church; James was granted an appearance of the risen Lord (1 Cor. xv. 7) and he was to follow Peter as head of the mother-church of Jerusalem, xii. 17, etc. It is strange that he was not now ranked with the apostles in place of Judas, but apparently only after James, the brother of John, had been killed, xii. 2. Probably the Lord's 'brother' had been converted too recently for him yet to be an apostle.

i. 15-end. THE DEATH OF JUDAS AND THE ELECTION OF MATTHIAS

(15) **And in those days Peter rose up in the midst of the brethren and said (and there was a crowd of persons together about a hundred and twenty), (16) 'Brethren, it was necessary for the scripture to be fulfilled, which the Holy Spirit spoke beforehand by the mouth of David about Judas who became guide to those who seized Jesus. (17) For he was numbered among us and got the allotted share of this ministry. (18) (Now this man purchased a field with the reward of his wickedness and falling headlong he burst in the middle and all his bowels gushed out. (19) And it became known to all the inhabitants of Jerusalem, so that that field was called in their language Akeldama, that is, Field of Blood.) (20) For it is written in the Book of Psalms, 'Let his quarters be desolate and let there not be a dweller therein', and, 'Let another take his overseership'. (21) It is necessary, therefore, that of the men who associated with us during the whole time in which the Lord Jesus came in and went out among us, (22) beginning from the baptism of John until the day on which He was taken up from us— one of these become with us a witness of His resurrec-**

tion.' (23) And they set forward two, Joseph called Barsabbas, who was surnamed Justus, and Matthias. (24) And they prayed and said, 'Lord, thou knower of the hearts of all, show which one thou hast chosen of these two, (25) to take the place of this ministry and apostleship, from which Judas lapsed to go to his own place'. (26) And they cast lots for them, and the lot fell on Matthias and he was reckoned with the eleven apostles.

(i. 15-end) Is the story of the election of Matthias historical? As Blunt says (*Acts*, 134 f.), it is quite natural and 'we cannot conceive any reason why such a tradition if invented should have been connected with a person of such secondary importance as Matthias'. The mode of election was unique so far as is known and did not conform to later methods as it would have done if the story had been a late invention. The modern motives for casting doubt on the story may be due to the desire to displace the Twelve from the high regard that they had in the early Church. Guignebert (*Le Christ*, 67 ff.) imagined that the Twelve were a creation called forth to meet the situation of the primitive community when it was realized that the original hope of the immediate Parousia had failed. In fact, the Twelve, now Eleven, had a special 'ministry' or deaconship (vs. 17), 'office', overseership or bishopric (vs. 20), and an Apostleship so unique that of all the apostles the Twelve were outstanding, cf. Luke xxii. 30, Rev. xxi. 12-14, cf. Appendix I.

(15) Peter appears at first in Acts as *primus inter pares*. Typologists could explain the number 120 by reference to the universalistic saying of pseudo-Zechariah viii. 23, which mentions ten men from the nations of every tongue who would wish to go with the Jews for they had heard that God was with them; if this saying could be twisted to mean that each tribe would have ten aliens, 120 would symbolize the ingathering of foreign nations. There is probably equally little significance in the fact that 120 is one of several 'triangular' numbers of the New Testament, being the sum of the series 1-15. In fact there probably were about 120 present and a later inventor would have exaggerated the number as wildly as Josephus did his

numbers. (16) Peter's speech may have been in Aramaic, but it may have come to Luke in an oral rather than a written form and representing the kind of way in which the primitive Jerusalem church presented the kerygma rather than what Peter said on this occasion (cf. W. L. Knox, *Acts*, 17). The lapse of Judas was thought necessary for the fulfilment of the Old Testament Scriptures, for in the Old Testament revelation of God's will was found the 'divine necessity' for the Passion and many of its events. (18-19) may be bracketed, as a writer's note rather than a supposedly Petrine statement. The account of Judas' death here differs from that in Matt. xxvii. 3-10; the latter may be the account current in Antioch or some other Palestinian city where Matthew was written; Luke's may be the account of the Church in Jerusalem (contrast Brandon, *op. cit.* 42 and 220). **Falling headlong,** contrast Matthew's 'he hanged himself'; *prenes* probably means 'flat' rather than 'swelling up', though F. H. Chase pleaded for the latter as denoting a medical disease (*J.T.S.* xiii, 1912, 278 ff.) and the Syriac, Georgian, and Armenian versions take it in this sense desiring to make Judas' death resemble that of other notorious traitors or villains. Luke was very familiar with 2 Macc., and he probably had in mind 2 Macc. ix. 8 f. with its description of the death of Antiochus Epiphanes. (19) **Akeldama** may represent 'Field of Blood' or possibly 'Field of Sleep', i.e. a cemetery; Matt. xxvii. 8 supports the former. It may be significant that in Palestine a barren soil could be termed a Field of Mot or Field of Death (Anath, after grinding Mot the god of corn sowed him; cf. M. R. Lehmann, *V.T.* 3, 1953, 361 ff.). (20) The first citation is from Ps. lxix. 25; 'this Psalm belongs to a group of Psalms of the Righteous Sufferer, which provided from early times many *testimonia* to the Passion of Christ' (C. H. Dodd, *The Fourth Gospel*, 1953, 301). Judas is to the Psalmist's villain as Christ is to his David. The second citation is from Ps. cix. 8, loosely quoted. (21 f.) It is assumed that one of the Twelve must be familiar with the earthly life of Jesus from the Baptism of John, with which the apostolic kerygma started and also must have witnessed to the fact that Jesus was risen. (For apostolic witness as an essential element of the kerygma see vs. 8 above.) It was one of Paul's difficulties that in a sense he could claim a knowledge of the risen Lord but not of the incarnate Christ; his apostleship had to be guaranteed by sufferings for Christ. (23) The two candidates were Judas Barsabbas ('son of the sabbath' or 'son of the aged one' or elder) called, as a Jew often ·was, also by a Gentile name, Justus, who according to Eusebius, *H.E.* iii. 39, on the authority of Papias who received it from Philip's daughters, cf. xxi. 9, drank poison unharmed, cf. Mark xvi. 9; and Matthias, a name which means 'Gift of God'. (24 f.) The prayer addressed to the 'Lord' was made to God, Yahweh or Yau, translated Kyrios (LXX) or Lord; or it was made to Jesus, who was 'our Lord', Maran, to the primitive Church (A. E. J. Rawlinson, *The New Testament Doctrine of the Christ*, 1926, 231 ff.). There is no need with *B.C.* iv to assume that Jesus was merely a superior saint who could be invoked. For **heart-knower** cf. the *Apostolic Constitutions*, iii. 7, 8. (26) Casting lots to learn God's will had been used in Old Testament times, cf. 1 Sam. xiv. 41 (LXX) with its reference to the Urim and Thummim, sacred lots in pre-exilic days; after Pentecost this method of learning God's will was not repeated. As L. S. Thornton showed (*J.T.S.* xlvi, 1945, 51-9), the Old Testament precedents for casting lots proved that God, not the community, still less chance, chose Matthias.

ii. 1-4. THE DAY OF PENTECOST

(1) While the day of Pentecost was being completed, they were all together in the same place. (2) And suddenly there was from heaven a sound like a strong blast of wind, and it filled the whole house where they were seated. (3) And there appeared to them tongues, as of fire, distributed to them and it rested on each one of them. (4) And they were all filled with Holy Spirit, and they began to speak with other tongues, even as the Spirit gave them utterance.

(1-4) Whatever the date of Acts, its early pictures of the Church and her doctrine are pre-Pauline, as Knox says (*Acts*,

80 ff.). He maintains that Pentecost, originally a harvest festival, had lost its agricultural meaning since Philo's day and had acquired at last a connexion with the giving of the Torah or Law. All that the Torah was to a Jew, Jesus was to Paul and the Holy Spirit to Luke, and more. There is no need to accept Harnack's thesis that this section comes from the 'inferior' Jerusalem B source or to prefer to it iv. 31 as the more historical. Yet it seems probable that Luke has taken over a source written or oral (Aramaic?) and has written it up under his firm conviction that the gift of the Holy Spirit to the Church at Pentecost inaugurated a new order and age, removed the curse of separation due to the sin of men at Babel (cf. Chase, *Credibility*, 40) and fulfilled such a prophecy as that of Isa. xxviii. 11 f. If one had to guess at the contents of Luke's source, it may have contained an account of the Twelve being equipped and commissioned to go to twelve different parts of the world. Perhaps Luke changed this into a picture of representatives from all the then known world being gathered together at Jerusalem and of the apostles being miraculously endowed with foreign tongues to speak to each, because Luke was going to relate not the contemporaneous mission of all the apostles to the whole world but the slow, gradual spread of the gospel from Jerusalem to Rome. (1) **All** refers probably to the Twelve, not to all Christians. **Together** translates a favourite and semi-liturgical word in Acts meaning almost 'in church', cf. i. 15. The Spirit's coming is conceived as that of God's breath or *pneuma* taking violent action as in Old Testament days, for, as Dupont observes (*Problèmes*, 97), the Holy Spirit is less interior and moral to Luke than to Paul and is seen in speaking with tongues and prophecy, in miracles and in guiding the missionary enterprise of the Church. (2) **The whole house** reminds one of the smoke that filled the house at Isaiah's call, Isa. vi. 4; cf. too the wind and fire (the earthquake would be inappropriate) of Elijah's experience, 1 Kings xix. 11 ff. (3) Ps. xxix. 7 f. with its picture of the Lord hewing the flames, and with its under-tones of earthquake, was probably in mind. As the divine presence or *Shekinah* rested on the pious Jew studying the Law, and as Paul hoped that the power of Christ would rest on him (2 Cor. xii. 9), so the purifying and consuming flame of the Holy Spirit

rested on each apostle. Luke iii. 16 had connected the Holy
Spirit with the eschatological fire, cf. Matt. iii. 11 f. Now the
'last days' had arrived and in Peter's speech below Luke is to
stress the eschatological nature of the gift of the Spirit. (4) The
common critical distinction made between Luke's and Paul's
presentations of the phenomenon, speaking with tongues,
associated with the gift of the Spirit, is too clear cut. Paul (1
Cor. xii, xiv) is said to have thought of it simply in terms of
ecstatic utterance unintelligible to a hearer without an interpreter, and Luke to have thought of *glossolalia* simply as speaking in a foreign language. But anyone who has been present
when others have been subject to strong emotional and spiritual
or even alcoholic (cf. ii. 15) pressure or stimulus may have
observed that words of complete gibberish together with words
suggesting a foreign tongue are mixed up when the 'censors' of
the psyche are removed. This fascinating subject can be studied
in G. B. Cutten's *Speaking with Tongues*, 1928; G. Pilkington,
*The Unknown Tongues discovered to be English, Spanish and
Latin*, 1831 (on the Irvingites), as well as in K. Lake, *B.C.* v,
note x, and his 'Glossolalia and Psychology' in *The Earlier
Epistles of St. Paul*, 1911, 241-52; cf. W. Shepherd, *A New
Survey of Science*, 1949, 482 ff. Paul was aware that under the
influence of the Holy Spirit certain inhibitions were removed
and that such removal was taken to indicate His presence, but
he preferred to *glossolalia*, of which he himself was more
capable than most (1 Cor. xiv. 18), the moral gifts of the
Spirit. 'Tongues' and their interpretation come last in his list
of Spirit-gifts, 1 Cor. xii. 8 ff. At the same time, those who
adopt the ordinary critical view tend to overlook that even to
Paul *glossolalia* may well have meant or included speaking in
foreign tongues (J. G. Davies, *J.T.S.*, N.S., iii, 1952, 229-31),
as well as unintelligible speech, not the latter alone. Though
Koine Greek and perhaps one or two Aramaic dialects would
have sufficed for anyone at a feast at Jerusalem in apostolic
days, both Luke and Paul may well have been familiar with
much the same phenomenon which included the use of foreign
terms or could be interpreted by hearers as such. The conclusion is too glib that Luke could not have been Paul's
companion.

ii. 5-13. THE WHOLE WORLD THROUGH ITS REPRESENTATIVES HEARS THE WORD OF GOD

(5) But there were dwelling in Jerusalem [Jews] devout men of every nation which is under heaven. (6) But when this sound was heard the crowd gathered and were thrown into confusion, because each one heard them speaking in his own language. (7) And they were all amazed and wondered, saying, 'Lo, are not all these which speak Galileans? (8) And how do we hear them, each of us in his own language in which we were born? (9) Parthians and Medes and Elamites and the dwellers in Mesopotomia, Judaea and Cappadocia, Pontus and Asia, (10) Phrygia and Pamphylia, Egypt and the parts of Libya which is near Cyrene, and residents in Rome, Jews and proselytes, (11) Cretans and Arabians, we hear them telling in our own tongues the mighty deeds of God.' (12) But all were amazed and at a loss, saying one to another, "What does this mean?" (13) But others mocked and said, "They are full of sweet wine".'

(5) Though B supports 'Jews', א omits and C puts it later; this word, like that for 'dwelling in' may have been interpolated from vs. 14. The word for 'devout' would then have general sense, though it may denote in particular those Gentiles who were connected with a synagogue, however loosely. But if 'Jews' is retained, it refers to members of the Dispersion who were in Jerusalem for the Feast of Weeks. (9-11) As S. Weinstock has said (*J.R.S.* xxviii, 1948, 43-6), to understand this list we need to follow up the suggestion of F. C. Burkitt that Luke is indebted to astrological geography. An ancient geographer might consider the signs of the Zodiac and allot the countries on or beyond his own horizon to each, as though the countries were under their 'influence'. Weinstock prints the list of Paulus Alexandrinus (fourth century A.D.), which probably had an older origin. He also prints the list in Acts of the names of countries in eleven groups corresponding to eleven of the twelve in the list of Paulus Alexandrinus; Syria is omitted in

Luke's list; was this because Acts or its source was compiled there? (9) **Judaea** must be wrong, being out of place in such a catalogue; it was probably inserted by a Christian Jew who found the omission intolerable. Possibly 'Armenia' should be inserted in its place, as Tertullian and Augustine (once in three citations) quote; but the Armenian text does not support this. Otherwise, we may recall Burkitt's own emendation 'Gorduian', i.e. Kurdistan, as E. E. F. Bishop does (*ibid*. xlii, 1952, 84 f.). Instead of saying 'all the world', Luke has made the reference precise, basing his language probably on an astrological catalogue. It was not his intention to say that all the regions mentioned were Christianized at an early date. (11) There is no need to suppose that **Cretans and Arabians** were added as an afterthought, for Cilicia and Crete correspond to Sagittarius, and the Red Sea and Indian region to Pisces in Paulus Alexandrinus' list. (13) Sweet or new wine would be unfermented; cf. vss. 4 and 15 for the suggestion that they were drunk.

ii. 14-36. PETER'S SPEECH

(14) But Peter stood with the Eleven and raised his voice and gave utterance to them, 'Men of Judaea, and all ye who dwell in Jerusalem, let this be known to you and give ear to my words. (15) For these men are not, as you suppose, drunk; for it is the third hour of the day, (16) but this is that which was spoken by the prophet [Joel]; (17) "And it shall be in the last days, saith God, that I shall pour out of my Spirit on all flesh, and your sons and your daughters will prophesy, and your young men will see visions and your old men will dream dreams. (18) Yes, even upon my slaves and upon my slave-girls in those days I shall pour out of my Spirit, and they will prophesy. (19) And I shall show wonders in the heaven above and signs in the earth below, blood and fire and vapour of smoke. (20) The sun shall be turned into darkness and the moon into blood, before there comes the great and notable day of the Lord. (21) And it shall be

that whosoever shall call on the name of the Lord shall be saved." (22) Men of Israel, hear these words: Jesus of Nazareth, a man God-attested to you by miracles, wonders and signs, which God did through Him among you, as you yourselves know, (23) Him, given up according to the appointed will and foreknowledge of God, you nailed up by the hands of lawless men and slew; (24) Whom God raised up, loosing the pangs of death, inasmuch as it was not possible for Him to be held by it. (25) For David says with regard to Him, "I foresaw the Lord before me always, for He is at my right hand that I may not be shaken; (26) On that account my heart rejoiced and my tongue was glad; and, besides, my flesh will tabernacle in hope. (27) For Thou wilt not abandon my soul to Hades nor give Thy Holy One to see corruption. (28) Thou hast made paths of life known to me, Thou wilt fill me with gladness at Thy presence." (29) Brethren, it is permitted to speak with boldness to you about the patriarch David, that he is both dead and buried and his tomb is with us to this day. (30) Therefore being a prophet, and knowing that God swore with an oath to him that He would set one of the fruit of his loins upon his throne, (31) he foresaw and spoke about the resurrection of Christ, that neither was He abandoned to Hades nor did His flesh see corruption. (32) This Jesus God raised up, of which we are all witnesses. (33) Being therefore exalted by the right hand of God, and receiving from the Father the promise of the Holy Spirit, He has poured out that which you see and hear. (34) For David did not ascend to the heavens, but he himself says, "The Lord said to my Lord, Sit on my right hand, (35) till I make thine enemies a footstool for thy feet." (36) So let all the house of Israel know for certain that God has made Him both Lord and Christ, this Jesus Whom you crucified.'

This speech falls into four parts and gives a proof that the long-awaited last events had arrived; the apostolic kerygma about the saving acts of Jesus; Old Testament citations in support of this and the consequent injunction, vss. 37 f., to repent, be baptized and receive the Holy Spirit. (15) The **third hour** from sunrise would be about 9 A.M. (16) 'Joel' should probably be omitted with the Western text; if testimonies were used in the primitive Church, they would be likely to be anonymous. (17-21) The citation of Joel ii. 28-32 follows the LXX much as we have the latter, though the Alexandrian text shows traces of closer harmonization with it than does the Western. A. W. Argyle (*J.T.S.*, N.S., iv, 1953, 213 ff.) has criticized the view that an Aramaïc original may underlie ii. 14-40 on the ground that the LXX is used and that the Septuagintal quotations and allusions are integral to the sense of the speech. His similar argument with reference to Septuagintal citations in Q (*E.T.* lxiv, 1953, 382) was answered by B. M. Metzger (*ibid.* lxv, 1954, 125); if an Aramaic account containing quotations from the Old Testament were reported in Greek by a writer familiar with the LXX, who seldom read the Scriptures in any other form, it is likely that he would give the quotations for the most part according to the LXX; it cannot be supposed that every discourse which, as reported to us, contains quotations from the Old Testament in the words of the LXX could not previously have existed in Aramaic. This citation from Joel probably formed an early Testimony, but it is odd, if this is so, that not more use of it was made apart from Rom. x. 13. (19) **Blood and fire and vapour of smoke** are words omitted in the Western text. (22) '*Nazoraios*' is the term usually employed to describe Jesus in the gospels and Acts, as '*Nazoraioi*' describes Christians in Acts xxiv. 5, though Mark prefers '*Nazarenos*'. It is well known that the Mandaeans are regularly called 'Nazarenes'; a whole literature has grown up about the relation of this sect to John the Baptist and to Christians. (To the references in *B.C.* v, 357, n. 3, must be added M. Black's *Aramaic Approach to the Gospels and Acts*, 2nd ed., 1954, 143-6.) Though scholars are less prone than before to the Mandaean fever, most would admit with Black that Mandaean tradition has roots which run deep into pre-Christian Persian and Babylonian thought; and that another root may have stretched westwards as far as the banks of the Jordan and lie as deep as the first or second centuries. If John the Baptist's followers were called *nasorayya*, i.e. keepers, guardians, or observers of certain rites and traditions, then the early name given to Jesus' disciples, and even to Him, may have arisen through belief that His disciples and John's were closely connected. In the popular mind Jesus may have seemed but a disciple of John Baptist and hence a 'Nazarene'. Etymologically '*Nazoraioi*' cannot have been derived from 'Nazareth', cf. Matt. ii. 23. Yet the early Christians were capable of false etymologies; they may have connected Jesus with Nazareth and, wrongly, with *neṣer*, the Branch, or with *nazir*, a Nazirite. (22) Christ's miracles are the fulfilment of the awaited signs (vs. 19), showing that the last series of events, the *Eschaton*, was at hand. When the Messianic King had come, His kingdom was on the threshold of invading this world-order and His miracles were signs of its coming. (23) The Cross is seen already to be no stumbling-block (1 Cor. i. 23), but part of God's preconceived plan. Possibly Luke meant by 'lawless men' the Romans, or, seeing that Luke is pro-Roman, he took this phrase from a source. (24) Aram. *ḥabalayya*, 'bonds', could mean 'pangs' too; hence 'to loose the pangs' is not unnatural, cf. Job xxxix. 2, which Polycarp i. 2 cites, unless he quotes this verse from Acts. (25-28) Cf. Ps. xvi. 8-11, LXX. It is argued that as David died, the Psalm must refer to one greater than David, i.e. the Messiah Jesus, whose body did not see corruption in the tomb. The fact of the empty Tomb on Easter morning is assumed, cf. i. 3. (29-36) Knox (*Acts*, 84 ff.) argues that there is a gap in the argument about Jesus being exalted and receiving the promised gift of the Spirit; he suggests that Luke's sources contained an allusion to Ps. lxviii, a Pentecostal Psalm in the modern Jewish, as in the Anglican, prayer-book and the Roman Breviary. Luke missed this allusion owing to his unfamiliarity with Rabbinic exegesis, according to which 'Thou hast gone up on high, thou hast led captivity captive' meant no more a triumphal procession of victor and captives in Jerusalem but the ascent of Moses to heaven to receive the Torah or Law; despite angelic opposition, Moses won this prize and brought it back to men. Similarly, Jesus, exalted to the Father's right hand, received as His prize the promised Spirit, which He poured out on His apostles. Dupont (*Problèmes*, 97) is not convinced by Knox's analogy between Moses and Jesus and allows only a faint echo of Ps. lxviii here; and Knox admits that the day of Pentecost as the new Sinai does not meet us elsewhere in Acts. (30) Cf. Ps. cxxxii. (LXX, cxxxi.) 11. M. Black (*Aramaic Approach*, 1st ed., 133) reconstructed the last clause on the basis of D's text taken to point to an Aramaic original, 'of the fruit of his loins He would raise up Christ upon his throne'. The variant 'heart' for 'loins' in the D text may point to an Aramaic source as Torrey suggests (*Documents*, 145). (32) **Witnesses,** cf. on i. 8 above. (33) Cf. vs. 31. The word **exalt** in the Greek was almost a technical term among early Christians for Christ being exalted to the right hand of God (cf. Dodd, *The Fourth Gospel*, 247 and 376, n. 2). (34) Cf. Ps. cx (LXX, cix) 1. Originally, 'A message from the Lord (Yahweh) to my lord (the king)', this phrase became an early Testimony to Jesus as Lord, and the whole Psalm a quarry for Testimonies; cf. Mark xii. 35-37, 1 Cor. xv. 25, Eph. i. 20, 22, Heb. *passim*, John xviii. 1, Rev. ii. 28. As T. W. Manson has said, 'David would not call the head of a restored Davidic kingdom "My Lord" any more than he would have so accosted Solomon. But if the kingdom which David saw by inspiration was the true kingdom of God, he [David] could indeed call the head of that kingdom, "My Lord"; for that kingdom is of a higher order than his and its head has nobility of a kind that does not rest on pedigree or power. He is greater than David or Solomon: and he is greater in his own way, not theirs' (*The Teaching of Jesus*, 1931, 267 n.). (36) The Resurrection is the final guarantee that Jesus is Lord or Kyrios and Messiah; for 'Lord' cf. on i. 24 above. Preaching to the unconverted, the apostles must inevitably have used language which in a later age would suggest that Jesus was 'adopted' by God the Father to divine Sonship at His Resurrection (cf. *B.C.* v. note xxix) instead of being 'God of God'.

ii. 37-42. THE RESULT OF PETER'S PREACHING

(37) But when they heard, they were cut to the heart and they said to Peter and to the rest of the apostles, 'What shall we do, brethren?' (38) And Peter said to them,

'Repent, and let each one of you be baptized in the name of Jesus Christ for forgiveness of your sins; and you shall receive the gift of the Holy Spirit. (39) For to you is the promise, and to your children, and to all that are afar, as many as the Lord shall summon.' (40) And with many other words he testified and kept exhorting them, saying, 'Be saved from this crooked generation'. (41) Now they who received his word were baptized and there were added on that day about three thousand souls. (42) And they were adhering firmly to the teaching of the apostles and the fellowship, the breaking of the bread and the prayers.

(37) A verb from Ps. cix (LXX, cviii.) 16 is borrowed to express contrition. (38) Repentance, Baptism, the forgiveness of sins and receipt of the Holy Spirit are linked together, but here there is no mention of the laying-on of hands, cf. Appendix 3. Some scholars seek to excise this verse as an interpolation, cf. *B.C.* i. 340; it is suggested that the full name 'Jesus Christ' betrays an editor's hand: originally, they maintain, this passage did not refer to water-baptism; and Pentecost was baptism with the Holy Spirit as opposed to John Baptist's water-baptism. But it seems likely that if Acts was edited, the editor was responsible for stressing the need for the laying-on of hands before the Spirit could be received, cf. viii. 15-17 and xix. 6, owing to the absence of 'editorial' reference to the laying-on of hands, it is probable that this verse is not editorial. Some apostles may have been John's disciples originally, and all may well have adapted his water-baptism to Christian use in the 'name of Jesus', i.e. in token of Christ's ownership, cf. Isa. iv. 1, Jer. vii. 10. (39) **Afar** may refer to distance or to far-away descendants, probably the former, cf. Isa. lvii. 19, Joel ii. 32. (40) Luke is no doubt producing the gist of the apostolic preaching as St. Peter was in the habit of delivering it. The pattern of that kerygma could end with an appeal to repentance. For the **crooked generation**, cf. Deut. xxxii. 5, Matt. xvi. 4, xvii. 17. The remnant of Israel had become the remnant of the Church, the link between them being Christ. (41) It may be possible to discover some deep Gnostic-Catholic symbolism in

the number 3000 and indeed number-symbolism was rife in
the first century A.D. But this figure is probably historical. This
verse marks the end of the first extract from Harnack's Jerusalem B source and as a summary may end a paragraph. (42)
The definite article before the nouns suggests that they are
semi-technical terms denoting not only a new basis for society
but also Christian liturgical custom. The best commentary on
this verse is L. S. Thornton's *The Common Life in the Body of
Christ*, 1941, 1-33, which examines all that apostolic fellowship
or partnership meant. Luke records this 'common life' because
he expects all Christians to share in it (cf. Easton, *Purpose*,
22 f.).

ii. 43-47. ASPECTS OF THE COMMON LIFE

**(43) But fear was on every soul, and many wonders and
signs were done through the apostles. (44) And all who
believed were together, and they had all things in
common; (45) and they used to sell their goods and
belongings and to divide them among all, as anyone had
need. (46) And daily adhering together with one accord
in the temple, and breaking bread at home, they par-
took of food in gladness and singleness of heart, (47)
praising God and finding favour with all the people. And
the Lord added day by day together those who were
saved.**

(43) The wonders and signs or miracles were evident tokens
that the Messianic kingdom was breaking through from the
'coming age' into the present one. After 'apostles' some MSS.
add 'in Jerusalem' and put the note of fear here instead of at
the beginning. (44) **Together,** cf. on vs. 47. (45) The primitive
community experimented in a 'communism' of a totally different kind from the modern all-embracing economic and political
form. It was voluntary (cf. v. 3 f.) and it was apparently an
unsuccessful experiment; the 'saints' of Jerusalem remained
so poor that St. Paul was glad to cement Gentile- and

Jewish-Christians together by a collection from the former for the latter, corresponding to the ½ shekel temple tax paid by every male Jew of the Dispersion to the Temple. The word **day by day,** applied in the Alexandrian text to the prayers, is applied in the Western text to 'divide', cf. vi. 1. (46) The Temple was still the centre of Christian devotions and Luke thought of Christians as the best kind of Jews, cf. iii. 1, v. 12, 20, xxi. 23. **Breaking bread,** cf. vs. 42, xx. 7, 11, xxvii. 35, Luke xxiv. 30. Every meal to a Jew had a religious significance; but the Christian, when he broke bread, would think especially of the Eucharist-Agape, the re-presentation of the Last Supper of Jesus with His disciples, when He had broken bread to give them His broken Body; for despite J. W. C. Wand, the Agape was probably not a late importation into Christianity but the relic of the original meal with the Eucharist as the continuation of the blessings by Jesus over bread and cup. One need not decide whether the Last Supper was a Passover meal or an anticipatory meal of some kind like a kiddush or sanctification meal or a chaburah or fellowship meal held before the Passover (contrast J. Jeremias, *The Eucharistic Words of Jesus*, Eng. trans., 1955), or whether it was of a more general character like the meal referred to in *Joseph and Aseneth* (G. D. Kilpatrick, *E.T.* lxiv, 1952, 4-8). It may have been a Passover meal according to an ancient sacerdotal calendar (without the Passover lamb and bitter herbs?) held two days before the legal Jewish Passover lambs were slain, cf. A. Jaubert, *R.H.R.* cxlvi, 1954, 140-73). (47) **Saved;** 'being saved' cannot refer merely to those being healed physically. 'Together', cf. i. 15, ii. 44 translates three Greek words which appear twice in the B text and three times in D in this passage and five times altogether in the first five chapters of Acts. C. C. Torrey (*C.D.A.*, 10 ff.) pointed to this phrase as his most interesting proof of an Aramaic original, written source; he rejects 'together' as a translation, postulating a Judaean Aramaic word meaning 'greatly' or 'exceedingly'; contrast H. F. D. Sparks, *J.T.S.*, N.S., i, 1950, 17 ff., who points out that 'exceedingly' is an impossible translation on four of the five occasions where the phrase occurs. M. Black also rejects Torrey's argument (*Aram. Approach*, 2nd ed., 9 f.).

Note on ii. 43-7

P. Benoit (*Mél. Goguel*, 1950, 1-10) has examined the 'summaries in Acts ii. 42-7, iv. 32-5, and v. 12-15'. In these sections he regards as secondary ii. 43-5, iv. 33, and v. 12b-14. ii. 43 is borrowed from v. 11-12a, hence the unexpected note of 'fear' in ii. 43a. ii. 44-5 is a summary of iv. 32, 34-5; 'sur ce point tout le monde est d'accord', though Benoit asks if it is not easier to derive iv. 33 from ii. 47a, before he goes on to derive v. 12b from ii. 46a as well as from iii. 11; v. 13 from ii. 47a and v. 14 from ii. 47b, cf. xiv. 1, xvii. 4, 12, and xviii. 8. A redactor has been at work on already existing summaries or recapitulatory pictures of the life of the primitive community. These three 'summaries' are in a different category from the other 'stops' (de Zwaan) in Acts, cf. Introduction, 11 (2) B.

iii. 1-10. THE LAME MAN CURED

(1) But Peter and John were going up to the Temple at the hour of prayer, the ninth hour. (2) And a man lame from his mother's womb was being carried, whom they would set daily at the door of the Temple which is called Beautiful, to ask alms from those entering into the Temple. (3) He seeing Peter and John going into the Temple asked to receive alms. (4) But Peter gazing at him together with John, said, 'Look at us'. (5) And he attended to them, expecting to receive something from them. (6) But Peter said, 'Silver and gold do not belong to me; but what I have, that I give you. In the name of Jesus Christ of Nazareth, walk.' (7) And he seized him by the right hand and raised him up, and immediately his feet and ankles were strengthened; (8) and jumping up, he stood and began to walk; and he entered with them into the Temple, walking and jumping and praising God. (9) And all the people saw him walking and praising God. (10) And they began to recognize him that this was he who sat for alms at the Beautiful gate of the Temple; and they were filled with awe and amazement at what happened to him.

(1-10) Like Jesus' miracles, those in Acts indicate that the Messianic Kingdom is on the very threshold; the Strong one, Satan, is bound and despoiled of his goods.

Goguel, *I.N.T.* iii. 181 f., 191, is willing to accept iii. 1-9 and 10b as authentic, though he thinks that iii. 1-iv. 22 is a doublet of v. 12-42 and that iii. 10a is secondary, breaking the 'organic connexion' between iii. 9 and 10b. In iii. 1 we have what Harnack took to be the opening of the Jerusalem A source; yet it seems to be a typical instance of the many 'signs and wonders' of ii. 43. (For Harnack's view see *B.C.* ii. 127 ff.) (1) Peter and John belonged to an inner circle of Jesus' disciples during His ministry and were leaders of the Church after the Resurrection, cf. Gal. ii. 9. Though in theory the John mentioned here might be John Mark or another John, for this was one of the commonest names even in the ancient world, the probability is that he was the son of Zebedee, cf. viii. 14 ff., cf. also Luke's identification of the two disciples sent to make ready the Passover with Peter and John, Luke xxii. 8. For worship at the Temple, cf. on ii. 46 above. The regular hours of sacrifice, according to Josephus, *Ant.* xiv. 4.3, were 'in the morning and at the ninth hour'. The D-text here seems to have been influenced by Lev. vi. 20 ff. (2) The exact identification of the 'Beautiful' gate of the Temple and the correct text of this passage have been much debated, cf. *B.C.* iv. 32 and v. note 35. Luke may have had in mind the Nicanor or the Shushan gate; if this chapter belongs to a new Jerusalem A source, its author may have imagined that the disciples lodged still in Bethany and that they entered therefore daily by the eastern or Shushan gate. (4) **Gazing;** this verb is found a dozen times in Luke and twice elsewhere in the N.T. It is characteristic of miracle-stories and is used of the healer and not, as in the Western text here of the healed person, though it is a different verb which is used with similar meaning. (6) The *dynamis* of the Kingdom worked through Christ and through those to whom He mediated His power. As R. Leivestad has said (*Christ the Conqueror*, 1954, 81), though in the Synoptic Gospels healings were performed in the name of Jesus even by those who were not real disciples, Mark ix. 38, cf. Matt. vii. 22, yet Luke rejects such magical usage in Acts xix. 13 ff. 'The mention of the mighty name will work only when used by those whom Jesus has authorised.' (7) See Introduction 2 (c). (10) A Form-critic like Bultmann would say that it is a characteristic of miracle stories to end on the note of astonishment or terror or approval on the part of those who witnessed the miraculous event (cf. his article in the *Journal of Religion*, vi, 1926, 347 ff.), but it would be difficult to imagine how else a popular account of a miracle could end, unless in a dramatic 'aposiopesis' or 'dying away into silence'.

iii. 11-26. PETER'S SPEECH IN SOLOMON'S COLONNADE

(11) And as he held Peter and John, all the people in amazement ran together to them in Solomon's colonnade. (12) And Peter seeing it answered the people, 'Men of Israel, why do you wonder at this or why do you gaze at us, as though by our own power or piety we had made him walk? (13) The God of Abraham and Isaac and Jacob, the God of our fathers, glorified His servant Jesus, whom you betrayed and denied in front of Pilate, when he decided to let Him go. (14) But you denied the Holy and Righteous One, and you begged that a man who was a murderer should be granted you, (15) and you killed the pioneer of life, whom God raised from the dead, of which we are witnesses. (16) And in the faith of His name, this one whom you see and know was strengthened by His name, and the faith which was through Him gave him this wholeness before you all. (17) And now, brethren, I know that it was in ignorance that you acted, as did your rulers too; (18) but God thus fulfilled what He foretold by the mouth of all the prophets, that His Christ should suffer. (19) Repent therefore and turn for the blotting out of your sins, that there may come seasons of refreshing from before the Lord, (20) and that He may send Jesus the Christ foreappointed to you, (21) whom heaven must receive until the times of restoration of all

things, which God spoke by the mouth of His holy
prophets from the beginning of the world. (22) Moses
said: "A prophet will the Lord God raise up from your
brethren, as He raised me. You shall hear him in all
things whatsoever he speaks to you. (23) And it shall be
that every soul which does not hear that prophet shall be
destroyed from the people." (24) And all the prophets
from Samuel and those following, as many as spoke, also
announced these days. (25) You are the sons of the
prophets and of the covenant which God covenanted to
your fathers, saying to Abraham, "And in thy seed
shall all the families of the earth be blessed". (26)
To you first God, having raised up His servant, sent
Him to bless you while turning each one from your
wickednesses.'

(11-26) This speech follows the pattern of the apostolic
kerygma (cf. the chart at the end of C. H. Dodd's *Apostolic
Preaching*), though the gist of the words may go back to the
preaching of Peter as Luke knew it. 'The construction of almost
every sentence in the speech is obscure, and some of it is scarcely
translatable, but the general meaning is plain' (*B.C.* iv. 34 f.).
Even if an Aramaic written source is not postulated, Luke may
have had the apostle's Aramaic speech in mind, as elsewhere
when composing Peter's speeches in Acts; if Luke inserted
Septuagintalisms, he did not do so to clarify the Greek style,
which may be intentionally awkward, although some of the
awkwardness may be due to the way in which Luke left his
material.

(11) The Western text makes the opening smoother than
the Alexandrian text, perhaps for lectionary purposes; at the
same time it has a curious grammatical howler which suggests
the influence of Semitic speech (cf. A. J. Wensinck's study of
the relation between D and its Semitisms to the non-Western
text of Luke, *Bulletin of the Bezan Club*, xii, 1937). (13) **Servant**
may also be translated 'child'. For the identification of Jesus
with the Suffering Servant, cf. iii. 26, iv. 27, 30, viii. 26-end,
cf. Matt. viii. 17, 1 Pet. ii. 22, Heb. ix. 28. On the other hand
Q, Mark, Paul, and 'John' are remarkably silent about such an

identification. F. C. Burkitt (*Christian Beginnings*, 1924, 35 ff.) deduced from this that Greek-speaking Christians were the first to apply the Songs of the Servant of the Lord in Deutero-Isaiah to Jesus. But if Isa. xlii. 1 was in the mind of Jesus from the moment of His baptism and if He had shown His originality in combining the ideals of Messiah and sufferer, then the germ of the identification was there from the start (cf. A. E. J. Rawlinson, *The Gospel according to St. Mark*, 1927, 251 ff., and *The New Testament Doctrine of the Christ*, 1926, 238 ff.), even if we have to turn to the later strata of the New Testament records for the explicit identification, as in Acts. V. Taylor (*The Names of Jesus*, 1953, 26 ff.) says: 'In view of the popularity of the Servant-conception in primitive Christianity, and its place in liturgical usage, in prayers (Acts iv. 27, 30, Didache ix. 2 f., x. 2) and in hymns (Phil. ii. 5-11), in early confessions (1 Cor. xv. 3) and in exhortations (1 Clem. xvi), it is a mark of the fidelity of the Evangelists to historic tradition that it [the Servant conception] emerges so rarely in the Gospels, and with manifest restraint in the sayings of Jesus. In the circumstances one cannot fail to be conscious of a healthy scepticism concerning the alleged activity of Hellenistic Christianity in the formation of the Servant-tradition.' For the 'glorification' of the Servant, cf. Isa. lii. 13, Behold my servant shall prosper, he shall be exalted and lifted up. **You betrayed;** as time went on, the Jews more than the Romans were blamed for the crucifixion of Jesus, cf. 1 Thess. ii. 15. The mention of Pilate is one of many points in Luke which the old baptismal Creed of Rome was to include; Pontius Pilate was procurator from A.D. 26-36; he roused the anger of the Jews foolishly and needlessly and owing to his tactless handling of a Samaritan rising he was relieved of his office and called to account at Rome. (14) **The Holy and Righteous one;** 'the Holy One' does not seem to have been generally accepted as a Messianic title, cf. Mark i. 24, Acts iv. 27, cf. the citation of Ps. xvi. 10 in ii. 27, xiii. 35. 'The Righteous One' is used in Acts three times in a Messianic sense, here, in vii. 52 and xxii. 14, cf. 1 Pet. iii. 18, James v. 6, and Enoch xxxviii. 22. V. Taylor (*The Names of Jesus*, 80-83) suggests that it was a title used in the primitive Church at Jerusalem, but that it passed out of use. One reason for such desuetude may

have been that Christians, e.g. at Damascus, had heard of the
sect from whom the 'Damascus document' or Fragment of a
Zadokite Work emerged, probably an early Essene sect closely
connected with that of the Qumran scrolls, who had had at one
stage of their history a 'Teacher of Righteousness' whose death
or 'gathering in' seems to appear from the 'Damascus document', ix. 39. According to H. H. Rowley this Teacher of
Righteousness, who appears also in the Testament of Levi, is
to be identified with Onias, as the 'wicked priest' is with
Menelaus, the 'man of scorn and untruth' with Antiochus and
the 'house of Absalom' with the Tobiads (*Analecta Lovanensia
Biblica et Orientalia*, ii. 30, 1952, and *Bulletin of the John
Rylands Library*, 30, 1952, 111-54; contrast Bo Reicke, *Symbolae
Biblicae Upsaliensis*, xiv, 1952, according to whom the Teacher
of Righteousness cannot be identified; cf. A. Dupont-Sommer,
V.T. i. 3, 1951, 200 ff.). According to the Damascus document,
this Teacher is different from the Messiah who would arise
forty years after him and from Aaron and Israel. **You denied;**
D. and Irenaeus (Latin) have a Greek word for 'you oppressed';
C. C. Torrey (*D.P.C.*, 141) suggests that *kdbtun* for 'you denied'
was translated from the Greek of Luke but misread as *kbdtun*,
which would suggest the Hebrew for 'you oppressed'; this
illustrates his theory that a midrashic Aramaic version of the
Greek of Acts represented by the Alexandrian text was translated back into Greek and has resulted in the Semitisms of D
and the Western text of Acts generally. (15) The **murderer,**
Barabbas, is contrasted with the 'pioneer' or 'author' of life,
cf. v. 31, Heb. ii. 10, xii. 2. As this word could be used of
quasi-divine founders of colonies (Delling, *T.W.N.T.*), did it
imply a comparison between Joshua and Jesus, both of whom
led God's people into a holy land? **Witnesses,** cf. i. 21, ii. 32,
etc. (16) This awkward verse may be derived from an Aramaic
(oral?) source; Torrey (*C.D.A.* 14 ff.) suggested that an original
Aramaic written source meant 'and by faith in His name He
has made whole this man whom you see and know'; or the
awkwardness may be due to lack of revision of an early draft
which led to scribal conflation of more than one clause. C. F. D.
Moule, following up an earlier form of this theory put forward
by his father, has suggested (*E.T.* lxv, 1954, 220) that possibly

the alternatives were (a) by faith in His name this man was saved, (b) His name made this man strong, (c) the faith which was through Him gave this man this perfect health; if all three clauses were left in Luke's unrevised text, an early scribe may have combined them all, instead of striking out two of the alternatives. This is a better solution than to suppose, as F. C. Burkitt did (*J.T.S.* xx, 1919, 324 f.), that a stop should be placed before 'this man whom you see . . .' and the clause 'by faith in his name' be considered part of verse 15. For the 'Name' cf. S. New, *B.C.* v, note 11, esp. pp. 132 ff. 'In the early chapters, and particularly those ascribed to the Jerusalem A source, the story is told of a great struggle between the Disciples and the Jewish authorities, which centred in the use of the Name of Jesus.' . . . 'Belief in Jesus (or in His Name), baptism, the remission of sins, the laying on of apostolic hands and the reception of the Spirit seem to have formed a single complex of associated ideas, any one of which might in any single narrative be either omitted or emphasized.' Cf. Appendix 3. (16) The noun translated 'wholeness' or 'perfect health' is a N.T. *hapax legomenon* (though the adjective for 'complete' is common) found in Chrysippus, Plutarch, and the papyri. The connexion between 'wholeness' and 'holiness' is not purely verbal. (17) Here even the Jews are not blamed for killing Jesus, cf. Luke xxiii. 34, which some scholars have wished to remove on inadequate textual grounds (cf. my *Alterations*, 8 f.). (18) The Jews would have denied that God foretold by the mouth of all the prophets that the Christ should suffer. The view that some Jews of the first century A.D. believed in a Suffering Messiah, cf. Brownlee, *B.A.S.O.R.* 132, December 1953, 8 ff., but that in controversy with Christians they abandoned this belief later has been maintained by W. D. Davies (*Paul and Rabbinic Judaism*, 1948, 276-84, cf. W. Manson, *Jesus the Messiah*, 1943, 171-4) has been denied by H. H. Rowley, *The Servant of the Lord*, 1952, 63 ff. Luke's, however, is a fair statement of early Christian belief based possibly on a loose compilation of Old Testament proof-texts; C. H. Dodd (*According to the Scriptures*, 92-6) has shown how deeply Isa. lii. 13-liii. 12 entered into Christian consciousness from the first. But for the Messiah to suffer *Crucifixion* was unthinkable to a Jew.

It is hypercritical to infer (cf. *B.C.* iv. 37) that '[the Christian view] could not have been put forward by Peter without more explanation'; for the speeches are mere summaries of what would have been said. (19) **Seasons of refreshing,** respite, or revival were apparently expected when or before the Messiah would return. (21) **Restoration** may mean 'establishment' of all that had been promised in the O.T. One is not compelled to accept Torrey's supposed Aramaic, 'until the fulness of the times of all that God has spoken'. The primitive Christian conception that Jesus must be 'received' or 'kept' till prophecy is completed should be noted. (22) C. H. Dodd (*According to the Scriptures,* 52-6) rather more tentatively than J. R. Harris (*Testimonies*) assigns this combination of Deut. xviii. 15, 19 and Lev. xxiii. 29 to a list of O.T. Testimonies, cf. Acts vii. 37, Luke ix. 35 (hear ye Him, not Moses or Elijah), Clem. Recog. i. 36. J. Dupont (*E.T.L.,* 1953, 321 ff.) suggests that the Deut. passage was a proof-text for Christians (as it was for the Qumran Sectaries), not only because it showed that Christ was predicted by Moses, but also because the 'raising up' of 'the prophet' could be taken to bear the secondary meaning of being raised from the dead. (24) The Greek is awkward. Torrey's conjectural emendation would run, 'And all the prophets who spoke from Samuel onwards through his successors announced these days' (*C.D.A.* 29 f.). The last days which the prophets had foretold had dawned and eschatology was 'in process of self-realisation' from the moment that Jesus had come announcing that the Kingdom was on the threshold. There was an organic connexion between what had been foretold, Jesus and His disciples and their teaching and above all His saving acts and the coming fulfilment, as there is organic connexion between seed and tree, ear of corn and harvest. (25) **Sons . . . of the covenant;** as Bruce notes, this is a primitive phrase, cf. the *Bene Q'yama* of the later Syrian Church. **In thy seed,** cf. Gen. xii. 3, xxii. 18, Gal. iii. 16. (26) **You first,** i.e. the Jews, cf. Rom. i. 16; **raised up,** cf. on vs. 16. But here the 'raising up' refers probably to God's sending His Son to save men, cf. Judges iii. 9.

iv. 1-4. THE ARREST OF PETER AND JOHN

(1) But when they were speaking to the people there came on them the priests and the captain of the Temple and the Sadducees, (2) being annoyed because they were teaching the people and announcing in Jesus the resurrection of the dead. (3) And they laid hands on them and put them in custody till the next day, for it was now evening. (4) And many of those who heard the word believed and the number of the men became about five thousand.

(1) In this section the style slips from Aramaic shadow into Hellenistic sunshine. Some MSS. read 'chief priests', as if Luke had in mind here the Temple guards; the officer of the Temple was either the Sagan or High Priest's adjutant who kept order in the Temple precincts, or one of his subordinates. The Sadducees may have derived their name from Zadok the priest who displaced Abiathar and to whose sons Ezekiel wished to restrict the office of priest; both Josephus and the N.T. treat them as a main party within Judaism, who denied the Resurrection life, cf. Mark xii. 28, Josephus, *B.J.* ii. 8, 14 and who rejected the developed angelology and demonology of post-exilic Judaism, for none of these was guaranteed by the Pentateuch. They formed the aristocratic and priestly party which was to perish in A.D. 70. (2) Christ's Resurrection proved that death is not the end, cf. 1 Cor. xv. 12. (3) The Sanhedrin seems to have had police powers of arrest and detention, and even of putting to death anyone who stepped into the inner courts of the Temple, not being a Jew. (4) The number 5000 may be historical; if Luke knew Mark when he wrote Acts, did he have in mind the Feeding of the 5000? This verse is not one of the 'rubrics' (Cadoux) or 'stops' (de Zwaan) intended to mark the progress of the gospel from Jerusalem to Rome.

iv. 5-12. THE EXAMINATION OF THE APOSTLES

(5) But it came to pass on the morrow that their rulers and elders and scribes were brought together in Jerusalem, (6) both Annas the high-priest and Caiaphas and John and Alexander and as many as were of high-priestly stock. (7) And having set them in the midst they began to inquire, 'By what power or by what name did you do this?' (8) Then Peter, filled with Holy Spirit, said to them: 'Rulers of the people and elders, (9) if we are asked this day about an act of benevolence to a sick man, by what he has been healed, (10) let it be known to you all and to all the people of Israel, that by the name of Jesus Christ of Nazareth, whom you crucified, whom God raised from the dead, by Him has this man taken his stand before you in health. (11) This is the stone which was rejected by you, the builders, becoming the head of the corner. (12) And salvation is in nobody else; for there is no other name under heaven given among men, by which we must be saved.'

(5) The rulers or priests together with the elders or presbyters and scribes made up the Sanhedrin which assisted from at least *c.* 198 B.C. the High Priest in the capacity of a judicial court, cf. *B.C.* i. 33 f., or in general to order the internal affairs of the Jews. (The latter attempted to trace the origin of the Sanhedrin back to the seventy elders of Num. xi. 16.) The scribes, usually of the Pharisaic party, were authorities on the law of Moses and its developments and their interpretation, while the elders exercised municipal and religious functions especially as judges with power to excommunicate from the synagogues. (6) **Annas** or Hananos (Josephus) was High Priest, A.D. 6–15; five of his sons became High Priests set up by the Romans, who like the Hasmonaeans and Herods set up whom they would; Luke (cf. Luke iii. 2) speaks as though both Annas and Caiaphas were High Priests in the procuratorship of Pontius Pilate, whereas Josephus recognizes only the latter, Joseph Caiaphas, who had been Annas' son-in-law (John xviii. 13) and who was High

Priest A.D. 18–36, during which time Annas was probably the power behind the throne. **John** may be short for 'Jonathan', the reading of D, who after being in and out of office from A.D. 36 was murdered in A.D. 66 by *Sicarii*. **Alexander** has not been identified. (7) **in the midst;** the late statement of *Sanhedrin* iv. 3 that this council sat in a semicircle 'like half a round threshing-floor' may be reliable; so 'each could observe another's face'. **The name;** cf. on iii. 16 and the experience of Christians that Jesus' name puts to flight the forces of evil, including evil spirits associated with sickness (Athanasius, *De Inc.* xxx. 5; Origen, *Contra Celsum* i. 6, 67). (8) Luke may have recalled the promise of Jesus to give His disciples the Holy Spirit when brought before adversaries, Mark xiii. 11, Luke xxi. 15. (9) **asked** may refer specially to a preliminary legal questioning, cf. J. Jeremias, *Z.N.T.W.* 36, 1937, 205-21. (11) Jesus was taken to be the 'Stone' of Ps. cxviii. 22, probably according to an early Testimony-list (cf. J. R. Harris, *Testimonies*, i, 1916, 26 f.), which may well have included that and the following verse of the Psalm, cf. Mark xii. 10 f., 1 Pet. ii. 7 (cf. Dodd, *According to the Scriptures*, 35 f.). The translation here may be from the Hebrew rather than the LXX. (12) **Salvation** and **life,** identical terms in Semitic speech, cover both physical and spiritual well-being.

iv. 13-22. PETER AND JOHN ARE SET FREE

(13) But seeing the boldness of Peter and John and perceiving that they were uneducated and common men, they wondered, and they recognized them, that they had been with Jesus. (14) But seeing the man who had been healed standing with them, they had nothing to gainsay it. (15) But commanding them to go out of the Sanhedrin, they consulted one with another, (16) saying, 'What shall we do to these men? For that a notable sign has been given through these men is evident to all that dwell in Jerusalem, and we cannot deny it. (17) But that it may spread no further to the people, let us warn them no

longer to speak in this name to anyone among men.'
(18) And having called them, they bade them cease
speaking or teaching in any way in the name of Jesus.
(19) But Peter and John said in answer to them, 'Whether
it is right before God to listen to you rather than to God,
judge yourselves. (20) For we cannot cease speaking of
what we have seen and heard.' (21) But they added to
their warning and let them go, not finding how to punish
them because of the people, because all were glorifying
God for what had happened. (22) For the man was more
than forty years old on whom this sign of healing had
been wrought.

(13) The **boldness** was of speech and bearing shown by un-
learned men and 'laymen' rather than unlettered and private
persons, as the words could mean. (19) Cf. Plato, *Apology*, 29 D,
'I shall obey God rather than you'. (22) The popular 'form' of
a miracle-story often includes a reference to the length of time
of a victim's disease; Luke's medical interests need not be
invoked here.

iv. 23-31. THE RETURN OF PETER AND JOHN AND THE PRAYER OF THE CHURCH

(23) But when they were let go they went to their friends
and announced all that the high priests and elders had
said to them. (24) And on hearing it, they lifted their
voices together to God and said, 'Master, Thou who
didst make the heaven and the earth and the sea and all
things that are in them, (25) who by the mouth of our
father David, Thy servant, by the Holy Spirit didst say,
"Why did nations rage and peoples imagine vain things?
(26) The kings of the earth stood up and the rulers were
gathered together, against the Lord and against His
Anointed." (27) For in truth there were gathered together in this city against Thy holy servant Jesus, whom
Thou didst anoint, both Herod and Pontius Pilate, with

the nations and the people of Israel, (28) to do whatever
Thy hand and Thy counsel had predetermined to be.
(29) And now, O Lord, look upon their threats and grant
to Thy servants with all boldness to speak Thy word, (30)
when Thou stretchest out Thy hand to heal and signs
and wonders are done through the name of Thy holy
servant Jesus. (31) And when they had prayed, the place
in which they were gathered together was shaken; and
they were all filled with the Holy Spirit and began to
speak the word of God with boldness.

(23) **friends**, lit. 'their own', cf. vs. 32. (24) **Master;** cf.
Luke ii. 29, Rev. vi. 10; this title suggests the despot and slave
relationship of God and man, cf. vss. 27 and 30 for the use of
'servant', though this word is not *doulos*, slave, but *pais*, which
could mean 'child'. (25) The Greek is awkward, as often in the
speeches in the first half of Acts, perhaps because Luke was
adopting a forced, Septuagintal style or because he was using
an Aramaic source. Torrey on his theory of a written Aramaic
source reconstructed the text to mean 'that which our father,
Thy servant, David said by command of the Holy Spirit'. On
H. W. Moule's theory (*E.T.* li, 1939–40, 396) Luke drafted a
clause and added alternatives which a copyist did not strike out
but combined; here 'who spake by the Holy Spirit' may have
had alternatives, 'of our father', and '(of) the mouth of David
thy servant', cf. C. F. D. Moule, *ibid.* lxv, 1954, 220 f., cf. on
iii. 16. On the latter view there is no need to explain how a
supposedly Aramaic source contained LXX quotations, but see
above on ii. 17. (26) Ps. ii. 1 ff. was Messianic to the author of
the Psalms of Solomon, xvii. 26, and to that of Heb. i. 5 and
v. 5. It may underlie Mark i. 11, ix. 7, Matt. iii. 17, and the
Western text of Luke iii. 22 (cf. Dodd, *According to the
Scriptures*, 31 f., 104-6). For Jesus as servant see on iii. 13
above; *pais* here may mean 'son' as in Ps. ii. 7. J. Dupont
has argued that the Christ theology of the primitive church
came logically before the Servant Christology, but the latter
could have followed soon after the former (*Problèmes*, 110).
(27) **Thou didst anoint;** in the primitive church when
Christological ideas were fluid, Jesus is spoken of as though

He became Messiah at His Baptism or at His death and resurrection (two events considered as one), cf. ii. 36, iii. 12. Luke, if he added Luke i-ii to his Gospel last of all, came to think of Jesus as 'Christ' from His birth. Luke alone refers to Jesus' trial before Herod Antipas (Luke xxiii. 6) as well as before Pilate (cf. on iii. 13); these stand for the 'kings' and 'rulers' respectively of the Psalm just cited. Was Luke, the pro-Roman, using a source which did not spare the Roman procurator the blame? (29) **Servants;** *douloi*, a different word from that applied to Christ, *pais*. (31) The **earthquake** may not have been taken to be a natural phenomenon so much as a divine affirmative in response to prayer, cf. Isa. vi. 4.

iv. 32-v. 11. TWO CONTRASTING PICTURES OF THE COMMON LIFE OF THE CHURCH

(32) But the multitude of those who believed had one heart and soul and not even one would say that any of his possessions was his own, but they had all things in common. (33) And with great power would the apostles give the testimony of the resurrection of the Lord Jesus; and great grace was upon them all. (34) For there was not even anyone in need among them; for as many as were owners of lands or houses sold them and brought the price of what was sold, (35) and laid it at the apostles' feet; and distribution was made to each according as anyone had need. (36) But Joseph, who was surnamed Barnabas by the apostles (which is translated, Son of exhortation), a Levite, a Cypriote by race, possessing a field, (37) sold it and brought the money and laid it at the apostles' feet.

(v. 1) But a certain man, named Ananias, with Sapphira, his wife, sold a property, (2) and kept back part of the price, his wife being privy to it too, and having brought some part, he laid it at the apostles' feet. (3) But Peter said, 'Ananias, why did Satan fill your heart to lie to the Holy Spirit, and to keep back part of the price of the land?

(4) While it remained, remained it not yours? And when it was sold, was it not in your power? Why did you conceive this affair in your heart? You have not lied to men but to God.' (5) When Ananias heard these words, he fell down and expired. And there was great fear on all who heard of it. (6) And the younger men arose, wrapped him up and carried him out and buried him. (7) And there was an interval of about three hours and his wife came in, not aware of what had happened. (8) And Peter addressed her, 'Tell me if you sold the land for so much'. And she said, 'Yes, for so much'. (9) And Peter said to her, 'Why was agreement made by you to tempt the Spirit of the Lord? Behold, the feet of those who buried your husband are at the door, and they will carry you out.' (10) And she fell down immediately at his feet and expired. And the young men came in and found her dead, and they carried her out and buried her by her husband. (11) And there was great fear on all the church, and on all who heard these things.

(32) 'In one matter Luke praises a standard even more rigorous than that actually taught by Jesus, for Luke is evidently delighted to tell of the extreme communism practised by the first believers. Still, he sets forth this extraordinary self-sacrifice not as a model that all Christians must imitate (vs. 4) but as a work of supererogation that distinguished uniquely the holy Church of Jerusalem' (Easton, *Purpose*, 35). **Multitude** may also mean ' crowd ' or ' congregation '. For these verses, cf. on ii. 43-7, above (Benoit's theory). (36) **Barnabas** in Acts is noted for (a) his generosity on this occasion, (b) his tolerance towards Saul in whose conversion he believed and whom he was willing to introduce to the apostles, and (c) his disinterested service with Paul when Barnabas takes second place (cf. R. O. P. Taylor, *C.Q.R.*, 1943, cxxxvi. 59-79). The derivation of his name ranges from 'son of Nebo' to 'son of a prophet' (*nabhi*); as *B.C.* iv. 49 says 'son of exhortation' would suit the name Manaen or Menahem better (xiii. 1), and it is possible that Luke, who pictured Barnabas as one who exhorted (xi. 23), confused the two names in a source-list. If so, perhaps Luke's

knowledge of Semitic languages was not very deep, cf. xiii. 8 on 'Elymas'.

(v. 1 ff.) It says much for Luke's honesty that he has included this second picture. Ph. Menoud (*Mél. Goguel*, 146-54) avoids the harshness of the story by supposing that 'natural' death occurred and cast a shadow on the early Church which was living in a new order of Life in Christ Jesus as part of His new creation; on Menoud's theory the couple did not die because they had sinned; but because they died it was thought that they must have sinned, according to a very primitive tradition to which Luke had access; so the emphasis is not to be put on the first sin in the Church but on the first death(s). This is a rationalization of the story for which Menoud admits that he has no evidence. It hardly does justice to the horror of early Christians at post-baptismal sin (cf. Heb. x. 26, etc.) or to the effect of the apostle's powerful words on a guilty conscience. The names of Ananias and Sapphira mean 'The Lord is gracious' and 'Beautiful'; and 'Sapphira' is found on an ossuary (burial urn) in Jerusalem. (2) **kept back,** or 'embezzled'; the verb is used of Achan's sins against God, Josh. vii. 1. (3) **Satan,** the Hebrew name for which the Greek equivalent was Diabolos, meaning Devil; originally Satan was the 'adversary', e.g. of Job, i. 6 ff., but later the name denoted the chief evil power opposing God (for a time), cf. the influence of Persian demonology. (5) **expired;** the word sometimes means 'fainted'; does this point to an original story in which Ananias merely swooned? This is improbable, for as *B.C.* iv. 51 says, the apostolic power to destroy is the necessary analogue to the power to heal and to make alive; cf. 1 Cor. v. 5. (6) **wrapped up;** this word may refer not so much to the winding in a shroud as to the removal from sight, cf. *B.C.* iv. 51 f. (8) **addressed;** the word for 'answer' was losing its strict meaning. (9) Both the idea of **testing** the Lord, cf. Exod. xvii. 2, and the phrase **at the feet of** suggest a strongly Semitic source, written or oral. (10) Though we may attribute her death to grief, terror, fear, and guilt, Luke probably took it to be due to the same apostolic power as killed Ananias. **The church;** this is the first of twenty-three occurrences of *ekklesia* in Acts, cf. Appendix 2.

v. 12-16. A SUMMARY OF PROGRESS

(12) And many signs and wonders were done by the hands of the apostles among the people. And they were all together in Solomon's colonnade. (13) But of the rest none dared to adhere to them but the people magnified them, (14) and more than ever believers were added to the Lord, multitudes both of men and women, (15) so that they carried out the sick even into the streets, and laid them on couches and pallets, in order that when Peter came his shadow might overshadow one of them. (16) There came together also the multitude of the cities around Jerusalem, bringing the sick and those troubled with unclean spirits, and they were healed, every one.

(12-16) Cf. Benoit's theory; see note on ii. 43-7 above. (12) On Benoit's theory, one is excused from discussing who are the **all**, 12b-14 being interpolated. (13) Unless we allow for a redactor's hand, the precise meaning of vs. 13 in conjunction with vs. 14 eludes one. Torrey emended on the basis of a supposed Aramaic original, 'of the elders no one dared join himself to them; nevertheless the common people magnified them' (*D.P.C.*, 96). (15-16) If Luke knew Mark's Gospel before he wrote Acts, it would not be unnatural for these verses to echo Mark vi. 56 and for Luke perhaps later to avoid repeating Mark in compiling his Gospel, cf. *E.T.* lxiv, 1953, 283 f.; cf. Acts i. 7 with Mark xiii. 32; Acts vi. 11 with Mark xiv. 58, 64; Acts xii. 4 with Mark xiv. 2; and Acts ix. 40 with Mark v. 40. The use here of Mark's word *krabbatos*, pallet, is especially striking. (15) Peter's **shadow** here has healing effect as do Paul's handkerchiefs and aprons (?), xix. 12. Without endorsing the Tübingen view that Peter's deeds were paralleled by Paul's in Acts, one may say that Luke consciously compared the two apostles, cf. Jacquier, *Actes*, xvii-xviii. The verb for **overshadow** occurs four times elsewhere in the N.T., always of the divine cloud of glory, the divine presence and power.

v. 17-32. ANOTHER IMPRISONMENT AND QUESTIONING OF THE APOSTLES

(17) But the High Priest stood up and all who were with him (the local party of the Sadducees) and were filled with indignation, (18) and they laid hands on the apostles and put them in public custody. (19) But an angel of the Lord by night opened the doors of the prison and brought them out and said, (20) 'Go and stand in the Temple and speak to the people all the words of this life'. (21) And when they heard it, they went in about dawn to the Temple and began to teach. But when the High Priest came and those that were with him, they called together the Sanhedrin and all the senate of the Sons of Israel and they sent to the prison to have them brought. (22) But when the officers came, they did not find them in the prison, and they returned and reported, saying, (23) 'We found the prison locked with every security and the guards standing at the doors. But when we opened it, we found nobody inside.' (24) And when they heard these words, both the captain of the Temple and the High Priests, they were at a loss about them, what this would mean. (25) And someone came and reported to them, 'Lo, the men whom you put in the prison are standing in the Temple and teaching the people'. (26) Then the captain went with the officers and brought them, without violence, for they feared the people, lest they should be stoned. (27) And they brought them and set them in the Sanhedrin, and the High Priest questioned them, (28) saying, 'We gave you strict command to cease teaching in this name, and lo, you have filled Jerusalem with your teaching, and you wish to bring upon us the blood of this man'. (29) But Peter answered, and the apostles, and they said, 'It is necessary to obey God rather than men. (30) The God of our fathers raised Jesus, whom you did away with, hanging him on a tree. (31) Him did God exalt by His right hand as pioneer and saviour, to give repentance to Israel and remission of sins. (32) And we are witnesses

of these words, and so is the Holy Spirit which God has given to those who obey Him.'

(17-32) 'The presence of dual sources is even suggested by parallelism of iv. 1 f. and v. 17-42', Moffatt, *I.L.N.T.* 2nd ed., 291, who sets out the parallels:

v. 17-42	iv. 1 f
(a) Annas [and all with him] arrest the apostles:	(a) arrest and arraignment of Peter and John before Annas.
(b) their miraculous release: arraigned before Sanhedrin:	(b) Answer: [If it is right in the sight of God, etc.]
(c) Speech of Peter and apostles [It is necessary, etc.]	(c) Release.

On the other hand, if Jeremias is right (*Z.N.T.W.* xxxvi, 1937, 205 ff.), legal action was taken according to Jewish procedure only after due warning; if Acts iv described the legal warning, v describes the legal action. Alternatively, on J. W. Swain's theory (*H.T.R.* 37, 1944, 34 f.) this imprisonment and Gamaliel's speech belong to the incidents of ch. xii.

(17) Dibelius is inclined to accept 'Annas' in place of '*anastas*', = 'standing up' (*J.R.* 21, 421 ff.), but 'Annas' is attested only by the African Latin text and may be due to the influence of iv. 6 **local;** *B.C.* iv. 56 and Bruce (140) accept this rendering, the participle of the verb 'to be' denoting what is current in time or local in place. (19) A belief in angels was deep-rooted in Hebrew thought and was developed in the Persian period of domination under the influence of Zoroastrian ideas. (20) **Life** in Semitic speech is the same as 'salvation'. (21) **and all the senate;** or 'even all the senate', for this is a redundancy due perhaps to Luke's consciously Septuagintal style. (24) It is striking that the Greek of 'what this would mean' (or 'come to') is a classical-sounding phrase found only in Luke's Gospel and Acts. (26) The D-text omits 'not' in front of 'with violence' probably accidentally. (28) According to Matt. xxvii. 25 the responsibility for the blood of Jesus was accepted by the Jews. (29) Cf. on iv. 19 above. The

Western text of *h* expands, 'And Peter answered and said to them, "Whom is it right to obey, God or man?" and he said, "God".' (30) Cf. Deut. xxi. 22 f. 'and you hang him on a tree . . . for a hanged man is accursed by God'. To Peter is ascribed the use of the same word, tree, for Cross, in x. 39, cf. 1 Pet. ii. 24. J. Schneider (*T.W.N.T.* 5, 1944, 38 f.) suggests that *xulon*, tree, is used instead of *stauros*, cross, owing to the influence of the LXX in contexts referring to a criminal's body being exposed after execution; the phrase 'to hang on (the) wood' indicates that the Roman method of execution by crucifixion was taken to be an equivalent for the Jewish penalty of stoning and then gibbeting. C. H. Dodd compares the *Baraita* in *Bab. Sanh.* 43, where it is reported that 'they hanged . . . Jesus on the eve of the Passover' (*J.T.S.*, N.S., v. 2, 1954, 244 f.). (31) **Pioneer and saviour,** cf. on iii. 15. The former word is taken to be a military metaphor, 'prince' or 'captain' (cf. C. P. M. Jones in *Studies in the Gospels*, ed. D. E. Nineham, 1955, 119), but the sense of pioneer is there, such as Moses was when he led God's people towards the promised land. Again, as God had raised up each judge of old to be a saviour or go'el of His people, so God had now raised up Jesus, cf. Judges iii. 9, etc. As Dupont observes, Jesus was not a Saviour after the manner of a deified emperor but as a liberator of the true Israel from their sins (*Problèmes*, 102). Heb. ii. 10, xii. 2 can pick up the phrase 'pioneer', the author being fully aware that it was an early title for Jesus, one 'which could be accommodated to his highly hellenistic point of view' (Knox, *Acts*, 79 f.). (32) **Witnesses,** cf. i. 8, ii. 32, etc. **Words;** *dabar* (Heb.) can mean an event as well as literally a 'word'; 'event' suits this context and that of x. 37 (where Peter is again the speaker).

v. 33-9. GAMALIEL'S SPEECH

(33) **But when they heard this, they were cut to the quick and wanted to kill them. (34) But there stood up one in the Sanhedrin, a Pharisee named Gamaliel, a lawyer honoured by all the people and he ordered them to put**

the men outside for a short time. (35) And he said to
them, 'Men of Israel, take heed to yourselves about these
men, what you intend to do. (36) For before these days
there arose Theudas, saying that he was someone, and a
number of men, about four hundred, attached themselves to him; he was slain and all, as many as obeyed
him, were dispersed, and came to nothing. (37) After him
arose Judas the Galilean, in the days of the census and
caused a rising of the people after him; he too perished
and all, as many as obeyed him, were scattered. (38) And
in the present instance I tell you, keep away from these
men and leave them alone, for if this plan or this work
be of men, it will be destroyed. (39) But if it is of God,
you will not be able to destroy them, lest you be found
fighting even against God!'

(33-9) For the anachronisms of this speech and for the
question whether Luke used Josephus' works, see Introduction
7 (a). Swain (art. cit.) suggests that Luke received a tradition
of another imprisonment of the apostles and that lacking
chronological evidence he inserted Gamaliel's speech here and
not in ch. xii. This would at least make the anachronisms less
glaring than they are in their present context, though it would
not settle the problem of Luke's dependence on Josephus. (33)
Cut to the quick; lit. sawn apart. (34) **Pharisee**; cf. *B.C.* i.
110-14. The name may have meant the 'separated ones' or
'the interpreters' (W. O. E. Oesterley) or even 'the Persianizers'
(T. W. Manson); at their best they taught much that Jesus
could adopt, e.g. belief in a resurrection life; at their worst they
fell under His condemnation on grounds which I. Abrahams
and T. Herford have failed to explain away in their modern
defences of Pharisaism. From being religious enthusiasts in the
days of John Hyrcanus, they and their scribes became ex-
pounders of the Torah and its interpretations, whereas according to the Gospels they seem often unable to rise above the
letter of the Law and of the interpretations of men; yet so far as
Judaism had a future after the rejection of Jesus and after A.D.
70, it was to lie with this party. Gamaliel was a descendant of
Hillel and, like him, a famous Rabbi; Paul is said to have been

his pupil once (Acts xxii. 3), and Montefiore's objection that Paul's criticisms of the Pharisees proves that he cannot have been educated by Gamaliel is flimsy; to a Christian repentance means more than the return of the prodigal son; it includes the Cross. (Cf. Knox, *S.H.E.P.C.* 26).

(35 f.) As Knox says (*Acts*, 23) after discussing the alleged inaccuracies, 'In any case the speech is not to be taken as a report or even a summary of what Gamaliel said. But the inaccuracies do not prove that Luke is not correct in his record of the fact which the speech implies, namely that the Pharisees led by Gamaliel refused to continue the policy of persecution on the ground that Christianity was not a political movement and that in religion it stood for much that the Pharisees held as against the Sadducees.' (37) **The census;** when Judaea became part of the imperial province of Syria on the deposition of Archelaus in A.D. 6, the legate Quirinius held a census, and Judas' revolt arose from fear of slavery being imposed by Rome after the census. Augustus' census of the Empire every fourteen years may have started before A.D. 6, though it is doubtful if it was held in the territory of a puppet king like Herod. Luke ii. 2 may refer to an earlier census, according to Luke, which took place in Herod the Great's reign; see *B.C.* iv. 61 f. **Were scattered:** yet, according to Josephus, Judas' became the 'fourth party' and from it the Zealots emerged. (38) The language is akin to that of Luke xx. 4 and xxiii. 51, which suggests that the actual wording here too is Luke's.

v. 40-2. THE APOSTLES' RELEASE

(40) **And they were persuaded by him, and summoning the apostles, they beat them and commanded them to cease speaking in the name of Jesus, and they let them go. (41) So then they went rejoicing from the presence of the Sanhedrin, because they were thought worthy to be disgraced on behalf of the name. (42) And every day, both in the Temple and at home, they did not stop teaching and preaching Jesus the Christ.**

(40) **name;** cf. on ii. 38. (41) **presence;** lit. face, has a Semitic flavour due to an Aramaic source or to Luke's conscious Septuagintalism. (42) **Jesus the Christ** or Jesus as the Christ; Christ or Messiah was not yet a proper name but a title of Jesus.

vi. 1-7. THE APPOINTMENT OF THE SEVEN AND A SUMMARY OF PROGRESS

(1) But in these days, when the number of the disciples was increasing, the Hellenists grumbled against the Hebrews because their widows were neglected in the daily ministration. (2) And the Twelve summoned the multitude of the disciples and said, 'It is not desirable for us to leave the word of God and to serve tables. (3) Therefore, brethren, look out from among you seven well-attested men, full of Spirit and wisdom, whom we shall set over this task, (4) but we shall give adherence to prayer and to the ministry of the word.' (5) And the saying was acceptable before all the multitude, and they chose Stephen, a man full of faith and Holy Spirit, and Philip and Prochorus and Nicanor and Timon and Parmenas and Nicolaus, a proselyte of Antioch. (6) And they set them before the apostles; and they prayed and laid their hands on them. (7) And the word of God increased and the number of the disciples multiplied greatly in Jerusalem; and a large crowd of priests were obedient to the faith.

(1) The word for **disciple** is not found in the N.T. outside the Gospels and Acts; in Acts it occurs here for the first time. Is this because Luke has now turned to use a new source? Cf. *B.C.* v, note 30. **Hellenists;** this rare word is usually taken to denote Greek-speaking Jews as opposed to Aramaic-speaking Jews or Hebraioi and to pure Greeks; but the word may denote Greek-speaking Jews whose sympathies and interests were opposed to those of the Hebraioi, cf. *B.C.* v, note 7. The story of Numbers xi. 1-24 (LXX) has influenced the choice of

language at least in this section; **grumbled**; here the noun is used, and in Num. xi. 1 the participle of the verb from the same root. **Ministration**; a dole for the needy was necessary when primitive Christian 'communism' ended in the poverty of the saints at Jerusalem, for whom Paul was constantly to beg money from his Gentile converts. It is unlikely that **the widows** were yet a separately organized section of the Church, as they became later. Christians would naturally strive to 'exceed the righteousness' of the Jews who had for their own people not only a weekly distribution each Friday among the poor, but also a daily collection of food for them ('the tray') which was made from house to house to support those in need of food for the morrow. (Cf. *B.C.* v. 148 f.) (2) **The Twelve;** cf. Appendix 1. Though it is true that Paul never calls the Twelve 'apostles' (cf. A. Fridrichsen, *The Apostle and his message*, 1947, 18 f., n. 12), it is probable that the Twelve and the apostles were two concentric circles, the apostles being wider. It is unlikely that Loisy was right in maintaining that the conception of the Twelve was not primitive and did not go back to Jesus Himself, cf. Mark iii. 14, Matt. xix. 28, Rev. xii. 1, cf. the 'Eleven', Acts i. 26, ii. 14, and 1 Cor. xv. 5. **To serve tables;** yet Stephen and Philip became noted for their preaching and evangelizing rather than for their administration. (3) **Look out;** this verb is used in Num. xxvii. 16 of the Lord 'appointing' someone. The noun from this verb would be episcopos or overseer or bishop. **Seven men;** it should be noted that the noun for 'deacon' is not used here, though 'service' (ministration) comes in vs. 1 and 'to serve' in vs. 2 (*Diakonia* and *diakonein*). (a) The older view was that here 'deacons' are meant. C. Gore (*The Church and the Ministry*, revised ed., 1921, 81 f.) could say, 'In these seven we must see (with most authorities ancient and modern) the prototype of the deacons. In the case of some of these first appointed deacons, their peculiar gifts as preachers sufficed to throw into the shade their humbler functions . . .' (b) Another view is that the characteristics of the three Orders of Bishops, priests, and deacons were to be found in the primitive undifferentiated ministry. Cf. W. K. L. Clarke (*Episcopacy, Ancient and Modern*, ed. by C. Jenkins and K. Mackenzie, 1930, 10 ff.). 'Were they the first deacons? Or were they really presbyters? Before answering the question we must try to understand the mind of the apostles. Certain passages of the LXX are so closely parallel to the narrative of Acts vi that some connexion is highly probable.' He goes on to tabulate the parallels between Num. xi. 1 ff. and Acts vi. 1 ff. and to compare Num. xxvii. 16 ff. and Deut. xxxiv. 9. He concludes: 'The narrative of Num. xi suggests that the Seven were presbyters and many scholars identify them with the presbyters of Acts xi. But the appointment of seven rulers or overseers with special care of Hellenistic Jews and of charitable relief can hardly be dissociated from the Palestinian institution of *parnasim* which . . . was probably one of the Jewish antecedents of the episcopus.' (c) Dr. A. M. Farrer is more definite (*The Apostolic Ministry*, ed. K. E. Kirk, 1946, 138 ff.): 'The supposition that the Seven are regarded by St. Luke as deacons is a very old error.' He finds the background of this section to be both Num. xi and Jesus' institution of the Seventy. 'There can be no reasonable doubt that a parallel is intended with the section in the Gospel where the Seventy are appointed to evangelize every place in Samaria whither the Lord Himself will come.' In taking the Seven to be presbyters and not 'deacons', Dr. Farrer concludes that Luke wanted to say with emphasis that the 'sending' of the elders is parallel to that of the apostles but does not carry the same commission. Codex B (Vaticanus) has 'let us look (or choose) out', which suggests that the choice of the Seven rested with the Twelve primarily, contrast vs. 6. **Spirit and wisdom;** cf. Isa. xi. 2 'a Spirit of wisdom and understanding' and the choice of Joshua in Num. xxvii. 16 ff., 'a man who has *pneuma* (spirit) in him and thou shalt lay thy hands upon him and thou shalt set him before Eleazar the priest. . . .' (4) Ministry of the word is contrasted with the ministry or service of tables. (5) **The saying,** etc.: a Semitic-sounding phrase possibly due to Luke's Septuagintal style. The choice fell on men with Greek names, though if they were Jews by race their Jewish names may have been lost; Nicolaus at least was a proselyte. Luke may have noted his Antiochene origin because Luke may possibly have come from Antioch himself or because he was interested especially in the Church there. It is uncertain whether Nicolaus became imbued with the errors of the Nicolaitans (Rev. ii. 6, 15);

though Hippolytus and Epiphanius thought so, Ignatius, who came from Antioch, Clement of Alexandria, and Eusebius do not connect him with the sect, which may have been an early Gnostic one. (6) The apostles stand to the Seven as Eleazar the priest had stood to Joshua; for the 'laying on of hands', cf. xiii. 3 (Barnabas). As S. New (Mrs. Lake) says, this gesture was well known not only in Judaism but also in other countries; it implies the passing of power, physical or spiritual, from one to another, cf. Appendix 3. It was used at the ordination of a Rabbi and termed the *Seminkha*, cf. Sanhedrin iv. 4 (*B.C.* v, note 11), but it is not certain that the Rabbis associated any gift of 'inspiration' with it. (7) is a summary or 'stop', cf. Introduction 11 (B).

vi. 8-15. THE ARREST OF STEPHEN

(8) But Stephen, full of grace and power, was doing great signs and wonders among the people. (9) But there rose up some of those of the synagogue which is called that of the Libertini, and of the Cyrenians, and of the Alexandrians, and of those from Cilicia and Asia, disputing with Stephen. (10) And they could not withstand the wisdom and the Spirit, with which he used to speak. (11) Then they secretly urged men who said, 'We have heard him speak blasphemous words against Moses and God'. (12) And they incited the people and the elders and the scribes, and they set upon him and seized him and brought him before the Sanhedrin, (13) and they put up false witnesses who said, 'This man does not stop speaking words against this holy place and the law. (14) For we have heard him say that this Jesus the Nazarene will destroy this place and will change the customs which Moses handed down to us.' (15) And gazing upon him, all who were sitting in the Sanhedrin saw his face as if the face of an angel.

(8) Picks up vs. 3 with its reference to Spirit and wisdom. Does **grace** here mean 'charm' as in Greek literature (cf.

N. P. Williams, *The Grace of God*, 1930, ch. i), or does it mean the loving, powerful help of God or His Spirit, as in Paul? **Great** may go with 'wonders' only, cf. Mark xiii. 22, Acts ii. 19 citing Joel iii. 3, ii. 22, 43, iv. 30; 'among the people' indicates that these were not portents in the heavens. (9) The origin of the synagogue system is unknown; reference may possibly be made to it in Ps. lxxiv. 8 (LXX. lxxiii); but in N.T. times 'synagogues were to be found throughout Palestine and Egypt and in every part of the Empire' (*B.C.* i. 161). While sacrifice could be offered only in the Temple, the reading and interpretation of the O.T. and prayer could be carried on in synagogues even in Jerusalem itself. A synagogue of the Alexandrians is known to have existed there (cf. *B.C.* iv. 68); this synagogue may have been frequented also by Jews from other parts of the Empire. It is possible, however, to take the five names here to refer (i) to one synagogue, as Hort did, or (ii) to two, if **Cyrenians** and **Alexandrians** explain Libertini or 'freedmen', while that of the Cilicians and Asians was the other, or (iii) to three, if the synagogue of the Libertini was separate from the other two, or (iv) to four if we bracket only the last two names together, or (v) to five if all five names imply a different synagogue. The Armenian and Syriac evidence suggests reading 'Libyans' in place of **Libertini,** cf. Beza's emendation 'Libystines'. But the textual evidence favours Libertini, among whom would be included Jewish freedmen or their sons. Paul may have belonged to the synagogue of those from Cilicia, though he was 'born free'. (10) **Wisdom and Spirit,** cf. vi. 3, vii. 10, 22. (11) The phrase about **secretly urging** or prompting may depend on Mark xiv. 56 ff., the details of our Lord's Passion being in Luke's mind. **Blasphemous words** should strictly have included blasphemy against the name of God, but here the sense is general. The contrast between Jesus and Moses as well as the parallels between them formed an undercurrent of Luke's thought. (14) Cf. Mark xiv. 58. (15) The Jews believed that Moses' face shone when he talked with God on Sinai (Exod. xxxiv. 29 ff., cf. Esther xv. 13, Enoch civ, 2 Cor. iii. 18). The Western text adds about Stephen, 'standing in the midst of them', which may be intended 'to make Stephen the middle-point of the whole scene' (Corssen), or may be due to the scribe's knowledge that it was the custom for the Sanhedrin to sit in a semicircle so that all could see the accused's face.

Note on Stephen's speech, vii. 2-53

(For the speeches in Acts, see Introduction, 12)

Very different views have been expressed about this speech which stands out from the others in Acts. Should it be regarded as an interpolation and omitted? F. J. Foakes Jackson (*J.B.L.* 49, 1930, 283-6) thinks so, maintaining that the speech is not relevant, that it is a summary of patriarchal history that everyone knew and that denunciation of the disobedience of the patriarchs had long been the theme of psalmist and prophet; and that as neither Jesus nor the Messiah is mentioned, nothing is lost by excision. He argues that vii. 55-60 would follow naturally on vi. 8-15, and he wonders if Luke took some ancient prophecy which denounced Israel's sin, putting it into Stephen's mouth because it seemed to Luke suitable to the occasion. As Foakes Jackson says in his commentary on Acts: 'By thus leaving out for the present the speech in ch. vii we have a very beautiful and well-conceived description of the death of the first Christian martyr, and we realize that the omission of the defence brings out the intentional parallelism between the trial of Jesus and of His proto-martyr.' Others too have noted, as Furneaux does (*Acts*, 1912, 90), a lack of obvious connexion between the speech and its setting; cf. *B.C.* iv. 69: 'This is not a rebuttal of the charges brought against him. It is an impassioned attack on the conduct of the Jews from the time of Joseph down to that of the speaker and on the importance which they attached to the Temple.'

On the other hand, the speech appears to many to have point and relevance where it stands. M. Simon (*J.E.H.* 2, 1951, 127-142) argues that it is the product of Judaeo-Christian thought, not Hellenist. He suggests that in Judaism there was already a section opposed to the Temple cult. Stephen stands in the line of Nathan, Hosea, Trito-Isaiah, and the Rechabites in demanding a non-material form of worship and claiming that the true Jew was one of the Dispersion. Whereas for Paul Christ merely overthrew the Old Covenant, for Stephen the Jewish Temple in itself marked a falling away from the authentic traditions of Israel. Stephen's unparalleled views are in contrast with those of the epistle to the Hebrews in regard to the relation of Christianity to the O.T. cultus. Simon suggests that Stephen belonged to the Jews of the Dispersion who contrasted the Temple, which they did not want, with the Tabernacle; the contrast in vss. 46 f. is not only between David and Solomon but also between the buildings in which each worshipped. Simon also finds the absence of any specifically Christian message significant, but explains it by the speech being part of primitive Christian theology.

R. P. C. Hanson (*Theology*, L, 1947, 142 ff.)—to whose essay this paragraph is deeply indebted—has wisely returned to Rackham's commentary on Acts (1901), according to whom the speech interpreted O.T. history in order to show that it revealed Jesus to be (1) Saviour, Redeemer, and so Ruler of His people; (2) the true prophet and mediator between God and His people; and (3) the Righteous One, i.e. the Fulfiller, and therefore the end, of the Law. 'Though the name of Christ is not once mentioned, Stephen is all the time preaching Jesus. . . . He preaches Him in His types, especially Joseph and Moses. Hanson adds to Rackham's points, (a) Stephen's attitude to the Temple was in line with John ii. 19, 21, "Destroy this Temple and in three days I will raise it up. . . . But He spake of the Temple of His body." God never allowed His people under the old covenant to have a permanent dwelling-place for Him, because the permanent tabernacle and shrine for Him was Jesus Christ, the house not made with hands. (b) Stephen agreed with Paul about the Law and the Law foretold Jesus.' On such a view it is unnecessary to suppose that the speech was broken off abruptly before the argument was finished.

B. S. Easton (*The Purpose of Acts*, 47 f.) thinks that two distinct charges were made against Stephen (a) that he attacked the Temple and (b) that he attacked the Law. These charges are answered separately, the answer to (a) in vss. 44-50 being carefully distinguished from the answer to (b); and these verses can be removed and the continuity of the speech improved. The Temple had no warrant in God's Law and so to depreciate the Temple can be no sin. Easton argues that the meaning is that even granting that the facts were as alleged by the persecutors, these facts constituted no crime; and that therefore the witnesses had had some truth on their side; Stephen had spoken in a derogatory way about the Temple, basing his words probably on Jesus' prediction of the Temple's overthrow. The witnesses spoke falsely in so far as they said that it would be Jesus who would destroy this place (vi. 14). On the other hand, according to Easton, the charge of speaking against the Law is vehemently denied. After a long introduction, vii. 2-19, designed to win the good-will of the audience, Stephen stresses that Palestine is

God's holy land and circumcision His covenanted gift. Moses is glorified; so marvellous a 'ruler and judge' is he that 'like unto Moses' is a title reserved for Jesus alone, while Moses' Law is no less than 'living oracles', delivered by angels (vii. 53). But this apologetic is a polemic. Moses was the type of Jesus, for the Jews had continually rejected Moses; in vii. 51-3 'Stephen unmasks his batteries'; the Jews of old rejected Moses, those of Stephen's day rejected Moses' successor. If Moses' Law was broken, not Stephen but the members of the Sanhedrin had broken it!

F. F. Bruce (*The Speeches in Acts*, 1942, 21) classifies this speech under the 'Apologetic speeches' and considers it an exposition which marked the decisive break of the new teaching with traditional Judaism. He asks whether Luke derived it from his 'Caesarean source', cf. vi-ix. 31 or, as Ramsay had suggested, from Philip, that is from one of the Seven, or even perhaps from Paul himself.

(Other contributions of note include: B. W. Bacon, *Stephen's speech, Biblical and Semitic Studies*, Yale Bicentenary Publications, 1901, 213-76; W. Mundle, 'Die Stephanusrede eine Märtyrerapologie', *Z.N.T.W.* 20, 1921, 133-47; W. L. Knox, *St. Paul and the Church of Jerusalem*, 1925, 43 ff., 54 ff.; B. Gärtner, *The Areopagus Speech and Natural Revelation*, 1955, 206 ff.)

vii. 1-29. STEPHEN'S HISTORICAL REVIEW

(1) And the High Priest said, 'Is this so?' (2) And he said: 'Brethren and fathers, hear me. The God of glory appeared to our father Abraham while he was in Mesopotamia, before he dwelt in Harran, (3) and he said to him, "Go out from your land and from your kinsfolk and come to the land which I shall show you".' (4) Then he went out of the land of the Chaldeans and dwelt in Harran; and after his father died, He changed his dwelling to this land in which you now dwell. (5) And He gave him no inheritance in it, not even a yard in length, and He promised to give it to him in possession, and to his seed after him, when he had no child. (6) But God spoke thus, that his seed would be a sojourner in a strange land, and they would enslave and ill-treat them for four hundred years. (7) And 'I shall judge,' said God, 'what-

ever nation they shall serve, and after this they shall go out and they shall worship me in this place'. (8) And He gave him a covenant of circumcision; and so he begat Isaac and circumcised him on the eighth day; and Isaac begat Jacob and Jacob the twelve patriarchs. (9) And the patriarchs, jealous of Joseph, sold him into Egypt; and God was with him, (10) and He rescued him from all his afflictions, and gave him favour and wisdom before Pharaoh, king of Egypt, and he made him governor over Egypt and all his house. (11) But there came a famine upon all Egypt and Canaan, and great affliction, and our fathers could find no food. (12) But Jacob sent out our fathers the first time to Egypt, hearing that there was grain. (13) And on the second visit Joseph was made known to his brothers, and the family of Joseph became clear to Pharaoh. (14) And Joseph sent and summoned his father Jacob, and all his kinsfolk, to the number of seventy-five souls. (15) And Jacob went down into Egypt and he himself died and our fathers. (16) And they were moved to Sychem and laid in the tomb which Abraham had bought for a sum of silver from the sons of Emmor in Sychem.

(17) But when the time of the promise approached, which God had granted to Abraham, the people increased and multiplied in Egypt, (18) until there arose another king over Egypt, who knew not Joseph. (19) He dealt craftily with our race and ill-treated our fathers, to make them expose their infants, that they might not be saved alive. (20) At which time Moses was born and was beautiful before God; and he was brought up for three months in his father's house; (21) but when he was exposed, Pharaoh's daughter adopted him and brought him up as a son for herself. (22) And Moses was trained in all the wisdom of the Egyptians and he was influential in his words and deeds. (23) But when the time of his fortieth year was being completed, it entered into his heart to visit his brethren, the sons of Israel. (24) And seeing someone wronged, he defended him and avenged the down-trodden one, smiting the Egyptian. (25) But he

thought that his brethren understood that God was granting them salvation through his hand; but they did not
understand. (26) And on the next day he appeared to
them as they were struggling and sought to reconcile
them to be at peace, saying, 'Men, you are brethren. Why
do you wrong one another?' (27) But he who was doing
wrong to his neighbour thrust him away, saying, 'Who
made you a ruler and a judge over us? (28) Do you want
to kill me as yesterday you killed the Egyptian?' (29) And
at this saying Moses fled, and became a sojourner in the
land of Midian where he begat two sons.

(1-8) As Hanson says, the inheritance, the seed, and the
promise all point to Christ, cf. Gen. xi. 27-xii. 5. Contrary
to Gen. xi. 31, it is said here that God's first appearance to
Abraham was even before he moved from Mesopotamia to
Harran, long before he reached the 'holy land' of which he
possessed not a 'foot's pace', vs. 5. The appearance of God to
Abraham in Ur is mentioned in Philo and Josephus. There are
many other discrepancies between the O.T. story and Stephen's
historical summary (see H. J. Cadbury, *B.A.H.* 102 ff.); the
speech or its source may be dependent on the LXX rather than
the Hebrew text. But deliberate divergence from the O.T. is
unlikely in view of the fact that Stephen's speech shares most
of the discrepancies with other Jewish writings. Luke is attack-
ing Jewish prejudices most subtly. As Cadbury says, 'In such
subtle references to Jewish prejudice perhaps more clearly than
in his more explicit use of external local colour is to be found
convincing evidence of our author's knowledge of the Jewish
environment of early Christianity. But he himself and his heroes
are reacting against it—and are doing so from a Christian stand-
point. Stephen's speech is written with an eye on the parallelism
between ancient history and the Jewish-Christian conflict.'
(2) **The God of glory,** i.e. the glorious God, cf. Ps. xxix. 3.
Harran or Charran was the classical Carrae. (5 ff.) God's
promise was not bound up with possession of the 'holy land'
but with the deliverance or 'salvation' (vs. 25) of His people.
(6) **Four hundred years,** cf. Gen. xv. 13, but contrast Exod.
xii. 40, 'four hundred and thirty'; both figures are probably too

large, cf. H. H. Rowley, *B.J.R.L.* 22, 1938, 243 ff. (8) Stephen
stresses that the rite of circumcision was given before the 'holy
land' became the Jews' place of worship pre-eminently. (9-16)
Joseph could be taken as an O.T. prototype to Christ. Rejected
by his brethren who wished to slay him, Joseph rose under
God's hand to a most exalted position: so Jesus after His cross
and Resurrection was made Lord over God's house and ruler
over His creation, cf. Ps. cv. 21, Gen. xli. 40 f. The Lordship of
Christ was a doctrine with Jewish rather than Hellenistic roots.
Both Joseph and Moses visited the brethren twice, cf. vs. 23 f.
So Christ's Second Coming would prove the ultimate deliverance of God's people. (15) For Jacob's death cf. Gen. xlix. 33.
According to the Alexandrian text the subject of 'died' could
be Joseph, but the Western reviser makes clear that it was
Jacob. Hanson (art. cit.) asks pertinently: 'Is Jacob thought to
be a type of Christ in that Christ went down to "the great city
which spiritually is called Sodom and Egypt, where also their
Lord was crucified?"' (Rev. xi. 8.) There Jacob died and was put
in a tomb bought by another. In any case it looks as if Luke or
his source has 'telescoped' (*B.C.* iv. 74) the burial of Jacob at
Hebron with that of Joseph at Shechem (*B.C.* iv. 74); Bruce
(*Acts*, 166) compares other instances of compression in this
speech. These may point to a lack of final revision. (16) Shechem
or **Sychem** (mod. Nablus) lies between Mt. Gerizim and Mt.
Ebal; the reference to a place so near the centre of the hated
Samaritan's place of worship, Gerizim, is intentional. (17-38)
Moses is a type of Christ who also came in the fullness of time
(cf. Gal. iv. 4) and at whose birth Herod slew the Innocents
(cf. vss. 18 f.). Jesus 'increased in wisdom and stature and in
favour with God and man' (Luke ii. 52); like Moses, Jesus was
mighty in deeds and words (Luke xxiv. 19). Like Moses (vss.
25 f., 39), Jesus was spurned by His brethren whom He was
'sent' down to deliver, preaching that brotherhood of man
which follows from the Fatherhood of God. God had sent Jesus
to be a greater saviour, deliverer, ruler, and judge than Moses,
'raising Him up' (cf. vs. 37) not only at His Resurrection but in
and through His ministry and revealing His nature especially
at the Transfiguration when both Moses and Elijah, both Law
and prophets, gave place to Him and His teaching ('Hear ye

Him'). (18) Cf. Exod. i. 8. (19) Exod. i. 10 and Judith v. 11 use the same Greek word for 'deal craftily' or 'exploit' of Pharaoh. (20) As the parallel between Moses and Jesus was in mind 'before God' may be parallel to 'with God and man', Luke ii. 52, used of Jesus: this is better than to suppose that 'before God' equals a prefix 'theo-', as in modern slang 'divinely', meaning 'very'. (22) According to Jewish legend Moses surpassed the Egyptians in their own wisdom, cf. Philo, *Vita Moysis*, i. 5; Josephus, *Ant*. ii. ix. 7-xi. 1. Similarly Philo and Josephus agree on the exceeding beauty of the infant Moses, cf. vs. 20. (25) The idea is introduced of a saviour (without O.T. support), in order to point from Moses to Jesus. (29) **sojourner;** cf. vs. 6 and the idea in vss. 36 and 44 of Israel being in the desert and the wilderness.

vii. 30-53. JESUS, LIKE MOSES BEFORE HIM, WAS REJECTED

(30) And when forty years were fulfilled, there appeared to him in the desert of Mount Sinai an angel in a flame of fire of a bush. (31) But when Moses saw it he wondered at the sight, and as he came near to look at it there was a voice of the Lord, (32) 'I am the God of your fathers, the God of Abraham and of Isaac and of Jacob.' But Moses trembled and did not dare to look. (33) And the Lord said to him, 'Loose the sandals from your feet, for the place whereon you stand is holy ground. (34) Surely I have seen the ill-treatment of my people which is in Egypt, and I have heard their groaning and I am come down to deliver them. And now come, I shall send you into Egypt.' (35) This Moses whom they denied, saying, 'Who made you a ruler and a judge?' God sent both as ruler and redeemer by the hand of the angel which appeared to him in the bush. (36) This is he who led them out, doing wonders and signs in Egypt, and in the Red Sea, and in the desert for forty years. (37) This is the Moses who said to the sons of Israel, 'A prophet will God

raise up for you from among your brethren, as He raised up me'. (38) This is he who was in the congregation in the wilderness with the angel who spoke to him on Mount Sinai, and with our fathers; he received living oracles to give to us; (39) to whom our fathers did not wish to be obedient, but thrust him away, and they turned in their hearts to Egypt, (40) saying to Aaron, 'Make for us gods who shall go before us, for this Moses who brought us from the land of Egypt, we do not know what has become of him'. (41) And they made a calf in those days, and they offered sacrifice to the idol, and they took pleasure in the works of their hands. (42) But God turned and delivered them up to worship the host of heaven, as it has been written in the Book of the Prophets, 'Did you bring me slain beasts and sacrifices for forty years in the wilderness, O house of Israel? (43) And you took up the tabernacle of Moloch, and the star of the god Rephan, the images which you made, to worship them, and I shall remove you beyond Babylon.' (44) The tabernacle of witness was in possession of our fathers in the wilderness, even as He who spoke to Moses arranged that he should make it according to the image which he had seen. (45) And when our fathers received this in succession, they brought it in with Joshua in taking possession of the nations, whom God thrust out before the face of our fathers, until the days of David, (46) who found favour before God and sought to find a tabernacle for the God of Jacob. (47) But Solomon built him a house. (48) Yet it is not that the Most High dwells in houses made with hands; (49) even as the prophet says, 'The heaven is my throne but the earth is the footstool of my feet. What sort of house will you build for me, saith the Lord, or what is the place of my rest? (50) Did not my hand make all these things?' (51) You stiff-necked and uncircumcised in heart and ears, you always resist the Holy Spirit. As your fathers were, you are also. (52) Which of the prophets did not your fathers persecute? And they killed those who announced beforehand concerning the coming of the Righteous One, whose betrayers and

murderers now you have become, (53) you, who received the law at the commands of angels and did not
keep it.'

(30 ff.) Cf. Exod. iii. 1-10. The parallel between Moses and
Jesus that Luke had in mind would suggest that here Luke
thought of the Lord's Baptism and the voice heard then from
heaven; the natural human awe of Moses contrasts with the
divine self-assurance of Jesus. (33) **Sandals,** cf. the reference
to Jesus' sandals, Luke iii. 16. (According to primitive ideas
contact with bare feet allowed the physically holy or separated
piece of ground to convey to those creatures on it its divine
power; later, to remove one's shoes on holy ground became an
act of reverence.) As Moses had to reverence God, so John the
Baptist reverenced Jesus. (35) Jesus is **Redeemer** as well as
Judge; the word for redeemer, used of God in Ps. xviii (LXX,
xix) 14 and lxxvii (LXX, lxxviii) is related in Greek to the word
for 'ransom' used by Jesus of Himself, Mark x. 45; cf. also
Luke xxiv. 21, where Moses again is mentioned. The wonders
and signs of Moses pointed to the greater ones of Christ, cf. ii.
22, x. 38. Jesus also was brought up from 'Egypt'; baptized in
the river Jordan, to which the Red Sea was a type, He had been
in the wilderness 'forty' days; for the final clause of this verse,
cf. Num. xiv. 33 and the Assumption of Moses, iii. 11, 'Moses
. . . who suffered many things in Egypt and in the Red Sea and
in the desert forty years'. (37) Cf. iii. 22 where Deut. xviii. 15, 19
is cited 'as though it were fulfilled solely in Jesus' (*B.C.* v. 372).
If Mr. C. F. Evans is right in maintaining that the central
section of St. Luke's Gospel, ix. 51-xviii. 14, follows the order
of the subject-matter of Deuteronomy and can be explained in
terms of it, Luke selecting and arranging his material 'in such a
way as to present it in a Deuteronomic sequence, his motive for
doing so . . . will have sprung from the conviction . . . that
Jesus was the prophet like unto Moses' (*Studies in the Gospels*,
ed. D. E. Nineham, 50). Cf. on xxvi. 23 f. (38) Moses was in the
old congregation or church, Heb. *qahal*, Greek *ekklesia*, as
Christ is in the new. **Angel;** for reverential reasons late Judaism
used the concept of angels to avoid mention of the divine name.
From this it was a step to treating angels as mediators between

God and Moses, for instance, in the giving of the law. But, as W. D. Davies has said, 'Only in two places in the N.T., in Gal. iii. 19, Heb. ii. 22, does this mediation [of the Law through angels] imply any inferiority, and is therefore associated with the notion that it was to change, and this is a specifically Christian development. . . . Stephen's meaning is that the Moses by whom even an angel speaks at Sinai was rejected by Israel, and in vii. 53, that although Israel had received the Law as it was ordained by angels—a great privilege—it had been nevertheless disobedient' (*H.T.R.* xlvii, 1954, 139). (38-43) Hanson (art. cit.) points out that Stephen's meaning is that if Israel had obeyed the 'living oracles' given them by Moses, they would not have worshipped idols but would have looked for and would have welcomed Christ, cf. Rom. x. 5, 16 ff. (39) Cf. Num. xiv. 3 f., Exod. xxxii. 1, 23. (42) It was a Jewish commonplace that the worship of idols led to such sins as immorality, cf. Wisd. xiv. 22, Rom. i. 24 ff. (cf. B. Gärtner, *The Areopagus Speech and Natural Revelation*, 102 ff.). (43) Luke follows mainly the LXX text of Amos v. 25-7, which differs from the Hebrew, having 'tabernacle' for 'Sikkuth' and 'of Moloch' for 'your king'; also 'the star of your god Raiphan' for 'Chiun your images, the star of your god'. On the other hand, Luke in having **beyond Babylon** differs from the Hebrew and the LXX text, 'beyond Damascus'; these variants show that this speech at least probably came to Luke in Greek and not Semitic dress. Amos with the Assyrian foe in mind gave a warning that the exile would be beyond Damascus; did Stephen use 'Babylon' because it became the Christian name for Rome? (1 Pet. v. 13, Rev. xviii. 2.) Or because the early Christians had some connexion with the Damascus sect, which was related to that of the Qumran sect from which the recently discovered Hebrew scrolls came? (It is significant that the Fragment of a Zadokite work or Damascus document makes the same citation from Amos as Luke does, cf. the Damascus Document ix. 4-9, cited by S. E. Johnson, *Z.A.T.W.* 66, 1-2, 1954, 115.) According to Westcott and Hort ('Select Readings' in *The New Testament in Greek*, 92), in the LXX of Amos v. 26, the form used is Raiphan or Rephan, which is similar to Repa or Repha, one of the names of the Egyptian Saturn (Seb). This was read in the LXX for the

Assyrian god Kaiwan or Chiun: Sikkuth in the Hebrew was probably intended to refer to the Akkadian Sakkut, god of the planet Saturn. (44-50) Hanson argues that the meaning is that the Tabernacle is the type of the Word who tabernacled among us, which was the reason for God having no permanent abode made for Himself. For the true dwelling-place of God, in whom dwelleth all the fullness of the Godhead bodily (Col. ii. 19), was to come. In the Epistle to the Hebrews the Platonic doctrine is developed of the earthly tent which is the copy of the heavenly. (45) While Stephen's main emphasis (cf. *B.C.* iv. 80) is probably on the tabernacle which from Joshua to David's time was the God-appointed place of worship, the reference to Joshua ('Jesus' in Greek) taking possession of the nations would carry to Christian ears the meaning that the Gentiles belong to Jesus. (46 ff.) The tabernacle appropriate to a pilgrim people was replaced by a standing Temple, but not till Solomon's day. **Made with hands** has an undercurrent of meaning denoting idolatry. (49) **Prophet;** Isa. lxvi. 1 f. Perhaps Luke and the author of the Epistle of Barnabas, who agree on the wording, drew this citation from a list of Testimonies. (51) W. L. Knox shows how the 'harsh consonants' in Greek, *k, p, t,* and *x* are heaped up in 51-3 as though the saint spat out his final comments (*S.H.E.P.C.* 15 n.). If he had preached Christ through types, he did not break off his speech before making his point and we need not suppose that he was interrupted before reaching his positively Christian message. (52) The prophets being inspired by God were sacrosanct and, in fact, were seldom subjected to violence; but see Matt. xxiii. 29 ff., Luke xvi. 47 ff. Zechariah was exceptional in being a prophet put to death. As *B.C.* iv. 82 suggests, probably some Jewish book of legends about the violent deaths of prophets gave rise to the idea that their martyrdom was usual. The word for **coming** was already a Messianic term (G. D. Kilpatrick, *J.T.S.* xlvi, 1945, 136-45). **The Righteous One,** cf. iii. 14. According to the Covenanters of Damascus, a new covenant was mediated by a 'Teacher of Righteousness', who was different from the Anointed One; who, it should be noted, is not from Judah but from Levi. The Covenanters aimed at producing in their common life that of Israel in the wilderness. In Acts the in-

fluence of Wisd. ii-iii. 1 and of Isa. liii and of their portrait of
the Righteous One is more prominent than in the writings of
the Damascus sect or the Qumran sect. (53) The argument is
that if the Jews had observed the Law they would have seen
that Jesus had been sent to do away with the Temple and the
customs of Moses. On the angelic mediation of the law, cf. on
vs. 42; Stephen does not, like Paul, take it as a sign of the Law's
inferiority that angels mediated it, cf. Gal. iii. 19.

vii. 54-viii. 1a. THE DEATH OF STEPHEN

**(54) But when they heard these things they were cut to
the heart and gnashed their teeth at him. (55) But he,
being full of Holy Spirit, gazed up to heaven and saw the
glory of God, and Jesus standing on the right hand of
God, (56) and he said, 'Behold, I see the heavens opened
and the Son of man standing on the right hand of God'.
(57) But they cried with a loud voice and closed their
ears and rushed together upon him, (58) and they cast
him out of the city and began to stone him; and the
witnesses put off their garments at the feet of a young
man called Saul. (59) And they stoned Stephen as he
invoked and said, 'Lord Jesus, receive my spirit'. (60)
And he kneeled down and cried with a loud voice, 'Lord,
place not this sin to their charge'. And having said this,
he fell asleep. (1a) Now Saul was consenting to his death.**

(56 f.) Knox (*Acts*, 76) notes that we have here the same
conception of Christ as in Mark xiv. 62, and he notes later that
Stephen's vision of the heavens opened and the Son of Man
standing on the right hand of God shows more affinity with
Mark's story of the Passion than with Luke's. (To the present
writer this would seem natural if Luke wrote Acts with Mark's
Gospel in mind and then wrote the Third Gospel later.) It is
possible that Stephen's dying words have come down to us; it is
also possible that details of his death have been assimilated to
the story of the Passion of Jesus; later martyrologies, e.g.

Martyrium Polycarpi, show the same tendency. It is less likely that the Passion story owed anything to the accounts of Stephen's death. Knox also suggests that Luke has preserved a Son of Man Christology current in the early Church for some time after the Resurrection, though it has disappeared from all other New Testament books than the Gospels. There can be little doubt that Jesus used this title 'Son of Man' of Himself in the Psalmist's sense of the phrase and Ezekiel's and in the apocalyptic sense of Daniel vii, and even perhaps in the sense in which it is found in the *Similitudes of Enoch*. Various theories have been advanced to explain why the Son of Man was seen standing rather than seated at God's right hand; did this indicate His readiness to vindicate the oppressed? (58) Was Stephen done to death by the mob lynching him? This was the view of the Western reviser. Or was there a more or less legal trial with 'witnesses'? Was Luke here combining two sources? Or did he assume the legality of the incident and impose it on his material, rather as he may later assume in xvii that Paul appeared before a duly assembled court? These questions are easier to ask than to answer. (59) Cf. Luke xxiii. 46. If these words were Stephen's, it is significant that Jesus' prayer to His Father can here be echoed and addressed to Jesus. (60) Cf. Luke xxiii. 34, which some MSS. omit probably wrongly (see my *Alterations*, 8 f.). (viii. 1a) If Saul was not a member of the Sanhedrin, he was at least a leading Pharisee. Perhaps the garments of Stephen, not the witnesses, were his perquisite if the Mishna rightly suggests that the criminal was disrobed (cf. vii. 58). In any case the influence on Saul of Stephen's death was profound. He was kicking against the pricks and the blood of the martyr was to become the seed of the Church.

THE EXPANSION OF THE CHURCH

viii. 1b-25. THE GOSPEL IS TAKEN TO SAMARIA

(1b) Now there arose on that day a great persecution against the church in Jerusalem; and they were all scattered throughout the regions of Judaea and Samaria, except the apostles. (2) But devout men helped in burying Stephen and made a great lament over him. (3) But Saul maltreated the church, going in from house to house, and dragging men and women away, he handed them over to prison.

(4) Now those who were scattered went their way preaching the word. (5) But Philip came down to a city of Samaria and began to preach to them the Christ. (6) And the crowds paid attention to what was said by Philip with one accord while hearing and seeing the signs which he did. (7) For many of those who had unclean spirits, crying with a loud voice, came out; and many paralyzed and lame were healed. (8) And there was much joy in that city. (9) But there was already a certain man named Simon in the city practising magic and astonishing the population of Samaria, saying that he was someone great. (10) They all paid attention to him, from the least to the greatest, saying, 'This man is the Power of God, which is called Great'. (11) And they paid attention to him because for a long time he had astonished them by his magic. (12) But when they believed Philip preaching the good news about the kingdom of God and the name of Jesus Christ, they were baptized, both men and women. (13) But even Simon himself believed and he was baptized and continued with Philip, and seeing signs and great miracles happening he was astonished.

(14) But when the apostles that were in Jerusalem heard that Samaria had received the word of God, they

sent to them Peter and John, (15) who went down and prayed for them that they might receive Holy Spirit; (16) for it had not yet fallen upon any of them but only had they been baptized in the name of the Lord Jesus. (17) Then they laid hands on them and they received Holy Spirit. (18) But when Simon saw that the (Holy) Spirit was given through the laying on of the apostles' hands, he brought them money, (19) saying, 'Give me too this power that anyone on whom I lay hands may receive Holy Spirit'. (20) But Peter said to him, 'May your silver go with you to destruction, because you thought to obtain the gift of God with money. (21) You have neither part nor lot in this word, for your heart is not straight before God. (22) Repent therefore of this your evil, and pray the Lord if, after all, the purpose of your heart may be forgiven you. (23) For I see that you are in the gall of bitterness and the bond of unrighteousness.' (24) And Simon answered and said, 'Pray for me to the Lord yourselves, that nothing of what you have said may come on me'. (25) Now after testifying and speaking the word of the Lord, they returned to Jerusalem, preaching the good news to many villages of the Samaritans.

(1b-3) Luke dovetails Stephen's burial into an account of Saul's persecution; vs. 2 comes in awkwardly, though it may be intended to stress the immediate expansion of the Church after the martyr's death. Luke implies that the stricter Jewish-Christian apostles were not affected, as were the Hellenists, by persecution, as though the observance of Temple worship safe-guarded the apostles. On the other hand it may be that all the apostles fled and the last three words of vs. 1 were added in view of vs. 14; but more probably the Jewish-Christians went into hiding, either in Jerusalem or elsewhere. In any case the Diaspora or Dispersion of the New Israel, corresponding to that of the Old Israel, began, cf. John vii. 35, 1 Pet. i. 1, James i. 1. (2) By using the Septuagintal word for **lament** Luke implies that a great hero has given his life for the people. What Joseph of Arimathea did for Jesus, devout men do for Stephen. (3) **Maltreated** may be too weak a translation of a word used of 'mangling' by lions and other wild animals. Paul himself was to be 'dragged away' later, xiv. 19. (4) **Now** or 'So then' marks a new paragraph. This one may have come to Luke from Philip, one of the Seven, or from his four unmarried daughters who prophesied, cf. xxi. 8 f. which picks up the reference to Philip at Caesarea in the course of a 'we-section'. Or it may have come from a written (Caesarean?) source. (5) **A city,** omitting the definite article attested by some Alexandrian MSS., may refer not to Samaria or Sebaste itself but possibly Gitta (*B.C.* iv. 89), the birthplace of Simon Magus, according to Justin. The Samaritans expected a Messiah, a *Taheb* or Restorer, possibly 'one who returns', cf. John iv. 25 ff. By taking the Gospel to the half-caste Samaritans, who were loathed by the Jews for their tainted blood and for their separate Yahweh-worship on Mt. Gerizim, Philip (and probably others unknown to us) launched that evangelization of non-Jews which Paul was to continue. (7) The obvious looseness of expression points to a lack of final revision of Acts. The cure of the paralyzed and lame showed that the Messianic hope was fulfilled (cf. Isa. xxxv. 3, 6). Both *B.C.* iv and Bruce point out that apart from raisings of the dead and exorcisms, healings of the lame and paralytic are specially frequent in Acts. (9-13) Simon the magician became a legendary figure among Christians as the first heretic of a Gnostic kind and as the arch enemy of St. Peter both in Samaria and at Rome. É. Amann (*D.T.C.* xiv (2), 2130-40) thinks that there is no necessary incompatibility between the idea of Simon as the oriental magician addicted to astral speculation and that of him as a divine incarnation; but after reviewing the evidence of Justin, the Apocryphal Acts, Hegesippus, Irenaeus, Clement of Alexandria, and Origen he is very cautious about identifying Simon the magician and the founder of the Simonian sect, cf. R. P. Casey, *B.C.* v, note xiii, who assumes the identity. (9) **someone great;** the word 'great' occurs three times in one form or another within two verses; perhaps 'megas' ('great') should be read as magos, magician, cf. *B.C.* iv. 96. (10) Adherents of the Simonian sect till *c.* 250 appear to testify that their founder claimed to be the expression of the power of Zeus and Yahweh; the Simonians in Rome may have taken a statue there erected to 'Semo Sancus, the god of oaths' as a statue to Simon; Justin assumed that origin for a statue there, cf. R. P. Casey, art. cit. 154 f. **The power of God which is called great;** an awkward phrase, which Wellhausen emended by supposing 'great' to be a translation of an Aramaic word for 'Revealer', while Torrey, also postulating an Aramaic original, took 'great' with 'God'. (11) This verse repeats the gist of 10; if this is not another indication of the lack of final revision of Acts, it was intended by Luke to stress the point that Christianity is far better and more impressive than any magic that paganism could produce. (12) Philip preached the sovereignty of God and the power and name or revealed character of Christ; the kerygma was that the Kingdom had drawn near in and through Jesus, His ministry, Cross, Resurrection, Ascension, and outpouring of the Spirit, and it often concluded with an appeal to repent and to be baptized. (14 f.) See Appendix 3 on the Spirit; the implication of this passage is that the Church was ruled by apostles and that Baptism did not confer as did the laying-on of hands by apostles or their emissaries the gift of the Holy Spirit, contrast x. 44 ff. (14) Peter still carries the leading role in the Church until he goes on his missionary travels when the leadership will pass to James (O. Cullmann, *Peter*, 35, 40); John is presumably the son of Zebedee, so often linked with Peter in the Synoptic Gospels and the early chapters of Acts. Mr. E. R. Annand has suggested, however, that this John is John Mark who was, in his view, the Beloved Disciple and the future author of the Fourth Gospel, as distinct from Mark the 'stump-fingered', the author of the Second Gospel (*Scottish Journal of Theology*, 9, 1956, 46-62). The possibility that John Mark is intended here was already noted in *B.C.* iv. 92. On the ordinary view, this John was the son of Zebedee, who became a pillar of the Church with Peter and James (Gal. ii. 9); like his brother he had once wanted to call down fire upon the Samaritans (Luke ix. 54). (18) 'Simon's professional instinct appears to have been reawakened' (Casey, art. cit., 151). He wanted to possess the gift and to sell it— hence 'simony', used of buying and selling spiritual powers. Some Alexandrian MSS. (B Cop. [sa]) omit 'holy'. (20) Luke uses an optative to express this wish, for which there is a parallel expression in Dan. ii. 5 (Theod.); this is a classical usage comparatively rare in the N.T. (cf. C. F. D. Moule, *Idiom Book of N.T. Greek*, 23). Peter's verdict is an instance of the use of the Church's power over sinners, cf. Matt. xvi. 19, xviii. 18, John xx. 23, 1 Cor. v. 3 f. (21-3) These verses are full of O.T. echoes, especially of Deut. xii. 12, Ps. lxxviii. 37, Jer. viii. 6, Deut. xxix. 18, Isa. lviii. 6, cf. *B.C.* ii. 99 where W. K. L. Clarke notes that in the first half of Acts the influence of the O.T. is far more marked than in the second. He suggests that in the first half Luke was relying less on his own powers of composition and that he had at his disposal reminiscences, written or otherwise, of the actual words used. (21) **Word;** Heb. *dabar* can also mean 'event', 'matter'. (24) It may be that Luke had in mind contemporary Simonians (Easton, *Purpose*, 22), but the Western text goes too far in adding of Simon: 'who did not stop weeping much'.

viii. 26-40. PHILIP AND THE CONVERSION OF THE ETHIOPIAN EUNUCH

(26) **But an angel of the Lord spoke to Philip, saying, 'Arise and go towards the south on the road which goes down from Jerusalem to Gaza'. This is deserted. (27) And he arose and went, and behold an Ethiopian, a eunuch, minister of Candace, queen of the Ethiopians, who was set over all her treasure, who had come to Jerusalem to worship, (28) was returning and sitting in his coach, and he was reading the prophet Isaiah. (29) And the Spirit said to Philip, 'Go up and join this coach'. (30) And Philip ran up and heard him reading Isaiah the prophet, and he said, 'Do you then understand what you are reading?' (31) And he said, 'How could I unless someone guide me?' And he asked Philip to come up and sit with him. (32) And the passage of the Scripture which he was reading was this, 'As a sheep to the slaughter was he led, and as a lamb dumb before his shearer, so he opens not his mouth. (33) In humiliation his judgement was removed. Who shall relate his generation? For his life is taken away from the earth.' (34) And**

the eunuch said to Philip, 'I pray you, about whom does the prophet say this? About himself? Or about some other man?' (35) And Philip opened his mouth, and beginning from this Scripture he preached to him the good news, Jesus. (36) And as they went along the road, they came to some water; and the eunuch said, 'Look, water! What prevents me being baptized?' (38) And he commanded the coach to stop; and they both went down into the water, both Philip and the eunuch; and he baptized him. (39) And when they came up out of the water, (the) Spirit of the Lord seized Philip; and the eunuch saw him no more, for he went on his way rejoicing. (40) But Philip was found at Azotus; and going through he preached the good news to all the cities, until he came to Caesarea.

(26 ff.) The influence of the LXX in colouring and even perhaps moulding parts of chs. viii-xii is well known, cf. *B.C.* ii. 101-3, where W. K. L. Clarke points out the resemblances between Acts viii. 26 and Zeph. ii. 4, Acts viii. 27 and Zeph. ii. 11 f., iii. 10; and Acts viii. 39 and Zeph. iii. 4. He refers also to the double meaning of 'Gaza', meaning not only the place but also 'treasure', cf. vs. 27, and to the possiblity that 'eunuch' and 'minister' represent the same Hebrew word, cf. Jer. xxxiv. 19. The influence of the story of Elijah also can be discerned, cf. 1 Kings xvii. 2, 9 f., 2 Kings i. 3, 15, cf. also Jonah i. 2, iii. 2 (F. H. Chase, *Credibility*, 66). At the same time there are aspects of the story which fit the Hellenic viewpoint, as Cadbury says (*B.A.H.* 15 ff.). Ethiopia, or rather Meroe, part of the Anglo-Egyptian Sudan, represented to Homer and Isaiah a geographical extreme beyond the borders of the Empire, though a military expedition under G. Petronius had invaded the land in 23 B.C. Strabo refers to an Amazonian type of queen at that date, a one-eyed Candace. Pliny the Elder mentions another queen in Nero's time, also Candace, which was not so much a name as a title for the queen-mother, the sun's consort and real power in the land. But Luke's main purpose is to show that the Gospel was taken not only to the half-caste Samaritans but even to one who because he was a eunuch could never have belonged

to the Old Israel, Deut. xxiii. 1, not merely to excite the romantic curiosity of his readers. (26) Both **angel** and 'spirit' of the Lord are synonyms for God in His acts of self-revelation. **Gaza,** the former Philistine town on the maritime plain was destroyed in 93 B.C., the new town being built near by, only to be destroyed in turn in A.D. 66. The word **deserted** may refer to Old Gaza or to New Gaza if Luke wrote after A.D. 66 (or if an editor added a note) or with less probability it refers to a deserted road (cf. R.S.V.), though the road is not a desert one till after Gaza (*B.C.* iv. 95). (27) The **eunuch,** interested enough in the O.T. to be reading Isa. liii, was probably connected loosely with Judaism. (28) **coach,** as *B.C.* iv says, is more appropriate a translation than 'chariot'. (30) **Understand;** English, unlike the Greek and Latin, cannot reproduce the similarity between this word and 'read'. Reading in the ancient world was usually done aloud, cf. Cadbury, *B.A.H.* 18 and 30, n. 29. (32 f.) cite Isa. liii. 7 f., part of the last and most famous Servant-song, Isa. lii. 13-liii. 12, which is constantly quoted or echoed by N.T. writers about Jesus, cf. C. H. Dodd, *According to the Scriptures*, 92-4, who says, 'practically every verse . . . is represented in one way or another in the N.T. and in almost every part of it. Its importance as a source of testimonia is manifest, and there is high probability, in view of its ubiquity, that its use as such goes back to the earliest period to which we have access.' Jesus may not have identified His role with that of the Suffering Servant; He may have put forward His claim to be a suffering Messiah, leaving it to His disciples to work out the identification of Him with the Suffering Servant for themselves. Whether the Servant was conceived originally to be the community (or an idealized part of it) or an individual, or, more probably, both, by that 'fluidity of reference' which enabled the Hebrew mind to pass from one to the other rapidly, yet for our present purpose we may note that the portrait of the Servant was taken by His Church to be that of Christ and that this passage contains perhaps the earliest but certainly the most explicit reference to the doctrine. (32) Jesus consciously kept silent at His Passion, cf. Mark xiv. 61, xv. 5, John xix. 9. (33) The Hebrew and the Greek are difficult to interpret exactly, but the general meaning is clear that the righteous Servant was oppressed unto death; the Church could say that Christ's humiliation came to Him not only at His trial but at His incarnation, cf. Phil. ii. 6 f. and his 'generation' may have meant to His disciples His contemporaries and followers and not His lack of physical descent. (35) Philip may be presumed to have handed on the Apostolic kerygma, cf. ii. 38. (37) The Western text has this verse, 'And Philip saïd, If you believe with all your heart, you may'. And he replied, 'I believe that Jesus Christ is the Son of God'. The motive of this scribal addition, which passed into the Byzantine text and so into that of Erasmus and the Textus Receptus, was to remove the difficulty felt at the sudden, almost unprepared, baptism of the eunuch. The addition, which was known to Irenaeus, may give a second-century formula of interrogation before Baptism (cf. J. N. D. Kelly, *Early Christian Creeds*, 31 ff.) which was still performed simply in the name of Jesus and not in the threefold name of the Trinity, Matt. xxviii. 19. (39) The word 'the' has to be supplied before Spirit. The Western reading here may be correct, 'Holy Spirit fell upon the eunuch, but an angel of the Lord caught away Philip', if 'holy' after 'Spirit' in the Greek down to 'angel' was omitted, perhaps accidentally, in the Alexandrian recension. On the other hand, the latter may be defended by treating the Western addition as an expansion intended to show that the Spirit fell on the convert after his baptism. But as Ropes (*B.C.* iii) admits, the geographical range of attestation for the Western reading here is widespread. Lampe (*The Seal of the Spirit*, 65) stresses the note of joy, i.e. spiritual joy, which came on converts after Baptism, cf. xvi. 34. Did this joy in itself denote the reception of the Spirit, cf. xiii. 52, 1 Thess. i. 6, 1 Pet. i. 8? (40) **Azotus**, Ashdod, was another originally Philistine town on the maritime plain. According to ch. xxi Philip was presumably settled at Caesarea with his family; this was a port, originally Strato's Tower, rebuilt by Herod the Great in honour of Augustus and hence called Caesarea Sebaste. Philip's house would become an inevitable meeting-place for Christians like Paul going overseas or returning to Palestine, and there Luke may have found many of his 'oral' sources which cannot be determined exactly.

ix. 1-19a. THE FIRST ACCOUNT OF SAUL'S CONVERSION

(1) But Saul, still breathing threat and murder against the Lord's disciples, went to the high priest, (2) and asked from him letters to Damascus for the synagogues, that, if he found any of the Way, men and women, he might bring them bound to Jerusalem. (3) But while he was going, it came about that he approached Damascus; and suddenly there flashed around him a light from heaven, (4) and falling to the ground, he heard a voice saying to him, 'Saul, Saul, why are you persecuting me?' (5) And he said, 'Who are you, Lord?' And he said, 'I am Jesus, whom you are persecuting. (6) But rise and go into the city, and it will be told you what you must do.' (7) But his travel-companions stood speechless, hearing the voice but seeing nobody. (8) And Saul arose from the earth; but when his eyes were opened, he saw nothing; and they led him by hand and brought him into Damascus. (9) And he was three days without sight and did not eat or drink anything.

(10) But there was a disciple in Damascus named Ananias; and the Lord said to him in a vision, 'Ananias'. And he said, 'Here I am, Lord'. (11) And the Lord said to him, 'Arise and go to the street that is called Straight, and ask in the house of Judas for a man of Tarsus named Saul, for behold, he is praying, (12) and he has seen a man named Ananias come in and lay his hands on him, that he might regain his sight'. (13) But Ananias answered, 'Lord, I have heard from many about this man, how much harm he did to thy saints in Jerusalem; (14) and here he has authority from the chief priests to fetter all who call on thy name'. (15) But the Lord said to him, 'Go, for this man is to me a chosen instrument, to carry my name before both Gentiles and kings and the children of Israel, (16) for I shall show him how much he must suffer for my name's sake'. (17) And Ananias went out and entered into the house, and he laid his

hands on him and said, 'Brother Saul, the Lord has sent
me, Jesus who appeared to you in the way by which you
came, in order that you may regain your sight and be
filled with Holy Spirit'. (18) And immediately something
like flakes fell from his eyes, and he regained his sight;
and he arose and was baptized; (19) and after taking
food he was strengthened.

(1 ff.) For the Conversion cf. xxii. 4 ff., xxvi. 9 ff., and Gal.
i. 13 f. Luke uses in Acts the threefold method of narrative
to emphasize the outstanding importance of this event. Luke
varies the wording in the three accounts, adapting each to its
circumstances; scribes, especially of the Western text, have
tended to harmonize the three accounts in Acts. It is to be
noted that much lay behind this 'sudden' conversion. Paul's
Hebrew training from his parents and Gamaliel, his early long-
ing for righteousness and perhaps his sense of the inadequacy of
the Law (but see Phil. iii. 6; Rom. vii may not be autobio-
graphical so much as a picture of Everyman or, if it is auto-
biographical, it may refer to Paul's post-conversion experiences)
and his memory of Stephen's faith and serenity on trial and in
death and, no doubt, the endurance of sufferings by countless
Christians whom he himself had persecuted, all are reckoned
among the pricks. (1) The number of Jews in Damascus and
their importance have been illustrated by the discovery of the
Damascus Document and more recently, though indirectly, by
that of the Qumran Scrolls, but see R. North (*op. cit.* in
Bibliography). According to Josephus the people of Damascus
massacred more than 18,000 Jews after A.D. 70 (*B.J.* ii. 20.2).
(2) **The Way;** Christianity was, for the disciples, the way of all
ways, the *derekh*, in which to walk, cf. xix. 9, 23, xxii. 4, xxiv.
14, 22, cf. xviii. 25. (4) Hearing the 'daughter of the voice', the
bath qol, of God was a means in late Judaism of learning His
will, after prophecy had ceased with Ezra; cf. Mark i. 11, ix. 7.
(5) It must be noted that the Lord's reply meant to Luke, as to
Paul, that in persecuting Christians, Saul had persecuted Christ,
the head of the body of the Church. (7) Contrast the minor
details of xxii. 9. (9) **Blind;** cf. C. G. Jung, *Contributions to
analytical Psychology*, tr. by H. G. and C. F. Baynes, 1945, 257.

'St. Paul had already been a Christian for a long time, only unconsciously; hence his fanatical resistance to the Christians,
because fanaticism is only found in individuals who are com-
pensating secret doubts. The incident . . . on the way to
Damascus marks the moment when the unconscious complex
of Christianity broke through into consciousness. . . . Unable
to conceive of himself as a Christian, on account of his resistance to Christ, he became blind and could only regain his sight
through . . . complete submission to Christianity. Psychogenetic
blindness is according to my experience always due to an unwillingness to see, that is to understand and to realize something that is incompatible with the conscious attitude. . . . Paul's
unwillingness to see corresponds with his fanatical resistance to
Christianity. This resistance is never wholly extinguished. . . .
It broke out in the form of fits . . . psychogenetic fits, which
actually mean a return of the old Saul complex, repressed
through conversion, in the same way that there had been previously a repression of the complex of Christianity.' Jung's thesis
is illuminating but quite incapable of proof, and his whole treatment of the subject eliminates the supernatural. **Did not eat or
drink anything:** was this due to shock? Or, less probably,
because Christians fasted before baptism, cf. *Didache*, vii. 4?
Or because fasting was supposed to be a cure for Paul's affliction? (10) According to xxii. 12 **Ananias was a devout man
according to the Law, well spoken of by all the Jews that lived
at Damascus.** A Jewish Christian, he had probably been converted independently of the apostles; was it for this reason that
Paul in Galatians overstresses his own independence of them?
Even so, why does Paul omit to mention the part played by
Ananias? Perhaps Paul in turn underestimated that part. (11)
The street that is called Straight; this is probably the main
street running from east to west, the modern Darb el-Mostakim.
Judas; either Luke was interested in those who acted as hosts to
early Christians or (*B.C.* iv. 102) such details are characteristic
of visions; both *B.C.* iv. 103 and Bruce note the close connexion
in Luke-Acts between prayer and vision. (12) Some MSS. have
'in a vision' after 'man', but ℵ A and 81, Alexandrian MSS.,
are among those which omit. The verb for 'regain sight' here
occurs in Mark x. 51. (13) **Saints;** the ordinary Pauline word

for Christians; it is significant that in Acts it is used only in this chapter and in xxvi. 10. This suggests that the author of Acts was familiar with Paul's vocabulary or even that Paul was Luke's source for this account of his conversion, cf. *B.C.* v. 380. **(15) Chosen instrument,** lit. vessel of choice, a Semitism. **(16) suffer;** cf. Mark x. 30, which perhaps Luke had in mind; there 'with persecutions' is as unexpected as the note of suffering struck here. **(17)** In his welcome of Saul as a brother Christian, Ananias calls Jesus 'Lord', the significant nominative being used; contrast his language in xxii. 14, which is sometimes said to give a more primitive account (*B.C.* v. 191). **(18) Flakes;** cf. *B.C.* iv. 104; Bruce, 202. The word is found in 'medical' writers of skin- rather than of eye-diseases. **(19)** The partaking of food was often meant to indicate that the cure of a patient was complete, cf. Mark v. 43 and R. Bultmann, *Journal of Religion* vi, 1926, 347 ff.; however, Luke may have known that Paul could now break his fast. **Strengthened;** a term used by the 'medical' writer Hippocrates.

ix. 19b-30. SAUL AT DAMASCUS

(19b) And he was with the disciples in Damascus for some days. (20) And immediately he preached Jesus in the synagogues, that this is the Son of God. (21) But all who heard him were astonished and said, 'Is not this he who in Jerusalem mauled those who call on this name? And here he has come for the very purpose of bringing them bound to the chief priests.' (22) But Saul increased all the more in power and threw into confusion the Jews that dwelt in Damascus, deducing that this is the Christ. (23) But when many days were completed, the Jews plotted together to kill him, (24) but their plot was made known to Saul. They kept watch on the gates day and night to kill him; (25) but his disciples took him by night and let him down through the wall, lowering him in a basket. (26) And when he came to Jerusalem he tried to join the disciples, and they all were afraid of him, not

believing that he was a disciple. (27) But Barnabas took
him and brought him to the apostles, and he related to
them how on the road he had seen the Lord, and that He
had spoken to him, and how in Damascus he had spoken
boldly in the name of Jesus. (28) And he was with them
going in and out at Jerusalem, speaking boldly in the
name of the Lord. (29) And he talked and argued with
those who spoke Greek; but they attempted to kill him.
(30) But when the brethren knew it, they brought him
down to Caesarea and they sent him off to Tarsus.

(19b) **Some days;** a very vague time link, cf. Introduction, 8.
In Gal. i. 15 ff. Paul says that he 'went into Arabia' at once after
his conversion; even if Paul is overstating his independence of
the Jerusalem apostles, his account is more likely to be historical, and if Luke means that Paul stayed in Damascus till he
went to Jerusalem, he was wrong. Bruce, however, suggests that
a short period of such activity as is described in these verses
may not be excluded. (20) **Son of God;** this is the only occasion
when this title is used of Jesus in Acts, and it is significant that
it occurs on Paul's lips, it being a frequent phrase in his letters.
Whereas in the Old Testament the phrase could be applied to
the chosen nation or its representative, the ideal king like David
or the coming Messiah, in New Testament times it is a striking
phrase for a monotheistic Jew to use, cf. Mark i. 1 (B D, etc.),
i. 11, iii. 11, and v. 7, ix. 7, xii. 6, xiii. 32, xiv. 61, xv. 39. To
deduce that Paul was the first Christian to put forward this
doctrine would be uncritical. It is even less likely that his pagan
converts, familiar with the 'gods many and lords many' of the
Hellenistic world, were allowed to import the doctrine through
Paul into the Church. (21) The amazement was due to Paul's
preaching the faith not to his use of the title. **Mauled;** the
word used by Paul to denote his persecuting acts, Gal. i. 13, 23;
here again Luke seems consciously to use Pauline language,
though he shows no knowledge of the extant epistles. To believe
that Paul was not an *agent provocateur* would test the charity
of a lesser man than Barnabas. (22) The Western text makes it
clear that it was Paul's spiritual strength, not physical, which
increased by adding '(in) the word'. **Deducing;** lit. 'putting

together', which probably means comparing texts of the O.T. with the known facts about Jesus, cf. xvii. 11. (23) **Many days;** according to Gal. i. 18 three years (i.e. probably over two years) were spent by Paul in Damascus, Arabia, and Damascus again; Luke's time-link is again very loose. Paul spent his time in Arabia or the Nabatean kingdom of Aretas probably in preaching rather than in 'retreat' or meditation. Aretas, a rather anti-Graeco-Roman ruler, is well known from references in pagan works and inscriptions, and his date would fit this episode. What is not so clear is his power in Damascus, for in 2 Cor. xi. 32 Paul says, 'In Damascus the ethnarch of Aretas the king guarded the city of the Damascenes to seize me and I was let down in a basket through a window over the wall and escaped their hands'. Rather than to suppose that Aretas was in possession of the city over which his representative was placed or that there were so many more Arabs than Jews there that Aretas appointed its governor, it is easier to assume that the ethnarch waiting for Paul was outside the city, perhaps a neighbouring sheikh, hoping to catch Paul as he emerged, cf. *B.C.* v. 193, and Cadbury, *B.A.H.*, 19-21. Or it may be that Luke or his source was wrong in placing the blame upon Jews and in assuming that they were inside the gates. In any case, the humiliating mode of escape for Paul the Roman citizen was the crowning insult which concluded his list of injuries. (25) **Basket,** cf. Mark viii. 8; Paul in 2 Cor. xi. 33 uses another word, *sargane*, but this one, *spuris*, is as old as the third century B.C. when it was used for a 'nose-bag' (*P.S.I.*). (26) Some apostles were still at large in Jerusalem apparently, cf. on viii. 14; according to Acts Paul was careful to preserve close contact with the Jerusalem authorities, cf. xi. 30, xv. 2, xvi. 4, xviii. 22, xxi. 17; 'Luke gives a Jerusalem frame to all of Paul's ministry' (Easton, *Purpose*, 19). Luke himself was no doubt more subservient to the apostles than Paul was, cf. Gal. ii, though the latter had the highest regard for the status of apostle, which he claimed. (27) In this passage it is implied that Paul and Barnabas are to be distinguished from the 'apostles'; contrast xiv. 4 and 14 where they are included in the term. In twenty-four out of twenty-six instances of the word in Acts it refers to the Twelve (or the Eleven), cf. Appendix 1. (28) If the Jews distinguished between Judaea and Jerusalem (cf. L. Finkelstein, *The Pharisees*, 1940, 24), Luke probably meant that Paul was known to Christians in the capital without being known to any outside, cf. Gal. i. 22 f. (29) The word translated **those who spoke Greek** is often interpreted to mean Greek-speaking Jews or 'Hellenists'. The reading in MS. A, 'Greeks', is probably an error, cf. xi. 20. (30) With this verse contrast xxii. 17 ff., according to which Paul was warned in a trance in the Temple to go, 'for I will send you far away to the Gentiles'. **Brethren** is a favourite term for Christians in Acts and in Paul's letters, cf. also John xxi. 23 and 3 John 3, 5.

ix. 31-43. PETER AT LYDDA AND JOPPA

(31) So the church throughout all Judaea and Galilee and Samaria had peace, being built up, and walking in the fear of the Lord and the comfort of the Holy Spirit, was multiplied. (32) And it came to pass that while Peter was going through all (the villages), he came down also to the saints who lived in Lydda. (33) And he found there a man named Aeneas, bedridden for eight years, who was paralyzed. (34) And Peter said to him, 'Aeneas, Jesus Christ has healed you; arise and lay for yourself'; and immediately he arose. (35) And all who lived in Lydda and Sharon saw him, and they turned to the Lord.

(36) But in Joppa there was a certain disciple named Tabitha, which is interpreted to mean Dorcas; she was full of good works and charitable deeds. (37) And it happened in those days that she fell ill and died; and they washed her and laid her in an upper room. (38) But as Lydda is near Joppa, the disciples, hearing that Peter was there, sent two men to him, exhorting him, 'Do not hesitate to come to us'. (39) And Peter arose and went with them and they took him when he arrived to the upper room. And all the widows stood by him lamenting and showing the tunics and cloaks which Dorcas had made when she was with them. (40) But Peter put them all outside and he kneeled down and prayed; and turning

towards the body, he said, 'Tabitha, arise'. And she opened her eyes and she saw Peter and she sat up. (41) And he gave her his hand and raised her up; and he called the saints and the widows and presented her alive. (42) And it became known throughout all Joppa and many believed on the Lord. (43) And it came to pass that he stayed for many days in Joppa with a certain Simon, a tanner.

(31) The 'third rubric' according to C. J. Cadoux marks this period as Pentecost, A.D. 40; see Introduction, 11 (B). The 'stop' points forward, however, to future progress as well as back to the past. Galilee; it is important to notice that Luke assumes the existence of Christians in Galilee, cf. xiii. 31, especially in view of recent tendencies to connect the appearances of the Risen Lord in Galilee, cf. Mark xiv. 28, xvi. 7 with some other form of His manifestation to disciples, cf. R. H. Lightfoot, *Doctrine and Locality in the Gospels*; C. F. Evans, *J.T.S.*, N.S., v, 1954, 3 ff. (32) The stories about Peter, ix. 32-xi. 18, may well pick up the threads of a (written?) source in viii. 25, in which case 'through them all' refers to the villages mentioned there; otherwise 'them' may mean various regions and cities, cf. Syr.^{vg}, or possibly the 'saints' mentioned later. **Lydda** or Diospolis is on the road from Ashdod to Caesarea; Joppa lies some twelve miles north-west of Lydda (vs. 38a may be an interpolation; it treats 'Lydda' as a feminine singular, not as here a neuter plural, cf. vs. 35). The saints that lived in Lydda may have been, like Mnason, xxi. 16, original disciples of Jesus; we must not be blinded by Acts to imagine that all Christ's followers reached Lydda, Damascus, or elsewhere from Jerusalem, or as a result of missions from Jerusalem alone. In miracle-stories ('Novellen' of the German Form-critics) references are often found to the length of the disease and persons are named; see the citation from Bultmann in A. H. McNeile's *Introduction to the Study of the New Testament*, 2nd ed., 50. This miracle may remind critics of those of Elijah and Elisha, 1 Kings xvii. 17 ff., 2 Kings iv. 32 ff., or of Christ's raising of Jairus' daughter, Luke v. 18 ff. But classification of this kind can never determine historicity. It can be argued also either

that the names of those cured, like Aeneas, point to a primitive tradition or, on the other hand, that the names vanished from the tradition before it was recorded, and that the names given are fictitious. (34) **Has healed;** the usual translation is 'heals'; the Greek word for either is the same, but the accent, unrecorded in primitive MSS., would differ, cf. H. J. Cadbury, *J.T.S.* xlix, 1948, 57 f. **Lay** might refer to a meal or a bed. The partaking of nourishment may indicate the completeness of the cure, cf. Mark v. 43. (35) **Sharon** is the fertile 'coastal plain' from Lydda to Carmel. It is an oddity of criticism that before the 'magic Sator square' (cf. McNeile, *op. cit.* 235, n. 2) was interpreted to be an anagram of *Pater noster* written in the form of a cross with A and O at the end of each arm, von Hardenburg suggested that the letters stood for a Latin sentence meaning 'The rose of Sharon lies open to Peter, though he is guilty'! (36) **Joppa,** mod. Jaffa, was in Jewish hands from 47 B.C. till it came under Roman rule in A.D. 6. Though the population included many Greeks, x. 45 implies that the Christians were ex-Jews. The feminine form of **disciple** does not occur elsewhere in the N.T. **Tabitha** is the Aramaic for gazelle, which in Greek is *Dorkas*, that is, used as a proper name. (38) **two men;** *B.C.* iv. 110 and Bruce, 212, note that two messengers are a common feature of Luke's narrative, cf. x. 7, xi. 30; according to Luke, even angels or messengers from heaven worked in pairs. (39) **The widows** in some churches later became a distinct ecclesiastical class, organizing charitable works. **Tunics and cloaks** denote the inner and outer garments respectively. (40) **Put outside;** Luke may have been influenced by (a) what in fact occurred, or (b) knowing that 'secrecy' was required according to the Novellen (cf. Bultmann), or (c) the story of Jairus' daughter, Mark v. 40; if Luke read Mark and was influenced by it in writing Acts (c) is most probable. Bruce comments, 213, that Luke in his Gospel frequently omits a Markan phrase which he introduces in Acts, as he does here. This would be natural if, as the present writer has suggested, Luke wrote Acts before he wrote the Third Gospel. The mention of the 'upper-room', of 'prayer', and of the eyes being opened is not necessarily a sign of dependence on 1 Kings xvii. 23 and 2 Kings iv. 33-35 (LXX), though Luke may have heard these passages read and the wording of the LXX may have influenced his mind perhaps subconsciously. (43) A tanner's occupation was 'unclean' to strict Jews; for this reason he may have lived outside the town, or if he mended nets he would naturally live by the sea. Luke liked to mention those who acted as hosts, cf. ix. 11, and probably did not mean to stress that Peter was not a strict Jew.

x. PETER AND THE CONVERSION OF CORNELIUS

(1) But a man in Caesarea, by name Cornelius, a centurion of the cohort that is called the Italian, (2) a devout man and one who feared God with all his household, doing many works of charity to the people and praying to God continually, (3) saw in a vision clearly, about the ninth hour of the day, an angel of God coming to him and saying to him, 'Cornelius'. (4) But he gazed at him and was terrified and said, 'What is it, Lord?' And he said to him, 'Your prayers and your works of charity have gone up as a memorial before God. (5) And now send men to Joppa and summon one Simon who is called Peter. (6) He is lodging with one Simon, a tanner, whose house is by the sea.' (7) And when the angel who spoke to him had gone away, he called two of the servants and a devout soldier from those attached to him, (8) and he related everything to them and sent them to Joppa. (9) And on the next day as they were journeying and drawing near to the city, Peter went up upon the housetop to pray about the sixth hour. (10) And he became hungry and wanted to eat; and when they were preparing it, he fell into a trance, (11) and he saw the heaven opened and some utensil descending, like a great sheet, lowered by four corners upon the ground. (12) In this were all the quadrupeds and reptiles and birds of heaven. (13) And a voice came to him, 'Arise, Peter, kill and eat'. (14) But Peter said, 'Not so, Lord, for I have never eaten anything common or unclean'. (15) And a voice came again a second time to him, 'What God has cleansed, do not call

common'. (16) And this happened three times, and immediately the utensil was received up into heaven.

(17) And while Peter was perplexed in himself what the vision which he had seen might mean, behold, the men who had been sent by Cornelius had enquired for Simon's house and they stood at the gate, (18) and they called and asked if Simon surnamed Peter was lodging there. (19) And as Peter was brooding about the vision, the Spirit said to him, 'Behold, three men are looking for you. (20) But arise and descend and go with them without hesitation; for I have sent them.' (21) And Peter descended to the men and said, 'Behold, I am he whom you seek; what is the reason for which you are here?' (22) And they said, 'Cornelius, a centurion, a righteous man and one who fears God and who is well attested by the whole nation of the Jews, was instructed by a holy angel to summon you to his house and to hear words from you'. (23) He called them in therefore and lodged them.

And on the next day he arose and went out with them and some of the brethren that were from Joppa went with him. (24) And on the next day they entered into Caesarea. And Cornelius was expecting them, having called together his kinsmen and near friends. (25) But when Peter's entrance took place, Cornelius met him and fell at his feet and worshipped him. (26) But Peter made him rise, saying, 'Stand up; I too myself am a man'. (27) And while he conversed with him, he went in and found many come together, (28) and he said to them, 'You yourselves know how unlawful it is for a man that is a Jew to be attached or make an approach to one of another race; and God showed me not to call any man common or unclean. (29) For this reason when I was summoned I came without any objection. So I ask why you sent for me.' (30) And Cornelius said, 'Four days ago to this hour I was praying at the ninth hour in my house; and behold a man stood before me in bright clothing, (31) and he said, "Cornelius, your prayer has been heard and your works of charity have been remembered before God. (32) Send therefore to Joppa and summon Simon who is surnamed Peter; he is lodging in the house of Simon, a tanner, by the sea." (33) So immediately I sent to you, and you have kindly come. Now therefore we are all present before God to listen to all that the Lord has commanded you (to say).' (34) And Peter opened his mouth and said, 'In truth I perceive that God is impartial; (35) but in every nation he who fears Him and works righteousness is acceptable to Him. (36) The word which He sent to the children of Israel, preaching the good news of peace through Jesus Christ (He is Lord of all) (37)—you know the story which took place throughout all Judaea, beginning from Galilee after the baptism which John preached, (38) Jesus of Nazareth, how God anointed Him with Holy Spirit and power; who went about doing good and healing all that were oppressed by the devil, because God was with Him. (39) And we are witnesses of all that He did both in the country of the Jews and in Jerusalem, Him also they killed, hanging Him on a tree. (40) Him God raised up on the third day and made Him visible, (41) not to all the people, but to witnesses that had been appointed beforehand by God, to us, who ate with Him and drank with Him after He rose from the dead. (42) And He commanded us to preach to the people and to witness that this is He who is ordained by God to be judge of living and dead. (43) To Him all the prophets bear witness, that every one who believes in Him receives remission of sins through His name.'

(44) While Peter was still pronouncing these sayings, the Holy Spirit fell on all who heard the word. (45) And the believers, who were from the circumcision, who came with Peter, were astonished that even upon the Gentiles was the gift of the Spirit poured out. (46) For they kept hearing them speaking with tongues and glorifying God. Then Peter answered, (47) 'Can anyone forbid the water, that these should not be baptized, who received the Holy Spirit, as we did also?' (48) And he ordered them to be baptized in the name of Jesus Christ. Then they asked him to remain for some days.

(x. *The conversion of Cornelius.*) Luke may have been uncertain about the order of events before Acts xvi-end and he
may have placed some of them in the wrong order, assuming
or suggesting that there was 'unilinear' development of events
one after the other, whereas some events that he records took
place at more or less the same time. If a Roman garrison was
established at Caesarea only after the death of Herod Agrippa,
xii. 20 ff., it is possible that xii. 1-17, Peter's escape from prison,
should come before x, as Cornelius was stationed at Caesarea;
it is even possible that Peter, when he escaped from prison and
went 'to another place', xii. 17, actually went to Lydda and
Joppa, ix. 32 ff.

Before Paul's doctrine (Rom. i-ii) was accepted that all, both
Jews and Gentiles alike, stand guilty before God, the inter-
mediate doctrinal stage may be assumed, according to which a
'good' Gentile was, by way of exception, taken to be included
in the Jewish synagogue (cf. W. C. van Unnik, cited by Dupont,
Problèmes, 74 ff.); the Church was not yet open to the Gentiles,
but the synagogue was enlarged. Hence the stress here on
Cornelius' good works, vss. 2 and 4; the **memorial before
God** which Cornelius made was as good as a pious Jew's meal-
offering; cf. vss. 35 and 42; Cornelius belonged in a sense to
the Jewish people. If so, this source goes back to a time when a
good Gentile was reckoned in the Church among true Israelites.
Cf. Appendix 3.

Dibelius is far more radical in his treatment; he suggests
(*Coniectanea Neot.* xi, 1948, 50 ff.) that a simple anecdote was
generalized and redacted by Luke to express a theological purpose. According to this 'primitive story' a centurion, Cornelius,
was warned by an angel to look for Peter; the latter also had a
revelation and arrived at Cornelius' house and preached; the
Spirit fell on his audience and baptism followed inevitably. The
anecdote told of the extraordinary circumstances in which a
Gentile had entered the Church, largely owing to his personal
piety. On the other hand, Dibelius argued, Luke made the
anecdote a peg for his doctrine that by the intervention of God's
will declared through His angel and His Spirit the Gentiles are
called to enter the Church without accepting the minute details
of the Jewish Law. Dibelius thinks that Luke has introduced

the vision of the clean and unclean animals for this purpose and that with the same motive Luke has accumulated the details of the infraction of the Law, as, for example, by letting Peter accept Cornelius' hospitality for several days in company with other Jewish-Christians, cf. Dupont, *ibid.* 72 f. But behind Dibelius' analysis there seems to lie a desire to reduce the supernatural element in Acts to nothing.

At all events the great importance that the episode has for Luke is seen in the length of and repetitions in x and xi. Luke treated the incident as the prelude to the Apostolic Council of Acts xv at which Peter's speech, xv. 7 ff., derived its justification from his part in the conversion of Cornelius. At the same time it is important to notice that two related but distinct problems arose in the early Church. (a) Should Jewish-Christians eat with Gentile-Christians? (b) Should Gentiles be circumcised before becoming Christians? It is probable that one problem would arise very soon after the other; it is also possible that in Acts x, xi, and xv Luke has imposed the later problem upon the earlier.

(1) **Cornelius** was a common name not merely because it had belonged to Sulla but because the latter had set free in 82 B.C. a large number of slaves who took his name. **The Italian** cohort was probably Cohors II Italica Civium Romanorum; an officer of this cohort is commemorated on an inscription near Vienna; it shows that this cohort helped to make Vespasian emperor in A.D. 69, but there is no certainty that it was at Caesarea as early as the reference in this verse, cf. *B.C.* v, 441, W. L. Knox, *Jerusalem*, 153 f., Cadbury, *B.A.H.* 59. As a centurion Cornelius would correspond to a modern sergeant-major and he would be almost certainly a Roman citizen, especially if he had finished his term of service and had settled in or near Caesarea, as the reference to his 'household', vs. 2, may suggest; contrast vs. 7. Bruce, 215, comments rightly on the large number of centurions mentioned favourably in the N.T. (2) **feared God,** cf. *B.C.* v. 86; this may have a quite general sense and does not imply that Cornelius belonged to a special 'class' of God-fearers attached to the synagogue, cf. xvi. 14, xviii. 7. The people would be that of the Jews. **Continually** may be a semi-technical term reminding Jewish-Christian readers of the meal-offering of Lev. ii, cf. vs. 4, or

the perpetual offering of incense, Exod. xxx. 8. (3) The time
would be about 3 P.M. (4) **Memorial**, cf. vs. 3 and contrast the
wording of x. 31. In later Judaism prayer, almsgiving and fasting
were recognized ways of atoning for sins besides the offering of
sacrifices in the Temple. (9) **The next day** is probably relative
to the messengers' start, not to the vision of Cornelius, cf. *B.C.*
iv. 114. For prayer at noon cf. Ps. lv. 17—but this was not one
of the usual hours of prayer. The psychological means through
which enlightenment came to Peter may have been (i) his increasing doubts whether to revise the Church's attitude to the
Gentiles and whether to accept Saul's attitude instead, (ii) the
awning on the roof or a sail of a boat on the horizon which
suggested a sail, (iii) his sense of hunger, vs. 10. In the *Hibbert
Journal*, 23, 1925, 339-41, B. H. Streeter argued that this vision
conformed to the laws of dream psychology in a way which
guarantees it as a reasonably accurate report of an authentic
occurrence, cf. W. L. Knox, *Jerusalem*, 153; Bruce, 217. (10)
Hungry; a rare word, the use of which is attested by the first
century A.D. eye-doctor, Demosthenes, who worked at Laodicea
on the Lycus (cf. F. W. Dillistone, *E.T.* xlvi, 1934-5, 380).
Cornelius' vision and Peter's form a set of 'double-dreams' of
which several are on record, cf. A. Wikenhauser, *Biblica*, 29,
1948, 100-11. (11) **saw;** lit. 'sees'; Luke seldom drops into
the historic present. *Skeuos* means an instrument or utensil
rather than a vessel. **Corners;** this may be a 'semi-medical'
word, for it is used by Galen and Hippocrates for the corners of
a bandage; but it is also used for the ends of ropes and sheets.
(12) Cf. Gen. vi. 20 LXX. (14) This protest seems to echo the
wording of Ezek. iv. 14. (15) **A second time;** cf. Jonah iii. 1.
Do not call; or 'stop calling'. (16) The repetition of the
incident in the dream, like the repetition in xi of the story,
stresses in Hebraic fashion the importance of the event. (17) As
B.C. iv. 115 f. suggests: 'It seems, at least in the immediate
context, to have been interpreted as referring to intercourse
with Gentiles rather than to the law concerning food'. Was this
interpretation due to Luke imposing the problem of the terms
of admission of Gentiles into the Church upon the problem of
social intercourse of Jewish-Christians with non-Jews? (19) **the
Spirit,** cf. the angel, x. 3. Both are the expressions of God's will

through Christ for men. **Three men;** perhaps the reading of B, 'two men', is preferable, the soldier, vs. 7, acting merely as an escort. (22) **Instructed;** directed or prepared, cf. Luke ii. 26. (23b) **Some;** six, according to xi. 12; does Luke increase the number of Jewish-Christians involved to heighten the enormity of unclean social contact with Gentiles? (25) According to the Western text, 'And as Peter was drawing near to Caesarea, one of the slaves ran ahead and announced his arrival; and Cornelius sprang forth and met him'. Perhaps this was a gloss based on knowledge of a custom of sending a slave to meet a notable person or it was intended to explain how Cornelius knew where to meet Peter. Either explanation is more probable than that the Western text is original and was abbreviated in the Alexandrian recension. (26) Cf. xiv. 14 f., Rev. xix. 10, xxii. 8 f. (28) **Unlawful;** *B.C.* iv. 117 'improper'. Bruce, 222, suggests 'tabu'. **Any man common;** J. R. Porter (*J.T.S.* xlvii, 1946, 171) rightly contrasts x. 14 with this verse, the former using a neuter, this verse a strong masculine. Porter suggests that the baptism of Gentiles was the main interest of Luke rather than the original problem whether Jews and Gentiles in the Church could meet at a common table; and that Luke touched up his narrative and obscured the original meaning here. (30) **Four days ago;** lit. 'from four days' or three according to modern reckoning, 'four' being perhaps an Aramaism here. In the Greek the first half of this verse is clumsy and points to a lack of final revision. D has 'fasting and praying', cf. the probable addition of 'and fasting' to Mark ix. 29 in many MSS. **Bright clothing;** cf. on i. 10. (34) Peter's speech reads awkwardly in Greek and suggests that Luke was consciously giving a Semitic flavour to his style. **Impartial,** a Hebraism from the word 'to accept or lift someone's face', i.e. 'to favour'. (35) **Works righteousness;** the Rabbis had elaborated rules for social intercourse between Jews and strangers dwelling in the land; the seven commandments known as Noachian, given by Noah to his sons, were directed against blasphemy, idolatry, fornication, blood-shedding, the use of meat containing blood, robbery, and civil disobedience, cf. *B.C.* v. 81. Righteousness also implied in late Judaism almsgiving in particular, cf. C. H. Dodd, *The Bible and the Greeks*, 42 ff. (36 f.) The harshness of the Greek text, so often a mark of the speeches in the first half of Acts, may be due not only to its Semitic idiom but also to its being a summary of the apostolic preaching or kerygma, the pattern of which is plain here; see above on i. 8 and Introduction, 12; cf. McNeile, *Introduction*, 2nd ed., 3; Knox, *Acts*, 17 f. There was a more or less fixed form of missionary preaching and Peter and Paul kept in the main to it, though there are individual variations in this section as in xiii. 38 ff. **He is Lord of all;** *B.C.* iv. 119 f. suggests that the words are not original; but if Col. i. 15-20 was part of an early Christian hymn, Luke could well have used such a phrase as this of Christ. (38) Both *B.C.* iv. 121 and Bruce, 226, note that this speech has the early Christology of Mark; the summary of the ministry here is comparatively rare in the kerygma. The influence of Isa. lx. 1 (LXX) may be detected. *Diabolos* for devil is used here as in Ephesians and the Pastorals; Paul preferred *Satanas*. (39) **Witnesses;** the apostolic witness was an integral part of the kerygma, cf. i. 8, 22, etc. **Tree;** cf. v. 30. (40) **On the third day;** Mark spoke of Christ's resurrection after three days, as does the Western text here; later evangelists, like some scribes of Mark, preferred 'on the third day', cf. my *Alterations*, 44. (41) The miracle of the physical resurrection of Christ was seen to be clinched by His eating and drinking after death, cf. i. 3 f., Luke xxiv. 13 ff. (42) **Ordained;** or appointed or determined, cf. ii. 23, xvii. 31. **Judge . . . dead;** *B.C.* iv. 122 rightly stresses the Son of Man Christology implicit in this phrase, cf. *ibid.* 155: 'It is, in general, the earlier views about Jesus which are given first in Acts. This seems to point to an historical basis in the Lucan presentation, in spite of editorial colour, sketchiness of statement, and many unhistorical details.' Jesus as Son of Man would be God's vicegerent to set up His kingdom and to udge all men. (43) **All the prophets;** the reference is to the Old Testament passages cited in chs. ii-iv, culled probably from an early list of Testimonies current in the Church. **Remission of sins;** cf. Jer. xxxi. 34, Luke xxiv. 46; Christ by His death and resurrection has transplanted the reprieved Christian into a New Order or Age, cf. O. C. Quick, *The Gospel of the New World*, 1944, 52 ff. The Church should be on earth the effective instrument of that New Order and in it the forgiveness of sins is always possible. (44) As Lampe says (*The Seal of the Spirit*, 66) of this passage, 'On one occasion Baptism follows the direct, unmediated bestowal of the Spirit . . . but this episode is in no way typical, it is a major turning-point in Luke's narrative—a second, purely Gentile Pentecost. . . . Possibly the Spirit is regarded as normally, but not universally, imparted before Baptism.' (45) **The Gentiles;** cf. Lampe, *ibid.* 47, 'Luke's conception of the dispensation of the Spirit . . . is coloured by his constant preoccupation with the Gentile mission as the climax of the Gospel'. Cf. Appendix 3. (46) By **speaking with tongues** here Luke may have meant the utterance of ecstatic cries of praise, cf. on ii. 1 ff. above, cf. 1 Cor. xii, xiv. The Western text, by adding 'other', stresses that foreign tongues were meant, cf. the variant in Mark xvi. 7. (47) The editors of *B.C.* i. 340 ff. argue that water-Baptism was unnecessary after Spirit-Baptism and that xi. 16 implies that water-Baptism was not in fact used on this occasion but interpolated by a redactor of Acts. This seems needlessly sceptical; the contrast was not between John's water-Baptism and Christian Spirit-Baptism but between the former and water-plus-Spirit Baptism which Jesus Himself had undergone, Luke iii. 21 ff. Cf. Appendix 3. As Rackham says, *Acts*, 159, though he had received the Spirit, Cornelius was afterwards baptized, and Saul, even after seeing the Lord and receiving his call, was baptized; these instances show the necessity of Baptism, testifying to the divine will that order should prevail in God's household. (48) Baptism was still in the name of Jesus; the use of the Trinitarian formula had not yet been adopted, cf. Matt. xxviii. 19, cf. my *Alterations*, 33 f.

THE GOSPEL AND THE GENTILES

xi. 1-18. THE AFTERMATH OF CORNELIUS' CONVERSION

(1) And the apostles and the brethren who were in Judaea heard that even the Gentiles had received the word of God. (2) But when Peter went up to Jerusalem, they who were of the circumcision argued with him, (3) saying, You went in to men who were uncircumcised and did eat with them? (4) But Peter began to make his explanation to them in order, saying, (5) 'I was in the city of Joppa, praying, and in a trance I saw a vision, some utensil descending, like a great sheet lowered by four corners from heaven, and it came as far as me. (6) And I gazed at it and observed and saw the quadrupeds of earth and the wild beasts and the reptiles and the birds of heaven. (7) And I heard also a voice saying to me, "Arise, Peter, kill and eat". (8) But I said, "Not so, Lord, for nothing common or unclean has ever entered into my mouth". (9) But a voice answered a second time from heaven, "What God has cleansed, do not call common". (10) This happened three times; and again everything was drawn up into heaven. (11) And behold, at once three men stood by the house, in which we were, sent from Caesarea to me. (12) But the Spirit told me to go with them without hesitation. And there came with me also these six brethren, and we entered into the man's house. (13) And he reported to us how he had seen the angel in his house standing and saying, "Send to Joppa, and summon Simon who is surnamed Peter, (14) who will speak to you words by which you will be saved, you and all your house". (15) And while I began to speak, the Holy Spirit fell on them, even as on us at the beginning. (16) And I remembered the word of the Lord, how

He said, "John indeed baptized with water but you shall be baptized with Holy Spirit." (17) If God therefore gave to them the same gift as also to us, when we believed on the Lord Jesus Christ, who was I to be able to hinder God?' (18) And when they heard these words, they fell silent, and they praised God, saying, 'So then even to the Gentiles God has granted repentance unto life'.

(1 f.) For the Western text, see Introduction 13; it seems that the Western reviser has sought to make Peter less subordinate than the Alexandrian text does to the Church in Jerusalem; the reviser may have had in mind viii. 25 and xv. 3. In either case the text implies that Peter was challenged for eating with Gentiles, not for baptizing them. (4 ff.) R. Liechtenhan connected vss. 4-18 with xv. 7-11, both Petrine 'defences', which may have been one unit originally. (5) The repetition of the Cornelius story, with minor alterations, is Luke's rather clumsy, Semitic way of stressing the event. (12) **Without hesitation;** the words may also be translated, 'without making any distinction'. The Western text omits. (15) **At the beginning;** i.e. presumably, at Pentecost.

xi. 19-26. THE CHURCH IN ANTIOCH

(19) Now those who were scattered after the tribulation which occurred over Stephen made their way as far as Phoenicia and Cyprus and Antioch, speaking the word to none except Jews alone. (20) But there were some of them, Cypriots and Cyrenians, who came to Antioch and began to speak even to the Greeks preaching as good news the Lord Jesus. (21) And the hand of the Lord was with them and a great number who believed turned to the Lord. (22) And the story was heard about them in the ears of the church which was in Jerusalem; and they sent out Barnabas as far as Antioch; (23) when he was present and saw the grace of God, he was glad and he began to exhort all to remain in the Lord in the purpose

of their hearts, (24) for he was a good man and full of Holy Spirit and faith; and a large multitude was added to the Lord. (25) And he went away to Tarsus to look for Saul (26) and when he found him he brought him to Antioch. And it came to pass that they were gathered together in the church even for a whole year, and that they taught a large multitude and that in Antioch the disciples were first called Christians.

Note on xi. 19 ff.

Luke's arrangement of his material is intended to emphasize the spread of Christianity from Jerusalem to the Gentile world through the Jews of the Diaspora and proselytes, ii. 9 ff., through Samaritans, viii. 5 ff., the Ethiopian proselyte (presumably), viii. 27; the half-Jewish, half-Gentile towns of Azotus and Lydda and Joppa, viii. 40, ix. 32, and then through Cornelius for whom the synagogue had had to enlarge, as it were, its borders, so that in a sense no exception had been made for him, and Jewish-Christians might have argued that Cornelius' conversion was no precedent for baptizing Gentiles. Now Luke shows how Gentiles were converted at Antioch. It is, of course, possible that some of these missionary efforts were more contemporaneous than Luke's narrative suggests and that his implication of gradual extension of the Gospel to full Gentiles is not altogether historical. Luke was concerned with only two focal points in an ellipse about Jerusalem and Rome and in the lines joining those two places, not with any spread of the Gospel towards Edessa or Alexandria, of which either he knew nothing or nothing had occurred when he wrote.

(19) The language shows that Luke consciously picks up viii. 4 and that he considered the story of the conversion of Judaea and Samaria, viii. 4 ff., to be parallel to the account of the Church in Antioch narrated here. Harnack believed that xi. 19 ff. belonged to a written source, the Jerusalem A source. Antioch-on-the-Orontes, the capital of Syria, was the third largest city of the Empire, coming after Rome and Alexandria with a population of about 800,000. B. M. Metzger (*The Biblical Archaeologist*, xi, 1948, 4) describes the part that it played in the life and fortunes of the early Church, its history,

the excavations undertaken there largely under the auspices of Princeton University; the marble statuette of the goddess of Fortune by Eutychides; the Charonion, which is a colossal relief carved in a limestone cliff near Antioch; the mosaic of the Phoenix and another probably referring to the cult of Isis; the extent of the Jewish community there and the massacre of Jews during Caligula's reign and the excavations at Seleucia Pieria, the seaport five miles north of that Orontes, which according to Juvenal 'flowed into the Tiber' (*Sat.* iii. 62); for the immorality especially of the neighbouring pleasure-garden of Daphne and the superstition of Antioch were notorious, cf. Propertius ii. 21. Despite Schürer, it seems that relations between Jews and Greeks in Antioch were remarkably friendly, cf. Josephus, *Ant.* vii. 3.3. The governor of Syria was usually a strong and reliable character, unlike the average procurator of Judaea. (20) **The Greeks;** the Alexandrian and Byzantine reading is 'Hellenists', which is wrong if the word means Greek-speaking Jews, but it may mean any Greek-speaking person. Here the contrast with the Jews is clear. For the title **Lord** applied to Jesus cf. on i. 24 above; the triple mention of 'Lord' here within two verses is curious; the word in the phrase **hand of the Lord** refers probably to Yahweh. The theory that Greek-speaking converts imported the worship of Jesus as 'Lord' from their knowledge of pagan cults of gods many and lords many is refuted by the early Christian use of the Aramaic Maran, as in *Maranatha*, 'our Lord'. 22a is a Semitic-sounding phrase and probably a conscious Septuagintalism. (22 f.) The choice of Barnabas was inspired; like some of the leaders in the Church in Antioch he was a Cypriot Jew and he would understand the position there; at the same time he had identified himself so closely with the 'poor' saints at Jerusalem that he could represent them; though not one of the Twelve, he came to bear the title of apostle; the verb here, *exapesteilan*, probably refers to an *ad hoc* commission, not to any permanent status as apostle, cf. Appendix 1. (24) Luke is not introducing Barnabas; he has done so in iv. 36; the saint's qualities were such that he could not condemn the good work at Antioch, cf. Knox, *Jerusalem*, 163, n. 15. (25) **to look for;** the text of B is at fault for once, 'to raise up'. But both readings suggest that Saul was

somewhat in obscurity. (26) **gathered together;** the word
might mean 'entertained as a guest'; the noun, Synaxis, came
to be used of the 'gathering together' of Christians for the
Eucharist. **Christians;** the ending -ianos is a Latinism and this
word is taken usually to refer to what was originally a nickname
given by those outside the Church, cf. Tacitus, *Annals* xv. 44.
E. J. Bickerman, however, insists that the word means 'to style
oneself'; he takes the Latin ending to denote 'a slave of'. Christians would be slaves of Christ. 'The name which the followers
of Jesus gave themselves officially at Antioch, *c.* A.D. 46, is a
precious relic which has survived from the short and obscure
period between Jesus and Paul. . . . They were officers of the
Anointed King in his Kingdom which was a present reality'
(*H.T.R.* 42, 1949, 109-24).

xi. 27-30. THE PROPHECY OF UNIVERSAL FAMINE AND THE FAMINE-RELIEF VISIT

**(27) But in those days prophets came down from Jeru-
salem to Antioch. (28) And one of them arose, named
Agabus, and made plain through the Spirit that there
would be a great famine over all the world, which took
place in the time of Claudius. (29) But of the disciples,
according as any had means, each of them decided to
send to minister to the brethren dwelling in Judaea, (30)
and they did so, sending it to the elders by the hand of
Barnabas and Saul.**

(27) *B.C.* iv. 130 stresses the part that prophets played in
early Christianity. 'It was essentially a prophetic movement'.
It is certainly implied in the *Didache*, xi ff., that prophets
were recognized leaders and that bishops and deacons were
tolerated locally (*c.* A.D. 100?). Agabus is mentioned later in
xxi. 10 as though he had not been mentioned before. Was the
name Agabus added here to that of an unnamed prophet? Or
did Luke derive this story of famine-relief from Agabus himself
or from an Antiochene source? Certainty is impossible. The

last suggestion is preferable perhaps as xi. 19-26 and xiii. 1-48 suggest an Antiochene source. If (and only if) Luke's source of information was Paul or Barnabas, it is unlikely that B. H. Streeter's suggestion following Renan is correct that Luke's source had in xi. 30 'Barnabas and x' and that Luke assumed wrongly that Barnabas' companion was Saul, cf. Dibelius, *T.L.Z.* lxii, 1947, 193-8, Streeter, *The Four Gospels*, 557, n. For the relation of this Pauline visit to Jerusalem, cf. the Introduction, 8, vi, cf. Dupont, *Problèmes*, 51 ff. **A great famine over all the world;** *B.C.* iv. 131 denies flatly that there was any famine over all the world under Claudius, allowing, however, a widespread one. As K. S. Gapp has said, 'the evidence of official documents among the papyri from Egypt and the wider sources, Pliny and Josephus, so supports Luke's account of the universal famine that the accuracy of his (Luke's) statement can no longer be challenged'. There was a famine in Claudius' reign in Egypt and in Judaea, the Egyptian one probably preceding that in Syria; the date is *c.* A.D. 46, when the renegade Jew, Alexander Tiberius, was procurator, or possibly one year earlier when Fadus was procurator, cf. *B.C.* v, 455. Luke may have derived his knowledge perhaps indirectly from records kept for the Emperor or for the Praefectus anonae, cf. Josephus, *Ant.* iii. xv. 3, xx. 2.5 and 5.2, Suetonius, *Life of Claudius*, xviii. 2. If queen Helena of Adiabene, who favoured Judaism, provided food, as Josephus relates, for those in Jerusalem during the famine, it is extremely likely that the distribution was made by the Jewish authorities and that no Christian benefited by this bounty. Did the early 'communistic experiment' of the Jerusalem Church lead to the poverty of the 'saints' there, who were continually the object of Paul's charity according to his middle and later letters? As Claudius ruled from A.D. 41-54, the language here used may suggest that Agabus' prophecy was made before 41 and, possibly, that Luke wrote at least after 54. If Luke's original source was Semitic, the word underlying *oikoumenē*, the (civilized) world, may have meant 'land', cf. Mark xv. 33 (*Gē*), i.e. the land of Palestine. But in view of the evidence, there is no need to restrict the famine in this way. (30) **The elders;** Easton (*Purpose*, 24 ff.) makes the good point that all Luke's readers are assumed to know perfectly well what these officials were; Easton supposes, no doubt rightly, that the appointment of Elders took place wherever the Gospel was taken. The Twelve had left, or were about to leave, Jerusalem, with the probable exception of James, the Lord's brother, who was to succeed Peter as head of the primitive community, when the latter went on his missionary travels. The elders would be responsible for administration, as the Seven had once been. It is possible, as Knox maintains (*Jerusalem*, 170 f. and 177, n. 33), that the Seven had been raised to Seventy and that James, the Lord's brother, had come to preside over them, just as the Sanhedrin consisted of Seventy members (cf. the Seventy appointed by Moses, Num. xi. 16) under the High Priest. Luke's record of our Lord's appointment of the Seventy (Luke x. 1 ff., written perhaps after Acts) may be anachronistic; Luke may have assumed that the Seventy Elders of Jerusalem, if they existed, dated back to the Lord Himself.

xii. 1-19. THE MARTYRDOM OF JAMES, THE SON OF ZEBEDEE AND THE ESCAPE OF PETER FROM PRISON

(1) But about that time Herod the king set his hand to maltreat some belonging to the church. (2) And he slew James the brother of John with the sword. (3) And when he saw that it was pleasing to the Jews, he proceeded to take into custody Peter also. They were the days of unleavened bread. (4) And he seized him and put him in prison, delivering him to four squads of four soldiers each to guard him, wishing after the Passover to lead him out to the people. (5) So then Peter was guarded in the prison, and prayer was made earnestly by the church to God for him. (6) But when Herod intended to lead him out, in that very night Peter was asleep between two soldiers, bound with two chains; and guards before the door were watching the prison. (7) And behold, an angel of the Lord stood over him and a light shone in the building; and he struck Peter's side and awoke him,

saying, 'Arise up quickly'. And the chains fell off his hands. (8) And the angel said, 'Gird on your belt, and put on your sandals', and he did so. And he said to him, 'Throw on your cloak and follow me'. (9) And he went out and followed him and he did not know that it was real, which was done by the angel, but he seemed to be seeing a vision. (10) When they had gone through the first guard and the second, they came to the iron gate that leads to the city, which opened to them of its own accord; and going out, they went on one street and immediately the angel departed from him. (11) And when Peter came to himself he said, 'Now I know really, that the Lord has sent His angel and delivered me from the hand of Herod and from all the expectation of the people of the Jews'. (12) And when he was conscious of it he came to the house of Mary the mother of John who was surnamed Mark where there were many gathered together and praying. (13) And when he knocked at the door of the gateway, a servant named Rhoda went forward to answer it. (14) And when she recognized Peter's voice, for joy she failed to open the gate but ran in and announced that Peter was standing before the gate. (15) And they said to her, 'You are mad'. But she maintained that it was so. But they said, 'It is his angel'. (16) But Peter remained knocking; and when they opened the door they saw him and were astonished. (17) But Peter signalled to them by hand to be silent and he related to them how the Lord had led him out of prison. And he said, 'Tell this to James and to the brethren'. And he departed and went elsewhere. (18) But when day came, there was no small commotion among the soldiers, as to what indeed had become of Peter. (19) And when Herod had had a search made for him and could not find him, he examined the guards and commanded them to be led off to their fate; and he went down from Judaea to Caesarea and stayed there.

(1 f.) **About that time**; a vague time-link. Herod died in A.D. 44 (Josephus, *Ant.* xix. 8, 2) and Peter's imprisonment and

escape took place before the famine-visit of xi, the famine being dated *c*. 46; Luke was probably using sources here and he has misplaced one of them. It may follow that xii. 25 is merely an attempt to pick up xi. 30, while historically Peter's early missionary work near Lydda was carried out at about the same time as that of Paul and Barnabas at Antioch, cf. Note on xi. 19 above. Dr. G. H. C. MacGregor (*Acts*, 155) gives an attractive reconstruction of the order of events as follows: (a) xii. 17 ff., Peter's escape from prison at Jerusalem and Herod's death, A.D. 44. (b) ix. 32-x. 48, Peter's tour through Palestine to Caesarea and the conversion of Cornelius, A.D. 44-5 and xi. 22-6, the work of Barnabas and Paul at Antioch (same dates). (c) xi. 28, the famine in Palestine. (d) xi. 2, Peter's return to Jerusalem, early in A.D. 46; and xi. 30, the 'famine-visit' of Paul and Barnabas, cf. Gal. ii. 1-10, the discussion at Jerusalem (same date). See *B.C.* ii. 156 f. Herod Agrippa I, son of Aristobulus and grandson of Herod the Great, had received from Caligula the tetrarchies of Philip and Lysanias and the title of king; in A.D. 39 the tetrarchy of Antipas, Galilee, was added. He boldly tried to dissuade Caligula from setting up his own statue in the Temple in A.D. 40, and when Claudius succeeded Caligula on the latter's assassination the territories of Judaea and Samaria were added to Herod's, in A.D. 41. (2) Herod tried to curry favour with the Jews with whose religion he sympathized as long as it did not conflict with his own interests, though he deposed Theophilus from the High Priesthood in favour of Simon son of Boethus. The persecution of Christians may well have been part of Herod's attempt to conciliate both Pharisees and Sadducees. The martyrdom of James the son of Zebedee fulfilled literally part of that prophecy of Mark x. 39 which gave rise probably to the legend that John his brother also died young as a martyr, cf. McNeile, *I.S.N.T.*, 2nd ed., 289 ff., contrast 287 ff. (3) **Proceeded**; the Semitic flavour of the Greek word is probably a conscious Septuagintalism. The feast could be named by using 'Passover' or by the days of unleavened bread which followed it, though technically the Passover day was Nisan 14 and not the rest of the eight days, cf. Luke xxii. 1. (4) The Passover is referred to because Herod presumably did not want an uproar during the feast, cf. Luke

xxii. 2; if Luke wrote Acts before the Third Gospel as we have it, but, after reading Mark, it would be natural for him to echo Marcan passages, like Mark xiv. 2, as he seems to do here, while he avoided Mark's phraseology later in revising the Third Gospel, cf. Bruce, *Acts*, 244. Both *B.C.* iv. 134 and Bruce (*ibid.*) cite Vegetius, *De re militari*, iii. 8, to the effect that the watches were divided into four, that it might not be necessary to watch at night for more than three hours. (7 ff.) Luke took the escape to be miraculous; the escape of Paul and Silas is the obvious parallel, xvi. 25 ff., though there 'a great earthquake' takes the place of the angel of the Lord; angelology is not so prominent in the second half of Acts as in the first. *B.C.* iv. 135 and Bruce, 245, give references to other stories of escape from prison current in the ancient world and both refer to Reitzenstein's *Hellenistische Wundererzählungen*. The 'form' of an escape story cannot of course decide the problem of its historicity. **Struck;** the Western text has 'nudged', which may come from a Semitic translation rendered back into Greek, cf. my *Alterations*, 81. (10) The Western reference to the seven steps down which Peter and the angel descended is often taken as an original note by Luke that has dropped out of the Alexandrian text, but cf. my *Alterations*, 62 f. It is probable that the prison was the tower of Antonia north of the Temple; there is little to be said for J. R. Harris' suggestion that the seven steps point to the Byrsa at Carthage. **Of its own accord;** a classical word, used of the gates of Olympus in Homer, *Il.* 5. 479; for doors supposed to open in this way *B.C.* iv. 136 quotes from Artapanus and Josephus. (12) **John . . . Mark;** either (a) this is Mark, the evangelist, who was Mary's son, a relative of Barnabas and a companion of Paul on the first missionary journey, xiii. 5, who 'deserted' at Perga, xiii. 13, and after being the bone of contention between Paul and Barnabas, went with the latter to Cyprus, xv. 37 f.; and who is mentioned in Col. iv. 10, Philem. 24 and 1 Pet. v. 13, which show that he was reconciled to Paul and was also with Peter probably at Rome later. This is the usual supposition. Or (b) this John Mark is not the evangelist, who was Mark the 'curt-fingered', perhaps a Roman Christian, cf. G. Dix, *Jew and Greek*. Certainly, Mark was a common name in the first century. **The house of Mary;** it is merely a guess that the Last Supper had been held here; it is sometimes urged that this is unlikely if Mark was the evangelist and Mary's son, or else he would have known the right date for the Last Supper in relation to the Crucifixion, whereas the Fourth Gospel gives a more consistent dating; but Mark's date has received the support of Dalman and Jeremias against John's, and the recent work of Jaubert points to our Lord (and Mark) following an ancient sacred calendar, while the Fourth Gospel followed the legal Jewish calendar for the Passover; this guess may not be incorrect. (13) **Rhoda** was not an unusual name for a slave-girl, meaning 'Rose' in Greek. It was the name later of the owner of Hermas, for whom the latter seems to have formed a sublimated affection, of which the *Shepherd* is the expression. (14 f.) The details suggest an eye-witness of the scene. (15) **Angel;** cf. the late Jewish belief in guardian angels who were supposed to resemble those in their charge. (17) There is little doubt that Peter was the leader of the primitive Church, as the early chapters of Acts suppose. Probably James, the Lord's brother, assumed that position, as O. Cullmann has argued (*Peter, disciple, apostle, martyr*, E.T., 1953, ch. ii) when Peter left Jerusalem and gave himself to missionary work for the Jewish Christian Church. Hitherto James had played, since his conversion, a 'somewhat leading role beside' Peter, Gal. i. 19, ii. 9; now on the strength of his unique relationship to Jesus, he stepped into that position of pre-eminence which Peter had enjoyed, and Peter would henceforth be answerable for his actions to the Mother Church in Jerusalem. It is significant that Luke can assume that his readers did not need to be told when or why James succeeded Peter. **Elsewhere** or lit. to another place; this phrase has been discussed at length because the Roman Catholic Church claims that Peter went at an early date to Rome and spent twenty-five years there, but there is no evidence for this; if xii. 17 ff. should precede ix. 32 ff. (see on xii. 1 above), 'elsewhere' means to Lydda and Joppa. Later, Peter appears at Antioch and, if Acts xv is historical, at Jerusalem, but presumably only in transit, cf. 1 Cor. ix. 5 which shows how Peter's wife went on his missionary travels. After leaving Jerusalem he did not continue to direct the work of the Jewish Christian Church, though he was the apostle for the circumcision, Gal. ii. 7 f., and indeed he was in the position of being 'afraid' of the circumcision party, *ibid.* ii. 12. The tradition that Peter reached Rome *c.* 42, supported by the apocryphal *Acts of Peter*, the *Clementine Recognitions* and *Clementine Homilies*, is abandoned by the best Roman Catholic scholars, cf. Cullmann, *op. cit.* 37 f. (18) **No small;** for this meiosis or understatement cf. xiv. 28, xv. 2, xvii. 4, xix. 23 f., xxi. 39, and xxvii. 20. Though these words are omitted here in D and d and some other MSS., they seem typical of Luke, and a similar litotes can be found in Acts xv.-end. (19) **Led . . . fate,** lit. led away, cf. Luke xxiii. 26; the Western text makes it clear that the death penalty was inflicted, perhaps because sometimes only a prison sentence was incurred when a prisoner escaped, according to some papyri. Caesarea, though the administrative capital of Judaea, is distinguished from it as was Jerusalem from Judaea by some Jews.

xii. 20-3. THE DEATH OF HEROD

(20) **And he was at strife with the Tyrians and Sidonians and they appeared before him in a body, and when they had won over Blastus, the king's chamberlain, they asked for peace because their country depended on the king's for its food-supply. (21) And on a fixed day Herod put on his royal robes, and sitting on his throne, he harangued them. (22) And the people began to call, 'It is the voice of a god and not of a man'. (23) And immediately an angel of the Lord smote him, because he did not give God the glory; and he was eaten by worms and expired.**

(20 ff.) For Josephus' account of Herod's death cf. Introduction 7 (c). His narrative differs so much from Luke's that the latter cannot be said to be dependent on him. According to Josephus, *Ant.* xix. 8, 2, on the occasion of a festival held in honour of the emperor Claudius, during the second morning of the festival, Herod Agrippa came into the Theatre at the moment when the sun rose and reflected his silver robe, the light of which so dazzled beholders that they acclaimed him a

god; Agrippa did not accept or reject the title, but a little later he saw an owl sitting above him and recognized it to be the messenger of the evil fate once prophesied to him: he was at once seized with internal pains and was taken home and died five days afterwards. (20) **At strife;** this word may mean 'furious' rather than 'at war with'; the Greek word is found in Polybius and Plutarch. Luke or his source and not Josephus refers to this quarrel, though the latter had mentioned (*Ant.* xviii. 6. 2) a quarrel between Herod Agrippa and Antigonus of Tyre. **Blastus;** a common name, but one which does not happen to occur elsewhere in the N.T. (23) **smote;** cf. the 'smiting' of the angel in verse 7 above. The Western text adds 'still living' after 'eaten with worms' to intensify the horrors of the disease. **Eaten by worms;** an adjective usually applied to crops or to a plant as in Theophrastus and in four papyri in an agricultural sense (Cadbury, *B.Λ.H.* 38, 54, n. 14) is applied to Herod because the ancients loved to dwell on the unpleasant deaths of tyrants, cf. that of Antiochus Epiphanes, 2 Macc. ix. 5 ff. Did Luke also imply that those who prosper in this world but reject Christ will perish like diseased cabbages?

xii. 24-5. A SUMMARY AND LINK

(24) And the word of God grew and multiplied. (25) And Barnabas and Saul returned to Jerusalem in completion of their mission, taking with them John surnamed Mark.

(24) A rubric or stop to mark the progress of the Gospel; according to C. J. Cadoux this rubric should be dated, Pentecost, A.D. 45, but contrast de Zwaan's arguments, see Introduction 11 (B). (25) 'From Jerusalem' makes better sense than **to Jerusalem,** but the latter is better attested textually. If Luke wrote 'to Jerusalem', perhaps by a slip of the pen, which went unrevised, instead of 'to Antioch', scribes would tend naturally to change 'to' into 'from'. Other explanations of 'to Jerusalem' have been advanced. (i) The Greek can be rearranged so as to be translated, 'having fulfilled their Jerusalem ministry', (ii) 'to Jerusalem' can be excised altogether as a

scribal gloss, (iii) The past participle, usually translated 'when they had fulfilled' can mean 'in order to fulfil', cf. xxv. 13; cf. C. D. Chambers, *J.T.S.* xxiv, 1922, 183 ff. and W. F. Howard, *ibid.* 403 ff. But on this view the reference to John Mark is obscure, for he was presumably at Jerusalem and was taken to Antioch. It may be, as Lake suggested, that this verse was intended to pick up xi. 30 and to show that Herod had died before the famine-visit (*Earlier Epistles*, 317 ff.). In any event, the words can hardly be made the basis of a theory of four rather than three Pauline visits to Jerusalem against the two of Galatians (contrast Dupont's *Problèmes*, 51 ff.).

Note on x-xii and Typology

It could be argued by a typologist, searching the Scriptures of the Old Testament, that the commission of Peter to go to Cornelius, his initial reluctance to do so but his subsequent obedience, leading to the gift of the Holy Spirit being conferred on the Gentiles, had its counterpart in the commission of Jonah to the heathen at Nineveh. Going further, the typologist might stress that Peter was in Aramaic Simon bar Jonah, though Luke refrained from giving him this name, and that the word of the Lord came to Jonah a second time before his final obedience enabled God to grant the Gentiles repentance unto life, to which Christian Baptism corresponds. The mention of Joppa as the place from which Jonah set out would be considered significant, cf. Acts ix. 36. Then the argument could be maintained that the king of Nineveh in the book of Jonah corresponds to the figure of Herod in Acts xii; Jonah went down to the waters of death and appeared to the king of Nineveh as one risen from the dead; the king repented and (a) put off his royal apparel and put on sackcloth, (b) came down from his throne to sit in ashes, and (c) proclaimed a fast, Jonah iii. 6 f.; Peter was smitten on the side, symbolically re-enacting Christ's Passion for Christ had been struck on the Cross in His side, while Peter lay in prison, which symbolizes the grave. After Herod heard the news of Peter's escape from prison, he reversed the actions of the repentant king of Nineveh by (a) putting on his royal robes, (b) sitting on his throne, (c) making an oration to those dependent on his land for food; the result was that Herod was worm-eaten (*skōlekobrotos*) and died, the *skōlex* being the worm in Jonah iv. 7 which devoured his gourd. On the basis of this 'parallelism' a typologist might maintain a connexion between the 'sign' of Jonah and the symbolism of death and resurrection with Christ in Christian baptism.

It may be that the pattern of events in the Old Testament sometimes foreshadows a similar pattern in the New, for the God of both Testaments is one. At the same time the pattern of interpretation of events, as opposed to that of the events themselves, may be due to Luke here or to his source, if he was familiar with the Jonah story. If so, these references should be added to those cited by W. K. L. Clarke, *The Use of the LXX in Acts*, B.C. ii. ch. iii. Luke may have listened to the Jonah story in a Christian church-house, while he was penning these chapters of Acts, and the details of the Jonah story or of a sermon based on the 'sign of Jonah' may have remained in his mind. A typologist is on uncertain ground if he argues from such instances that Luke's wording was the direct result of the inspiration of the Holy Spirit, cf. the present writer in *The Bible To-day*, 78 f. If Luke had wanted to make the 'parallels' more explicit, he could have done so.

A Note on the First Missionary Journey, xiii-xiv

Harnack argued that chs. vi-vii, xi. 19-30, and xiii. 1-3 belong together as parts of the Antiochean source; *B.C.* iv. 141, however, suggests that vi-vii are derived from the Jerusalem tradition(s) of Stephen's death and that xi. 19-30 may be the Jerusalem tradition of the founding of the Church in Antioch and that xiii. 1-3 was based on an original Antiochean source which held that Barnabas and the others mentioned were prophets working in the power of the Spirit and not emissaries from Jerusalem, cf. Gal. ii. 11 f. Macgregor, *op. cit.* 164, suggests that the break between the two halves of Acts should be placed at xiii. 1 and not as Harnack supposed at xv. 35; the details of xiii-xiv point to Luke's use of a reliable oral source perhaps, e.g. Timothy, for these chapters which are on a par in this respect with the later chapters in Acts.

xiii. 1-12. IN CYPRUS

(1) **And there were in Antioch in the local church prophets and teachers, both Barnabas and Simeon who is called Niger and Lucius the Cyrenian and Manaen, a**

foster-brother of Herod the tetrarch, and Saul. (2) And while they were performing their service to the Lord and fasting, the Holy Spirit said, 'Separate indeed for me Barnabas and Saul for the work to which I have called them'. (3) Then they fasted and prayed and laid their hands on them and sent them away. (4) Now they, being sent out by the Holy Spirit, came down to Seleucia and from there they sailed away to Cyprus. (5) And when they arrived in Salamis, they began to proclaim the word of God in the synagogues of the Jews; and they had John also as attendant. (6) And going through the whole island as far as Paphos, they found a certain man, a magician, a false prophet, whose name was Bar-Jesus, (7) who was with the proconsul Sergius Paulus, a man of intelligence. This man summoned Barnabas and Saul and sought to hear the word of God. (8) But Elymas the magician, for so is his name interpreted, resisted them, seeking to pervert the proconsul from the faith. (9) But Saul, who is also Paul, being filled with Holy Spirit, gazing at him (10) said, 'O full of all guile and all unscrupulousness, you son of the devil, enemy of all righteousness, will you not cease perverting the straight ways of the Lord? (11) And now, behold, a hand of the Lord is upon you and you shall be blind, not seeing the sun for a time'. And immediately there fell on him mist and darkness and as he went about he sought for someone to lead him by the hand. (12) Then the proconsul saw what had happened and he believed, being astonished at the teaching of the Lord.

(1) Nothing certain is known apart from this verse of **Simeon, Lucius, or Manaen;** Simeon the 'Black' may have come from Africa and may possibly be Simon of Cyrene, Luke xxiii. 26. The ordinary Roman praenomen, Lucius, is hardly likely to point to Luke himself or to be identical with the Lucius mentioned in Rom. xvi. 21; if Luke wrote Acts and refrained from divulging his identity except through using 'we' occasionally, it is unlikely that here he would give it away, though in course of time scribes inevitably identified Lucius of Cyrene

with Luke, cf. the fourth-century evidence of the *Prophetiae ex omnibus libris* known to us from ninth-century MSS., the underlying Greek text of which has been reconstructed by Zahn and would mean, 'Now there were in the church prophets and teachers, Barnabas and Saul, on whom the prophets laid their hands, Simeon who is called Niger and Lucius of Cyrene who remains until the present and Titus of Antioch and Manaen foster-brother of Herod the tetrarch, who were warned by the Holy spirit . . .'; cf. Ephrem Syrus (fourth century) commenting on Acts xii. 25, 'But Saul and Barnabas who carried food for the saints in Jerusalem returned with John who was called Mark and so did Luke of Cyrene. But both these are evangelists and wrote before the discipleship of Paul and therefore he used to repeat everywhere from their gospel.' These scribal hypotheses need not be taken seriously, cf. Cadbury, *B.C.* v, note xxxvii. 'Manaen' can mean 'Comforter', Menahem and this attribute may have been given wrongly to Barnabas, cf. iv. 36, though if Luke was a Jewish-Christian he is hardly likely to have made such a mistake. Foster-brother or companion became a title of honour for those who had been at court either adopted by or closely connected with the ruler. (2) The reference to fasting here and in vs. 3 should be compared with Matt. vi. 16 and Mark ii. 18 f. as well as contrasted with the original text of Mark ix. 29. (3) Was this laying-on of hands by the prophets and teachers of Antioch the sign of an *ad hoc* commission? This is more probable than that it denoted Saul's elevation to the apostolate, though it has been noted often that the two missionaries are not called apostles till after this event. The area covered in the first missionary journey was, or was meant to seem, a natural extension of the work of the Church in Antioch; the names in vs. 1 are of Jewish Christians and it was to Jews in Cyprus that Barnabas and Paul were sent, there being no indication that they were sent there to convert Gentiles. However, it can be argued that 'Luke's conception of the ceremony described here was something very much more than a service of parting benediction' (Easton, *Purpose*, 18). Luke and his readers may have thought of it in terms of the 'ordination' service of their own day, cf. 1 Tim. iv. 14, and contrast Gal. i. 1, where Paul claims that he was an apostle not from men nor through man but through Jesus Christ. To Barnabas the Cypriote the mission was to his own home country. (4) Luke notes frequently the seaport where a journey began or ended; Seleucia was the port of Antioch and sixteen miles west of it, taking its name from Seleucus Nikator, who had founded it three centuries earlier. The strategic importance of Cyprus, placed on the shipping lines to Syria, Asia (Minor), and to Greece (cf. H. Metzger, *Les Routes de S. Paul*, 12) is all too well known in the modern, as in the ancient, world. After belonging to Cleopatra's children, it became an imperial province in 27 B.C. under a *legatus pro praetore*; but Luke refers rightly to the governor as '*anthupatos*' or proconsul, the courtesy title of the propraetor, for in 22 B.C. it had become a senatorial province. Metzger notes that the cult of Aphrodite was well known on the island, but Luke refers not to them but to the Jews who were numerous enough on the island since the days when Herod the Great had acquired a half-share of the copper-mines from Augustus. Seleucia lies 130 miles north-east of Salamis, the chief town of Cyprus, on the east coast. (5) **John . . . an attendant**, cf. on xii. 12 above. Was John an attendant in the sense that a Jewish Chazzan was a minister or *huperetes*? Luke uses this word (later?) in his Prologue, Luke i. 2 where eye-witnesses and ministers of the word are coupled together. The papyri show that this word was often used of an official in charge of documents; the apostles would need such a helper, perhaps to furnish proofs from the Old Testament that Jesus was the Christ and perhaps to draw up simple catechetical forms for converts to learn by heart or perhaps to interpret their sermons to a Greek-speaking audience (cf. Papias' description of Mark as Peter's *hermeneutes* or interpreter). (6) Paphos, on the west coast of Cyprus, is ninety miles from Salamis. Bar-Jesus or Son of Joshua is written out in D in a way that attempts to represent the Hebrew. (7) Luke uses the story of Sergius Paulus because (a) it shows a Roman official favouring and even adopting Christianity, (b) it proves the superiority of Christianity over even a form of magic which could impress a Roman official and (c) it balances the story of Peter and Simon Magus, viii. 14 ff., suggesting that Paul was as good an apostle as Peter. It is not improbable that a magician should be among the companions of a proconsul who shared the prevalent religious curiosity such as that which Vespasian and Titus took in a Jewish sorcerer, Josephus, *Ant.* viii. ii. 5. **Sergius Paulus,** cf. *C.I.L.* vi. 4. ii, 3116, No. 31545, where Sergius Paulus is mentioned as a Curator of the Tiber in the reign of Claudius; if this is the same person, he took office probably in Cyprus later, cf. *B.C.* v. 458. (8) The difficulty here is that 'Elymas' cannot be a translation of 'Bar-Jesus'. Bruce, 256, accepts the theory that Elymas is probably a Semitic word akin to Arabic *'alim,* wise, learned; but as *B.C.* iv says, 'Why should a Jew in Cyprus at the court of a Roman consular governor be called by an obscure Arabic nickname?' The confusion may be due to textual error; there is some Western evidence for reading *Hetoimas,* 'ready' and the root of 'Bar-Jesus' is a Semitic word for 'to be like', 'to be worthy', 'to be equal'. 'One who is *par* to a task is obviously *paratus*' (G. R. Driver). If *Hetoimas* is the right reading, Luke may well have followed a similar Semitic source to the one used by Josephus when he spoke of a Cypriote sorcerer 'Atomos' whom Felix is said to have used to procure Azizus' wife, Drusilla (*Ant.* xx. 7, 2), cf. my *Alterations,* 68. The alternative is to suppose that 'interpreted' should be understood to mean 'he was also known as'. The addition in the Western text of 'since he was listening with great pleasure to them' is unnecessary; a line of about twenty-three letters, as this is in Greek, is frequently otiose in the Western text. (9) As Saul moved westwards he was known more by his Roman name of Paul. Many Jews had a double name, e.g. Joseph Caiaphas, and some had a Roman one similar to the Jewish; it is unlikely that Paul took his name for the first time from Sergius Paulus, cf. my *Augustine, Confessions,* Bk. viii, 48, for patristic suggestions; cf. *B.C.* iv. 145 f. (10) **Son of the devil;** so far from being 'Bar-Jesus', son of salvation, he was the devil's son; in the genuine Pauline epistles we find '*Satanas*' used, not '*diabolos*' for devil, though the latter occurs in Ephesians and the Pastorals; **straight ways,** a conscious Septuagintalism, cf. Isa. xl. 3, Mark i. 3, cf. also Hos. xiv. 9 (10, LXX), Prob. x. 9. (11) The apostles assumed that they had power to punish for spiritual offences, cf. Matt. xvi. 16-19, xviii. 18, John xx. 23, 1 Cor. v. 3, 2 Cor. x. 6. The word for **mist** is as old as Homer,

who uses it of the mist over a dying man's eyes, *Il.* 5, 696.
(12) 'The statement that he believed . . . can hardly be interpreted as meaning less than that he was baptized, the omission
of any mention of the baptism of believers being common, as
in xiii. 48, xiv. 1, xvii. 34, xviii. 18', Knox, *Jerusalem*, 208, cf.
Appendix 3; contrast *B.C.* iv. 147, which suggests that the proconsul was not baptized but that his courtesy was mistaken for
conversion!

xiii. 13-43. PAUL'S SERMON AT ANTIOCH IN PISIDIA

(13) But Paul and those with him set sail from Paphos
and came to Perga of Pamphylia; but John departed from
them and returned to Jerusalem. (14) And they themselves went through from Perga and came to Pisidian
Antioch, and going into the synagogue on the sabbath
day, they sat down. (15) And after the reading of the Law
and the prophets, the chiefs of the synagogue sent to
them, saying, 'Brethren, if there is in you any word of
exhortation to the people, say it'. (16) And Paul arose
and motioned with his hand and said, 'Men of Israel and
you that fear God, listen. (17) The God of this people
Israel chose our fathers and raised on high the people in
the sojourn in the land of Egypt, and with a high arm he
led them out of it. (18) And for about forty years he bore
their manners in the wilderness. (19) And destroying
seven nations in the land of Canaan, he gave them their
land to inherit it for about four hundred and fifty years.
(20) And after that he gave them judges until Samuel the
prophet. (21) Thereupon they asked for a king and God
gave them Saul the son of Kish, a man of the tribe of
Benjamin, for forty years. (22) And after removing him
He raised up David for them to be king, to whom he
witnessed and said, "I found in David the son of Jesse a
man after my own heart, who will do all my wishes".
(23) It was from this man's seed that God according to

His promise brought to Israel a saviour Jesus, (24) John having preached beforehand in view of His coming a baptism of repentance to all the people of Israel. (25) And as John was completing his course, he said, "What do you suppose me to be? I am not He. But behold, there comes after me one whose sandals for His feet I am not worthy to unloose." (26) Brethren, sons of the race of Abraham, and those among you who fear God, it is to us that the word of this salvation has been sent. (27) For the dwellers in Jerusalem and their rulers, not knowing Him and the utterances of the prophets which are read every sabbath day, fulfilled them in condemning Him. (28) And though they found no cause for death, they asked Pilate for Him to be killed. (29) And when they had finished all things written about Him, they took Him down from the tree and placed Him in a tomb. (30) But God raised Him from the dead, (31) and He was seen for many days by those who had gone up with Him from Galilee to Jerusalem, who are now His witnesses to the people. (32) And we preach to you the good news of the promise made to the fathers, (33) that God has fulfilled this for our children in raising up Jesus; as also in the second psalm it is written, "Thou art my son, this day have I begotten Thee". (34) But that He raised Him from the dead no more to be about to return to corruption, thus He said, "I will give to you the holy, the sure things of David". (35) Wherefore also in another psalm He says, "Thou shalt not give thy holy one to see corruption". (36) For David indeed, having served the purpose of God in his generation, fell asleep and was added to his fathers and saw corruption (37) but He did not see corruption whom God raised. (38) Let it be known to you, therefore, brethren, that through Him forgiveness of sins is proclaimed to you; (39) and from all from which you could not be set free by the law of Moses, by Him every believer is set free. (40) Take care then that there come not on you that which was spoken in the prophets, (41) "Look, you scoffers and wonder and disappear, for I work in your days a work which you will not believe, if anyone recount it to you ".' (42) And as they went out, they besought that these things might be spoken to them on the next sabbath. (43) And when the synagogue was dissolved, many of the Jews and of the worshipping proselytes followed Paul and Barnabas who spoke to them and began to persuade them to remain in the grace of God.

(13) 'Those around Paul' (literally) may indicate that Paul is now the leader. **Perga**; no mention is made here of the port of Attalia, south-west of Perga, which the apostles were to visit on their return; did they pick up some of their companions there? **Pamphylia;** a large district with the mountains of Lycia on the west, those of Pisidia to the north and those of Cilicia on the east, was a poor region, joined to Lycia from A.D. 43 for some twenty years, and then again to Galatia. **John departed;** Luke gives no reason. It may be that John felt that Cyprus had been the proper sphere of their work; he and Barnabas were to return to it later after Paul's quarrel over Mark with Barnabas. Perhaps Paul fell ill with malaria, as Ramsay suggested, and for a cure sought the high ground of the mainland as well as the return route overland to Tarsus, if necessary. Or was Mark shocked at the conversion of a Gentile, Sergius Paulus? The day was yet to come when, if this Mark was the evangelist, his gospel would show that while Jesus had ministered rarely to non-Jews during His ministry, He had thrown open the King-dom of heaven by His Passion to all believers (M. Kiddle, *J.T.S.* xxxv, 1934, 45 ff.). If Mark had had such scruples, it is easier to understand Paul's ultimate reconciliation with him (Col. iv. 10) than it would be if his departure now were due merely to cowardice (cf. Knox, *Jerusalem,* 209). (14) As H. Metzger remarks, *op. cit.* 18, from Perga to Antioch in Pisidia 'the route is long and often painful, sometimes even dangerous. The imperial police had no doubt not yet completely suppressed the raids of Isaurian robbers.' Pisidian Antioch; cf. W. M. Ramsay, *H.D.B.* i. 104, who says that the name Antioch towards Pisidia (Strabo, A.D. 19) or Pisidian Antioch . . . gave place to the name Antioch of Pisidia; the Alexandrian MSS., including P45, have Pisidian Antioch; the rest, Antioch of Pisidia.

Sabbath; the original text of D does not make sense here, but it may be due to corruption from a variant 'second Sabbath day' (cf. the variant in Luke vi. 1), which would agree with Ramsay's theory that at least a Sabbath elapsed before Paul preached; but this suggestion of a second Sabbath is probably due to the failure to understand that *metaxu* in vs. 42 means 'next' and not 'middle'. (15) **The reading;** *B.C.* iv. 148 and Bruce, 260, show what the first century A.D. synagogue service contained, (a) The Shema', Hear, O Israel, etc., (b) Prayer by the leader, (c) Old Testament lections usually from the Law, (d) a sermon by any person considered suitable (cf. Luke iv. 16), (e) a blessing. The lections used on this occasion are not specified, but as Cadbury has said (*B.C.* v. 409), on the basis of *etropophoresen* in vs. 18 and *hupsosen* in vs. 17 they have been conjectured to have included Deut. i and Isa. i at least. **The chiefs of the synagogue** would appear a mixture of modern vergers and lay-readers, though other suitable persons could be chosen to conduct the prayers and to preach, and though this title became honorific and could be applied even to women and children when it became hereditary. Paul's dress probably proclaimed him a Pharisee and the invitation for him to speak would be natural. (16) **You that fear God** seems here more than a semi-technical description for those loosely connected with the synagogue, cf. x. 3, xv. 21. (17 f.) In one respect Paul's speech is like Stephen's; it assumes that God controls history and it starts therefore with a summary of events from the Exodus to David's time. The speech is compressed and does not give in vss. 23 f. the Messianic hope as Paul must have done on such occasions; yet the gist of the argument that Old Testament hopes have been fulfilled and that Jesus is David's promised son, is clear; Knox, however, argues (*Jerusalem*, 210) that the speech is hardly to be regarded even as an actual summary of what St. Paul said but rather as a summary of the sort of things which he was in the habit of saying to an audience of Jews and Gentiles familiar with Judaism, based on speeches actually heard by Luke on such occasions. (For this reason Knox thinks it useless to connect this speech with any special set of lections, see above on vs. 15.) (17) Ropes, *B.C.* iii. 120, suggests omitting 'Israel' with the Byzantine text. The

language is consciously Septuagintal, however, cf. Exod. vi. 1, 6.
(18) **He bore their manners,** *etropophoresen,* is better attested
textually than *etrophophoresen,* he cared for them, nourished
them, which occurs in most MSS. of Deut. i. 31 and also in
2 Macc. vii. 27. The Heb. *nasa,* endure, carry, could be translated by either Greek word. (19) **Seven nations,** cf. Deut. vii. 1,
Josh. xiv. 1. (19-20) The note of time as given here is that of
the Alexandrian, Armenian, and Latin Vulgate text; the **450
years** would include the period of the sojourn in Egypt, the
wilderness wanderings, and the time from the entry into Canaan
to the distribution of the land, cf. Josh. xiv. On the other hand,
the Western and Byzantine texts take the 450 years with reference to the 'judges'; the Western reviser may have taken the
Hebrew, not the LXX, text of the Book of Judges, and added
up all the years allotted to the judges, assuming, as modern
scholars do not, that these were all successive and not at all
contemporaneous, though there is no other indication that Jews
adopted this system of chronology for Judges. Ropes, however,
thinks that the Western reading, for once, represents better the
text of Luke here, whereas *B.C.* iv. 151 supports the Alexandrian text, 'because the Western text seems to have disregarded the plain statement of 1 Kings vi. 1, whether the
Hebrew or the LXX be followed'. (For the modern views of
the O.T. chronology of this period, see H. H. Rowley, *B.J.R.L.*
22, 1938, 243-90.) **Samuel,** after Moses, was the first of the
prophets as well as the last of the Judges and one who exercised
the sacrificial office of the priest; it is surprising that he is not
treated in the N.T. as a 'type' of Christ. (21) The reference to
Saul, the son of Kish, would be appropriate in the mouth of
another Benjamite Saul, cf. Philip. iii. 5. **Forty years;** this is
part of Jewish tradition, cf. Josephus, *Ant.* vi. 14.9 (but contrast
the 'twenty years', *ibid.* x. 8.4). (22) Cf. Ps. lxxxix. 21 (lxxxviii,
LXX) combined with 1 Sam. xiii. 14, cf. I Clem. xviii. 1. See
The N.T. in the Apostolic Fathers (1905), 49, according to which
the phenomena are complicated, but Clement may have been
quoting Ps. lxxxviii while influenced by a recollection of Acts,
unless both were dependent on a collection of O.T. Testimonies,
already current in apostolic times; cf. J. R. Harris, *Testimonies.*
All my wishes (or 'will'), cf. Isa. xliv. 28. (23) **Brought,**

ēgagen, is like 'raised up', *ēgeiren,* in uncial Greek letters; the former is the text of Bℵ (Alexandrian), the latter of C 33 (inferior Alexandrian) and D (Western) and many late MSS. as well as Judges iii. 9. (24 f.) A 'specimen kerygma' put into the mouth of Paul shows that Luke believed that Paul, like Peter, had adopted the pattern of apostolic preaching, cf. ii. 14-39, iii. 13-26, iv. 10-12, v. 30-32, x. 36-45. Paul's object on this occasion would have been to prove Jesus to be the promised Messiah, not to give an outline of his own theology, as Windisch seems to assume that Paul should have done, *B.C.* ii. 336 ff. (24) **In view of;** lit. before the face of; a Septuagintalism, cf. iii. 20, etc., and Mal. iii. 1. (25) **I am not he;** i.e. the coming Messiah. A full statement of Messianic doctrine at this point would be unnecessary. **One ... unloose,** cf. Matt. iii. 11, Luke iii. 16 (possibly a Q saying, unless Luke copied Matthew), Mark i. 7, John i. 27. Bruce, 266, points out that both Acts and John have 'worthy' as opposed to 'sufficient', and that this is one of the many points of contact between Luke and John which suggest to him that the son of Zebedee was, directly or not, one of Luke's informants. (26) **Fear God;** cf. vs. 16 above. **This salvation;** Luke is not thinking of the Greek *sōteria,* which must have been used so much as of its Semitic background, the word for 'life' and 'salvation' being the same in Aramaic. (27 ff.) Ropes has reconstructed the original form of the Western text of this passage in a detached note, *B.C.* iii. 261-3, a translation of which would run as follows: 'For the dwellers in Jerusalem and the rulers of her, not understanding the writings of the prophets that are read on every sabbath, fulfilled them and though they found no cause of death in him they judged him and delivered him to Pilate for destruction; but as they were completing all things written about him, they besought Pilate after He was crucified for Him to be taken down from the tree and gaining their request they took Him down and laid Him in a tomb.' Though the reference to 'judging' is better placed and the sense is clearer than in the Alexandrian text, yet this Western text is no doubt a revision and the Alexandrian is nearer to what Luke wrote; the difficulty is due to Luke's compression of the kerygma; this has led to Pilate's guilt (cf. iii. 13) being transferred to the Jews entirely and to the omission of any reference to Joseph of Arimathea (but cf. John xix. 31). (28) Luke loves to note that Christ and His disciples have been found innocent before the authorities. (30) God who had raised up David in one sense, vs. 22, had raised up His Son, in a deeper sense. The pattern of the kerygma is adapted here to the speaker; whereas Peter had hinted that Jesus is Son of Man, x. 34 ff., here Paul maintains that He is Davidic king, cf. Rom. i. 1-3 (cf. *B.C.* iv. 155). (31) Easton (*Purpose*, 19) thinks this verse is the strongest assertion made by Luke of Paul's inferiority to the original disciples; but Luke is repeating an element in the pattern of the kerygma known to all and acknowledged by Paul himself, cf. 1 Cor. xv. 1-8. If Paul included here a reference to his own vision of the Risen Lord, we may discern yet another gap in the discourse. (32) **The promise,** cf. vs. 23, was that of Davidic kingship. (33) The textual evidence strongly favours reading 'to our children', not 'to us their children'; but the sense seems to demand the latter. Was the former a slip of the pen by Luke, left unrevised? Or did he write originally 'to us and to our children' (Chase, *Credibility*, 187 n.) or 'to us, the children' (Ropes, *B.C.* iii. 124)? Chase compares Ps. Sol. viii. 39. The 'raising up' of Jesus here is probably not merely a reference to His resurrection but also to His coming and His glorification, i.e. to the whole series of saving events outlined in the kerygma. **Second psalm;** third-century Hebrew and Latin psalters put Pss. i and ii together as Ps. i, hence the Western text has 'first' here; P[45] and probably 0142 omit the number. The second Psalm was Messianic to the Jews as well as to Christians, Ps. ii. 7 becoming a Christian proof-text which could be applied to the Baptism of Jesus as in the Western text of Luke iii. 22 or to the whole saving act of God through Christ (as here) or to His exaltation at the Ascension, as in Heb. i. 5, v. 5. The Western text continues with the universalistic phrases of Ps. ii. 8. (34) **The holy, the sure things of David;** a citation from the LXX of Isa. lv. 3 and not the Hebrew which means 'the sure mercies of David'. The point of this obscure phrase is that the quotation to follow, from Ps. xvi. 10, 'Thou shalt not give thy holy one to see corruption', could be taken according to Rabbinic exegesis to interpret Isa. lv. 3. Jesus is the Holy One, and the promises of God about Him are faithful and sure. This Rabbinic-sounding connexion between two O.T. phrases is strengthened by the alteration of the verb 'I will make a covenant' in Isa. lv. 3 into 'I will give' to link up with the second quotation. Paul could beat the Rabbis at their own exegesis (cf. Gal. iv. 21-v. 1) if he wished, as Luke no doubt knew. (36) The argument, as so often in Acts, is that as the promise of incorruption after death was not fulfilled for David, it must have been fulfilled for David's son. **Served the purpose** (or 'counsel') **of God;** this translation suggests perhaps too strongly, the casting aside of a worn-out instrument. Another, inferior, rendering could be 'after he had served his generation by the counsel of God', but cf. vs. 22. **Fell asleep;** cf. Judges ii. 10, 1 Kings ii. 10. (38) **To you** is emphatic, picking up the dative, 'to you' in vs. 34. (38 f.) **Forgiveness of sins,** cf. ii. 38, iii. 19, x. 43; the promised forgiveness of sins to the repentant is available to those who are, as Paul would have said, 'in Christ', whereas for the Jew repentance with prayer and almsgiving and study of the Law covered sins, quite apart from sacrifice, which was mainly for ritual offences. Incorporated by Baptism into Christ and made a member of the New Order, the Christian participates in far more than the forgiveness of sins, though that is essential, through Christ, cf. O. C. Quick, *The Gospel of the New World,* 54. As *B.C.* iv. 157 points out, John ii. 3 f. and i. 12 come very close to Acts on this point. (39) The meaning probably is that Jesus could set free the believer from the 'guilt and power' of *every* sin, and that the Jewish Law had been unable to do that. It can hardly mean that the Law could set free from some sins, while Jesus could do so from the rest, though B. W. Bacon (*The Story of Paul,* 103) took it thus. The verb for 'set free' is *dikaioun,* often translated inadequately, 'to justify' or 'to acquit'; man is indeed declared free, acquitted or reprieved at the bar of divine justice through faith in Christ, but as Quick observes 'to acquit' conveys too narrow and legal a metaphor; rather it means 'to set right' with God; incorporated in Christ's Body, one is given a new life in Him and becomes a new creation, part of His New Order. By using this Pauline word, Luke shows that he is adapting the kerygma to the speaker. Windisch, magnifying the differences between Paul's epistles and this speech says, 'This sentence about justification is obviously an endeavour to put into Paul's mouth a phrase with a genuinely Pauline ring about it. But even this seems to be a misunderstanding of Paul's teaching. Faith seems to be a supplement of strict observance of the Law.' But this is to take vs. 39 as Bacon did. Paul's teaching in Romans is that the Law, to use a modern metaphor adopted by N. P. Williams, is a hot fomentation to bring to the surface of man's nature the poison of sin in him; vss. 38 f. do not contradict this view of the Jewish Law. (40 f.) A citation probably from a list of prophetic Testimonies, including Hab. i. 5 (LXX). (42) Hort's quite possible reconstruction of the text would do away with the verb in vs. 42, *parekaloun*, or as Chrysostom may have read, *exioun*, and to read *axiountōn* for *exiontōn* and to run the sentence on to vs. 43, 'When they approved of these things (or words) being spoken (of) to them on the next sabbath . . .' (*The N.T. in Greek, Notes on Select Readings*, 95 f.). *Metaxu* in the sense of 'next' is found in Josephus, *B.J.* v. 4, 2 as well as in Plutarch, Barnabas, 1 Clement cf. Acts xxiii. 25, Western text. (43) **Grace** is another Pauline word which was reminted by him and passed into Christian currency, cf. xi. 23. From graciousness and favour it came to mean the powerful help of God through His own free gift to men, Christ being the personification of that loving help. (Cf. N. P. Williams, *The Grace of God*, 1930, ch. i.)

xiii. 44-52. THE AFTERMATH OF THE SERMON

(44) **And on the following Sabbath almost the whole city was gathered together to hear the word of God. (45) But when the Jews saw the crowds, they were filled with jealousy, and with blasphemy they contradicted the sayings of Paul. (46) And Paul and Barnabas spoke boldly and said, 'It was to you first that it was necessary for the word of God to be spoken. Since you thrust it away and judge yourselves not worthy of eternal life, behold, we turn to the Gentiles. (47) For thus has the Lord com-**

manded us, "I have put thee as a light of the Gentiles, for thee to be for salvation to the end of the earth".' (48) And the Gentiles heard and were glad and they glorified the word of God; and as many as were appointed to eternal life believed. (49) And the word of the Lord was borne throughout the whole region. (50) But the Jews incited the God-fearing women of honourable rank and the chief men of the city and they stirred up persecution against Paul and Barnabas, and they cast them out of their borders; (51) but they, shaking the dust of their feet off against them, came to Iconium. (52) But the disciples were filled with joy and Holy Spirit.

(xiii. 44) **The whole city;** an artistic exaggeration, cf. Posidonius ap. Athenaeus, *Deipn.* v. 48, 212b. **Word of God;** the textual evidence for this and for 'word of the Lord' is evenly balanced here. (45) One argument of the Jews must have been that failure to insist on keeping the Law opened the door to moral catastrophe. **Blasphemy;** probably against Jesus rather than against Paul. (46) The prior claim of the Jews to hear the Gospel is recognized, cf. Rom. i-iii; though Paul clearly converted Jews when he could, he deliberately turned now to the Gentiles, cf. xviii. 6, xix. 9 f., xxi. 19, xxvi. 20, xxviii. 28. **Eternal life;** lit. life of the age (to come), which through Christ has become a present possibility. (47) Words addressed to the Servant of the Lord (Isa. xlix. 6) are applied here to the apostles and (later?) in Luke ii. 32 to Christ Himself. (48) **glorified,** *edoxazon*; D has, 'received', *edexanto*. **Appointed to eternal life,** cf. on vs. 46; ordained, inscribed or enrolled (a meaning found in papyri) are translations suggesting that the full number of those who are to live in the coming age are already written in the book of life, cf. Rev. xiii. 8, Luke x. 20. The ideas of predestination implied in this phrase were common in Judaism of the period, cf. Strack and Billerbeck, *Kommentar zum N.T. aus Talmud und Midrasch,* ii. 726. (50) For *sebomenas* as a description of the women cf. an inscription on the seats of the ancient theatre at Miletus which describes it as the 'place of the Jews and God-worshippers' (*theosebioi*). (51) **Shaking the dust off,** cf. H. J. Cadbury, *B.C.* v. 269-71; the gesture may denote scorn and anger or the desire to avoid further responsibility and also on this occasion, used against Jews to whom it symbolized an act of purification, it denoted a wish to be free from 'Gentile' contamination! **Iconium,** mod. Konia, was described by Xenophon as the easternmost city of Phrygia, *Anab.* i. ii. 19. Though many ancient writers describe it as Lycaonian, the natives thought of themselves as Phrygian. In 36 B.C. Amyntas of Galatia was given this town by Antony, but at his death in 25 B.C. it became part of the Roman province of Galatia; see W. M. Ramsay, *H.D.B.* ii. 443 ff. About 120 miles as the crow flies, north-east of Attalia, where the apostles had landed, it stood on an important road-junction; cf. *B.C.* v. 225.

xiv. 1-7. PREACHING IN ICONIUM

(1) And it came to pass in Iconium that they went together into the synagogue of the Jews and so spoke that a great multitude both of Jews and Greeks believed. (2) But the Jews who did not believe incited and inflamed the souls of the Gentiles against their brethren. (3) So then they stayed a long while, uttering boldly about the Lord, who witnessed to the word of His grace, granting signs and wonders to be done through their hands. (4) But the multitude of the city was divided; and while some were with the Jews, others were with the apostles. (5) But when there was an onset both of the Gentiles and of the Jews with their rulers to insult and to stone them, (6) they became aware of it and fled down to the cities of Lycaonia, Lystra and Derbe, and the surrounding region; (7) and there they were preaching the good news.

(1) **Together;** cf. the somewhat similar phrase in ii. 47; but some, like Bruce (277), translate this 'after the same manner', i.e. as at Antioch. (2 ff.) These verses present awkward phrases, smoothed out in the Western text, which point to a lack of final revision by Luke. (2) The Western text has, 'But the chiefs of the synagogue and the rulers (of Iconium) raised persecution

and made the minds of the Gentiles hostile to the brethren. But the Lord soon gave peace'. The last clause prepares the way for vs. 3. **The Gentiles** of vs. 2 may mean the leading citizens, while vs. 3 refers to work among the populace; there is no need to take vs. 3 before vs. 2. (3) **A long while;** the Apocryphal *Acts of Paul and Thecla* fill up the picture with legendary details, only a few of which may be based on fact, like the description of Paul, 'A man of small stature, with his eyebrows meeting and a rather large nose, somewhat bald-headed, bandy-legged, strongly built, of gracious presence; for sometimes he looked like a man and sometimes he had the face of an angel'. (4) **Apostles;** see Appendix 1. Barnabas may have been one who had seen the Lord during His ministry or after His resurrection. The Western text (D, Syr.^hl.mg) adds, 'cleaving to them because of the word of God'. (6) Luke derived probably from local knowledge the idea that Iconium was not in Lycaonia (which it was, officially) because the natives were more Phrygian than Lycaonian. **Lystra** lies about twenty-three miles south-west of Iconium, and **Derbe**, though it has not been identified with complete certainty, is marked by A. H. M. Jones (*The Cities of the Eastern Roman Provinces*, map) thirty miles south-east of Lystra. Lystra, mod. Zoldera, made a Roman colony in A.D. 6, maintained a close connexion with Pisidian Antioch where a statue records that it was erected by citizens of Lystra, some eighty miles away. (Cf. Jones, *op. cit.* 133-6; and Sir W. M. Ramsay, *St. Paul the Traveller . . .* 110 f.) Knox, as against Ramsay, finds no technical implication behind the word for 'region' (*Jerusalem*, 212) and he may be right in supposing that the apostles spent their time, probably during the winter, waiting to return to Iconium and until new magistrates there were installed. Not speaking Lycaonian, they could not hope to make many converts locally.

xiv. 8-18. THE CURE AT LYSTRA

(8) And there was a man sitting in Lystra, whose feet were useless, lame from his mother's womb, who had never walked. (9) He was listening to Paul speaking, who

gazed at him and saw that he had faith to be made whole (10) and said in a loud voice, 'Rise on your feet, upright', and he leaped and began to walk. (11) And the crowds, seeing what Paul had done, lifted up their voice, saying in the Lycaonian dialect, 'The gods have become like men and are come down to us'; (12) And they tried to call Barnabas Zeus and Paul Hermes, since he was the leader in speaking. (13) And the priest of Zeus-which-is-before-the-city brought bulls and garlands to the gates and wanted to offer sacrifice with the crowds. (14) But when the apostles Barnabas and Paul heard it, they tore their clothes and rushed out into the crowd and cried and said, (15) 'Men, why are you doing this? For we too are men of like feelings as you, bringing good news to you to turn from these vain things to the living God, who made heaven and earth and sea and all things in them, (16) who in past generations allowed all the nations to walk in their own ways; (17) and yet He did not leave Himself without witness, for He did good, giving you rains from heaven and fruitful seasons, filling your hearts with food and gladness.' (18) And saying this, they hardly restrained the crowds from offering them sacrifice.

(8 ff.) The parallelism between this story and that of Peter's cure in iii. 2-8 is no doubt intentional; 'lame from his mother's womb', 'gazing at', and the leaping and walking of the cured man are common to both accounts. (8) Note the 'triple beat' of the phrases to stress the man's disability. (9) The element of faith found here is absent from the story of iii. 2-8. (11) As John Chrysostom observed, it was only by their acts that the natives' intentions became plain to the apostles. (12) The names of Greek gods suggest that the Hellenization of the local gods of Asia Minor was already taking place rather than that Luke has interpreted Lycaonian gods in Greek terms; contrast the note in *B.C.* iv. 164 with Cadbury's later, more cautious, statement in *B.A.H.* 23. It is striking, however, to find that among the pagans the legend was current which Ovid, *Metam.* viii. 626 ff., recounts how in this region Zeus and

Hermes visited the peasants Baucis and Philemon. But these gods, Jupiter and Mercury in Latin form, are found combined in various cults over a wide area, as in Samothrace (Eitrem, *Coniectanea Neotestamentica*, iii, 1938, 12). If evidence of the third century A.D. is significant, weight should also be given to two inscriptions from the region of Lystra, to which W. M. Calder drew attention, both of them in Greek; one refers to priests of Zeus and the other is on a statue of Hermes with a sun dial consecrated to Zeus, cf. *E.T.* xxxvii, 1926, 528. **Leader in speaking;** Hermes was the god of oratory; *B.C.* iv. 164 and Bruce, 283, cite Iamblichus, *De mysteriis Aegypt.* 1, which speaks of Hermes as a god, 'the leader of words'. (13) The Western text refers to 'The priests of the local Zeus-before-the-city', which may be correct; the Western reviser often shows local knowledge of places in the Levant. **Garlands** of wool were to adorn the victims; the gates would be those of the city rather than of the Temple or of the house where the apostles stayed. (14) The language of Judith xiv. 16-19 may have been in Luke's mind; a Hebrew woman had brought 'shame' on the royal house of Assur; and now two Hebrew Christians had put to shame the 'vanities' of the pagan cults. (15 ff.) The speeches hitherto had been addressed to Jews or their adherents; now, as in xvii, a purely Gentile audience is addressed. The arguments used here, as in xvii, are in the Jewish-Christian tradition; whereas the Greek, being polytheistic, could not pursue a polemic against idols consistently, the Jew, being exclusive, attacked idolatry because it led to apostasy, cf. the semi-credal saying in 1 Thess. i. 9, 'You turned to God from idols, to serve the living and true God', cf. Rom. i. 21, viii. 20. (Cf. B. Gärtner, *The Areopagus Speech and Natural Revelation*, 227 f.) **Of like feelings;** God is impassible (cf. von Hügel, *Essays and Addresses*, 2nd series, vii), man is passible and perishable; for *homoiopathes*, cf. Wisdom vii. 3, James v. 17. (16) **Allowed,** cf. Rom. i. 18 ff., iii. 25 for God's past forbearance towards sin; in Romans Paul argues that in the past sinners had been allowed to lapse into idolatry and immorality, God giving them up to their own devices, while here the argument is that God has excused the errors due to past ignorance. (17) **And yet;** cf. xvii. 27. **Food and gladness;**

C. C. Torrey thinks that the Greek is a mistranslation of an
Aramaic which had 'from all' in place of 'food', *J.T.S.* xx,
1918–19, 327; but Knox (*Acts*, 70 n.) thinks this unlikely and
suggests that the whole clause is a careless paraphrase of
Xenophon, *Memorabilia*, iv. 3, 5 f., where Socrates argues in
favour of providence from the fact that man's need of food has
been met by the provision of the fruits of the earth and suitable
seasons which provide not only what we need but also what
gladdens us. The words for 'doing-good' and 'fruitful' are
both as old as Herodotus. (18) At the end of this verse some
MSS., including P45 C and 33 (Alexandrian) as well as Western,
add 'but to go each to his own home', which rounds off this
section well, perhaps for lectionary purposes, cf. the gloss in
the following verse in C 33 81 and other MSS. including D,
'And when they stayed there and taught, there came against
them Jews . . .'

xiv. 19-28. PREACHING IN DERBE AND THE RETURN JOURNEY

**(19) But there came Jews from Antioch and Iconium, and
when they had persuaded the crowd they stoned Paul
and dragged him outside the city, thinking him to be
dead. (20) But when the disciples surrounded him, he
rose up and entered into the city; and on the next day he
went off with Barnabas to Derbe. (21) And when they had
preached the good news to that city and had made many
disciples, they returned to Lystra and to Iconium and to
Antioch, (22) strengthening the souls of the disciples,
exhorting them to remain in the faith and (saying) that
'it is through many tribulations that we must enter into
the kingdom of God'. (23) And when they had appointed
elders for them in every church, praying with fasting,
they committed them to the Lord in whom they had
believed. (24) And going through Pisidia, they came to
Pamphylia. (25) And when they had spoken the word in
Perga, they came down to Attalia. (26) And from there**

they sailed off to Antioch, from which they had been dedicated to the grace of God for the work which they had fulfilled. (27) And when they arrived, and had gathered the church together, they related all that God had done with them and how He had opened a door of faith to the Gentiles. (28) And they spent no little time with the disciples.

(xiv. 19) As the Jews in Pisidian Antioch stir up trouble at Lystra, so the Jews of Thessalonica will stir up trouble in Beroea, xvii. 13. **Stoned**; cf. 2 Cor. xi. 25, 'Once was I stoned'; 2 Tim. iii. 11, which mentions Antioch, Iconium and Lystra and persecutions there, may depend on a knowledge of Acts and may not be a genuine fragment of a Pauline letter. (20) The Western text answers the inevitable question, 'What were Paul's companions doing all this time?' by suggesting that they surrounded him and held him up till he recovered in the evening. Vs. 21 picks up vs. 7, but this does not prove that vss. 8-18 have been interpolated; on Schwartz's view of Acts, xiv. 21-6 are due largely to the editor and are inserted to make the narrative smooth, while Barnabas is supposed to have left Paul at Iconium and returned to Antioch alone, Paul continuing the journey as xvi. 4 ff. relates. This theory is incapable of proof and the text can be taken as it stands, cf. *B.C.* v. 227 ff. (22) Knox suggests that on this return Paul's main object was to preach to the converted and not to make new converts; at the same time, even if new magistrates had been appointed in the cities, Paul's bravery in revisiting these places where he had been persecuted is too obvious for Luke to need to stress it. **Faith** here almost means 'orthodoxy', cf. xiii. 8, xv. 9, xxiv. 24, and the use of this word in the Pastorals. **We** does not point to a 'we-section' but is an instance of a general use of the first person plural, 'we Christians'; contrast, however, Knox, *Jerusalem*, 214 f. The phrase, **Kingdom of God,** is used in its futurist sense, not in that of 'realized eschatology'. It was a phrase which Paul was to use less and less as he moved westwards, owing to the ease with which opponents could interpret it as seditious. Like the Master, the Christian disciple has to suffer before entering into glory, cf. Luke xxiv. 26, Rom. viii.

17-25. (23) The word for **appoint** had lost its meaning of
'elect by show of hands', cf. 2 Cor. viii. 19, Josephus (of the
High Priest), *Ant.* xiii. 2.2; cf. Knox, *Jerusalem*, 216. Luke
mentions the appointment of elders or presbyters here as
typical of Paul's methods which he adopted wherever he
founded a Christian community; the appointment was in the
hands of the authorities, not those of the rank and file of the
Church, though Acts vi. 1-6 stresses the part played by the
community in choosing its officers. As the Church was the new
and true Israel, it adopted inevitably the lines of organization
of the old Israel. The local synagogue, and the town itself if it
was Jewish, was governed by a body of Jewish elders to which
the rulers of the synagogue might well belong. The Christian
elders would be appointed as here by having hands laid on
them if possible, by an apostle, with prayer and fasting, and it is
possible that outside Jerusalem the system that probably grew
up there of James the Lord's brother being surrounded by a
large body of elders (seventy?) was copied and paved the way
for the growth of the monepiscopate elsewhere than in Jerusalem. The word 'elder' was used also in pagan circles, in
Egypt for officers both civil and religious, and in Asia Minor
for officers of various guilds (Deissmann, *Bible Studies*, 154 ff.
233 ff.). More important than the different titles for officers in
the Church, elders (presbyters or priests), overseers, cf. xx. 28,
'those over you', cf. 1 Thess. v. 12, 'leaders', Heb. xiii. 17,
were their functions of administration, teaching, and discipline.
It is not significant that Galatians fails to mention such officers;
Paul's letters assume a large stock of knowledge common to
him and his readers and Luke is describing what Paul did to
organize the Church wherever there were no 'older Christians'
to be found. (24) There must be some reason for Paul not
returning overland to Tarsus and Antioch. Had he already converted sufficiently the Christians in Cilicia during the 'hidden
years' after his own conversion? Or was it simply for the sake
of the new converts? 'After Paul and Barnabas extend their
work as far as Derbe, they retrace their steps through all the
other communities in Asia Minor—Luke lists the cities in-
dividually by name—confirming the neo-Christians in the faith
and establishing a regularized ministry', cf. xvi. 1-5, xviii. 23,

xx. 1-6 (Easton, *Purpose*, 15). (25) The apostles returned, going down to Attalia, the port of Perga, from which ships sailed normally straight to Syria, not via Cyprus. (26) They reported to the Church in Antioch, not Jerusalem, because the work done was an extension of the Church in Antioch; Luke with his pro-Jerusalem bias carefully notes this point. (27 ff.) *B.C.* iv suggests that while these verses may be the true end of the account of the first missionary journey, they may mark an editorial transition between a probably 'Antiochian' narrative in xii and xiv, and a probably Jerusalem narrative in xv.

Note on the Epistle to the Galatians and the Churches of Chapters xiii and xiv

A full discussion of the North Galatian and the South Galatian theories belongs to a commentary on Galatians. The present writer inclines to the South Galatian theory, taking the view that Christians in Pisidian Antioch, Lystra, Iconium, and Derbe were addressed in 'Galatians' and not Christians in the north around Ancyra, Pessinus, and Tavium. As Sir William Ramsay pointed out, 'Galatian' was the only comprehensive term to cover churches in Antioch, Iconium, Lystra, and Derbe and their men of divers nationalities and political institutions, and in Paul's day it was not a misnomer. During the fourth to third centuries B.C. some Celtic tribes, having set out from the North Sea board, occupied the Danube basin and even invaded Greece after Alexander the Great's death in 323; a wave of Celts passed from Thrace into Asia Minor and settled in the Bithynian kingdom around Pessinus, Ancyra, and Tavium; at the head of this tribe were twelve tetrarchs whom Pompey limited later to three; Julius Caesar recognized one of these, Deiotarus, as king and the latter's grandson, Castor, reigned from 40–36 B.C., being displaced by Mark Antony in favour of Amyntas and having his kingdom of Galatia in the narrow sense enlarged by part of Phrygia, Lycaonia, Pisidia, Pamphylia, and Western Cilicia. When Amyntas died in 25 B.C., Rome took over his territories; part of Lycaonia and western Cilicia became the kingdom of Antiochus; and Pamphylia became a separate province, while the rest became part of the wider province of Galatia. This wider 'Galatia' included the four cities under discussion as opposed to Ancyra, Pessinus, and Tavium in the north which belonged to Galatia proper. Inhabitants of the four cities in the south would not have objected to the term 'Galatian', as J. B.

Lightfoot argued, even if they were politically rather than racially Galatian, any more than Paul objected to being called Roman. Apart from Ancyra (mod. Ankora), the district in the north was undeveloped country and the four cities in the south lay nearer to Paul landing on the south coast of the mainland and they were placed strategically on highways along which it was Paul's custom to take the Gospel. If Paul was ill (cf. Gal. iv. 13) when he visited the Galatians, he is not likely to have journeyed several more hundred miles north than Pisidian Antioch when a well-populated area was at hand. It is not necessary to interpret xvi. 6, xviii. 23, and xix. 1 to fit the North Galatian theory, and, apart from these ambiguous references, Acts makes no reference to Paul's work in Galatia. To clinch the argument, Barnabas is mentioned in Gal. ii. 1 as a person well known to the readers; but he was Paul's companion only on the first missionary journey, i.e. to the southern cities. It is also probable that Gal. iv. 14, 'You received me as a messenger of God', is an allusion to the name Hermes conferred on Paul at Lystra, Acts xiv. 12, and it is even possible that 'the marks of the Lord Jesus', Gal. vi. 17, were scars left by the stoning at Lystra, Acts xiv. 19. However, not all scholars who accept the South Galatian view, place it, as W. L. Knox, before the Council meeting of Acts xv, see Introduction, 8 vi (h). Many continental and American scholars indeed cling to the North Galatian theory, cf. McNeile, *I.S.N.T.* 146.

According to Bruce, 287, it is during the 'no little time' of Acts xiv. 28 that it is best to place the incident at Antioch, Gal. ii. 11 f., when Paul rebuked Peter face to face for withdrawing from table-fellowship with Gentiles out of fear of those of the circumcision party. Knox, however, puts this incident at Antioch earlier, before the mission to Cyprus and 'Galatia', suggesting that the decision to undertake the first missionary journey was the result of the difficult situation produced by the controversy at Antioch, though he admits that the text of Acts does not support this hypothesis (*Jerusalem*, 191 ff.). On the other hand, Lake's reconstruction of events, based on a distinction of sources, is as follows (*B.C.* v. 203).

	Galatians	Antioch source	Jerusalem source
1. Paul's visit to Jerusalem	Gal. ii. 1-2	Acts xi. 27-30	—
2. The Council of the Apostles.	Gal. ii. 3-10	—	Acts xv. 3-29
3. Paul's return to Antioch	Implied by Gal. ii. 11	? Acts xii. 25	Acts xv. 30
4. Peter's arrival in Antioch	Gal. ii. 11	—	—

	Galatians	Antioch source	Jerusalem source
5. The arrival of emissaries from James	Gal. ii. 12	Acts xv. 1-2	—
6. A quarrel of Paul against Peter and Barnabas	Gal. ii. 13-14	? Acts xv. 36 ff.	—

Lake suggests that possibly the mission to the Gentiles in Acts xiii-xiv should be inserted between 3 and 4, but he accepted Schwartz's view as more probable. In this way he reconciled the order of events in Acts with that in Galatians, the more important source historically; on this view the dispute in Acts about circumcision and the Law should have been about social intercourse.

XV. 1-29. THE APOSTOLIC CONFERENCE

(1) And some came down from Judaea and began to teach the brethren, 'Unless you are circumcised after the custom of Moses, you cannot be saved'. (2) And when Paul and Barnabas had no small discord and debate with them, they arranged for Paul and Barnabas and some others of them to go up to Jerusalem to the apostles and elders about this problem. (3) So then they, being sent on their way by the church, went through both Phoenicia and Samaria, relating the conversion of the Gentiles; and they caused great joy to all the brethren. (4) And when they were come to Jerusalem, they were received by the church and the apostles and the elders and they reported all that God had done with them. (5) But some arose of the party of the Pharisees, believers, and said, 'It is necessary to circumcise them and bid them keep the law of Moses'. (6) And the apostles and the elders were assembled to see about this matter. (7) And after much dispute Peter arose and said to them, 'Brethren, you know that in days of old God made choice among you, that through my mouth the Gentiles should hear the word of the gospel and believe. (8) And God who knows the heart bore witness to them, giving the Holy Spirit to them, even as to us too. (9) And He made no

distinction between us and them, cleansing their hearts by faith. (10) So now why do you test God by putting a yoke on the neck of the disciples, which neither our fathers nor we were able to bear? (11) But through the grace of the Lord Jesus we believe that we shall be saved, even as they too.' (12) And the whole crowd fell silent and listened to Barnabas and Paul recounting all the signs and wonders that God had done through them among the heathen. (13) And after they stopped speaking, James replied and said, 'Brethren, listen to me. (14) Simeon has recounted how God first visited the Gentiles to take from them a people for His name. (15) And with this agree the words of the prophets, as it is written, (16) "After this I shall return and I shall rebuild the tent of David which has fallen and I shall rebuild the ruins of it and I shall set it straight again, (17) that the rest of men may seek the Lord, and all the nations on whom my name has been called, (18) saith the Lord who makes these things known from the beginning (of the world)". (19) Therefore I give judgement that we cease to trouble those from the Gentiles who turn to God. (20) But that we write to them to abstain from the pollutions of idols and from fornication and from what is strangled and from blood. (21) For from the generations of the beginning Moses has had in every city those who preach him, being read on every sabbath in the synagogues.' (22) Then it seemed good to the apostles and the elders together with the whole church to choose men from among them and to send them to Antioch with Paul and Barnabas, namely, Judas who is called Barsabbas and Silas, leading men among the brethren, (23) writing by their hand; 'The brethren, apostles and elders, to the brethren in Antioch and Syria and Cilicia from among the Gentiles, greeting; (24) Since we heard that some of us went out and troubled you with words, upsetting your souls, to whom we gave no instructions, (25) it seemed good to us when we were met together to choose out men to send to you with our beloved Barnabas and Paul, (26) men who have dedicated their lives for the sake of our Lord

Jesus Christ. (27) **Therefore we have sent Judas and Silas, making the same report themselves also verbally. (28) For it seemed good to the Holy Spirit and to us to put no further burden on you than these essentials, (29) that you abstain from what has been offered to idols, and from blood, and from things strangled and from fornication. If you keep yourselves from these things, you will do well. Farewell.'**

(1 ff.) As Bruce (290) says, we gather from vs. 24 and Gal. ii. 12, if that is the right parallel, that those who came down from Jerusalem had some commission from the Jerusalem Church, the terms of which they exceeded when they tried to impose the conditions mentioned here; on the other hand, according to the Schwartz-Lake hypothesis (*B.C.* v. 204), in order to fit the Jerusalem account into the Antiochian frame Luke has had to insert some editorial phrases to make the Jerusalem account to appear as the story of another incident, and he has forced this verse into connexion with the circumcision controversy instead of identifying it with the controversy over table-fellowship. The Western text has, 'Unless you are circumcised and walk according to the custom of Moses . . .'; this makes the Jewish-Christian demands more sweeping and it may be derived from vs. 5. (2) **They arranged;** who are 'they'? Those from Jerusalem? But would the Jewish-Christians have had authority to summon Paul and Barnabas to the mother-church? Or did Luke think that they had, even if they had not? Or does 'they' refer to the leaders of the Church in Antioch? (Cf. *B.C.* iv. 170 f.) Or was Luke using an impersonal plural, best translated by a passive, 'it was arranged', leaving the question open? The Western text assumes the authority of the Jewish-Christians—but this text tends to favour the claims of the mother-church. It can, of course, be argued that here the Western text is nearer to the original and that the Alexandrian recension is due to a scribe who knew Galatians and who altered the text to prove Paul's 'independence' of the Jerusalem apostolate. But it is more likely that the Western text is secondary here, due to a scribe who knew those parts of the Pauline epistles which stress the necessity of maintaining the *status quo*

either for the slave or for the circumcised and who assumed the authority of the mother-church over both Paul and the Church of Antioch; this impression is strengthened by the apparent dependence of the Western scribe of vs. 2 on 1 Cor. vii. 8, 20, 24, and 40, cf. *B.C.* iii. 139. **Apostles and elders;** cf. vs. 4; whereas in xi. 30 only 'elders' were mentioned as being in Jerusalem, here we find 'apostles' too. If Acts xv is rightly placed, this may indicate that the apostles (apart from James, the Lord's brother, who was probably reckoned by Luke among the apostles and not the elders, despite *B.C.* iv. 171) had fled from persecution but had now been able to return to Jerusalem. On the Schwartz-Lake hypothesis the phrase would be editorial. (3) Phoenicia, cf. xi. 19 ff.; Tyre, cf. xxi. 3 ff. (4) The stress is on what God has done with them, not on what they have done for Him. (5) **To circumcise them.** Whom? All Gentiles on the usual interpretation, or perhaps those like Titus in particular among Paul's companions who were uncircumcised. (6) Some critics who identify this visit with that of Paul described in Gal. ii hold that this verse denotes a private conference, cf. Gal. ii. 2 ('but privately before those who were of repute'), while they take vs. 7 to refer to the public conference. **Matter;** lit. 'word', hence 'subject'; some MSS. have 'question'. (7) P⁴⁵ (Chester Beatty) has a curious repetition here (in error) of the phrase in vs. 2 relating to the discord between Paul and Barnabas. **Days of old;** lit. from the days of the beginning. **Made choice among you;** there is no need with Torrey (*C.D.A.* 21 f.) to suppose an original Aramaic 'you' (accusative) for 'among you', or even to cite Neh. ix. 7 as a parallel. **The gospel;** it is significant that Luke in Luke-Acts uses this noun only twice, here (by Peter) and in xx. 24, though he uses the verb, to preach the good news, often; as Paul and Mark use the noun frequently, the rarity of the noun in Luke may well point to his historical accuracy or to his sense of what was historically appropriate. (8) **Who knows the heart;** this adjective occurs in i. 24 but not elsewhere in the N.T. **Giving;** a timeless aorist participle. (9) **Made no distinction . . . cleansing;** these words occurring in connexion with Cornelius, x. 15, 20, xi. 2, 9, 12, link this speech closely with the Cornelius story, cf. J. R. Porter, *J.T.S.* xlvii, 1946, 169-74. (10) **Test God;** cf. Deut. vi.

16, cited by Jesus, Luke iv. 12. To put another burden on the Gentiles, when God has given them His Spirit would be to make trial of Him and to doubt that His will is clear. **Nor . . . able to bear;** Jesus had condemned the scribes and Pharisees for binding heavy burdens grievous to the bearer upon men, Matt. xxiii. 4. Cf. Rom. vii for Paul's attitude to the Law. This verse and the following seem very Pauline in sentiment. (11) **Grace** and **saved** have a Pauline ring, cf. on xiii. 43. Alternative translations of the aorist infinitive here would be (a) we are saved, (b) so as to be saved, cf. ℵ D, (c) we have been saved. Cullmann rightly stresses that Peter's position as a mediator was very difficult and that he was much nearer Paul's position than James'. (12) Before 'fell silent' the Western text has 'the elders agreeing together with the words spoken by Peter', an addition to give Peter more prestige, Peter often being singled out for special emphasis in the Western text, cf. my *Alterations*, 57. Peter was in fact no longer head of the Jerusalem Church, James having taken his place; but Peter was responsible for the 'Jewish-Christian mission' as Cullmann has shown, *op. cit.* 43, and responsible to the Jerusalem Church! He speaks as a missionary and not as an administrator. **Barnabas and Paul;** after xiii. 7 Paul's name has been put first with the exception of xiv. 14, where the order of names is dictated by the reference to Zeus before Hermes (Bruce, 295); was the order here due to Luke's use of a Jewish-Christian source? **Signs and wonders;** cf. ii. 22 f.; these showed that God's kingdom was breaking in even upon the Gentile world. (13) **Stopped speaking;** lit. kept silence. Though Knox (*Jerusalem*, 233, n. 39) implies that Peter is still head of the mother-church, it is clear that James has replaced him; this is corroborated by Paul putting James before Peter and John in Gal. ii. 9 as well as by Peter's lapse at Antioch being due to those who had come from James and who are presumably those of the circumcision whom Peter *feared*! (Gal. ii. 12). As head of the Church James gives the decision, vs. 19 now; and later he will receive Paul on the latter's last visit to Jerusalem, xxi. 18, cf. *B.C.* v. 55 f. The contents of xxi show James' Jewish-Christian sympathies, while the present context makes clear that he was no extremist; he could argue that to be circumcised without

keeping the whole Law in each particular would be useless for
Gentiles to attempt, though Jewish-Christians like himself tried
to do so. His reputation for strictness and asceticism earned
him the title, 'the Just'; for this and for the story of his
martyrdom see Hegesippus (Eusebius, *H.E.* ii. 23) and Josephus,
Ant. xx. 9. 1. (14) Simeon = Heb. Shim'on; it is striking that
Luke should put into James' mouth the 'Hebrew' form of this
name found elsewhere in the N.T. only in 2 Pet. i. 1. Chrysostom for some reason did not identify this Simeon with Peter
but with the Simeon of Luke ii. 29-32! E. R. Smothers (*H.T.R.*
xlvi. 4, 1953, 203-15) concludes that Chrysostom was wrong,
but he also questions Giet's theory (*R.Sc.R.* xxxix. 203) that
Simeon here was Simeon called Niger of xiii. 1, another
Antiochene. **Visited;** both *B.C.* iv. 175 and Bruce, 297, stress
that this word implies a providential visitation. **People;** the
New Israel in place of the Old; Strathmann (Kittel, *T.W.N.T.*
iv. 53) maintains that Luke's usage is based on the LXX. (15)
The prophets; i.e. the Book of the Twelve Prophets. (16 f.)
The citation is from Amos ix. 11 f.; the latter begins, 'In that
day I shall raise up . . .' For the **Tent** or Tabernacle cf. Ps. xiv
(xv). 1 and compare the note on 'people' above. (17 f.) C. C.
Torrey, claiming an Aramaic original for i-xv, finds it difficult
to account for James' undoubted use of the LXX not the
Hebrew text; the literal translation of the Hebrew would be,
'. . . and will build them as in the days of old that they may
inherit what remains of Edom and of the other nations over
which my name is named'. The LXX has 'they will seek' for
'they may inherit' and 'man' ('adam) for Edom, taking 'man'
as subject not object; the result is that the LXX means not that
Israel would possess the lands but that the heathen would be
converted. Torrey's explanation (*C.D.A.* 38 f.) that the Hebrew
text would have suited James' purpose admirably but that he
used a variant text, is unconvincing, the alleged reason being
that the standard text of the Prophets was not yet established.
(18) The Western text puts a stop after 'Lord' and reads a
separate sentence, 'Known to Him from the beginning if the
world is His work'; here again this text seems secondary, the
motive of the scribe being to separate James' comment from
the text of Amos cited; for the comment cf. Isa. xlv. 21. (20) Cf.

29. The contents of the apostolic decree have been much debated, cf. *B.C.* iii. 265-9 and v. 204-11; cf. my *Alterations*, 72 ff. The textual evidence falls under three heads: (a) the Alexandrian text has four phrases, pollutions of idols, fornication, what is strangled and blood; (b) the African Latin text of Tertullian omits 'what is strangled' and the European Latin does the same and adds the negative form of the Golden Rule; (c) a (Caesarean?) text of Acts represented apparently by P⁴⁵ (Chester Beatty), Origen (*Contra Celsum*, viii. 29) and Eth. omit 'fornication'. The omission in (c) is probably due to the difficulty found in including among food regulations a moral prohibition against 'fornication' (which may merely mean marriage within the prohibited Levitical degrees, cf. Num. xxv. 1, rather than general sexual irregularity). For 'what is strangled', i.e. with the blood still in the meat, cf. the Koran, *Sura*, 5. 3, which includes 'things strangled' among food-taboos (J. R. Harris, *E.T.* xxv, 1913-14, 200). The Western text (b) seems secondary as it is a threefold moral prohibition of idolatry, unchastity, and blood-shedding (or murder). To postulate the scribal alteration of an original food-law (mainly) concerning foods offered to idols, things strangled and blood-drinking, into a moral law is easier than to suppose that the original moral law was turned into a food-law plus a ban on 'fornication'. A knowledge of the commands supposed to have been given to the sons of Noah (cf. *B.C.* v. 208) and therefore binding on all mankind, including the three prohibitions of the Western text, would lead a reviser easily to cut out 'what is strangled' and to adopt the moral demand. The fourfold prohibition of the Alexandrian text is no doubt original. 'One problem has at least been settled' (Dupont, *Problèmes*, 70)! The main object of this decree was to regulate the conditions under which Jewish-Christians could meet Gentile-Christians at table, including the table of the Eucharist and the Agape and as Easton has said, 'The four points of the Decree are precisely those of Lev. xvii-xxviii, essential laws that bind not only the Israelites but also the "strangers and sojourners" as well' (*Purpose*, 16). And the verb 'to abstain from' would suit such a food-law; to use such a verb of murder, etc., as the Western text implies would be slightly absurd. The question may be

asked whether the Decree belongs to a later date than the apostolic conference, even if the latter is rightly put in xv. For in Acts xxi. 25 James refers to the Decree as if Paul had not heard of it before, though James may there be repeating what Paul already knew or Luke may be reminding his readers of what they had already read, cf. Dupont, *op. cit.* 68 f. Yet if Paul did not know the exact terms of the Decree till a late date, it might be easier to understand why he did not refer to it in writing to the Galatians (if he did so after the Council) or in his letter to the Corinthians on meats, unless he wished to argue from first principles in writing to Gentile converts. Finally, the negative form of the Golden Rule, found in some places in the Western text, is Jewish in tone; it is implied in Tobit iv. 15, cf. Hillel, *Shabbath*, 31a, *Didache*, i. 2, and is found in the *Diatessaron* of Tatian, cf. G. Dix, *J.T.S.* xxxiv, 1933, 242 ff. (21) probably picks up vs. 17 ('all the nations') as J. H. Ropes, *J.B.L.* xv, 1896, 75 ff., suggested, but the obscurity of the argument here points to a lack of final revision by Luke. Knox (*Jerusalem*, 234) suggested tentatively that the meaning was that while Moses has failed for so long to convert the Gentiles, in spite of the fact that his works are read in the synagogue every Sabbath, yet he has succeeded in converting some; and so any Christians anxious to learn the Mosaic law as well as Christianity can do it by attending the synagogue still, while those who prefer not to combine Judaism with Christianity can rest content with the essentials common to both. (22) **It seemed good;** or 'it was voted'. **To choose;** the participle is in the accusative; the dative would have been better Greek; the same applies to 'writing', vs. 23, which is in the nominative; Luke's source (Paul? Silas?) probably said, 'They decided to choose . . . and send . . . and write' and Luke's account was left unrevised. **Judas called Barsabbas** was probably the brother of Joseph, i. 23; **Silas** (Western text, Sileas) is a fairly common Semitic name. The two represented the Jewish-Christian and the Hellenist points of view. Unless the plural in xvi. 37 is used loosely, Silas was, like Paul, a Roman citizen, and it is his Latin *cognomen* Silvanus which appears in the Pauline epistles. He may have been a joint author (with Timothy?) of the Thessalonian Epistles (cf. their salutations) or at least of 2 Thess., and he was the messenger who took 1 Pet. to its destination perhaps, or at any rate the scribe who penned it (1 Pet. v. 12); E. G. Selwyn thinks that he was joint author with Peter of that Epistle too. If so, he could write 'good Greek'. If one were to take this suggestion still further, are some pieces of 'scholarship prose' (Knox, *Acts*, 9) found in Acts due ultimately to Silas? It is perhaps odd that later tradition was to distinguish between Silas and Silvanus. (23) **Brethren;** this is in apposition to **the apostles and elders;** Torrey claims this as an Aramaism, *C.D.A.* 39. (24 ff.) K. Lake (*B.C.* v. 211) follows Harnack and Weiss against Zahn in thinking that Luke composed this letter to recapitulate what he has narrated and—though Lake admits doubt here—that Luke did not have an actual copy of the letter before him; Lake's cautious conclusion is that some letter expressing the apostolic views was sent about this problem on this or some other occasion. Perhaps Luke's source originally had no more than a reference to the decision to send a letter, and Luke filled out as best he could such a bare reference. (24) The Jewish-Christian emissaries are repudiated. If the original Decree was addressed to Gentiles only in Syria and Cilicia as well as Antioch, we have another reason why Paul would not quote it in writing Rom. xiv, cf. on vs. 20 above. After 'souls' (i.e. 'minds') some MSS. add, 'saying that you should be circumcised and keep the law' from vs. 5 and other MSS. have this addition at the end of this verse. (26) **Dedicated** or devoted (Bruce) is a better translation than 'risked' or 'hazarded their lives', cf. *B.C.* iv. 180. There is an unfortunate lacuna from vss. 26-38 in P[45]. (28) The emphasis on **the Holy Spirit** is typical of Luke, but his words are doubtless true of the experience of the early Church. (29) The Western text omits 'what is strangled' again, and adds again the negative form of the Golden Rule, cf. vs. 20, and after 'Farewell' it adds 'being borne along by (in) [the] Holy Spirit', a line of twenty-three Greek letters probably, the approximate length of many Western additions to Acts.

xv. 30-5. THE AFTERMATH OF THE COUNCIL

(30) So when they were despatched, they came down to Antioch and gathering the multitude together, they handed on the letter; (31) and when they had read it they rejoiced at the exhortation. (32) Both Judas and Silas, being themselves also prophets, exhorted the brethren in many words and gave them strength. (33) And when they had spent some time, they were despatched in peace by the brethren to those that had sent them. [(34) But it seemed good to Silas to remain there.] (35) But Paul and Barnabas passed the time in Antioch, teaching and preaching the good news of the word of the Lord, with many others also.

(30) **So** or 'so then' marks a new paragraph. (32) **Exhortation**; or 'comfort', cf. vs. 32. There may not be a reference here to xiii. 1. (33) **Spent**; lit. 'made', cf. Prov. xiii. 23. As Luke seldom concerns himself with the minor characters in the story or their movements, there may be some reason for his stressing the return of Judas and Silas, followed by a note of time spent by Paul in Antioch; was it to prove that he and Barnabas were quite independent of the emissaries from Jerusalem? (Knox, *Jerusalem*, 246 f.) Vs. 34 is found in some secondary Alexandrian MSS. and in others including the Western D; but the better Alexandrian MSS. omit. The scribes were so influenced by vs. 40 that they overlooked that Paul could have sent for Silas again after the latter's return to Jerusalem.

xv. 36-41. THE SECOND MISSIONARY JOURNEY OPENS WITH A DISPUTE

(36) And after some days Paul said to Barnabas, 'Let us return indeed and visit the brethren in every city in which we preached the word of the Lord, to see how

they are'. (37) But Barnabas wanted to take John also, who is called Mark, with them. (38) But Paul did not think it right to take with them one who had withdrawn from them in Pamphylia and who had not gone with them to the work. (39) And there was an outbreak of irritation so that they parted one from the other and Barnabas took Mark and sailed off to Cyprus; (40) but Paul chose Silas and departed, being dedicated to the grace of the Lord by the brethren. (41) And he went through Syria and Cilicia, strengthening the churches.

(36) *B.C.* iv. 182 and Bruce, 305 f., point out that 'after some days' in the second half of Acts is common, as 'so then' has been in the first half to mark a new beginning. (38) Cf. xiii. 13. **Not . . . to take,** lit. to stop taking. (39) **Irritation;** a semi-medical term found also in Hippocrates and Galen. Luke does not gloss over the quarrel. Barnabas before (or about) this time had become involved in the table-fellowship dispute at Antioch, Gal. ii. 13, showing that his natural sympathies lay with the Jewish-Christians, and it was equally natural for him to side with his nephew (or cousin) Mark and to take him to his own homeland, Cyprus, to work among Jews. Paul was thereby relieved of strengthening the Church again in that island. (40) The choice of Silas was wise. He was probably a Roman citizen, cf. on xv. 22 and xvi. 37, like Paul who could claim, if driven to it, the privileges of such citizenship for both of them; Silas was *persona grata* in the mother-church at Jerusalem and probably a good Greek speaker, cf. on xv. 22. (41) It is strange that Luke tells us so little of the Church in Syria-Cilicia (one administrative province) which Paul had presumably founded, cf. Gal. i. 21. If Luke was a native of Antioch, which is doubtful, he would probably have said more. The Western text adds at the end 'and handing on the commands of the elders', and though it does not refer to the apostles too, intends probably to emphasize the subordination of Paul to the mother-church.

xvi. 1-5. THE STRENGTHENING OF THE CHURCHES ALREADY FOUNDED

(1) And he went down also to Derbe and to Lystra; and behold, there was a certain disciple there named Timothy, son of a converted Jewish woman, but his father was a Greek; (2) He was well attested by the brethren in Lystra and Iconium. (3) Paul wanted him to go out with him and he took and circumcised him because of the Jews who were in those places; for they all knew that his father was a Greek; (4) and as they went through the cities, they handed over the decrees on which the apostles and elders that were in Jerusalem had decided, for them to keep. (5) So then the churches were strengthened in the faith and they increased in number daily.

(1) **There;** presumably Lystra rather than Derbe, though Origen accepted Derbe. Lois and her daughter, Eunice, Timothy's mother, were probably among Paul's first converts in this area, unless 2 Tim. i. 5 is purely fictional. (3) *B.C.* iv. 184 suggests that the story of Timothy here is due to a confused and perhaps erroneous memory of the story of Titus, Gal. ii. 3. But Paul was willing to become a Jew to save Jews (cf. 1 Cor. ix. 19-23), and over a half-Jew he could safely compromise. **Was a Greek;** the tense used suggests that Timothy's father was dead. (4) **The decrees;** *B.C.* iv. 185 suggests that whatever the truth was, Luke wished to represent Paul as the delegate of the Jerusalem apostles in a way which conflicts with the epistle to the Galatians. Yet Paul may well have delivered the decrees in fact, if he thought that the Galatian churches were within the scope of the misson from Antioch, and especially if he wrote the letter to the Galatians before the Council meeting and was now able to say that the mother-church supported his own views. (5) The good progress of the Church is noted, cf. vi. 7, ix. 31; this summary closes the account of the Apostolic Council while it opens the account of Paul's travels on part of which Luke accompanied him.

PAUL IN GREECE AND AT EPHESUS

Note on xvi. 6 f., cf. xviii. 23

The geographical and ethnological problems raised by these verses are complicated, cf. Knox, *Jerusalem*, 236-9; K. Lake, *B.C.* v. 228-39; Foakes Jackson, *Acts*, 150 f.; and Bruce, *Acts*, 309 f.

It is possible that Luke was concerned only to bring Paul as speedily as possible from the last town on his travels, Iconium, to Troas; in doing this he stresses that God's Spirit overruled Paul's desire to make for the Greek-speaking cities of the coastland of Asia, such as Ephesus, and led him to go in a north-westerly direction, avoiding Ephesus on the left and Bithynia on the right; and Paul may well have passed through, without preaching in the districts mentioned, despite Ramsay. Probably this verse refers to more than the part of Phrygia belonging to the Roman province of Galatia, around Antioch and Iconium and indeed to the border country between Phrygia and Galatian territory, where both languages were still spoken and where Paul's Greek would hardly be understood. Luke's phrase is intended probably to cover the country between Iconium and e.g. Dorylaeum. Near the latter Paul would have reached a point 'opposite Mysia', xvi. 7. It is extremely improbable that he penetrated into the country of Galatia proper around Ancyra, Pessinus, and Tavium. If Paul turned north or north-east at Pisidian Antioch, it is probable that he did not go then so far north even as H. Metzger's map (*op. cit.* 23) suggests, before turning westwards. The language of xviii. 23 is often compared with that of xvi. 6, and K. Lake links the two passages closely together. It is possible that the second phrase is a mere periphrasis for the first, Luke being fond of slight alterations in a second account of a narrative, but Knox, *Jerusalem*, 238, distinguishes between the two verses.

One theory which deserves mention is that of Schwartz (cf. *B.C.* v. 237), who assumed that Paul's visits to Jerusalem according to xi. 30 and xv were one and the same and who suggested that the missionary journeys which followed each visit were also to be identified; if so, Luke added an end to one and a beginning to another account of the same tour; on this view xiv. 21-8 is editorial, and so also is xv. 36-xvi. 9. Both passages 'rush' Paul from Derbe to Jerusalem and from Jerusalem to Troas; the latter passage is certainly remarkable for its omission of any events or even names of towns through which Paul passed, but as Lake goes on to say, there are considerable difficulties in the way of accepting this theory, especially with regard to Barnabas, quite apart from the fact that it makes the author of Acts rather untrustworthy as an historian and probably not a companion of Paul later.

xvi. 6-40. PAUL IN PHILIPPI

(6) And they went through the Phrygian and Galatian region, being prevented by the Holy Spirit from preaching the word in Asia. (7) And coming opposite Mysia, they tried to go to Bithynia but the Spirit of Jesus did not allow them; (8) and passing by Mysia, they came down to Troas. (9) And a vision in the night appeared to Paul; a certain man of Macedonia was standing and exhorting him and saying, 'Cross over into Macedonia and help us'. (10) And when he saw the vision, at once we sought to go into Macedonia, inferring that God had summoned us to preach the good news to them.

(11) So setting sail from Troas we ran a straight course to Samothrace, and on the following day to Neapolis, (12) and from there to Philippi, which is a chief city of the region of Macedonia, a colony; and we were passing the time in that city for some days. (13) And on the sabbath day we went outside the gate by the riverside where we supposed that there was a place of prayer, and we sat down and talked to the women who had come together. (14) And a certain woman, named Lydia, a purple-seller of the city of Thyateira, one who worshipped God, listened; and the Lord opened her heart and she attended to the words spoken by Paul. (15) And when she was baptized, and her household, she exhorted us, saying, 'If you have judged me to be faithful to the Lord, come into my house and stay'; and she put pressure on us. (16) And it came to pass that as we went to the place of prayer, a girl, having a spirit of divination,

met us, who provided much profit for her masters by
soothsaying. (17) She followed after Paul and us and
cried, saying, 'These men are servants of the most High
God, who proclaim to you a way of salvation'. (18) And
she kept doing this for many days. But Paul was ex-
asperated and turning to the spirit he said, 'I charge
you in the name of Jesus Christ, come out of her'. And
it came out that very hour.

(19) And when her masters saw that the hope of their
profit was gone, they seized Paul and Silas and dragged
them to the market-place before the rulers. (20) And
bringing them to the magistrates, they said, 'These men
are Jews and they cause trouble in our city, (21) and they
proclaim customs which it is not lawful for us, being
Romans, to adopt or keep'. (22) And the multitude made
a combined assault on them. And the magistrates
tore the clothes off them and commanded them to be
beaten. (23) And when they had laid many stripes on
them, they threw them into prison, charging the warder
to keep them safely; (24) and he, having received such a
charge, thrust them into the inner prison and made their
feet fast in the stocks. (25) But about midnight Paul and
Silas were praying and singing hymns to God, while the
prisoners listened to them. (26) But suddenly there was a
great earthquake so that the foundations of the prison
were shaken; and at once all the doors were opened and
the bonds of all of them were undone. (27) And the
warder awoke and saw the doors of the prison opened,
and he drew his sword and was about to kill himself,
thinking that the prisoners had escaped. (28) But Paul
called in a loud voice and said, 'Do yourself no harm;
for we are all here'. (29) And he called for a light and
sprang in and trembling he fell down before Paul and
Silas. (30) And he conducted them out and said, 'Masters,
what must I do to be saved?' (31) And they said, 'Believe
in the Lord Jesus and you will be saved, you and your
household'. (32) And they spoke the word of the Lord to
him with all that were in his house. (33) And taking them
in that hour of the night he washed their stripes and he

was baptized and all who belonged to him immediately.
(34) And conducting them up into his house he laid a
table and he rejoiced, having made his act of faith in
God with the whole household.

(35) And when it was day, the magistrates sent the
lictors, saying, 'Let those men go'. (36) And the warder
reported the words to Paul, 'The magistrates have sent
that you may be let go; so go now and depart in peace'.
(37) But Paul said to them, 'They have beaten us publicly,
uncondemned, though we are Romans, and have cast us
into prison; and now is it in secret that they cast us out?
Not so; but let them come themselves and lead us out.'
(38) And the lictors reported these words to the magistrates. And they were afraid when they heard that they
were Romans. (39) And they came and begged them and
led them out and asked them to depart from the city.
(40) And when they left the prison, they went to Lydia's
house and saw the brethren and exhorted them and
departed.

(6) **Asia**; Luke meant the Aegean coast near Ephesus rather
than the whole Roman province of Asia (*B.C.* v. 229), a small
part of the modern 'Asia Minor'. (7) The timeless aorist participle suggests that Paul was prevented from preaching in 'Asia'
before, not after, leaving the Phrygian and Galatian region.
Mysia was a proverbially undefined area of north-western Asia
(Minor) south of the Hellespont and Propontis; see Ramsay,
H.D.B. iii. 465. **Bithynia**-Pontus was one administrative district north-east of Mysia; it had been a senatorial province since
74 B.C. The presence of Jews there who (later?) became Christians is indicated in 1 Pet. by the O.T. citations and allusions,
if 1 Pet. i. 1 correctly describes its destination. Paul would
naturally have wished to go to such places as Nicaea, Nicomedia,
and Byzantium itself. **The Spirit of Jesus**, a rare phrase best
attested by B and D; weaker textual evidence supports 'the
Spirit of the Lord' (Armenian, the Holy Spirit); possibly a
prophet speaking in Jesus' name, possibly a vision of the Risen
Lord Himself, or a blinding flash of inward illumination was
the medium of revelation. Nock has noted the crescendo in

vss. 6-10, 'Holy Spirit' . . . 'Spirit of Jesus' . . . 'God' (*Gnomon*, 25, 1953, 497 n.). Paul was not a person to change his plans constantly, cf. 2 Cor. i. 17 ff., except under divine guidance. (8) At first Paul may have felt that his 'guidance' prompted him to return to Syria by sea, but the Gospel was to be brought into Europe. (9) **Man of Macedonia;** the identification with Luke himself is quite conjectural; it may be correct if the tradition of Luke's original connexion with Antioch is false or if Luke made Philippi a second home. Certainly, the next verse opens a we-section, vss. 10-17, but it suggests perhaps that Luke was already in Paul's party. A psychologist might say that the dream was due to Paul's unrealized desire to reach a district like Achaia where Greeks and Jews lived side by side, where adherents to the synagogues promised a ready harvest for the Gospel and where contact with Ephesus and Jerusalem by sea would be easy to maintain. Macedonia had been divided into four districts with republican federative leagues, but since 146 B.C. it was subjected and became a province administered by a propraetor with rank of proconsul; it was commonly connected with the province of Achaia or Greece under its own legate, though it took precedence before it. See W. P. Dickson, *H.D.B.* iii. 196. (11) The wind must have favoured the travellers for another journey from Philippi to Troas in the other direction took five days, xx. 6. **Samothrace,** rising to 5000 feet, was an unforgettable landmark. **Neapolis** (mod. Cavalla), one of the main ports of Macedonia, was at the end of the Via Egnatia which ran to Dyrrachium (Durazzo) on the route to Rome; was it at Neapolis that Paul's hopes were raised to see Rome one day? (12) Some nine miles from Neapolis lay **Philippi,** now deserted, a chief city of the district; Thessalonica or Amphipolis might have claimed such a title more justly, cf. *C.I.G.* 1967; but some MSS., notably Alexandrian, suggest the slight emendation *protēs* for *protē*, 'of the first district', cf. my *Alterations*, 61 f. It is possible that Luke took a local pride in Philippi, cf. above on vs. 10. **A colony** would normally denote a semi-military outpost of Roman veterans enjoying Roman citizenship, and forming the nucleus of the local population. (13) Knox is probably right in saying (*Jerusalem*, 250) that Paul was anxious to press on to Thessalonica and that at first he had no intention of preaching in any but the large centres of civilization. The river mentioned would be the Gangites (Angites) which flows into the Strymon, cf. W. A. McDonald, *B.A.* iii. 1940, 20. **We supposed;** if *enomizeto* is read (for *enomizomen*) as in the Western text, a possible translation is, 'it was usual', i.e. prayer was usually made, cf. Cop^sa. Foreign cults had to be practised 'outside the gate', and Schürer's contention that a synagogue is denoted is unnecessary. (14) If **named** is an interpolation, for 'Lydia' translate 'a Lydian woman'; for Thyateira is in Lydia and Lydia was noted from Homeric times for its purple-dyers, cf. *C.I.G.* 3496 ff. **Worshipped God;** this suggests that she was loosely attached at least to the local synagogue. **Opened her heart;** cf. 2 Macc. i. 4. (15) Cf. the later generosity of the Church in Philippi, Phil. iv. 10, 16. (16 ff.) These verses describe what took place before and after meeting Lydia. **Divination** conveys an allusion to the snake (Python) in which the Pythian god, Apollo, was supposed to be embodied at Delphi. Used in the plural of ventriloquists, as by Plutarch, this word in the singular could denote the serpent slain by Apollo or the place, Pytho being the name of the region in which Delphi lay. Profit; lit. 'work'. (17) **The most High God;** cf. Jewish title for Yahweh, El Elyon; the Greek *Hypsistos* was the name for Yahweh not only among Greek-speaking Jews but also among Gentiles who worshipped Yahweh without accepting all the demands of Judaism; at the same time the name occurs, e.g. on the Bosphorus inscriptions to denote the supreme God of a semi-Jewish, semi-syncretistic cult, cf. *B.C.* v. 93-6. **Salvation;** as deliverance from the powers governing the fate of man or the material world, this was common ground in the cults of the age, cf. Knox, *Jerusalem*, 251. Luke is purposely using language which a pagan could understand but which meant more to a Christian. The we-section concludes at vs. 17; was Luke left behind at Philippi to organize the Church there? If so, Paul picked him up at Troas, xx. 5. (19) Here, as in xix. 23 ff., the pockets of the pagans were affected so that they became hostile to Paul. The *agora* at Philippi has been uncovered; the city prison and civic buildings bordered on it, McDonald, art. cit. 20 ff. **The rulers** normally in a colony like Philippi would be *duoviri* (or elsewhere *quattuorviri*) and *aediles*. (20) **The magis-**

trates would be included among the 'rulers' of vs. 19, as the less general term. The anti-Semitic tone of the accusation is remarkable; new religions were tolerated by the Romans, so long as there was no moral scandal or seditious disturbance in which case the technical charge of proselytizing for Judaism in a colony, i.e. among citizens, would lie. (22) The Greek might mean that the magistrates tore their own clothes, but this is unlikely. (23 ff.) A Form-critic might collect stories of escape from prison and find in them certain features in common, e.g. the security employed, the inmost prison, the stocks or their equivalent, the cheerfulness of the prisoners under adverse conditions, an unexpected deliverance, cf. Acts v. 17 ff., xii. 7 ff., and the *Acts of Thomas*, 154 ff. or Euripides' *Bacchae*, 443 ff. But the form in which a miracle story is told can give no clue at all to its historicity, cf. McNeile, *I.S.N.T.* 2nd ed., ch. iii. 49 ff. (24) **The stocks**, lit. the wood, cf. Euseb. *H.E.* v. 1, 27 (*Letter of the Churches of Vienne and Lyons*). (27) **Awoke;** for the Greek cf. I Es. 3, 3 and Josephus, *Ant.* 11, 3, 2. **To kill himself,** cf. xii. 19. (29) **Sprang in;** the Greek word is not found elsewhere in the N.T. but occurs in the LXX, Amos v. 19. (30) The Western text has an additional line of twenty-four letters, 'having made the rest secure', which adds nothing to our knowledge. (33) **Washed their stripes,** lit. washed them from their stripes, cf. the construction of Heb. x. 22. For this 'sudden Baptism' cf. viii. 36 ff. (34) **Laid a table;** an archaistic expression as old as Homer. (35 ff.) It is striking that in these verses there is no reference to the earthquake, an omission which the Western text of vs. 35 has tried to remedy. Does this lack of reference point to an interpolation of the story of the earthquake into the original account? Not necessarily. (35) **The lictors** or police carried bundles of rods with axes bound together with them by a red fillet. (37) By the Valerian and Porcian laws Roman citizens were exempt from beating; if anyone cried out that he was a Roman citizen, presumably he had to furnish proofs, but what these were is unknown. Such a cry during a mob riot might well go unheeded, cf. 2 Cor. xi. 25, 'Thrice was I beaten with rods'; but in xxii. 24, threatened with the far more terrible scourge, he claimed exemption as a Roman citizen with success. (39) The additional material of the

Western text seems intended to stress the subservience of the magistrates. (40) No mention is made here of the overseers (bishops) and deacons of Philippi, whom Paul mentions in Phil. i. 1. Luke has apparently assumed their appointment and does not mention it on all ocasions.

xvii. 1-15. PAUL IN THESSALONICA AND BEROEA

(1) And journeying through Amphipolis and Apollonia they came to Thessalonica, where there was a synagogue of the Jews, (2) and according to Paul's custom he went in to them and for three sabbath days he reasoned with them from the scriptures, (3) explaining and expounding that it was necessary for Christ to suffer and rise from the dead, and that 'this is the Christ, even Jesus whom I proclaim unto you'. (4) And some of them believed and cast in their lot with Paul and Silas, both a great multitude of worshipping Greeks and not a few of the leading women. (5) But the Jews were filled with envy and took certain wicked men of the market-place mob and collected a crowd and set the city in an uproar and they made an assault on Jason's house and sought to bring them out to the people. (6) But when they did not find them, they dragged Jason and some brethren to the city-rulers, crying out, 'These men who have overturned the world are come here too. (7) And Jason has received them; and all these men act contrary to Caesar's decrees, saying that there is another king, Jesus.' (8) And they disturbed the multitude and the city-rulers who heard this. (9) And they took security from Jason and the rest and they let them go. (10) And the brethren immediately sent Paul and Silas off by night to Beroea; and when they arrived, they went off to the synagogue of the Jews. (11) Now the latter were more noble than those in Thessalonica, for they received the word with all willingness, searching the scriptures daily to see if these things were so. (12) So then many of them made an act

of belief, and not a few of the women of good class and of the men. (13) But when the Jews from Thessalonica knew that in Beroea also the word of God was proclaimed by Paul, they came there too, upsetting and troubling the crowds. (14) And then immediately the brethren sent Paul away as far as to the sea; but Silas and Timothy remained there. (15) But those who conducted Paul brought him as far as to Athens; and receiving a command for Silas and Timothy to come to him as quickly as possible, they went away.

(1) The journey was along the famous Via Egnatia and may have been completed on horseback, thirty miles a day; Amphipolis was about thirty-three miles from Philippi and lay on the river Strymon, and Apollonia was about thirty miles from Amphipolis, which was a leading city in the first region of Macedonia, cf. on xvi. 12. The Western text, which often shows knowledge of the geography, implies a pause at Apollonia. **Thessalonica,** originally Thermē, became the capital of the second region of Macedonia and the seat of the provincial government. It lay thirty-seven miles from Apollonia. There is no inscriptional evidence for the existence of a synagogue there (and the better MSS. speak of 'a' not 'the' synagogue), but there may have been many if the Jews were both numerous there and influential. (Cf. Knox, *Jerusalem*, 261, 270.) (2) We do not know how long Paul was there either before he was asked to preach or after the third Sabbath before he left, but he was probably engaged during the other days too in controversy as well as in earning a living, cf. 1 Thess. ii. 9. **Scriptures;** probably testimonies or proof-texts listed from the O.T. current in Church as pointing to Jesus as Christ. (3) **Explaining;** opening up so as to connect, cf. Luke xxiv. 32; **expounding;** setting side by side and comparing. It is possible that the doctrine of the suffering Messiah was held by some Jews even in pre-Christian days, see on xxvi. 23 below, cf. on iii. 18. The Cross and Resurrection are the heart of the apostolic preaching of Paul as of Peter. Even if Luke was not present, the message of Paul was so familiar that he could drop into direct speech. (4) **Worshipping** (God) may not denote a special class of

adherents of the synagogue. **Leading women;** the Greek could also mean 'wives of the leading men'. (5) **Market-place mob;** the one word in Greek suggests ill-bred loafers of the *agora*, who were liable to be agitators, cf. *B.C.* iv. 204. **Jason** (another form of Joshua or Jesus) had 'received' Paul and, whether a Christian or not, he could be held responsible in some measure for the trouble. (6) **City-rulers;** politarchs. Inscriptions show that Thessalonica had five or six of these rulers, and the technical term used correctly here was one almost peculiar to Macedonia. **Overturned;** cf. xxi. 38, Dan. vii. 23, and Gal. v. 12 as well as P. Mag. Par. 1. 2244; Knox suggests that the Jews expelled from Rome under Claudius (in A.D. 49 if Orosius is correct) were connected with Christianity ('Judaeos impulsore Chresto assidue tumultuantes Roma expulit', says Suetonius) and that the politarchs of Thessalonica knew of the troubles in Rome and were alarmed accordingly. He is probably right too in suggesting that Paul's use of the term 'the Kingdom of God' aroused suspicion of anti-imperial sedition outside Palestine; Paul learned later to avoid this use of 'kingdom' and 'king' in this connexion as it carried to Greek ears the connotation of the Empire and the Emperor. (9) **Took security;** i.e. contracted a legal bond probably, as Ramsay suggests, not to harbour Paul any more (*P.T.R.C.* 231); that this was not the end of the persecution of Christians in Thessalonica is clear from 1 Thess. ii. 14, cf. ii. 3, where the 'hindrance' to Paul may have been this agreement. (10) **Beroea** (mod. Verria) is about fifty miles from Thessalonica; it is in Beroea and Athens that Paul preaches to Gentiles, though in Beroea they are half Jews, and in Athens Paul preached to them as an afterthought. At Verria there is still a Jewish community (McDonald, art. cit. 24). (11) **More noble;** *B.C.* iv. 106, 'more generous'; Moffatt, 'more amenable'. The word is used of good birth but carries the meaning of good manners. The examination of the O.T. scriptures to see if Paul's preaching of Christ agreed with them may have been based on or may have led to a collection of 'Testimonies' made at an early date in the Church. The Western text adds a line of twenty-one Greek letters, 'even as Paul announced'. (12) The theory has been advanced that 2 Thess., with its strong Jewish-Christian arguments and with its O.T. citations, may have been sent to Beroean Christians, while 1 Thess. was sent, perhaps later, to Christians at Thessalonica. The only name of a Beroean Christian known to us is Sopater, cf. xx. 4. The Western text has here 'and of the Greeks and of those of good class many men and women'. This is better grammar and seems a typically Western note to lessen the prominence of women in the Church. (14) The Alexandrian text is intended probably to imply that Paul went to Athens by sea, but the Western text that he went there overland; in the latter text the words for 'sea' (*thalassa*) and 'Thessaly' may have been confused. Silas and Timothy remained at first to establish the community at Thessalonica. (15) The movements of Silas and Timothy recounted here are sometimes contrasted with those reflected in 1 Thess. But (a) Luke was not concerned with details of the movements of the minor characters of his story and (b) it is easy to reconcile both accounts by supposing that Acts xviii. 14 is correct but that they rejoined Paul in Athens, 1 Thess. iii. 1, and that then Timothy returned to Thessalonica (*ibid*. vs. 2) and Silas went elsewhere, possibly to Philippi, while Paul went on to Corinth where both rejoined him (1 Thess. iii. 6, Acts xviii. 5).

xvii. 16-34. PAUL AT ATHENS

(16) But while Paul was waiting for them in Athens, his spirit was stirred in him on seeing the city full of idols. (17) So he reasoned with the Jews and the worshippers in the synagogue and in the market-place every day with those that came his way. (18) But some of the Epicurean and Stoic philosophers encountered him; and some said, 'What would this retailer of scraps say?' But others said, 'He seems to be a herald of strange gods', for he was preaching the good news of Jesus and of the resurrection. (19) And they took hold of him and brought him to the Areopagus, saying 'Can we know what is this new teaching of which you speak? (20) For you bring strange things to our ears; we wish to know therefore what these things

mean.' (21) Now all the Athenians and resident foreigners spent their time on nothing else than to say or to hear something new. (22) But Paul stood in the middle of the Areopagus and said, 'Men of Athens, I perceive that in everything you are somewhat given to religiosity. (23) For as I passed along and saw your objects of worship, I found also an altar on which was written, "To an unknown god". So what you worship without knowing, that I proclaim to you. (24) The God who made the world and all things in it, being Lord of heaven and earth, does not dwell in shrines made with hands. (25) Nor is He served by human hands as though He needed anything, He Himself giving to all life and breath and all things. (26) And He made from one every race of men to dwell on the earth's entire face, having determined appointed epochs and the bounds of their habitation, (27) that they should seek God in the hope that they might feel after Him and find Him; and yet He is not far from each one of us. (28) For in Him we live and move and have our being, as certain also of your poets have said, "For we are also His offspring". (29) Being therefore the offspring of God, we ought not to think that the Godhead is like gold or silver or stone, carved work of the art or imagination of man. (30) So then God overlooked the times of ignorance but now He orders men to repent, all of them everywhere, (31) inasmuch as He has set a day on which He intends to judge the world in righteousness by the man whom He appointed, providing assurance of this to all by raising Him from the dead.'

(32) But when they heard of the resurrection of the dead, some mocked, but others said, (33) 'We will hear you again on this subject'. So Paul departed from their midst. (34) But some men attached themselves to him and made an act of faith; among them also was Dionysius the Areopagite and a woman named Damaris and others with them.

(16) It seems to have been no part of Paul's original plan to preach at Athens, but that while waiting he felt compelled to

do so. Athens had given way politically and commercially to Corinth, though culturally she could live still on her past, remaining the university city *par excellence* of the ancient world, and a 'free and allied city' even under Rome since 146 B.C. Some scholars have maintained extreme positions about this speech, some holding that it is almost a verbatim account of what Paul said and that the references to the Agora, the Areopagus, the Stoics and Epicureans and their philosophies as well as to the city being full of idols and its inhabitants marked by intellectual curiosity are derived from an eye-witness account: while others hold that Luke wanted to place Christianity in the setting of contemporary culture and perhaps from a knowledge of Paul's 'Areopagite' disciple invented the whole story. If the latter theory were true, Luke would have made Paul's success at Athens much more resounding than he does in vs. 34. The truth lies between the two extremes; there is a genuinely historical kernel to the narrative, cf. *B.C.* iv. 208, and Paul's arguments were those which Luke had good reason to believe were the kind of arguments presented by Paul to a Gentile audience as opposed to a Jewish one. Dibelius, who denies the historicity of this speech, finds Paul's indignation at variance with the speech; but as Nock remarks, why should anger have blinded Paul to his duties as a Christian? **Stirred;** cf. Xenophon, *Cyr.* 6. 25. (18) Epicurean philosophers, whose centre at Athens was the 'Garden', were followers of Epicurus (*fl.* 300 B.C.); they believed in the atomic basis of the universe, the atoms being in a state of continuous and fortuitous re-formation, so giving rise to new structures; pleasure (in the best sense) was their aim, in a life free from 'disturbance'. The Stoics followed Zeno (*fl.* 300 B.C.) and owed their name to their meeting in the *Stoa Poikile*; they believed in the eternity of the four elements, earth, air, fire, and water, and they aimed at living 'according to nature'. In practice the ethics of the two schools were similar. **Retailer of scraps;** one who picks up scraps of learning is inadequately described as 'babbler' or 'cock-sparrow', though the Greek means 'seed-picker' and could be used of a rook by Aristotle. **Jesus and the resurrection;** if this was the phrase used by Paul, his hearers may have thought that he spoke of Jesus and Anastasis, two divine beings. (19) The

powers of the ancient court of the Areopagus had been dimin-
ished by the Romans, but it seems that it retained its right to
try cases of murder and questions involving morality and
religion; if it controlled the right of lecturing on religious
matters, it or a committee may well have summoned Paul before
it. But the proceedings seem here to have been informal and
the meeting may have been held on the ancient site, the hill
north-west of the Acropolis, not in the Agora itself where a
formal session of the court was held in the first century. If it
was a formal meeting of the Areopagus as a court, it probably
met not on the hill of Ares or Mars but in the Stoa Basileios in
the Agora; the phrases in vss. 22 and 33, 'in their midst', are
often taken to indicate a formal rather than informal meeting,
though on rather slender evidence. But Luke is probably re-
cording an informal meeting 'before the education commission
of the Areopagus court' (B. Gärtner, *The Areopagus Speech and
Natural Revelation*, 59). **Religiosity;** the noun is used in xxv.
19, where Festus speaks contemptuously and the meaning is
'superstition'. But the adjective here would not be intended
to alienate good-will but to express 'respect for or fear of the
supernatural' (A. Richardson in his *T.W.B.B.* 253). (23) **To an
unknown god;** there is no certain inscriptional or literary
evidence yet discovered for the existence of an altar to an
unknown god (singular) but to unknown gods (plural). To the
latter Pausanias witnesses as having been on the road from
Phalerum to Athens (i. 1. 4 and cf. v. 14. 8) and there is a
well-known altar of the second century from Pergamum, the
fragmentary inscription of which has been taken to mean 'to
(the) unknown gods', though it could also stand for 'to the most
holy gods'. Further, according to Diogenes Laertius (i. 110),
Epimenides the Cretan was summoned to Athens to purify the
city with sacrifices to ward off a pestilence and sheep were
sacrificed, where they rested, to the appropriate god, altars to
unnamed gods being set up. So the pagans protected themselves
against the jealousy and anger of unknown deities. It is possible
that Paul saw such an altar in or near Athens and adroitly used
the singular for the plural in his sermon. For the appeal to
natural revelation (rather than 'natural theology' (Gärtner)) cf.
the speech at Lystra, xiv. 15 ff. **Without knowing,** cf. and

contrast John iv. 22. Gärtner brings out the argument well
(*op. cit.* 238); 'An altar to an unknown God conveys, to Paul,
that the Athenians have acknowledged that God is unknown
to them. He was brought within their ken by His revelations,
which are accessible to all, but the men of Athens have made
Him an unknown God. . . . The whole of their ignorance is
manifested in their worship, particularly when they even erect
an altar to a God Whom they do not know, but Whom they
ought to have known. But now, with the coming of Christ, the
unknown God is made known to all.' (24 ff.) Either Paul or
Luke or both could use 'scholarship Greek prose' as here, when
occasion demanded. As Gärtner shows (*op. cit.* 211) 'made with
hands' had in Old Testament-Jewish texts the connotation of
idolatry, cf. Isa. xvi. 12, LXX, xxi. 9, and of 'nothingness',
cf. 'served by human hands'; cf. also Acts vii. 25, Mark xvii. 24.
Gärtner takes Dibelius to task for minimizing the Old Testament connotation here. (25) In the O.T.-Jewish tradition God
is the preserver of His creation and the God of history, cf.
Gärtner, *op. cit.* 175 ff. It is true that the Epicureans would
have endorsed the first half of this verse, the Stoics the second
half, and that Paul (or Luke) knew that the Greek mind could
play on the words 'Zeus' and '*zoē*' (life). Like Paul's language
in 2 Cor., it is fundamentally Jewish but could appeal also to
the educated Greek. The phrase '*zoē kai pnoē*' ('life and breath')
is striking. The triadic structure of life—breath—all things, cf.
vs. 28, was a common linguistic device in current religious
literature, as Gärtner (*op. cit.* 201) observes, comparing Rom.
xi. 36, to which Norden and Dibelius have failed to adduce
any convincing Stoic 'parallel'. (26) The Western, Syriac, and
Armenian texts have 'blood' after 'one', but the other MSS. are
probably right, 'one' referring to Adam; Bruce (336) notes that
the Athenians boasted that they had sprung from the soil of
their native land; the Jew could claim that he was descended
from Abraham; and the Stoic insisted on the unity of all mankind; but Paul's contrast was between unredeemed man, one
in Adam, and redeemed man, one in Christ, cf. Rom. v. 12-
vi. 11. Dibelius interprets 26b philosophically by eliminating
any reference in epochs (or seasons) and bounds to the course of
history as though Paul is depicted as arguing philosophically

for God's existence from the organization of the seasons and the inhabited zones of the earth; Gärtner rightly rejects this, *op. cit.* 147 ff., and urges that 'historical epochs' is meant, while 'bound' belongs to a land-surveyor's vocabulary and means the boundary-line between two inhabited areas of the earth. 'Both language and content exclude any argument for God's existence here; what we have is a reference to the revelation of God provided in the life of the nations' (Gärtner). Similarly Pohlenz's theory that we should find another argument here of a philosophical kind (that for God's existence, based on the one *e consensu gentium* which was familiar to the Stoics) is to be rejected. At the same time Luke (or Paul) may have purposely used language which the Jew would recognize and yet which the Gentile would find not totally unfamiliar. One point about this verse, and indeed the whole speech, is that in the Greek 'k', 'p', and 't' occur frequently, as if the argument was delivered with 'explosive' force, cf. on vii. 51. (27) At creation God made men to inhabit the earth and to seek Him through obedience, service, and praise; again Gärtner rightly links this thought with the O.T.-Jewish tradition and warns us against reading into the words a philosophical meaning akin to Stoic ideas that man has an innate urge to seek to know God's existence from his knowledge of the world (*op. cit.* 152 ff.). The uncertainty of finding God (vs. 27b) does not accord with Dibelius' philosophical interpretation. Man's quest for God has resulted in ignorance, and this in false worship and idolatry, cf. Rom. i. 18 ff. 'To feel after' denotes the groping and fumbling of a blind man, cf. Isa. lix. 10, Deut. xxviii. 29, Job v. 13, xii. 25, cited by Gärtner. **Not far;** this phrase and the next verse are often explained as Stoic; this passage 'does not merely border on Stoic pantheism, it is nothing else but that' (J.Weiss, *History of Primitive Christianity*, i. 241); cf. Dio Chrysostom's *Olympic Oration*, xii. 28, 'for he is not far from the godhead'. But the connexion may be quite accidental; and Dio Chrysostom's thought as a whole is quite different from that of Acts xvii, cf. Gärtner, *op. cit.* 162 ff. (28) At first sight it seems again that Paul (or Luke) is using Stoic thought, according to which man's reason is derived from God and leads him to find God, even guaranteeing to man the success of his search. Certainly,

'For we also are his offspring' is the fifth line of Aratus'
Phaenomena, though found before him in a poem ('Hymn to
Zeus', 4) of Cleanthes. With far less certainty the phrase 'in
him we live and move and have our being' (the word for 'live'
being a play on 'Zeus') has been treated as a poetic allusion,
cf. K. Lake, *B.C.* v. 246-51; in the Syriac commentary of
Isho'dad of Merv, based probably on the work of Theodore of
Mopsuestia, the following comment is made on the latter phrase
and on 'As certain of your own sages have said'—Paul takes
both of these from certain heathen poets. Now about this, 'In
him we live, etc.; because the Cretans said as truth about Zeus,
that he was a lord; he was lacerated by a wild boar and buried;
and behold, his grave is among us; so therefore Minos, son of
Zeus, made a laudatory speech on behalf of his father; and he
said in it, The Cretans carve a tomb for thee, O high and holy
one! Liars, evil beasts and slow bellies! For thou art not dead
for ever; thou art alive and risen; for in thee we live and are
moved and have our being, so therefore the blessed Paul took
this sentence from Minos; for he took again, We are the offspring of God from Aratus, a poet . . .' This citation includes a
phrase that occurs in Titus i. 12, which is attributed by Clement
of Alexandria to Epimenides the Cretan, who may therefore
have been the author of the whole poem from 'The Cretans
carve' to 'have our being'. However, though some scholars
assign 'in him we live . . . being' to Epimenides writing on the
'tomb of Zeus', perhaps in his poem, *Cretica*, yet M. Pohlenz
has advanced strong reasons for doubting this hypothesis
(*Z.N.T.W.* 42, 1949, 101-4) and Dibelius has now abandoned
the idea that Epimenides is quoted. But the point of the phrase,
even of the Stoic-sounding 'move(d)', is that man depends
entirely on God, the source of life, and the one true God, as
opposed to all idols. The argument is the typically Jewish one
which sets the Creator against the creatures, cf. Rom. i. Man,
the highest form of life on earth, is akin to God and man-made
images cannot be God. (Cf. Gärtner, *op. cit.* 222.) On the text
of this verse see my *Alterations*, 69; 'your poets' may be right,
but the Alexandrian text has 'our'; possibly the word 'poets'
was interpolated; Syr. and Arm. have 'sages'. 'Our' poets might
indicate that Paul was citing consciously a Cilician poet Aratus

or that he was siding with the Greeks against the 'barbarians'. (29) **Gold and silver;** cf. Ps. cxv. 4, Isa. xl. 18, cf. Wisdom xiii. 5. (30 ff.) Burkitt pointed out (*J.T.S.* xv, 1913–14, 462) that the remarkable thing about this famous speech is that for all its wealth of pagan illustration its message is simply the Galilean gospel, 'The Kingdom of God is at hand; repent and believe the tidings'. So far Paul has said little that would offend a Gentile audience; now he goes on to demand repentance from sin and to speak in terms of the Son of Man Christology (without using 'Son of Man'), cf. vii. 56, for Christ will judge the world in righteousness; this part of the speech is in line with 1 Thess. i. 9 ff.; even if Dibelius were right in saying that the speech is at variance with Paul's thought expressed in his letters, could not Paul be 'all things to all men' to save men? (30) **Overlooked,** cf. xiv. 16 and Rom. iii. 25 as well as Rom. i. 18 ff. The worship and knowledge of God go together; failure to accept God's universal self-revelation leads to idolatry; while in Rom. i the culpable nature of man's ignorance is brought out, here God's forbearance is stressed, cf. Gärtner, *op. cit.* 168 f. (31) **A man,** i.e. the 'Son of Man' of the Gospels, a phrase which would have been unintelligible to a Greek audience. Insistence on the coming of the 'Day' appears in all the Pauline letters, even those of the imprisonment; like Peter, cf. x. 42, Paul knew that Christ was future Judge and that this was part of the apostolic faith (but contrast T. F. Glasson, *Hibbert Journal*, 56, 1952–3, 1 ff.). (32) To the Greeks the body was a tomb; the *sōma* was a *sēma*; while some assented to the doctrine of the immortality of the soul, all would have been perplexed or amused by a doctrine of a resurrection of the body, that is, of the whole man. Bruce (*Speeches*, 18) aptly refers to Aeschylus' *Eumenides*, 647 f., where the god Apollo is represented as saying, on the occasion when that very court of the Areopagus was instituted by the city's patron goddess, Athene, 'But when the earth drinks up a man's blood once he has died, there is no resurrection'. (33) It may be incorrect to over-emphasize the 'failure' of Paul's preaching in the university city, but it is true that he went on to Corinth 'in fear and trembling' and that at Corinth he fell back on the central fact of Christ crucified, 1 Cor. i. 20–5, ii. 2. (34) **Dionysius the**

Areopagite; according to Eusebius, *H.E.* iii. 4, 10 and iv. 23, 3, he became bishop of Athens according to his namesake of Corinth (*fl.* A.D. 170); the famous fifth-century writings attributed to him are spurious. **Damaris** (possibly from Damalis, which means 'heifer'); the Western scribe either omits mention of her in keeping with the usual tendency of his text towards women (so D) or like *e* adds '*mulier honesta*', which the scribe of D may have known but omitted, giving the adjective, *euschēmōn*, cf. xvii. 12, to Dionysius instead! The entire sentence in Greek shows a lack of finish out of keeping with the rest of the chapter and indicates an absence of final revision.

xviii. 1-17. PAUL AT CORINTH

(1) **After this he departed from Athens and came to Corinth.** (2) **And finding a certain Jew, named Aquila, of Pontus by race, recently come from Italy, and Priscilla his wife, owing to Claudius having decreed that all Jews should depart from Rome, he approached them,** (3) **and because he was of the same trade he stayed with them and they continued working; for they were tent-makers by trade.** (4) **And he reasoned in the synagogue on every sabbath day and was persuading Jews and Greeks.** (5) **But when Silas and Timothy came down from Macedonia Paul was engaged with the word, testifying to the Jews that the Christ was Jesus.** (6) **And when they withstood and reviled him, he shook out his garments and said to them, 'Your blood be upon your own head; I am clean; from now I shall go to the Gentiles'.** (7) **And he removed from there and came to the house of one named Titius Justus, a worshipper of God, whose house was attached to the synagogue.** (8) **And Crispus, the ruler of the synagogue, made an act of belief in the Lord with all his household; and many of the Corinthians heard and believed and were baptized.** (9) **But the Lord told Paul during the night by means of a vision, 'Fear not but speak and do not keep silent.** (10) **For I am with you and**

nobody will set on you to do you harm; for I have much people in this city.' (11) And he resided for a year and six months, teaching among them the word of God.

(12) But when Gallio was proconsul of Achaia, the Jews set themselves against Paul with one consent, and brought him to the judgement seat, saying, (13) 'This fellow, contrary to the law, is persuading men to worship God'. (14) But when Paul was about to open his mouth, Gallio said to the Jews, 'If it were wrong-doing or knavery, O Jews, it would be reasonable for me to tolerate you. (15) But if the questions are about a word and names and a law that you have, see to it yourselves; for I do not wish to be a judge of these matters.' (16) And he drove them away from the judgement seat. (17) And they all laid hold of Sosthenes, the ruler of the synagogue, and beat him in front of the judgement seat. And Gallio paid no attention to these things.

(1) **Corinth**, the 'Vanity Fair' of the ancient world (A. H. Hunter), was favoured geographically to become a centre of sea and land routes; at Lechaeum, the port on the Corinthian gulf on the west side, cargo could be taken off and shipped again at Cenchreae, the port on the Saronic gulf to the east, or vice versa, so as to avoid the long journey round the Peloponnese. Notorious for its immorality, Corinth had had, according to Strabo, more than 1000 sacred prostitutes attached to the temple of Aphrodite, though, as Knox observes, there is no evidence that this system was restored after the destruction of the original city, and Pausanias (*fl.* second century A.D.) leaves no room for it in his account of Corinth (*Jerusalem*, 276). The problem of the incestuous Christian is discussed in 1 Cor. v and the low moral standards of the city are reflected in the support which the Christian Church there gave at first to the offender. The vast cosmopolitan population could worship in any of the many temples in Corinth, including those put up for the observance of Egyptian mysteries, cf. W. A. McDonald, *The Biblical Archaeologist*, v, 1942, 3, 36-48. It is typical of Paul that he seems to have been more at home working among the Corinthians than he had been in the university city of

Athens. Whereas his Corinthian correspondence tells us much about the Church there, Luke used his material to show either that Christians are the true Israel, as opposed to the persecuting Jews, and that Rome should allow the Church those privileges to the Jews which Julius had confirmed (Josephus, *Ant.* xiv. 10. 2) or that if Rome persecuted the Church, she acted less tolerantly than the wisest of her governors, such as Gallio, a man renowned for his 'sweetness' (Seneca) and his 'wit' (Dio). (2 f.) The Western text has a longer and smoother version than the Alexandrian text. Aquila (Latin, 'Eagle'), like his namesake who translated the O.T., came from Pontus, i.e. Pontus-Bithynia or possibly the more easterly kingdom of Pontus. Priscilla, the colloquial form of Prisca, 1 Cor. xvi. 19, etc., as Paul calls her, is usually placed before her husband as though she were the more influential or more active Christian. There is something to be said for connecting Aquila and Priscilla with those named in the cemetery of the *gens Acilia* in Rome, but less for connecting them with the *gens Pontia*, though it has been suggested that 'of Pontus' may be a mistake for 'of the *gens Pontia*'. They accompanied Paul to Ephesus, xviii. 18, and set up a church-house there, 1 Cor. xvi. 19. Rom. xvi. 3 implies that they returned to Rome, but this chapter may well have been addressed originally to Ephesus, cf. McNeile, *I.S.N.T.*, 2nd ed., 157 f.; 2 Tim. iv. 19, if a genuine Pauline fragment, suggests that they stayed in the east. Claudius' edict is probably that which Suetonius mentions, *Claudius*, 25, 'He drove out from Rome the Jews as they were incessantly causing disturbances, the ringleader being Chrestus', cf. *B.C.* v. 459 ff. According to Orosius (fifth century A.D.) this edict was put out in Claudius' ninth year, i.e. January 25, A.D. 49–January 24, 50, which may well be correct whatever Orosius' source may have been. Dio Cassius (lx. 6. 6) reports that the large number of Jews made the decree ineffective. Perhaps Chrestus was the name of a person or a mistake for 'Christ', in which case the riots may have been between Jews and Christians; if Christians were already in Rome by A.D. 49, they had probably reached the capital in the course of trade and business; Acts does not relate the conversion of Aquila and Priscilla, who were probably Christians, not Jews, when Paul met them. (3) **Tent-makers;**

or more generally 'leather-workers', working with the famous
Cilicium, goat-hair cloth of Cilicia, as the reading of *h* suggests
(see my *Alterations*, 76); the omission of 'for they were tent-
makers', twenty-four letters in Greek, in D gig. is probably an
early omission of a whole line by accident. It is possible that the
trio had a shop 'not far from the point where the road from
Lechaeum led into the market-place' (McDonald, *op. cit.* 39).
(4) **The synagogue;** Deissmann (*L.A.E.* 16, n. 7) reproduces
the relics of a crude inscription over the door of a synagogue
at Corinth, dated 'with some reservation' between 100 B.C. and
A.D. 200, meaning, 'Synagogue of the Hebrews', but as
McDonald says (*op. cit.* 41), 'The careless style of the lettering
indicates that the inscription, and presumably the synagogue to
which it belonged, is considerably later than the time of Paul'.
Though it is not unreasonable to suppose that a synagogue
existed in the same area, no existing foundations have yet been
associated convincingly with the lintel. (5) **Engaged with;**
more than once the Philippian converts helped Paul financially,
cf. Phil. iv. 15 ff.; if this was such an occasion, Paul was set
free to concentrate on preaching instead of earning a living as
well. (6) **Shook out,** cf. on xiii. 51; he repudiated them as
heathen. **Blood . . . head,** cf. 2 Sam. i. 16, Matt. xxvii. 25.
(7) To remain in contact with adherents of the synagogue, Paul
stayed near by. Titius Justus; 'Titius' arose perhaps from the
last two letters of *onomati*, by name, being repeated by dittography (Ropes, *B.C.* iii. 173), cf. D, etc. But, as Goodspeed
says, *onomati* is absent from A, the chief ancient support for
the omission of Titius and the full name was Gaius (*praenomen*)
Titius (*nomen*) Justus (*cognomen*); Goodspeed identifies him
with the Gaius of Rom. xvi. 23, *J.B.L.* 69, 1950, 382 f. Later
scribes changed Titius to Titus, the easier reading, with ℵ, or
omitted the word altogether, on this view. But does the full
name imply Roman citizenship? Cf. on vs. 15 below. (8)
Crispus was one of the Corinthians whom Paul baptized, cf.
1 Cor. i. 14 where he implies that his own main task was to preach,
while his companions, no doubt, baptized for him, cf. John iv. 2.
Ruler of the synagogue, cf. on xiii. 15. **Act of belief;**
once again the tense implies a single act, no doubt, of baptism.
(11 f.) The date of **Gallio's** proconsulship is fixed fairly exactly

by the Delphi and other inscriptions, cf. Introduction, 11 A (2). It provides the chronological centre-point for Paul's life. The restored text of the four fragments of the inscription is given in *B.C.* v. 461, and allowing for the fact that we do not know how long Paul's stay overlapped with Gallio's or when exactly in the latter's term of office Paul appeared before him, we may suppose that Paul's trial took place between the summer of A.D. 51 and a year later or that of 52 and a year later. If vss. 11-12 imply that Paul arrived in Corinth a year and six months before Gallio, Paul probably reached there in the spring of 49 or of 50. (12) **Gallio,** son of the elder Seneca and adopted son of the wealthy Lucius Junius Gallio, was brother of Mela, father of the poet Lucan; he was brother also of Lucius Seneca, the philosopher and the tutor of Nero. Gallio's illness at Corinth, his subsequent consulship, his voyage to Egypt to ward off the threat of consumption, his initially successful pleading for his own life when Nero put Seneca to death, but his eventual fall and death at Nero's command lie outside the scope of this commentary. **Proconsul;** it says much for Luke's accuracy that he names the titles of officials accurately, cf. Introduction, 9; Achaia was governed by a proconsul from 27 B.C.–A.D. 15 and from A.D. 44 onwards. **Judgement seat;** McDonald, *op. cit.* 44, suggests that this was the well-built stone platform at the central point of the Agora and beneath a Christian church and not the Bēma of the official audience chamber, which may have been the Basilica behind the south Stoa. (13) **The law;** Jewish or Roman? Knox, *Jerusalem,* 279, favours the former emphatically in view of the normal use of *nomos* for the Torah in the N.T. (15) A judge deals with acts not with verbiage about names (or is this a reference to titles, e.g. 'Messiah'?) or with the 'law' of a subject people. If there had been any evidence that Roman citizens had been converted at Corinth, Gallio could not have spoken thus; but there was no law against proselytizing among provincials. The importance of Gallio's decision was profound; had the verdict gone against Paul, the Jews could have quoted it against him from Jerusalem to Rome, cf. Knox, *ibid.* 267. (17) The obscurity of this verse suggests a lack of final revision; who was Sosthenes? Who beat him? And why? The name is comparatively rare, and he probably is the Sosthenes of 1 Cor. i. 1 and a Christian when that epistle was penned. All may mean the Jews who took vengeance on a prominent Jew who was attracted to Christianity, when they could not punish Paul, or it may mean the Greeks, who were encouraged by Gallio's attitude to work off an anti-Semitic prejudice. *B.C.* iv. 228 suggests, improbably, that both Jews and Greeks beat him. The Western text reads 'all the Greeks'. Gallio paid no attention; he was completely impartial. This does not mean that he was superciliously indifferent, as the proverbial phrase suggests to modern ears, 'Gallio cared for none of these things'.

xviii. 18-28. PAUL'S BRIEF VISIT TO SYRIA AND PALESTINE

(18) But Paul, after waiting yet for many days, bade farewell to the brethren and sailed off to Syria (and with him Priscilla and Aquila), having had his head shaved in Cenchreae, for he had a vow. (19) And they went down to Ephesus and he left them there. And he himself went into the synagogue and reasoned with the Jews. (20) And when they asked him to stay longer, he refused, (21) but bade farewell, and said, 'I shall return to you again, if God is willing', and he set sail from Ephesus. (22) And he came down to Caesarea and he went up and saluted the church and went down to Antioch. (23) And after passing some time there, he went away, going through the Galatian country and Phrygia in order, strengthening all the disciples. (24) And a Jew named Apollos, an Alexandrian by race, a learned man, mighty in the scriptures, came down to Ephesus. (25) He was instructed in the way of the Lord; and being fervent in spirit, he spoke and taught accurately the things about Jesus, knowing only the baptism of John. (26) And he began to speak boldly in the synagogue. And when they heard him, Priscilla and Aquila took him and expounded to him more accurately the way of God. (27) And when

he wanted to cross over into Achaia, the brethren encouraged him and wrote to the disciples to receive him.
When he arrived there, he contributed greatly to those
who had believed through grace. (28) For he refuted the
Jews with vigour, in public, showing by the scriptures
that the Christ was Jesus.

(1 ff.) It is possible, though not certain, that Luke, anxious
to get Paul from Corinth to Ephesus and at the same time
to show that the Jerusalem Church agreed with his missionary
aims, interpolated vss. 18-23 on the basis of Paul's last visit
to Jerusalem. The Western text shows an assimilation of this
passage to the other, the similarities having been noticed. Some
critics maintain that Paul is unlikely on two occasions to have
fulfilled a vow at Jerusalem or to have paid two visits both
clouded over with the sense of his coming doom; others add
that the motive of an insertion here may have been to attribute
to Paul a larger part in the formation of the Church in Ephesus
than he had, in fact, or to present the relations between Paul and
the Church in Antioch in a more favourable light than they had
been since his quarrel with Barnabas. At the same time it is
not unlikely that Paul did pay two such visits and that on each
occasion a vow was performed, cf. *B.C.* iv. 229. Even so, Luke's
account is extremely condensed. One reason for this may have
been that Paul wished perhaps to arrange secretly with James
and other leading Christians in Jerusalem for his collection from
his converts for the mother-church, which would serve as a
cement to bind the Jewish-Christians to the Gentile-Christians,
cf. Knox, *Jerusalem*, 284 ff. Another reason may have been that
Luke no longer accompanied Paul, having been left at Philippi,
cf. xx. 6, and so in after days Luke had no clear recollection of
Paul's visit on this occasion. (18) **His head shaved;** whose?
Probably Paul's, though the Greek might be taken to point to
Aquila's, as *h* apparently took it. Priscilla and Aquila were to
set up a church-house in Ephesus, becoming fellow-workers
with Paul who 'risked their lives' for him, cf. Rom. xvi. 3 f.
Cenchreae, cf. on xviii. 1, cf. Rom. xvi. 1; there was a Church
there of which Phoebe was deaconess; from the Church in
Corinth under Paul the gospel had gone out widely, unless Rom.

xv. 19 is a pardonable exaggeration. **A vow,** cf. Num. vi. 5, 18, the Priestly writer did not regard a Nazirite vow as lifelong, any more than Paul; contrast pre-exilic practice. Despite scanty evidence for the cutting of the hair at the beginning and not at the end of the period of the vow, this seems to have been the custom followed here by Paul, or assumed to have been followed by him by Luke, who suggests that Paul was as a result in haste to reach Jerusalem, vs. 20, cf. the Western text of vs. 21. Paul's vow would prove to his colleagues at Jerusalem that he remained a good Jewish-Christian. (19) **Ephesus,** the chief market or business centre of Asia Minor 'this side of the Taurus' (Strabo, xiv. 1, 24) was the largest city in the very wealthy (Roman) province of Asia. On the trade routes between east and west, it was the centre also of the worship of Artemis (Diana); cf. Ramsay, *H.D.B.* i. 720; J. T. Wood, *Discoveries at Ephesus,* 1877; M. M. Parvis, *B.A.* vii, 1945 (with F. V. Filson), 61-80. (21) The Western text has an addition which may be a correct note, 'I must at all costs keep the coming feast at Jerusalem'. (22) **The church;** at Caesarea? at Jerusalem? Probably the latter, as the phrase 'went down to Antioch' indicates, cf. Knox, *Jerusalem,* 289, who calls it a grotesque misunderstanding to suppose that Caesarea is meant; however, it may be urged that if Paul went to Jerusalem, his doings there would have been recorded and that, as Streeter said, the word for 'going up' by itself can hardly mean to the capital (*J.T.S.* xxxiv, 1933, 237). It is usual to take this and the following verses to point to the beginning of the 'third missionary journey', but as Menoud has said, there is room for serious doubt whether this division corresponds to Luke's plan (*New Testament Studies,* i, 1954, 44 ff.); Menoud takes the journey from Jerusalem, xv. 30, to Jerusalem again, xxi. 15, to be a single one. (23) **The Galatian country and Phrygia;** cf. on xvi. 6 above; Knox (*Jerusalem,* 238) argues that this phrase does not indicate exactly the same region as that of xvi. 6; as far as Pisidian Antioch the route may have been the same as before, but from that point St. Paul, instead of turning north-west, may have gone straight in a westerly direction till he reached Ephesus, though Lake suggests that the phrase here is a mere stylistic variation of that in xvi. 6 (*B.C.* v. 239). There is no need, with the exponents of the North Galatian hypothesis, to suppose that Paul visited the country around Ancyra, Pessinus, or Tavium or that the words, 'the upper country', xix. 1, mean that. 'Strengthening all the disciples' refers to the converts made in and near Antioch, Lystra, Iconium, and Derbe. (24 ff.) Little is known of the arrival of Christianity in Alexandria or the rest of Egypt, and it would be rash to accept Professor Brandon's contention that the Jewish-Christians fled to Alexandria in A.D. 70. But from the studies in the Jung Codex by Puech, Quispel, and van Unnik and to judge from the commentaries on the Fourth Gospel by Gnostic Christians there in the second century A.D. as well as from the papyrological discoveries of the same date of the Fourth Gospel or of Gospel 'mosaics', it would seem that a form of Christianity was known there at least early in the second century. Acts, here and in xix. 1-7, implies that there were 'disciples' in Alexandria and elsewhere who knew something of the faith about Jesus but not of the doctrine of Baptism into Him or of the gift of the Spirit through Baptism, being familiar only with the baptism of John the Baptist. It may be that in some early Church circles the latter conferred the status of 'disciple' loosely and that Luke or his source was aware of this conception, cf. Appendix 3. Hence the term 'disciples', xix. 1, and hence too the omission of any mention of Apollos' baptism here, unless that is assumed by Luke. **Apollos;** the text of D has Apollonius, which is derived probably from the Latin side, d. Some Alexandrian MSS., including ℵ, read Apelles here, but this is a mere assimilation to Rom. xvi. 10. **Learned;** or educated; this word came to have a secondary meaning, 'eloquent', in the first century A.D. **Scriptures;** i.e. the Old Testament; from Luther to T. W. Manson the suggestion has found favour that Apollos was the author of the Epistle to the Hebrews, with its arguments based on the Old Testament Tabernacle and sacrificial system. (27) The visit of Apollos to Achaia is corroborated by 1 Cor. i-iv, where Paul contrasts the wisdom of God with that of men (including Apollos) and where Paul denounces party strife, a party having formed around Apollos, as around Cephas and around Paul, 1 Cor. i. 12, cf. iii. 6, iv. 9. The Western text gives a revision of this verse, probably on the basis also of

1 Cor. xvi. 12. (28) **Scriptures;** this again would point to the use of proof-texts from the O.T. and their surrounding contexts, cf. C. H. Dodd, *According to the Scriptures,* which were probably in current usage in the Church. The testimonies taken to point to Jesus formed a solid core of Messianic teaching for those who were 'more accurate' about the 'Way'. It is not unreasonable to suppose that Apollos used the allegorical methods of interpretation which Alexandrian scholars had applied to Homer and to Philo. J. H. A. Hart (*J.T.S.* vii, 1905, 16-28) suggests that Apollos elaborated the parallels between the Old and the New Israel; 'As the deliverance of the Old Israel was effected, under God, by two leaders, so it was now at Corinth. In his anxiety to render an honour to St. Paul, Apollos naturally represented himself as another Aaron, the mere mouthpiece of the second Moses. Pharoah, who knew not the Lord and hardened his heart, was present in the person of the unbelievers—Jews and Greeks—who persecuted the faithful. With them were the wise men (Exod. vii. 11) and the scribes (*ibid.* vs. 6) standing by to deride the folly of the tongue-tied preacher, who could only repeat, again and again, his naked message, the proclamation of the crucified Messiah. And, as of old, God's despicable envoys triumphed over the magicians and their taskmasters.' It is possible that Luke had Exod. vii in mind when he wrote this section.

xix. PAUL IN EPHESUS

(1) And it came to pass that while Apollos was in Corinth, Paul went through the upper regions and came to Ephesus and found some disciples, (2) and he said to them, 'Did you receive (the) Holy Spirit when you made your act of belief?' And they said, 'Why, we have not heard even if there is a Holy Spirit'. (3) And he said, 'Into what then were you baptized?' And they said, 'Into the baptism of John'. (4) And Paul said, 'John baptized with a baptism of repentance, telling the people to believe on the one coming after him, that is, on Jesus'. (5) And

when they heard, they were baptized into the name of the Lord Jesus. (6) And when Paul laid hands on them, the Holy Spirit came upon them and they spoke with tongues and prophesied. (7) And the men were in all about twelve.

(8) And he went into the synagogue and spoke boldly for three months, reasoning and advancing what concerns the kingdom of God. (9) And when some were hardened and disbelieved, speaking evil of the Way before the multitude, he set himself apart from them and separated the disciples, reasoning daily in the hall of one Tyrannus. (10) This took place for two years so that all that dwelt in Asia heard the word of the Lord, both Jews and Greeks. (11) They were no ordinary miracles that God wrought by Paul's hands, (12) so that handkerchiefs and aprons were carried off from his body even for the sick, and diseases were driven away by them and evil spirits came forth. (13) And some also of the wandering Jews, exorcists, tried to name over those that had evil spirits the name of the Lord Jesus, saying, 'I adjure you by Jesus whom Paul preaches'. (14) And there were seven sons of one Sceva, a Jew, a high priest, who did this. (15) But the evil spirit answered and said to them, 'Jesus I know and Paul I know, but who are you?'. (16) And the man in whom was the evil spirit leaped on them and dominated all of them and prevailed against them, so that they fled naked and wounded from that house. (17) And this became known to all the Jews and Greeks who dwelt at Ephesus. And fear fell on them all and the name of the Lord Jesus was magnified. (18) And many of those that had made an act of belief came, confessing and reporting their magic spells. (19) And many of those that practised magic arts collected their books and burnt them before them all. And they reckoned the price and found it fifty thousand drachmas. (20) So powerfully did the word of the Lord increase and prevail.

(21) And when this was completed, Paul purposed in spirit to pass through Macedonia and Achaia and to go

to Jerusalem, saying, 'After I have been there, I must see Rome also'. (22) And he sent into Macedonia two of those who ministered to him, Timothy and Erastus, and he himself spent time in Asia. (23) And about that time there was no small disturbance about the Way. (24) For one Demetrius, a silversmith, who made silver shrines of Artemis, provided no little profit for the craftsmen. (25) He called them together and workmen engaged in similar ways and said, 'Men, you know that by this business we have our wealth. (26) You both see and hear that not only at Ephesus but almost throughout all Asia this fellow Paul has persuaded and perverted a large crowd, saying that they are not gods that are hand-made. (27) Not only do we have this trade in danger of being exposed but also the shrine of the great goddess Artemis is in danger of being reckoned at nothing and her greatness in danger of being destroyed, she whom all Asia and the world worship.' (28) And when they heard it and were seized with anger, they began to cry out, 'Great is Artemis of the Ephesians'. (29) And the city was filled with confusion. And they rushed with one accord to the theatre, seizing Gaius and Aristarchus, Macedonians, Paul's travel-companions. (30) And when Paul wanted to enter among the populace, the disciples did not let him. (31) But some of the Asiarchs also, being friendly to him, sent to him and begged him not to commit himself to the theatre. (32) But different people uttered different cries; for the assembly was in confusion and the majority did not know why they had come together. (33) And from the crowd they prompted Alexander, the Jews thrusting him forward. And Alexander motioned with his hand and wanted to make his defence to the people. (34) But when they realized that he was a Jew, a single cry went up from them all as they shouted for about two hours, 'Great is Artemis of the Ephesians'. (35) And when the town clerk had pacified the crowd, he said, 'Men of Ephesus, what man is there who does not know that the city of the Ephesians is the temple keeper of the great Artemis and of the image which fell from Zeus? (36) So,

as these points cannot be contradicted, it is necessary
for you to be pacified and to do nothing rash. (37) For
you have brought these men, who are neither temple-
robbers nor blasphemers against our goddess. (38) If then
Demetrius and his fellow-craftsmen have a case against
anyone, courts are held and there are proconsuls; let
them accuse each other. (39) But if you pursue some
other matter, it shall be settled in the lawful assembly.
(40) For actually we are in danger of being charged in
connection with this day's revolt, there being no cause
for it; and we shall not be able to give an account about
it in connection with this gathering.' (41) And when he
had said this, he dismissed the assembly.

(1 ff.) Many readers would agree with Knox (*Jerusalem*,
309) that this section is of poor quality, however vivid, as compared with the general level of the book; the reason that Knox
suggests is that Luke may have expected his readers to be
interested for local reasons in Paul's labours in Ephesus but
had no means of obtaining better information. A Form-critic
might say that the preceding incident in xviii. 24 ff. with its
reference to one who had known only the baptism of John
suggested the insertion here of xix. 1-7. It is certainly strange
that Luke tells us comparatively little of Paul's Ephesian
ministry but selects this story. It is only from 1 Corinthians and
other Pauline epistles that the situation facing Paul at Ephesus
can be reconstructed. *B.C.* iv. 235 f., while stressing rightly that
Luke's interest throughout this chapter lay in 'the supernatural
power of Christianity and its obvious rightness, as witnessed by
the highest Gentile authorities, in its disputes with the Jews
and with the Greek rabble', makes the most of the apparent
discrepancies between Acts and the Pauline epistles here.
Certainly, Luke's account of Paul's sufferings at Ephesus
would have been welcome, cf. 2 Cor. i. 8, iv. 9 ff., vi. 4 ff., xi.
23 ff., cf. 1 Cor. xv. 28 ff. And Luke makes no mention of a
'flying-visit' paid to Corinth apparently by Paul from Ephesus
before his 'severe letter', cf. 2 Cor. xii. 14, ii. 1; ii. 4, vii. 8 f.
(See McNeile, *I.S.N.T.* 2nd ed., 139-42.) Nor does Luke
mention many of the twenty-seven Christians named in Rom.

xvi. (1-16), a chapter probably sent to the Church in Ephesus (cf. McNeile, *ibid.* 157 f.).

(1) Ramsay took the **upper country** to mean the more hilly route from Pisidian Antioch to Ephesus, passing through Trallia. But though this is possible, it is not necessary; xix. 1 picks up xviii. 23; the words of Col. ii. 1 are sometimes taken to mean literally that Paul had not even passed through the Lycus valley. 'Upper country' probably means the region above and behind Ephesus; it does not denote the North Galatian district, nor is the adjective to be called a medical word, despite Hobart, *The Medical Language of St. Luke*, 1882, 148, even if it could be used in connexion with emetics! (2) Cf. on xviii. 24 ff. above. The Western text softens the reply thus, 'We have not even heard that some receive Holy Spirit'. (4) It is probable that when Acts and the Fourth Gospel were written, John the Baptist's followers had a strong and compact group in and near Ephesus; there was need to show that the Baptist was inferior to Jesus and that the influence of the former had to 'decrease' if that of Jesus was to 'increase'. (5) The inept Western addition 'for remission of sins' overlooks that John's Baptism had been for this. (6) As with the converts at Samaria, viii. 14 ff., so here Baptism is followed by the laying on of hands by an apostle, and that in turn by the gift of the Holy Spirit, cf. Appendix 3. There is no indication here that Luke took 'speaking with tongues' to mean the gift of foreign languages rather than ecstatic utterance, cf. on ii. 4 ff. Lampe, *op. cit.* 75 f., would see in the laying on of hands here as elsewhere an indication of yet another decisive moment in missionary history; Ephesus was the centre of the Gentile mission and the laying on of hands would be the token of association in the apostolic or missionary work of the Church. If Lampe's suggestion is right, is the number 'twelve' in the next verse significant? Luke's favourite 'about' with numbers may be disregarded. Does this section point to the existence of a primitive 'college' of Twelve at Ephesus, reorganized perhaps by Paul, who governed the Church there? (8) **advancing;** lit. 'persuading'. **The kingdom of God;** Paul did not normally use this phrase, intelligible enough as it was in Palestine, as he went farther westwards, cf. on xvii. 6. *B.C.* iv. 239 recognizes that here the phrase may be

used either in its eschatological sense or as a synonym for the Christian Church. Probably it includes both, Christ being the fulfilment of the promised Kingdom, though its future consummation is still awaited, and the Church being an integral part of the good news about the Kingdom, cf. Appendix 2. (9) **Hardened;** the same verb is used as in Exod. vii. 3 of the hardening of Pharaoh's heart. **Hall;** presumably a familiar lecture-hall owned or used by one Tyrannus. A famous Western reading here of (probably) twenty-two letters in the Greek, runs, 'from the fifth to the tenth hour', i.e. during the siesta from 11 A.M. to 4 P.M., cf. Martial iv. 8. This may be an original line of about twenty-two letters which has dropped out, but cf. my *Alterations*, 63 f., cf. Dibelius and Kümmel, *Paulus*, 74. **Two years;** during this period Christianity spread probably to the churches in the Lycus valley, Epaphras being the missioner sent by Paul, cf. Col. i. 7 (Alexandrian reading) and also to the seven Churches of Asia, Rev. i. 9-iii. 22. G. S. Duncan (*St. Paul's Ephesian Ministry*) has maintained that Paul was imprisoned three times at Ephesus and that all the 'captivity epistles' were written from there and not from Rome. Contrast C. H. Dodd, *B.J.R.L.* 24, 1934, 72 ff. (12) **Handkerchiefs,** a word from the Latin *sudarium*, sweat-rag, and **aprons,** from the Latin *semi-cinctium*, apron, would be used by Paul in his trade as a leather-worker or tent-maker. Like the tassel of Jesus' garment or the shadow of Peter, so Paul's possessions conveyed healing power, cf. Luke viii. 44, Acts v. 15. (13) For Jewish exorcists, cf. Matt. xii. 27, Luke xi. 19 (Q), and for those using Jesus' name cf. Mark ix. 38-41, Luke ix. 49 f. A Paris magical papyrus has the following: 'I adjure thee by the God of the Hebrews, Jesus'. Later, Rabbis condemned the use of the name of Jesus by exorcists. (14) **Seven;** this may not be correct, since the word translated 'all' in vs. 16 usually means 'both' in Greek, though in late Greek the meaning 'all' is found, cf. *B.C.* iv. 242. Perhaps 'seven' came in as a marginal note, 'z̄' meaning 'Query', and was later put into the text as a numeral, 7 (A. C. Clark, *Acts*, 370 ff.), or perhaps 'Skeua' gave rise to the Hebrew form for 7, Sheva' (Moulton and Milligan, *V.G.T.* 577a), unless a note 'Skepsai' = 'check' came to form 'Sceva' in the text, cf. *B. of B.C.* xi. 14 and xii. 77. Otherwise one must suppose that only two of the seven sons were actually attacked by demons. **A high priest;** this is the reading of the Alexandrian text and of P³⁸, the Michigan papyrus (which usually supports D, though it omits 'Sceva', having 'Jews' instead) against the simple 'priest' of D, which is due probably to the Latin '*sacerdos*' of *d*. We are not told that Sceva himself was at Ephesus nor that he was a Jewish high-priest, though this is usually assumed; but B. E. Taylor (*E.T.* lvii. 8, 1945-6, 222) quotes from Mommsen's *Provinces of the Roman Empire*, 1, 345 ff., to show that Ephesus had not only Asiarchs but also pagan high-priests like other Asian cities. Their duty was to supervise the emperor-cult and temple-worship. Sceva may well have been a renegade Jew. (15) The two words translated 'know' differ in Greek, but the distinction sometimes made between knowing by hearsay and knowing personally cannot be pressed. (17) The Form-critic might say that this is a typical ending on a note of awe which marks the 'Novellen' or miracle-tales; it is, however, likely to be true and a story of this kind told in popular form is likely to relate this 'fear', though *B.C.* iv. 242 suggests that vss. 17-20 are editorial. (18) The verb for **confess** is sometimes used of praising God and sometimes, as here, of confessing sins, cf. Mark i. 5, Matt. iii. 6. **Spells,** lit. practices, but the word is used in two magical papyri of magic spells. (19) **Magic arts;** *perierga*, Lat. *curiosa*, cf. Plutarch, Alexander, 2. Ephesus was noted for magic, the books containing magic incantations being called 'Ephesian writings', cf. Bruce, 360. The word **drachmas** has to be supplied.

(21) Luke intends to make it clear that Paul was not forced to leave Ephesus by the riot; he had intended to do so before. **Rome;** the Epistle to the Romans, despite the omissions in G *g*, was addressed to the Church in Rome, cf. Rom. i. 11-15, xv. 23 f.; written about A.D. 57, it shows that Paul then hoped to visit Rome and Spain. (22) **Timothy,** last mentioned in xviii. 5 (at Corinth), probably joined Paul in Ephesus, returning to Corinth, 1 Cor. xvi. 10 f., later. **Erastus,** cf. Rom. xvi. 23, 'Erastus, the city treasurer' (of Corinth). 2 Tim. iv. 20 also mentions an Erastus who remained at Corinth. He may be identified, according to some scholars, with the Erastus who was aedile at Corinth according to an inscription discovered

there, 'ERASTUS . PRO . AED . S . P . STRAVIT', cf. *B.A.* v, 1942, 3, 46; 'Erastus, in return for his aedileship laid (this pavement) at his own expense'. (23) **About that time**; probably towards the end of his stay at Ephesus. (24) **Silver shrines**; B omits 'silver', no doubt by accident. Votive terra-cotta and marble shrines in miniature with the goddess Artemis inside certainly existed and perhaps also silver ones, cf. Deissmann's reference to an inscription at Ephesus according to which C. Vibius Salutaris presented a silver image of Artemis to be put in the assembly (*L.A.E.* 112 ff.). However, according to E. L. Hicks, *Expositor* i, 1890, 401 ff., 'shrine-maker' (*neōpoios* or *naopoios*) was a technical term for a warden of the temple at Ephesus; if so, Luke may have been led quite naturally to mistake the meaning of this word, if he was not at Ephesus with Paul. Hicks went on to identify the Demetrius here mentioned in Acts with Demetrius a *neōpoios* mentioned in an inscription dated *c.* A.D. 50. **Artemis**; cf. L. R. Taylor, *B.C.* v. 261-6, who says, 'She seems to have been a form of the great Asiatic mother-goddess, a divinity of fertility'; she acquired the name and many of the attributes of Artemis (the Roman Diana), the maiden huntress. Artemis Ephesia is commonly thought to be represented on images as a many-breasted goddess; cf. the plates showing such statues reproduced by R. Tonneau, *R.B.* xxxviii. 29, 5-34 and 321-63. But Seltman suggests that the protuberances originally depicted clusters of dates ('The Wardrobe of Artemis', in *Numismatic Chronicle*, 1952, 33-51). (27) **Shrine**; the temple of Artemis had been one of the seven ancient wonders of the world; a reconstruction of the west portico and a plan of the temple are reproduced in *B.A.* viii, 1945, 3, 65 and 67 by M. M. Parvis, cf. J. T. Wood, *Discoveries at Ephesus*, 1877, and D. G. Hogarth, *The Archaic Artemisia*, 1908. The capacity of the temple has been variously estimated as 56,000 (Renan), 50,000 (Jacquier), 23,000 (Navarre), cf. Tonneau, art. cit. 19. (29) **Gaius** was probably from Doberus, a place in Macedonia, cf. the Western text of xx. 4; like Aristarchus, he could be called a Thessalonian. (31) **Asiarchs**; Luke gives the correct title for these anually elected officers as literary and inscriptional evidence corroborates, cf. L. R. Taylor, *op. cit.*, who describes them as the foremost men of the province of

Asia, chosen from the wealthiest and most aristocratic inhabitants of the province. She goes on to show that probably before Paul's time some Asiarchs were 'chief-priests' of the cult of the Emperor, cf. on xix. 14 above, and all the latter were Asiarchs; later the two titles became more or less synonymous. Luke loses no opportunity of stressing the friendliness of the authorities to St. Paul or the Gospel. (32)· **The assembly** (*ekklesia*); did Luke have in mind a properly constituted assembly or a riotous meeting? Did the town clerk treat the latter as though it were the former? Or was Luke being ironical in using the legal term? (33) **From the crowd;** or 'some of the crowd'; for Luke this is careless Greek. **Prompted;** this may be the correct translation for *sumbibazo*, but the Western text has *detraxerunt*, 'pulled down'. The normal sense of the Greek is 'bring together', 'instruct', or 'infer', cf. ix. 22. The textual variants point to scribal bewilderment. An **Alexander** is mentioned in 1 Tim. i. 19 f. as one who had rejected conscience and made shipwreck of the faith; cf. 2 Tim. iv. 14, 'Alexander the copper-smith did me much evil'. If these are genuine fragments of Pauline writings, they may well refer to the Alexander of this context. Was he a Jew put up by the Jews in Ephesus to distinguish between Judaism and Christianity? And is the obscurity here in Luke's narrative due to his desire to claim for the Christians the privileges accorded to Judaism? (34) B (alone) has the cry twice, 'Great is Artemis of the Ephesians' at this point, probably owing to dittography. (35) The **town clerk,** scribe of the *demos* or people's secretary, was a most influential figure in Ephesian political life, cf. A. H. M. Jones, *The Greek City*, 1940, 239. **Temple keeper** had been a title of individuals, e.g. of a Jewish temple keeper attached to a synagogue in Egypt. A well-known inscription from Priene mentions one who was a temple keeper of Artemis in Ephesus, cf. *C.I.G.* 2972. Other cities of Asia were given this title as keepers of the imperial cultus and in the second century A.D. at least Ephesus was doubly temple keeper, both of the emperor's cult and of Artemis. **The image which fell from Zeus** or from the sky was probably a meteorite, which could be claimed at least to be of superhuman workmanship; meteorites were venerated by Greeks and Romans; there was one even in a synagogue at

Abydos (*E.R.E.* x. 371), cf. Ramsay, *H.D.B.* i. 605. The claims of the town clerk were justified not only by the temple of Artemis being the biggest bank in Asia Minor but by relics also of the worship of Artemis Ephesia in more than thirty places outside that city and by the fact that she was worshipped more widely by private persons than any other deity known to Pausanias, iv. 31. 8. (37) **Temple-robbers,** cf. Rom. ii. 22. (38) **Courts;** lit. market-days or market-assemblies, and so the assizes held on those days. The proconsul or his delegate would preside; Luke uses the plural, **proconsuls,** perhaps because the successor to M. Junius Silvanus had not entered yet on his office, Silvanus having been poisoned, thanks to Agrippa, in A.D. 54. (39) The **lawful assembly** was still nominally the final authority, though in Paul's day it served chiefly to pass legislation sent from the Senate. But such autonomous power as a city had could be removed by Rome for any blatant disregard of law and order, cf. Tacitus, *Ann.* iv. 36; xiv. 17. (40b) The Alexandrian text is clumsy and may be due to lack of final revision or, as *B.C.* iv. 252 suggests, it may be due to the inclusion of legal or technical language of the indictment supposed. The Western text omits 'about it' (lit. 'concerning which') and 'not'. If 'cause' in 40a is translated by 'charge', cf. Luke xxiii. 4, then the sense may require a negative, 'there being no charge about which we cannot give account'.

Note on the Corinthian Correspondence

Quite apart from the riot at Ephesus, Paul had had much to cast him into the deepest despair there, cf. 2 Cor. i. 8, if a probable reconstruction of part of the letters to Corinth may be cited here, cf. McNeile, *I.S.N.T.* 138-42. A personal offender against Paul, not necessarily the same as the incestuous man of 1 Cor. v. 1 f., had been allowed by the majority of the Church at Corinth to go unpunished. Paul's authority was being undermined and the success of the gospel message at Corinth endangered. Though Acts does not relate it, Paul had probably paid a flying-visit to Corinth to subdue the offender, only to fail in this purpose; if 2 Cor. x-xiii is part of the 'sorrowful letter' which he wrote after his return to Ephesus, it shows how deeply Paul felt, not so much because his pride had been wounded as because his converts whom he loved were rebellious and because his 'failure' at Athens appeared now to have been followed by failure too at Corinth. The collection for the poor of the mother-church at Jerusalem, on which Paul rightly set so great a value, could not be organized solely from Ephesus; and plans perhaps already made for the collectors to meet at Ephesus had had to be changed. Hence his departure from Ephesus, xx. 1 ff. It was during the course of his journey in Macedonia that he met Titus again, for the latter had gone ahead to Corinth to make a report on the reception there of the 'severe (or sorrowful) letter'. Titus' report was good so that from utter despondency Paul's spirits were raised to such heights of jubilation that the letter which followed, mainly 2 Cor. i-ix, is almost incoherent in its gratitude to God and to his Corinthian converts.

PAUL IS BROUGHT TO ROME

xx. THE JOURNEY TO GREECE AND TO MILETUS

(1) And when the uproar ceased, Paul summoned the disciples and gave them an exhortation, and after bidding them farewell, he went out to go into Macedonia. (2) And after going through those parts and exhorting them at great length, he came into Greece. (3) And he spent three months (there), and when a plot was formed against him by the Jews, as he was about to set sail for Syria, he made up his mind to return through Macedonia. (4) And there accompanied him as far as Asia Sopater, son of Pyrrhus, a Beroean; and of the Thessalonians, Aristarchus and Secundus; and Gaius a Doberian and Timothy; and Tychicus and Trophimus, men of Asia. (5) These went ahead and awaited us in Troas. (6) And we sailed away after the days of unleavened bread from Philippi and we came to them at Troas in five days, where we stayed seven days.

(7) And on the first day of the week, when we were gathered together to break bread, Paul addressed them, intending to depart on the morrow, and he protracted his discourse till midnight. (8) And there were many lamps in the upper room where we were gathered together. (9) And a young man, named Eutychus, sat at a window, and being heavy with sleep, as Paul's address continued for a long time, he was overcome with sleep and fell down from the third floor and was taken up dead. (10) And Paul went down and fell upon him and embracing him he said, 'Do not be disturbed; for his life is in him'. (11) And when he had gone up and had broken bread and tasted it, he conversed for a long time till dawn and so departed. (12) And they brought the boy alive and were immeasurably consoled.

(13) And we, going on to the ship, set sail for Assos, intending to pick up Paul from there, for he had arranged it so, intending himself to go on foot. (14) And when he met us at Assos, we picked him up and came to Mitylene. (15) And sailing away from there on the next day we came down opposite Chios and on the second day we passed by Samos, and on the following day we came to Miletus. (16) For Paul had decided to sail past Ephesus that he might not have to spend time in Asia; for he was hastening, if it were possible for him, to be in Jerusalem for the day of Pentecost.

(17) And from Miletus he sent to Ephesus and summoned the elders of the church. (18) And when they were come to him, he said to them, 'You know how from the first day that I came into Asia I have been with you the whole time, (19) serving the Lord with all humility and tears and testings which fell to me by the plots of the Jews; (20) how I kept back nothing of what was profitable from announcing to you and from teaching you publicly and from house to house, (21) testifying to the Jews and to the Greeks repentance towards God and faith towards our Lord Jesus Christ. (22) And now, behold, I go bound in the spirit to Jerusalem, not knowing what will meet me there, (23) except that the Holy Spirit witnesses in every city saying that bonds and tribulations await me. (24) But I make my life of no account as of any value to me, that I may finish my course and the ministry which I received of the Lord Jesus, to testify the gospel of the grace of God. (25) And now, behold, I know that you all will see my face no longer, you among whom I went about preaching the kingdom. (26) Wherefore I testify to you this day that I am pure from the blood of all men. (27) For I did not keep back from announcing to you the whole of the counsel of God. (28) Take heed to yourselves and to all the flock, in which the Holy Spirit has set you as overseers, to shepherd the church of God which he purchased with the blood of His own. (29) I know that there will come to you after my departure grievous wolves, not sparing the

flock; (30) and from yourselves shall men arise, speaking perverse things, to draw away the disciples after them. (31) Therefore watch, remembering that for a period of three years I did not cease night and day admonishing each one with tears. (32) And now I commend you to God and to the word of His grace, which is able to build you up and to give you an inheritance among all those that are sanctified. (33) I coveted no man's silver or gold or raiment. (34) You yourselves know that these hands ministered to the needs of myself and of those with me. (35) I showed you everything, how that so labouring you should help the weak, and remember the words of the Lord Jesus, how He Himself said, "It is more blessed to give than to receive".' (36) And when he had said this, he kneeled down and prayed with them all. (37) And there was great lament from all, and they fell on Paul's neck and kissed him, (38) being most of all sorry for the word which he had said, that they would see his face no longer. And they escorted him to the ship.

(2) **Greece**; i.e. Achaia. (3) **Three months,** probably during the winter of A.D. 56-7 (C. J. Cadoux) if he left Ephesus in 55; but Bacon thought that this period was from January to March, 55. Luke's account is extremely condensed, and in fact Paul or his messengers may have gone far afield if the reference in Rom. xv. 19 is to be taken literally that the gospel had been preached in Illyricum. The Western text is a revision showing lack of insight. Whereas Paul's journey to Jerusalem was necessary if the collection for the saints was to be taken personally, the Western text ascribes the reason for the journey to the Jews' plot; and whereas the route through Macedonia was chosen to avoid murder on the high seas, the Western reviser makes this choice of route due to the inspiration of the Holy Spirit, in typical fashion. The Jews may have plotted both to kill Paul by sea and to steal the collection money. (4) The Western reading Doberios or Douberios used of Gaius is undoubtedly right. A. C. Clark drew attention to it, and pointed to the existence of Doberes in Macedonia, cf. xix. 29. The Alexandrian reading, 'of Derbe', is the easier one and therefore wrong. Here Clark

'scored at least one bull's-eye' (B. H. Streeter, *J.T.S.* xxxiv, 1933, 238), cf. Lagrange, *Critique textuelle*, 397 f. and *R.B.* 42, 1933, 426. Those named in this verse may have been the agents commissioned by each church to carry its collection to the mother-church, Luke perhaps representing Philippi and Paul Corinth. Sopater may possibly be the Sosipater of Rom. xvi. 21, where he appears alongside Timothy, Lucius, and Jason. If Lucius were Luke, it would be tempting to see in Rom. xvi. 21 two of Paul's present companions named. But it is unlikely that Lucius there means our author. **Tychicus;** cf. Col. iv. 7 f. repeated in Eph. vi. 21 f., cf. Tit. iii. 12, 2 Tim. iv. 12; the Western text has 'Eutychus', an assimilation to vs. 9;Trophimus cf. 2 Tim. iv. 20; according to xxi. 29 he was an Ephesian; it is to this verse that the Western text seems to assimilate, reading 'Ephesians' for 'Asians'. (5) The beginning of another we-section which continues to vs. 15 and is picked up at xxi. 1. (6) If Paul had hoped to keep the Passover and the days of unleavened bread in Jerusalem, he had found himself compelled to keep them at Philippi instead. (7) **The first day of the week;** Sunday, unless Luke means that the first day began on the Saturday night at 6 P.M. according to Jewish reckoning; but Paul departed probably on Monday morning, not Sunday. **To break bread;** was this an ordinary meal in so far as any meal taken by Jews or Jewish-Christians was ordinary and without special religious significance? Was it a social meal corresponding to the *Ḥaburah* or fellowship-meal which may have been held in primitive times in conjunction with the Eucharist or *Berakah*? Did Paul separate the former from the latter after the disorders at Corinth, cf. 1 Cor. x, xi? As in ii. 42, xxvii. 35, it is uncertain what is meant. (8) **Lamps;** instead of *lampades*, D but not its Latin side, *d*, has *hypolampades*, 'look-out holes'; did the Western scribe have the 'window', *thuris*, of vs. 9 in mind? Probably 'lamps' or 'lights' is right, and they are mentioned because Luke felt perhaps that the heat thrown off by them and the hypnotic effect that they can have on an audience helped to send Eutychus to sleep. (9) **Dead;** Luke did not mean that Eutychus was unconscious but dead, as he may himself have verified, though *B.C.* iv. 256 suggests that this verdict was the opinion of those who picked up Eutychus. The parallels in

the next verse to the raising of the widow's son by Elijah,
1 Kings xvii. 17 ff., and of the Shunammite's son by Elisha,
2 Kings iv. 34 ff., corroborate that Luke had a real raising from
the dead in mind. At the same time it must be admitted that
W. K. L. Clarke (*B.C.* ii. 103) decides in favour of the probability that nothing more is demonstrated than that these
chapters of Acts are composed in a strongly Septuagintal style.
(10) **His life is in him;** these words have suggested to some
critics that according to some hypothetical source used by Luke
Eutychus suffered concussion, not death; but as this is a
we-section Luke did not have to rely probably on sources.
(12) The Western text has, 'And as they were giving him
salutations, they (or "he") brought the youth alive'. There is
no need on Form-critical grounds to assume that Eutychus was
the one who broke and ate bread in vs. 11, on the analogy of
other cures ending with a note of command with reference to
the patient's ability to eat which proclaimed the completion of
his cure. (13) **We;** the Armenian catena, and possibly the Old
Syriac text, read, 'I, Luke, and those with me', cf. *B.C.* iii. 442.
Certainly the Armenian translator found these words in Ephraim
Syrus' text; but too much weight should not be given to a
variant lacking general support. (13-16) Knox, *Acts*, 58, thinks
that Luke incorporated his notes of the journey as they stood,
while they have a 'freshness' which makes them very good
reading, which a Greek public would appreciate; but Dibelius
thinks that the detail serves merely an edificatory purpose.
Assos is on the mainland of Mysia facing south towards
Lesbos; some inferior MSS. read 'Thasos', the island east of
Amphipolis; so P41 Syr.vg.hl and possibly Cop.sa. While the boat
went round Cape Lectum, Paul had time to go overland from
Troas to Assos. **Mitylene** is on the east side of the island of
Lesbos. (15) **Passed by;** the meaning of *paraballo* is obscure,
but it probably means passing by rather than crossing to or
touching at. Paul left Ephesus twenty miles on his left on his
course past Samos. After 'Samos' the Bezan text, D, with
P41 Cop.sa have 'and after remaining at Trogyllium', cf. my
Alterations, 64. Perhaps an original line of twenty-two letters
dropped out from the Greek of the Alexandrian tradition or else
the Western reviser shows here, as elsewhere, a good knowledge

of the geography of the Levant or derived his knowledge from Strabo's *Geography*, xiv. 1, 12-14. (17) **Miletus** is about thirty miles from Ephesus measuring in a straight line across the mountains. (18 ff.) This is the sole occasion in Acts when a speech by Paul to Christians is recorded, and it is therefore different in style from others attributed to him; this difference may also be due to Luke having been present on this occasion and to his noting the gist of what was actually said, though little more than the gist is recorded. It strikes a curiously apologetic note, implying that Paul's detractors have been at work in Ephesus, and it includes warnings both that his friends will see him no more and that false teachers will appear. In his article on farewell discourses in the New Testament and in Biblical Literature (*Mélanges Goguel*, 155-70), J. Munck has adduced 'parallels' to this speech from 1 Tim. iv. 1 ff. and 2 Tim. iii. 1 ff., Gen. xlvii. 29-1. 14, Josh. xxiii-xxiv. 32, 1 Sam. xii, Deut. i-iii, Tobit xiv. 3-11, and elsewhere. He thinks that Paul's speech as recorded here is an excellent example of a Farewell Address with its prediction of the difficulties that will arise after the speaker's death. It is said to be a mark of such discourses to hold oneself up as a model, cf. vss. 33-5. 'We have here a N.T. figure who (a) before setting out for martyrdom gathers the elders of Ephesus to address to them as his last words definite teaching; (b) exhorts those whom he is going to leave; (c) gives himself as a model for they must imitate his life and tireless zeal for the community; (d) foretells the persecution which the community will suffer, and the coming, after his death, of false teachers' (art. cit., 161). These four points may well be in line with a normal farewell discourse and if 'Luke' was not Paul's companion and if Acts was written late in the first century, the author may have derived his ideas here from a standard type of farewell speech current in late Judaism. But it is more probable that Paul or Luke followed the main trend of a Farewell Discourse consciously or otherwise and that the form of a narrative cannot determine the historical value.

(19) **Serving the Lord;** a typical Paulinism, cf. Bruce, 378. **Humility;** here used in its good sense, as of a child looking up, contrast Col. ii. 23, where it is used in a bad sense as of a servant looking down. **With tears;** a Pauline trait, cf. Bruce

(*ibid.*). **Testings;** or trials; Luke under-emphasizes Paul's
sufferings referred to in 1 Cor. xv. 32, xvi. 9, 2 Cor. i. 8-10,
xi. 23. (21) Instead of saying that Paul taught repentance and
faith to Jews and Greeks, Luke indulges in a chiasmus. (22)
Bound; probably metaphorical, 'under the compulsion of'.
But this is not to accept Wedell's theory (*Theology*, l, 1947,
366-72) that every reference in Paul's last letters to prison or
bonds is a metaphor. (23) Has Luke anticipated the prophecy
of the disciples at Tyre, xxi. 4, or that of Agabus, xxi. 11? Or
had Paul already received a similar warning? (24) Ropes translates (*B.C.* iii. 196) the Alexandrian text, 'I make of no account
my life, as precious to myself', while *B.C.* iv. 260 suggests
another translation of the same text, 'I do not regard for myself
my life as a thing even worth mentioning'. The awkwardness
of the Greek led to alteration in the Western text and the
Byzantine. But the sense is clear enough and corroborated by
Paul's letters, cf. Bruce, 379. **That;** *hōs* is sometimes used in a
final sense, cf. *L.S.J.* 2039, Luke ix. 52; or perhaps *hōstē*
teleiōsai should be read, 'so as to finish', the first '*-te*' having
dropped out accidentally. **Finish my course;** cf. 2 Tim. iv. 7.
'The writer of 2 Timothy appears to have drawn his knowledge
of Paul's career in iii. 11 from Acts' (Knox, *Acts*, 41); he is an
important link between Paul and Ignatius. **The ministry . . .**
Jesus; again typically Pauline phrases, Bruce, 379. (25) **The**
kingdom (D adds 'of Jesus'; the Byzantine text 'of God') is
the subject of the Gospel of the grace of God, cf. vs. 28. *B.C.* iv.
261 poses the alternatives for the meaning of the Kingdom, the
coming judgement or the Church; 'I think the latter, but the
matter is not susceptible of proof'. But in view of the work
done since 1938 on the Apostolic Preaching (e.g. by Dr. C. H.
Dodd), one may say that the Kingdom is both present and
future and that to a Jewish mind the thought of the Messianic
community was bound up with that of the Messiah. The prediction in this verse has been taken in opposite senses (i) that
Acts was written before Paul's martyrdom, otherwise an allusion
to his death here would have been made explicitly, (ii) that this
is such an allusion and that Acts was written after his martydrom.
(26 f.) If Paul had 'watered down' the gospel (cf. 2 Cor. ii. 7),
he would have been answerable to God for the lives or souls of

the converts, cf. the warning to the shepherds of Israel; Ezek. xxxiv, esp. 10, Jer. xxiii. 2, Zech. x. 3, xi. 16. (28) **Overseers,** guardians or bishops; this word is found in the LXX as a translation of the Hebrew word from the root *pqd*, the verb meaning 'attend to', 'visit', or 'appoint'; hence 'observe' with care, 'attend to' mostly used of sheep as in Jer. xxiii. 2 figuratively, cf. Zech. x. 3, xi. 16; 'seek' with interest or desire, 'visit graciously', 'visit upon', hence 'injure'; 'appoint' (hence for passive participle pl. 'appointed ones, officers'); 'assign' or 'deposit' and in Hiph. 'set over', 'make an overseer', 'commit', 'entrust'. The noun from this root means 'oversight', 'mastery', 'visitation' in the abstract and of a person 'commissioner', 'deputy', 'overseer', one commissioned for a special duty or as a permanent deputy of a king, priest, or Levite. See *B.D.B.* 823-4; cf. Appendix 1. Cf. LXX of Num. xxi. 14, 4 Kingd. xi. 15, xii. 12, 2 Chron. xxxiv. 12, 17, 1 Macc. i. 51; cf. Philo, *Quis Rer. Div. Haer.* 30; Josephus, *Ant.* x. 4, 1 and xii. 54; cf. *Fragments of a Zadokite work* where the 'Censor' appears, whose duty it is to command, examine, instruct, receive alms or accusations, cf. the *Epimeletes* (Manager) of the Essenes and the Inspector of the *Manual of Discipline*, vi. 10 ff. and 19 ff. In the N.T. Christ is the Chief Shepherd and Bishop of souls, 1 Pet. ii. 25, cf. v. 2; *episcopoi* appear in Phil. i. 1, cf. 1 Tim. iii. 1 ff., Titus, i. 5-9. Here the *presbyteroi* or elders of Ephesus are called *episcopoi*, though the former may have been the wider term. The connexion of 'shepherding' and 'overseeing' is to be noted, cf. the *Zadokite Document* cited above, xvi. 3, 'As the shepherd with his flock he shall loose all the bands of their knots'. See Beyer, Kittel, *T.W.N.T.* ii. 595-617. **The Church;** see Appendix 2. **Of God;** this, rather than 'of the Lord', is original, as attested by B and ℵ. The verse goes on to speak of the 'blood of His [i.e. God's] Own [Son]'. As the Greek of the latter phrase could be mistranslated to mean 'with His own blood', the later scribes would tend to substitute 'Lord' for 'God' to avoid Patripassian implications. **His Own;** cf. Col. i. 13. (29) **Departure;** the word usually means 'arrival', but cf. Josephus, *Ant.* ii. 4. 18, iv. 8. 47. **Grievous wolves;** if this is not a mere literary touch based on the 'usual pattern' of the farewell-discourse (see above), it may be taken to imply that

Luke knew that the Church in Ephesus after Paul's day had trouble with false teachers (cf. Easton, *Purpose*, 22). In the message to the Church in Ephesus (Rev. ii. 2 ff.) we hear of evil men calling themselves apostles when they were not, of the Church there abandoning its first love and of its hatred of the Nicolaitans. (31) **Watch;** as Dr. P. Carrington has suggested, there seems to have been a primitive catechetical pattern of instruction summed up in the words 'Strip away; then obey; watch and pray; stand and stay'. (*The Primitive Christian Cathechism* suggests '*Deponentes, subiecti, vigilate, state*'.) (32) Some MSS., including B, have 'Lord' for 'God'. The reference to the message of God's freely given, undeserved favour and benefaction is Pauline in sentiment, the 'word' not being the O.T. revelation but that of God in Christ, who is God's 'unspeakable gift', 2 Cor. ix. 15. (33) The sudden change of theme may be due to (a) Luke's account being a very short summary of Paul's speech and (b) Luke's knowledge of Paul's habitual change of moods. **Raiment;** as *B.C.* iv. 262 says, this was part of a man's wealth in the ancient world. (34) **These hands;** a vivid touch, suggesting that Luke remembered how Paul gestured as he spoke. (35) **Everything;** or 'in all things' or 'always'. In the Thessalonian letters Paul had had to warn his converts not to play truant in view of the Parousia but to work or toil, 1 Thess. v. 14, 2 Thess. iii. 6 f., 11. This saying of Jesus may have been in a collection of *Ipsissima Verba* of Jesus known to Luke, cf. the implications of 1 Cor. vii. 6, 10, 12, 40; a similar saying occurs in 1 Clem. ii. 1. *B.C.* iv. 263 asks why Luke did not use this saying in the Gospel; the answer may be that Luke wrote Acts before the complete Third Gospel. (38) **No longer;** cf. on vs. 25.

xxi. 1-16. THE JOURNEY TO JERUSALEM

(1) **And when it happened that we set sail and were drawn away from them, we came on a straight course to Cos, on the next day to Rhodes and from there to Patara. (2) And finding a boat crossing over to Phoenicia, we embarked and set sail. (3) And we sighted Cyprus**

and leaving it on the left, we sailed to Syria and came down to Tyre; for there the boat was discharging her cargo. (4) And seeking out the disciples, we stayed there seven days; and they told Paul through the Spirit not to go to Jerusalem. (5) And when we had put a finish to those days, we went out and were on our way, all of them escorting us with their wives and children as far as outside the city. And kneeling down on the shore we prayed and bade farewell to each other, (6) and embarked on the ship, while they returned to their own homes.

(7) But having completed the voyage from Tyre, we came down to Ptolemais and greeted the brethren and stayed one day with them. (8) And on the morrow we went away and came to Caesarea; entering into the house of Philip the Evangelist, one of the Seven, we remained with him. (9) And he had four unmarried daughters who prophesied. (10) And while we waited many days, a prophet named Agabus came down from Judaea. (11) And he came to us and took Paul's girdle, and bound his own hands and feet and said, ' Thus speaks the Holy Spirit, "So shall the Jews bind in Jerusalem the man whose girdle this is and they shall deliver him into the hands of the Gentiles".' (12) And when we heard this, both we and the local people begged him not to go up to Jerusalem. (13) Then Paul answered, 'What are you doing, weeping and breaking my heart? For I am ready not only to be bound but also to die in Jerusalem for the sake of the name of the Lord Jesus.' (14) And when he would not be persuaded, we fell silent, saying, ' The will of the Lord be done '. (15) And after those days we made our arrangements and went up to Jerusalem. (16) And some of the disciples came from Caesarea with us, bringing Mnason, a Cypriote, a primitive disciple, with whom we should lodge.

(1) **Cos**, a small island off Caria; **Rhodes** is the famous, larger island south-west of Caria; **Patara** is a harbour on the coast of Lycia. For the Western addition after Patara, 'and

Myra', found also in P⁴¹, see my *Alterations*, 64 f. (2) The
change of boats was due probably to the desire to make a
speedy journey on a boat going direct to Phoenicia without
stopping on the way. (3) The voyage, 400 miles from Patara
direct to Tyre, left Cyprus to the north. The word for **discharging cargo** is sometimes used of jettisoning it. (4) This
verse provides another indication that Acts does not and could
not relate all the details of the spread of the gospel, e.g. to
Tyre, but cf. xi. 19. Critics who express surprise that Paul
could afford to spend seven days at Tyre if he was in a hurry to
reach Jerusalem forget that transport in the unchanging East
is slow and often unavailable. **Through the Spirit;** perhaps
this means by ecstatic utterance. But Paul also believed that he
was guided by the Spirit to go on, xx. 22, and Acts does not
attempt to reconcile the two commands, not to go, and to go to
Jerusalem. (5) **Put a finish;** a curious phrase, sometimes used
of finishing a book or a building or a piece of furniture. (7) The
verb for **complete** (cf. 2 Macc. xii. 17) is used in Xenophon of
Ephesus (second century A.D.) to mean 'continue'. The journey
from Tyre was probably by sea. **Ptolemais,** Acre or Acco, a
fortress on the coast twenty-five miles south of Tyre. (8) **Philip**
was last mentioned in viii. 40 as being at Caesarea, which is
thirty-two miles from Acco, though rather more by the coast
road. **The evangelist;** to distinguish him from Philip the
Apostle, though later tradition confused the two (Eusebius,
II.E. iii. 31, 3, cf. v. 17. 3). (9) Harnack suggested that Philip's
daughters were Luke's sources for parts of Acts, *Luke the
Physician*, 155 f. (10) **Agabus,** cf. xi. 28; Luke speaks here as if
he had not been mentioned before, which may indicate the use
of sources. On the Roman view Jerusalem was not the capital,
but Caesarea was. (11) Acted or prophetic symbolism was
common among the Hebrews, cf. 1 Kings xi. 29 ff., Isa. xx. 2 ff.,
Ezek. iv. 1 ff. The prophet was considered to set in motion a
train of events culminating in the one symbolized. His act was
almost 'sacramental'; inspired by God, it was an act with
power. (13) **Breaking;** the verb suggests to pound or to pummel
like a washerwoman, hence to bleach, whiten. Paul felt their
request like a blow at his heart, quite apart from his natural
fears. Bruce, 388 f., rightly stresses Luke's parallel between

Jesus going up steadfastly to die at Jerusalem and Paul's 'Passion narrative'; this would be all the more natural if Luke wrote Acts with Mark in mind. (14) Cf. Luke xxii. 42. (15) **Made arrangements;** the verb means to provide oneself with necessities for a journey and also to saddle horses for it. The Western variant, 'bidding farewell', is an easier, inferior reading. (16) **Some;** this has to be supplied and the simple genitive in this sense is awkward in Greek. The Western text presupposes a break in the journey from Caesarea to Jerusalem at a village where Mnason acted as host; to many this has seemed plausible, but Knox takes it to be probably an inference from the text (*Jerusalem,* xxvi). Like Philip and Agabus, Mnason belonged to the circle of those who had been Christians apparently before Paul's conversion and who had connexions with the Gentile-Christian Church.

xxi. 17-36. PAUL IN JERUSALEM; HIS ARREST

(17) And when we came to Jerusalem, the brethren received us gladly. (18) And on the next day Paul entered in with us to James, and all the elders were present. (19) And he greeted them and related in each particular what God had done among the Gentiles through his ministry. (20) And when they heard it, they began to glorify God. And they said to him, 'You see, brother, how many thousands of believers there are among the Jews; and they are all zealous for the law. (21) But they were informed about you that you are teaching all the Jews who are among the Gentiles to revolt from Moses, telling them not to circumcise their children and not to walk after the customs. (22) What then? For they will certainly hear that you have come. (23) So then, do as we say to you; we have four men who have a vow on them. (24) Take these men and purify yourself along with them, and pay their expenses that they may shave their heads and all will know that there is nothing in the information that they have heard about you, but that you yourself walk keeping the law. (25) But with regard to the Gentiles

who have made their act of faith, we sent a letter with
our judgement that they should keep themselves from
what is offered to idols and from blood and from what is
strangled and from fornication.' (26) Then Paul took the
men and on the next day he purified himself with them
and entered into the Temple, announcing the completion
of the days of the purification, till the sacrifice was
offered on behalf of each one of them.

(27) And when seven days were about to be completed, the Jews from Asia, seeing him in the Temple,
threw all the crowd into confusion and laid hands on
him, crying, (28) 'Men of Israel, help! This is the man
who teaches all men everywhere against the people and
the law and this place; and moreover, he has brought
Greeks into the Temple; and he has defiled this holy
place.' (29) For beforehand they had seen Trophimus the
Ephesian in the city with him and they supposed that
Paul had taken him into the Temple. (30) And the whole
city was moved and there was a concourse of the people;
and they seized Paul and dragged him outside the
Temple; and immediately the doors were shut. (31) And
while they sought to kill him, a report came up to the
chief captain of the band that the whole of Jerusalem
was in an uproar. (32) At once he took soldiers and
centurions and ran down upon them; and when they
saw the chief captain and the soldiers, they stopped
beating Paul. (33) Then the chief captain approached and
seized him and ordered him to be bound with two chains,
and he enquired who he might be and what he had done.
(34) And different men in the crowd called out differently; unable to know for certain on account of the
tumult, he ordered him to be led into the castle. (35) And
when he was on the stairs, so it was that he was carried
by the soldiers on account of the violence of the crowd;
(36) for the multitude of the people kept following, and
crying, 'Away with him'.

(17) **We**; cf. xxvii. 1; probably Luke was with Paul for a
longer time than these two verses would imply by themselves.

(18) Paul is carefully marked off from 'us' as the limelight is to be on him. James is undoubtedly head now of the Church in Jerusalem, having taken Peter's place; **all the elders;** these may, as Knox suggests, have numbered up to seventy, forming a presbyterate 'college' under James. (20) Paul's mission had been slandered and the Church could glorify God when it heard the truth. **Thousands;** lit. tens of thousands. J. Weiss (*The History of primitive Christianity*, 49) notes the numbers of Christians given in Acts; 120 (i. 15); 3000 more at Pentecost (ii. 41); 5000 (iv. 4), cf. v. 16, vi. 1, viii. 1, xi. 19; he says, 'The picture of a steady course of growth and of a divinely guided if gradual expansion is strictly in accordance with the plan of the author. . . . The figures . . . result mainly from conjecture and are probably exaggerated.' (His translator, F. C. Grant, in a footnote is more cautious about the last remark.)

(21 ff.) Many critics have doubted whether Paul, the champion of Gentile-Christian rights and of freedom from the Jewish Law, could have undertaken the role that Luke says that he did. Would it be such a compromise that his principles would be sacrificed? Even if Paul could have performed such an act in the Temple, would he have agreed with the motive expressed in vs. 24b for so doing? Windisch (*B.C.* ii. 320 f.), making the most of the alleged discrepancies between the Epistles of Paul and Acts, rejects this account and urges that it would have been an act of hypocrisy if it had been performed. Paul, however, had lived as a Pharisee and in 1 Cor. ix. 19 f. he expresses his readiness to go as far as he could to become as a Jew to win Jews and though not under the Law to be as under it. He could be gloriously inconsistent, if it was inconsistency to behave like a Jew in the mother-church at Jerusalem. But the motives expressed in vs. 24 were probably not his own, but James'. (23) **A vow;** to judge from the reference to the shaving of heads, this was a Nazirite vow of temporary duration, the minimum being of thirty days, cf. Num. vi. 13-20; Paul identified himself with the men either at the time of completion of the vow or in the effacement of a ritual defilement contracted in the course of the thirty days. (25) Cf. the apostolic decree of xv. 20, 29. Was James now telling Paul the terms of that decree for the first time? Probably he was merely reminding him (or Luke was

reminding his readers) of them. The argument is compressed, as often in speeches. The decree has made clear what a Jewish-Christian demands of a Gentile and so Paul can with a good conscience act as a Jew with Jews. (26) **Entered;** the imperfect tense here may be used of a single act, cf. vs. 18, or it may imply that Paul had to present himself for each of the four men in turn. (27) Jews from Asia up for Pentecost probably recognized Paul and Trophimus. Luke makes clear that the trouble started with Jews, not Jewish-Christians. **The Temple;** the implication was that Paul had taken Gentiles beyond the Court of the Gentiles and within the Court of Israel ignoring the barrier on which Greek and Latin notices warned Gentiles against going within on pain of death, cf. Josephus, *B.J.* v. 52; J. A. Robinson, *Ephesians*, 160, on ii. 14. (30) **Shut;** presumably by the Sagan or his men, cf. on iv. 1. (31) The guards on duty on the castle Antonia would observe the events. It would not take long for the chief captain or tribune and part of his cohort to run down the two flights of stairs to the outer court. (33) **He might be;** Luke uses the optative, comparatively rare in the N.T., cf. C. F. D. Moule, *Idiom Book of the N.T.*, 23, 150, 155. (34) **Castle;** probably the fortress Antonia, north-west of the Temple, cf. Josephus, *B.J.* v. 5, 8. (36) **Away with him,** i.e. to death, cf. John xix. 15.

xxi. 37-xxii. 21. PAUL IS ALLOWED TO SPEAK

(37) And as he was to be led into the castle, Paul said to the chief captain, 'Is it allowed for me to say something to you?' And he said, 'Do you know Greek? (38) Are you not that Egyptian who before these days revolted and led out into the desert four thousand men of the assassins?' (39) But Paul said, 'I am a Jew, of Tarsus in Cilicia, a citizen of no mean city. I beg of you, permit me to speak to the people.' (40) And when he had permitted him, Paul stood on the steps and beckoned with his hand to the people. And when there was a great silence, he addressed them in the Hebrew tongue, saying, (xxii. 1) 'Brethren

and fathers, listen now to me, as I make my defence to you'. (2) And when they heard that he addressed them in the Hebrew tongue, they kept a deeper silence; and he said, (3) 'I am a Jew, born in Tarsus of Cilicia, but brought up in this city at the feet of Gamaliel, trained according to the strictness of the ancestral law, being zealous for God, as you all are to-day. (4) I persecuted this Way unto the death, binding and delivering both men and women to prison, (5) as also the chief priest and all the body of elders witness for me; from them too I received letters to the brethren and went to Damascus to bring those also that were there in bonds to Jerusalem to be punished. (6) And it came to pass that as I journeyed and came near Damascus, about midday suddenly a great light shone round me from heaven. (7) And I fell to the ground and I heard a voice saying to me, "Saul, Saul, why are you persecuting me?" (8) And I answered, "Who are you, Lord?" And he said to me, "I am Jesus of Nazareth whom you are persecuting". (9) And those who were with me saw the light but they did not hear the voice of Him that spoke to me. (10) And I said, "What shall I do, Lord?" And the Lord said to me, "Rise up and go into Damascus, and there it shall be told you about all that is arranged for you to do". (11) And as I could not see for the glory of that light, I was led by the hand by those that were with me, into Damascus. (12) And one Ananias, a pious man according to the law, attested by all the Jews who dwelt there, (13) came to me and stood by me and said to me, "Brother Saul, receive your sight again", and in that same hour I received my sight, looking upon him. (14) And he said, "The God of our fathers has appointed you beforehand to know His will and to see the Just One and to hear a voice from His mouth. (15) For you shall be a witness for Him to all men of what you have seen and heard. (16) And now what are you to do? Rise up and be baptized and wash away your sins, calling on His name." (17) And it came to pass that when I returned to Jerusalem and was praying in the Temple, I was in a trance (18) and I saw Him saying to me,

"Hasten and go out quickly from Jerusalem, for they
will not receive your testimony about Me". (19) And I
said, "Lord, they themselves know that I was imprison-
ing and beating those that believe in Thee from one
synagogue to another. (20) And when the blood of
Stephen, Thy witness, was shed, I also was standing by
and giving consent and keeping the garments of them
that slew him." (21) And He said to me, "Go, for I shall
send you far away to the Gentiles".'

(37) **Know Greek**, i.e. know (how to speak) Greek. (38)
That Egyptian; see Introduction, 7 (b). **Assassins,** Greek
sikarioi from the Latin *sica*, a dagger. *B.C.* iv. 277 deprecates
the translation ' assassins ', as this was the name of an Arab
sect who used hashish at the time of the Crusades to stimu-
late themselves to murderous exploits; ' terrorists ' might be
better. (39) As often, there are three short clauses here. The
understatement **no mean city** conveys a suggestion of a
Greek sense of superiority, even if Euripides, *Ion*, 8, was
not in mind, cf. *B.C.* iv. 278, Cadbury, *B.A.H.* 32 f. The
latter says, ' In other passages also " not mean " is shown in
its context to imply pre-eminently Greek '. (40) **Hebrew**, i.e.
probably Aramaic, cf. *B.C.* v. 63. (xxii. 3) Paul now stresses his
Jewish origins, as well as his Tarsian citizenship, but not his
Roman. **Gamaliel;** *B.C.* iv. 279 discusses whether Paul could
have been a pupil of Gamaliel, as Paul's ' statement of the Jewish
doctrine of the Law is so gross a caricature of anything which he
could have learnt from Gamaliel' and as Paul omits reference
to the Jewish doctrine of repentance. But Paul's own conversion
and all his subsequent experience proved to him that the constant Jewish error was to seek salvation by 'works of the Law',
and the contrast between faith and works became almost an
obsession with him. At all events, Paul had learned how to
argue like a Rabbi, whether from Gamaliel or another, cf. Gal.
iv. 22-31. **Zealous;** cf. Gal. i. 14, 'being exceedingly zealous
for the traditions of my fathers'. These words are insufficient
to prove that Luke had a copy of Galatians before him; no
doubt he had heard Paul on the subject often enough, cf. ix. 21;
for the Pauline sentiments expressed here, cf. Rom. x. 2, Phil.

iii. 4-6. (4) **Way,** cf. on ix. 2. (5) **Body of elders.** By this Luke means the Sanhedrin, cf. Luke xxii. 66. (6 ff.) The second of the three accounts of Paul's conversion given in Acts. If Luke adopts the clumsy Semitic method of emphasizing a point by repeating it three times, yet he introduces each time variations in detail. (6) **Midday,** cf. Deut. xxviii. 28 f. for noonday blindness as well as for confusion of mind and madness and groping in the dark. (7) Cf. ix. 4; again the implication is that to persecute Christians is to persecute Christ or His Body, the Church. (10) **Arranged** or appointed, not predetermined. (12) Addressing Jews, Paul speaks of Ananias as a pious Jew in terms differing from the other accounts of the conversion. If Ananias was a Christian who owed little or nothing to the Church in Jerusalem himself and acted simply as God's intermediary, then Paul's claim to be independent of the Church in Jerusalem (Gal. i-ii) does not contradict this passage. (14) If these were not Ananias' words, Luke shows artistry in his choice of Jewish-Christian phrases put into his mouth. **The Just One;** cf. on iii. 14. (15 f.) As the apostolic kerygma included apparently the element of apostolic witness (cf. on i. 8), Paul could claim as an apostle to witness like the other apostles to what he had heard and seen of the Lord, though probably he had not seen Him in the flesh, despite the superficial interpretation of 2 Cor. v. 16. (16) A reference to Baptism and washing away of sins is typical of the conclusion to the Kerygma. **His name;** Baptism was at first into Jesus' name; later the threefold formula of Matt. xxviii. 19 was evolved. (17) Luke probably meant that Paul received this vision during his first visit to Jerusalem after his conversion, and he may have assumed that the three years spent by Paul in preaching (or in retreat?) in 'Arabia', Gal. i. 17, had not occurred, even if Luke knew of it. It is less likely that the visit here referred to was the second one, as Ramsay suggested, cf. 2 Cor. xii. 2 ff. (20) **Witness,** *martus*, is almost 'martyr' here though it bears the wider meaning. (21) Dr. Farrer, after believing that Mark's gospel was intended to finish at xvi. 8, later suggested that it had a brief ending; if Luke knew that ending, is it not likely that the gist of it was similar to the injunction here given to Paul? This would not conflict with Mr. C. F. Evans' view that Mark meant

the Gentile world by 'Galilee' and that in Mark xiv. 28 and
xvi. 7 Jesus promised to lead His disciples there, *J.T.S.* n.s., v,
1954, 3-18.

xxii. 22-30. PAUL UNDER ARREST

(22) **And they heard him as far as this word and they
lifted up their voices saying, 'Away with such a fellow
from the earth, for it is not fitting for him to live'. (23)
And they cried out and tore their clothes, and threw dust
into the air, (24) and the chief captain ordered him to be
brought into the castle, bidding him to be examined with
scourges that he might know for what reason they
shouted against him. (25) And when they stretched him
out for the whip, Paul said to the centurion standing by,
'Is it lawful for you to scourge a man that is a Roman
and uncondemned?' (26) And when the centurion heard
it, he came to the chief captain and reported, saying,
'What are you about to do? For this man is a Roman.'
(27) And the chief captain came to him and said, 'Tell
me, are you a Roman?' And he said, 'Yes'. (28) And the
chief captain answered, 'I obtained this citizenship at a
great price'; and Paul answered, 'But I was even born
one'. (29) And at once those about to examine him
departed from him. And the chief captain was afraid,
realizing that he was a Roman and that he had bound
him.**

(30) **And on the morrow, wanting to know for sure
what was the accusation made against him by the Jews,
he loosed him and ordered the chief priests and all the
Sanhedrin to come together and he brought Paul down
and set him before them.**

(22) Both *B.C.* iv. 281 and Bruce, 405, agree that Paul's
mention of the Gentiles was 'the last straw' to the crowd. It is
also agreed that the Jews did not object to Gentiles being
proselytized but to Paul doing it on his own terms of equality
with the Jews and of Law-lessness. (24) It was customary for

Romans to use the barbarous scourge on slaves and aliens to
beat the truth out of them. (25) **For the whip** (lit. whips); or
'with thongs'. Paul could appeal to the Valerian and Porcian
laws against inflicting humiliating punishments on Roman
citizens. (28) For the Western text, see my *Alterations*, 70; it
suggests a cynical remark by the chief captain, 'I know at what
sum I obtained this citizenship', meaning, 'Even a disreputable-
looking person like you can obtain it nowadays', but Paul's
reply suggests that the Alexandrian text is correct. Many guesses
have been made how Paul's forebear(s) could have obtained
citizenship. If Jerome is right (*De viris illustr.* 5) that Paul's
parents came from Gischala in Palestine to Tarsus, it is possible
that they earned citizenship by helping Mark Antony, as *B.C.*
iv. 284 suggests. **Departed;** there is humour in Luke's description of the torturers' exit. **Bound;** i.e. for flogging.

xxiii. 1-11. PAUL BEFORE THE SANHEDRIN

**(1) And Paul gazed at the Sanhedrin and said, 'Brethren,
I have lived freely, with a good conscience towards God
until this day'. (2) But the high priest Ananias commanded those that stood by him to smite him on the
mouth. (3) Then Paul said to him, 'God is about to smite
you, you plastered wall. Do you indeed sit judging me
according to the Law and contrary to the Law command
me to be smitten?' (4) And those that stood by said, 'Are
you reviling God's high priest?' (5) And Paul said, 'I did
not know, brethren, that he was high priest; for it is
written, "Thou shalt not speak evil of the ruler of thy
people".' (6) And when Paul knew that one part was of
the Sadducees and the other of the Pharisees, he cried
out in the Sanhedrin, 'Brethren, I am a Pharisee, son of
a Pharisee; it is for the hope and resurrection of the
dead that I am being judged'. (7) And when he said this,
a dissension of the Pharisees and Sadducees took place
and the multitude was divided. (8) For the Sadducees
say that there is no resurrection, nor angel nor spirit;**

but the Pharisees confess both. (9) And there was a great outcry and some of the scribes of the party of the Pharisees arose and contended, saying, 'We find no evil in this man. But what if a spirit or an angel spoke to him?' (10) And when there was great dissension, the chief captain was afraid that Paul might be torn apart by them and he commanded the detachment of soldiers to snatch him from their midst and to bring him into the castle.

(11) And on the next night the Lord stood by him and said, 'Be brave! For as you bore witness to the things concerning me unto Jerusalem, so must you bear witness also unto Rome.'

(1 ff.) The historicity of this whole scene has been doubted for various reasons. Would the Jewish Sanhedrin have been given an opportunity by a Roman official of judging one who claimed Roman citizenship? But in addition to the reason given in xxii. 30, Lysias may have wished to confront Paul with men who knew not only his 'crime' but also his claim to be a Roman citizen. It is unknown how proof of citizenship was provided if it was demanded of those who were not ex-veterans of the Roman army. It was probably done by personal reference, though Acts, like all other ancient sources, may take this for granted. Again, would Paul have claimed to be a Pharisee? Would he not, as Windisch argues (*B.C.* ii. 333), have been a hypocrite to do so? 'A personal friend could not possibly have represented Paul as denying his convictions in order to save his life'. But just as many Anglo-Catholics are strict in obeying the rules and customs of the Catholic Church without enforcing their observance on others, so Paul the Pharisee (cf. 2 Cor. xi. 22 ff., Phil. iii. 4-6) may well have lived and dressed in Palestine as a Pharisee, though he would have been the first to maintain that Christianity is not a baptized Pharisaism. Besides, xxiv. 21 reads like an apology for his claim. As Knox says, *Acts*, 97 n., 'It would be strange if Luke was so ignorant of the situation that he could represent Paul as speaking to this effect in xxiii. 6, and yet sufficiently aware of it to make Paul feel some doubts as to the justification of his action in using the words in xxiv. 21 '.

Again, it is urged that Paul's reference to the Resurrection is beside the point and that if he had made it, it would have been ignored by the sophisticated members of the Sanhedrin. But recent political trials have shown that the accused often takes an opportunity not to answer the charge against him but to preach his faith, and Paul may well have felt that if there is no Resurrection he was of all men most miserable in undergoing sufferings for nothing and that the Jewish doctrine of the after life was a convenient apple of discord to throw among men who were not judges so much as enemies. Finally, Luke was in a better position than we are to know how heated the Pharisees and Sadducees of the first century A.D. were when they discussed the Resurrection. (1) **Lived freely;** lit. 'lived as a free citizen', cf. 2 Macc. vi. 1, xi. 25. **Conscience,** cf. xxiv. 16 (where Paul is again speaking); though the full sense of conscience is not found in Greek philosophy or in the O.T., the Hellenistic world, where Jew and Greek met, saw the growth of the word, cf. Wisdom, xvii. 11. It appears fully without being named in Matt. vi. 22 f., and the word occurs in Rom. ii. 15, ix. 1, xiii. 5, 1 Cor. viii. 10. J. P. Thornton-Duesbury rightly criticizes the comment in *B.C.* iv. 286 that the idea of a guide for conduct is not included in the term (Richardson, *T.W.B.B.* 52). (2) **Ananias,** son of Nebedaeus, was High Priest from 48–c. 58. 'A bold man in his temper and very insolent; he was also of the party of the Pharisees, who are very stern in judging offenders more than all the rest of the Jews' (Josephus, *Ant.* xx. 9. 1 f.). He was murdered by robbers (Sicarii? Zealots?) in A.D. 66. If Luke knew of his murder when he wrote Acts, this may be an indication that Acts was written after 66, though even so vs. 3 need not be a 'prophecy after the event'. (3) *B.C.* iv. 287 has a needlessly sceptical note to the effect that the relation of a whitewashed wall to hypocrisy is very obscure. But cf. Matt. xxiii. 27; Jesus meant that a fair outward show is sometimes a cover for a mass of corruption. Paul (and Luke) may have known this phrase as one of the *ipsissima verba* of Jesus. A reference to Ezek. xiii. 10-16 (a wall daubed with whitewash) is preferred by some commentators. (4) Luke seems to have had access to some 'Johannine' traditions and this incident is not unlike that of John xviii. 22. (5) Paul may have known another

high priest before in Jerusalem or may have failed to recognize
the high priest if the chief captain presided or possibly if Paul's
eyesight was faulty. He cites Exod. xxii. 28. (6) Cf. Phil. iii. 5.
Hope and resurrection, i.e. hope of the resurrection, not
hope of the Messiah and Resurrection. (8) Cf. Mark xii. 18 ff.
and Josephus, *B.J.* ii. 8, 14. **Both;** if 'spirit' and 'angel' mean
the same, as Chrysostom took it, this is a possible translation;
otherwise *amphoteroi* means 'all' as probably in xix. 16 above.
The Sadducees' denial of angelic or spiritual beings is not
mentioned elsewhere. (9) Scribes and Pharisees overlapped one
another, cf. Mark ii. 16 and its variant readings with parallels
in Matt. and Luke. As the Pharisaic scribes could side with
Jesus in His controversy with the Sadducees over the Resurrection, Luke xx. 39, so they agree now with Paul. **Spirit or
angel;** here presumably synonymous, see on the previous verse.
(10) **Detachment of soldiers;** the word usually means 'expedition', 'campaign', 'armament', or 'host', but here presumably those on duty in the castle. (11) **Jerusalem ... Rome;**
cf. i. 8.

xxiii. 12-35. THE PLOT AND THE JOURNEY
TO CAESAREA

**(12) And when it was day, the Jews laid a plot and bound
themselves by a curse, saying that they would not eat or
drink until they had killed Paul. (13) And there were
more than forty who made this conspiracy. (14) These
went to the chief priests and the elders and said, 'We
have vowed with a curse on ourselves not to taste anything till we have killed Paul. (15) Now therefore lay
information before the chief captain with the Sanhedrin
that he may bring him down to you, as though you were
going to make a more exact enquiry into his affairs; but
before he approaches, we are ready to kill him.' (16) But
the son of Paul's sister heard of the ambush and came
and entered into the castle and reported it to Paul. (17)
And Paul summoned one of the centurions and said,**

'Take this young man off to the chief captain for he has something to report to him'. (18) So then he took and brought him to the chief captain and said, 'The prisoner Paul summoned me and asked me to bring this young man to you, as he has something to say to you'. (19) And the chief captain took him by the hand and withdrew and enquired privately, 'What is this that you have to report to me?' (20) And he said, 'The Jews plotted to ask you to bring Paul down on the morrow to the Sanhedrin as if you were going to make a more exact questioning about him. (21) Do not therefore be persuaded by them; for more than forty of their number are lying in wait for him and have vowed themselves not to eat or drink till they have killed him; and now they are ready, awaiting your promise.' (22) So then the chief captain dismissed the young man, charging him to 'tell nobody that you have laid this information before me'. (23) And he summoned two of his centurions and said, 'Prepare two hundred soldiers to go as far as Caesarea and seventy horsemen and two hundred *dexiolaboi*, from the third hour of the night'; (24) and he told them to provide animals that they might set Paul on them and bring him safely through to Felix the governor, (25) and he wrote a letter after this fashion; (26) 'Claudius Lysias to the most excellent governor, Felix, greeting. (27) This fellow was seized by the Jews and was about to be killed by them and I came on him and with the detachment rescued him, learning that he is a Roman. (28) And wanting to know the cause for which they accuse him, I brought him down to their Sanhedrin. (29) I found him accused about questions of their law, but with no charge worthy of death or bonds. (30) And when it was revealed to me that there would be a plot against the man, at once I sent him to you, ordering also his accusers to speak against him before you.'

(31) The soldiers then, as they had been commanded, took Paul and brought him by night to Antipatris. (32) And on the next day, letting the horsemen depart with him, they returned to the castle. (33) The others came

**and entered Caesarea and gave the letter up to the
governor and set Paul also before him. (34) And when he
had read it and asked from what province he was and
learned that he was from Cilicia, he said, (35) 'I will try
your case when your accusers also are present'; and he
ordered him to be guarded in Herod's palace.**

(12) **Plot,** cf. xix. 40. Rabbinic custom would allow dispensation from such vows if they proved impossible (Mishna,
Ned. iii. i, 3), and it was against such rash vows that Jesus
protested, Matt. v. 34 f. (13 ff.) The Western text is fuller and
more vivid but gives nothing which an intelligent scribe could
not have deduced from the text. (15) It has been urged that this
incident is a fabrication and that Paul would have gone to
Caesarea as the first stage of his journey to Rome, quite apart
from this 'plot'. But apart from a certain anti-Jewish tendency
in Luke, more pronounced still in the Western reviser, there
appears to be no motive for a 'fabrication' and the vivid details
suggest an eyewitness account. (16) Nothing else is known of
Paul's sister or nephew. The Latin African text supposes that
the nephew was drawn into the plot, which he betrayed; but
the scribe misunderstood 'came', taking it to mean 'being
present', i.e. at the plot. (20) **You were going to;** *mellōn,* as
B, A, 81 read, does not make such good sense as *mellon,* it,
the Sanhedrin, were going to, cf. vs. 15. The late *mellontes,*
'they', etc., is an obvious emendation. (23) The escort seems
far too large if *dexiolaboi* refers to persons; this word is not
found again till the sixth century, and it is so uncertain that
B.C. iv. 293 suggests (in place of the usual 'spearmen') 'led
horses', so eliminating the presence of 200 men and substituting
animals which would be needed to make the journey, of eighty
miles in all, possible in twenty-four hours. The variant,
dexioboloi, in A, 'slingers', is easier textually, but otherwise as
difficult as 'spearmen'. The third hour; between 9 and 10 P.M.
(24) **Felix** the governor was procurator from A.D. 52 to 59; he
was the brother of Claudius' favourite and freedman, Pallas.
After some success in putting down trouble in Judaea (Josephus,
B.J. ii. 13, 2) both his harshness and his failure to quell anti-
Semitic risings in Samaria led to his recall; Tacitus (*Hist.* v. 9)

says of him, 'With all manner of cruelty and lust he exercised the power of a king with the mind of a slave'. (26) **Claudius;** the name taken probably from the Emperor's when Lysias bought his freedom. **Most excellent;** or 'Your Excellency', a title which was a courtesy one in addressing a freedman, and reserved usually for those of the equestrian order from which all procurators were drawn. (27 ff.) If Luke did not see the document, he shows artistry in compiling a letter which does credit to Lysias by suppressing such facts as the important one that Paul was about to be flogged before his Roman citizenship was known. (29) Luke stresses again that Roman officials found the faith harmless. (30) The Greek shows traces of confusion, pointing to a lack of final revision, cf. *B.C.* iv. 295, Bruce, 418. (31) **Antipatris,** cf. vs. 23; though the exact site is not known, it may be Kulat Ras el 'Ain (G. A. Smith, *H.A.H.L.* 23 C 3); the party probably travelled down into the plains to Lydda then north to this place, rather than via Bethel through the hills. But see Cadbury, *B.A.H.* 64 f. (34) **What;** not 'what kind of' as the word would imply in classical Greek. For the question cf. Luke xxiii. 6. (35) **Try your case;** this is a technical term for holding a hearing, cf. Dittenberger, *O.G.I.S.* 335, 71, Job ix. 33. **Herod's palace;** or *praetorium.* The governor's residence was often a large house taken over for the purpose; here it had been the palace built by Herod the Great.

xxiv. 1-9. THE SPEECH OF TERTULLUS

(1) And after five days the high priest Ananias went down with some elders and an orator, one Tertullus; and they laid information before the governor against Paul. (2) And when he was summoned, Tertullus began the accusation saying, 'As we have enjoyed a long peace, thanks to you, and as this nation has benefited by many reforms, thanks to your foresight, (3) we accept them in every way and in every place, most excellent Felix, with all thankfulness. (4) But, that I may not delay you longer, I beg you of your kindness to hear us briefly. (5) For we

found this man a pestilent fellow, one who stirs up
revolts among all the Jews throughout the world and a
protagonist of the sect of the Nazarenes. (6) He tried also
to defile the Temple; and we laid hands on him. (8) You
can learn from him by personal examination of all those
things of which we accuse him.' (9) And the Jews also
joined the attack, saying that it was so.

(1) **Five days**; presumably after the events of xxiii. 33.
Tertullus may have been a Jew, especially if vs. 7 is authentic,
where 'our Law' is used; but the name was not rare. (2) **Peace
. . . reforms**; contrast on xxiii. 26 above; but the 'winning of
goodwill' at the opening of an orator's address meant nothing.
Bruce, 421, rightly notes that Luke's language is reminiscent
of 2 Macc. iv. 6. (4) **Delay**; or possibly, from another root,
'weary': **kindness**; the word translated by Matthew Arnold as
'sweet-reasonableness', a strange word to use of Felix. (5 f.)
The political charge of being a ringleader of sedition was the
most serious. **Nazarenes**; cf. on ii. 22. (6) **We laid hands on**;
a slight euphemism for mob-lynching! Vs. 7 is found only in
the Western text, 'and we wished to judge him according to our
law, but Lysias the chief captain came and with great violence
took him out of our hands, and commanded his accusers to come
before you'. Though this addition is impressive and is often
put among the Western readings which may well be authentic,
having been preserved in a second-century recension but having
dropped out of the Alexandrian recension, yet it may not be
genuine; it would make Lysias, not Paul, the antecedent of 'him'
in vs. 8, but the word for 'examine', cf. xxviii. 18, suggests
that a prisoner rather than an official was the object of the
inquiry. Cf. my *Alterations*, 70 f.

xxiv. 10-21. PAUL'S SPEECH BEFORE FELIX

(10) And Paul answered, when the governor beckoned
to him to speak, 'Knowing that you have been a judge
for this nation for many years, I willingly plead in my

own defence, (11) for it is in your power to learn that it is only within the last twelve days that I came up to Jerusalem to worship, (12) and they did not find me arguing with anyone or causing an uprising of the people either in the Temple or in the synagogue or in the city. (13) Nor can they prove the present charges against me. (14) But I confess this to you, that according to the Way, which they call a sect, thus worship I the God of our fathers, believing all things that are according to the law and written in the prophets, (15) having hope in God, which these men themselves cherish, that there is to be a resurrection both of the just and of the unjust. (16) In this also I exercise myself to have a clear conscience towards God and towards men at all times. (17) Now, after many years I came to bring alms and offerings for my nation; (18) they found me engaged in this, purified in the Temple, without a crowd and without tumult. (19) But some Jews from Asia—who ought to have been here before you and to accuse me, if they had anything against me. (20) Or let these men themselves say what wrong they found in me, as I stood before the Sanhedrin, (21) except this one utterance which I made as I stood among them, "It is for the resurrection of the dead that I am being judged this day before you".'

(10) Paul knew as well as Tertullus how to aim at winning good will. **Many years;** nine at the most, including Felix's term of office in Samaria. (11) **Twelve,** cf. xxi. 27 and xxiv. 1. **To worship,** i.e. as a pilgrim. (14) **the Way,** cf. ix. 2. **Our fathers;** the Christians claim the family portraits of the patriarchs and all such privileges as Julius Caesar had given to the Jews. (15) **These men,** presumably the Pharisees. The mention of the resurrection of the unjust as well as of the just is striking, but cf. Dan. xii. 2, John v. 28 f. The definite hope here expressed stands in contrast with the uncertain hopes found elsewhere whether only the righteous would rise again and when that would be, cf. *B.C.* iv. 301 f. (16) **I exercise myself;** a N.T. *hapax legomenon*, from which 'asceticism' was derived. In classical Greek it could mean to go into training, to take

254

pains, cf. the Pauline metaphors from the Isthmian games in
1 Cor. ix. 23 ff. **Clear,** 'unharmed', *B.C.* iv. 302, is better than
'void of offence'. (17) **Alms and offerings,** cf. Paul's references to his collection for the saints, i.e. the poor Christians at
Jerusalem impoverished by the early voluntary communism (cf.
that of the Qumran sect), cf. ii. 44 f. and by the famine (xi. 28),
1 Cor. xvi. 1 ff., 2 Cor. viii-ix, Rom. xv. 25 ff. As male Jews of
the Dispersion paid ½ shekel to the Temple, so they of the
Christian Dispersion paid their gifts to the mother-church of
Jerusalem and were thus cemented into unity with her. It is
striking that Acts does not say more about this collecting for
the saints, which was constantly in Paul's heart. (19) The break
in the sentence according to the Alexandrian, not Byzantine,
text is a typically Pauline *anacoluthon.* From Asia, cf. xxi. 27.
(20 f.) These verses may express Paul's uneasiness after throw-
ing his apple of discord into the midst of the Sanhedrin, xxiii.
6 ff., for using such an argument or it may be the reiteration
that the doctrine of the Resurrection, based on that of Jesus,
was the real bone of contention between Jews and Christians,
though the better Jews should accept it; this bone was a
doctrinal, not political one.

xxiv. 22-7. PAUL'S CASE IS DEFERRED

(22) But Felix put them off, knowing more exactly the
subject of the Way, saying, 'When Lysias, the chief
captain comes down, I will give judgement in your case',
(23) giving orders to the centurion for him to be guarded
and to have respite and that none of his friends should
be prevented from ministering to him.

(24) And after some days Felix appeared with Drusilla
his wife, a Jewess, and he summoned Paul and listened
to him about the faith in Christ Jesus. (25) But when he
reasoned with him about righteousness and self-control
and the judgement to come, Felix, being frightened,
answered, 'For the present go your way but I shall take
another opportunity and summon you again'. (26) He
hoped at the same time also that money would be given

him by Paul; therefore he summoned him even more frequently and conversed with him. (27) And when a period of two years was complete, Felix was replaced by Porcius Festus, and wanting to show favour to the Jews, Felix left Paul in bonds.

(22) **Put off;** reserved for decision after mature reflection, cf. 'Pronuntiavit amplius' (Blass). (23) **Respite;** or relaxation. (24) **Drusilla,** the third wife of Felix, was a daughter of Herod Agrippa I; she had married Azizus, king of Emesa c. A.D. 53, but Felix won her away with the help of Atomos, a Cypriote magician, cf. on xiii. 8. (25) The three subjects chosen were appropriate in view of Felix's greed, sexual lust, and future doom. **Opportunity;** it is uncertain whether Felix was fobbing off Paul or if Drusilla's information about Christianity and Paul's words had roused his real interest. (26) The *Lex Julia de repetundis* forbidding the taking of bribes from prisoners was honoured by provincial governors more often in the breach than in the observance. (27) **Two years;** from the date of Paul entering prison? Or from the date of Felix's appointment as procurator? The former seems more natural, but the latter is well supported by modern scholars who accept on the basis of Josephus, *Ant.* xx. 8, 9. and Tacitus, *Ann.* xiii. 14, the date A.D. 55 as that of the fall from imperial favour of Pallas, brother of Felix and the one who shielded Felix after his recall to Rome. According to Lake, if Felix was recalled in the early spring of A.D. 55, Pallas would just have had time to protect him. In this case the summer of A.D. 55 is the most probable year for the entry of Festus upon his office (*B.C.* v. 466, 471). On the other hand, Josephus' chronological notes are far from reliable and Lake's chronology for the last years of Paul's life is very compressed, cf. Introduction, 11, and see below on xxv. 1. It has been suggested that Paul wrote some, if not all, of his 'imprisonment letters' from Caesarea, if he did not write them from Ephesus or, as the traditional view maintained, from Rome; and that Luke spent the two years in collecting material for his Luke-Acts, making perhaps, as Streeter suggested, an early draft of Gospel material such as Proto-Luke in or near Caesarea (*The Four Gospels*, 218).

xxv. 1-12. PAUL BEFORE FESTUS

(1) Festus therefore entered on his province and after three days went up to Jerusalem from Caesarea. (2) And the chief priests and leading men of the Jews laid information against Paul. (3) And they asked a favour against him and begged Festus that he would send for him to Jerusalem, forming a plot to kill him on the way. (4) So then Festus answered that Paul was being kept at Caesarea but that he himself was on the point of leaving shortly. (5) 'Therefore', he said, 'let the men of power among you go down with me and if there is anything amiss in the man, let them accuse him.' (6) And having spent not more than eight or ten days among them, he went down to Caesarea, and on the morrow he sat on the bench and commanded Paul to be brought. (7) And when he came, the Jews who had come down from Jerusalem stood about him, bringing many and serious charges against him, which they were not able to prove, (8) Paul making his defence, 'I have done nothing wrong either against the law of the Jews or against the Temple or against Caesar'. (9) Then Festus, wishing to confer a favour on the Jews, said in answer to Paul, 'Do you want to go up to Jerusalem and there be judged on these matters before me?' (10) But Paul said, 'I stand before Caesar's judgement-seat, where I ought to be judged. I have not wronged the Jews, as you also know quite well. (11) Now if I am a wrongdoer and have done anything worthy of death, I do not plead to escape dying; but if there is nothing in these men's charges, no one can make a present of me to them. I appeal to Caesar.' (12) Then Festus, after conferring with the council, answered, 'You have appealed to Caesar; to Caesar you shall go'.

(1) The date of Festus' entry upon office, according to Eusebius, was A.D. 55–6 and he seems to have been governor for about four years. Bruce would make the date of his entry upon office c. 58, on the ground that Pallas, though out of favour, may still have had influence to use for his brother (cf. on xxiv.

27), and many scholars would accept a later date than Lake does, e.g. A.D. 60 (Zahn and Lightfoot), A.D. 59 (Plooij) and Lake himself admits (*B.C.* v. 466 f.), 'It is possible that Festus did not reach the province until the year after the recall of Felix, so that Paul may have left Caesarea in 56 and reached Rome in 57'. Only Acts and Josephus tell us anything of Festus, who belonged apparently to the gens Porcia. (3) Luke writes as though the same trap was prepared as before by the Jews, but it may have been their real object to get Paul before the Sanhedrin in Jerusalem, without Festus in the chair (vs. 9), so that they could do him 'legally' to death. Knowing this, Paul was forced to appeal to Caesar. (8) This is but the gist of Paul's answer to the charges brought against him, as against Jesus, Luke xxiii. 2. (9) What little is known of Festus shows him in a good light as a governor faced with a situation that could not be mended. But Luke, usually anxious to show that Rome officially favoured Christianity, does not spare Festus now. (10) B (Vaticanus) has 'Standing before Caesar's judgement-seat, I am standing where I ought to be judged'. But though ℵ supports B for the first 'standing', other MSS. omit it; even B sometimes has a word twice by mistake (dittography), cf. xix. 34. (11) **Plead to escape**; beg off. Though this passage does not imply that only Roman citizens could exercise the right of appeal to the Emperor, that right was probably so limited; what had been an appeal to the people originally was now to the Emperor alone (*provocatio ad Caesarem*) and the right of appeal from one magistrate to another (*appelatio*) coincided apparently with the *provocatio* to the Emperor. The questions that can be asked about the rights of appeal cannot all be answered, cf. Cadbury, *B.C.* v. 316 ff. Though Acts suggests some answers, it does not supply sufficient evidence. (12) **Council;** the assessors who helped a magistrate with their advice.

xxv. 13-27. PAUL BEFORE AGRIPPA AND BERNICE

(13) And after an interval of some days Agrippa the king and Bernice came down to Caesarea to give a welcome

to Festus. (14) And as they were spending many days there, Festus laid Paul's case before the king, saying, 'There is a man left by Felix, a prisoner. (15) When I came to Jerusalem, the chief priests and the elders of the Jews brought information about him, asking for a verdict against him. (16) I answered them that it is not a custom of the Romans to hand over anyone as a gift before the accused has his accusers face to face and has an opportunity of defence on the charge. (17) So when they came together here, I made no delay; I sat next day on the bench and I ordered the man to be brought. (18) And when his accusers stood up, they brought no charge of the wrongs that I supposed, (19) but they had some questions about their own religiosity to put to him and about one Jesus who was dead and who, Paul maintained, is alive. (20) And being at a loss over questioning about such matters, I asked if he wanted to go to Jerusalem to be judged there on these matters. (21) And when Paul appealed to be kept for the decision of the Emperor, I ordered him to be kept till I should send him to Caesar.' (22) And Agrippa said to Festus, 'I too would like to hear this man myself'. 'Tomorrow', he said, 'you shall hear him.' (23) And on the morrow when Agrippa came and Bernice with much pomp and entered into the audience-room with the chief captains and outstanding men of the city and when Festus had given the order, Paul was brought in. (24) And Festus said, 'King Agrippa, and all men present with us, you see this man, about whom all the multitude of the Jews petitioned me both in Jerusalem and here, crying out that he ought to live no longer. (25) But I realized that he had done nothing worthy of death; and when he appealed to the Emperor, I decided to send him. (26) And I have nothing definite to write about him to my lord. Therefore I brought him before you, and especially before you, king Agrippa, that when the examination has been conducted, I may have something to write. (27) For it seems to me unreasonable to send a prisoner without also signifying the charges against him.'

(13) Herod Agrippa II, son of Agrippa I, was a boy of 17 at Rome when his father died in A.D. 44. He received the tetrarchy of his uncle Herod of Chalcis when the latter died and exchanged this in 53 for the tetrarchies of Philip and Lysanias. He had already had the oversight of the Temple, and later Nero gave him cities in Galilee and Peraea. Rabbinical records point to his interest in Jewish questions. He tried to avert war with Rome, but took her side when it came and, like the renegade Josephus, was rewarded by Rome. He died about the beginning of the second century. Rumour suggested that he had incestuous relations with Bernice, his sister, who was about 50 when she heard Paul speak on this occasion, as her younger sister, Drusilla, had done. She too espoused the cause of Rome later and had intimate relations with Titus. There is no need to assume that because Acts ix. 15 had prophesied that Paul would stand before kings, so Luke has created this whole incident to fulfil the prophecy. To give a welcome; the aorist participle is timeless and expresses purpose here. (15 ff.) Festus puts the best possible construction on his own behaviour. (16) Luke may have heard of such a defence of Roman justice or he thought it appropriate here. (19) **Questions;** or points under dispute. **Religiosity;** or superstition, cf. xvii. 22. (22) As both the power of appointing to the High Priesthood and the custody of the sacred vestments had been given to this Herod in A.D. 49, and as he might be regarded as the 'secular head of the Jewish state' (cf. *B.C.* i. 26), he might be taken to have an interest in Paul. **I would like;** or I rather wanted; this may be a 'desiderative imperfect' (Moule, *op. cit.* 9, cf. 151) intended 'to soften a remark and make it more diffident or more polite', cf. Rom. ix. 3; but *B.C.* iv. 312 suggests that it means, 'I had wished', the parallel being the desire of another Herod to see Jesus (Luke iv. 9, xxiii. 8). (23) **Pomp;** cf. Diogenes Laertius, 4. 53. **Audience-room;** the *Digest* (iv. 18) uses the same word of the room used by the Emperor for hearing trials; but here the inquiry is quite informal. **Chief captains** or military tribunes; they were in command of each of the five cohorts at Caesarea and were probably non-Jewish by extraction. Paul's claim to be a Roman citizen was no doubt mentioned but not recorded here. (24) **Multitude** or body, community in a semi-official

political sense, cf. 1 Macc. viii. 20. (26) **my lord;** the title
Kyrios was a divine predicate attached to earthly rulers throughout the Eastern world. It was a cult-name in Caesar worship and
in the mystery religions; it is found on an inscription dated
62 B.C., used of Ptolemy XIII; used of Herod the Great and of
Agrippa I and II, it was used more and more of the Emperors
Caligula, Claudius, Nero, and Domitian (Vincent Taylor, *The
Names of Jesus*, 39 ff.). (27) The picture of the puzzled Roman
official, bewildered by a doctrine of the Resurrection, and
seeking advice from a Palestinian princelet, is so naïve that it
must be true.

xxvi. PAUL'S SPEECH BEFORE AGRIPPA II

(1) And Agrippa said to Paul, 'You are permitted to speak
on your own behalf'. Then Paul stretched out his hand
and began to make his defence: (2) 'With regard to all
the charges, king Agrippa, brought against me by the
Jews, I think myself happy to be about to make my
defence before you, (3) especially as you are expert in
all the customs and problems among Jews; therefore I
beg you to hear me patiently. (4) Now, all the Jews know
my manner of life from my youth which was originally
among my own nation in Jerusalem, (5) for they have
known from the first, if they would testify, that I lived a
Pharisee according to the strictest party of our religious
cult, (6) and now I stand judged for the hope of the
promise made by God to our fathers, (7) to which our
twelve tribes hope to attain, worshipping strenuously
night and day. (8) It is for this hope, O king, that I am
accused by Jews. Why is it judged unbelievable among
you that God raises the dead? (9) Now, I thought to
myself that I ought to do many deeds contrary to the
name of Jesus of Nazareth. (10) And I did so too in
Jerusalem; and I shut up in prisons many of the saints,
having received authority from the chief priests and
when they were put to death, I voted against them. (11)
And I punished them often throughout all the synagogues

261

and I used to compel them to blaspheme; and being exceedingly mad with them, I persecuted them as far as cities outside. (12) So I was going to Damascus with authority and commission from the chief priests (13) and at midday I saw on the way, O king, a light from heaven shining about me and my fellow-travellers with more than the brightness of the sun. (14) And when we all fell to the ground, I heard a voice saying to me in the Hebrew tongue, "Saul, Saul, why are you persecuting me? It is hard for you to kick against the pricks." (15) And I said, "Who are you, Lord?" And he said, "I am Jesus, whom you are persecuting. (16) But arise and stand upon your feet; for it was for this reason that I appeared to you to appoint you a minister and a witness both to the things in which you have seen me and to those in which I shall appear to you, (17) delivering you from the people and from the Gentiles, to whom I send you, (18) to open their eyes and to turn them from darkness to light and from the power of Satan to God, that they may receive remission of sins and an inheritance among those sanctified by faith set on me." (19) Hence, King Agrippa, I was not disobedient to the heavenly vision, (20) but I proclaimed first to those at Damascus, then also in Jerusalem, and through all the land of Judaea, and to the Gentiles, that they should repent and turn to God, performing works worthy of repentance. (21) It was for that reason that the Jews seized me in the Temple and tried to do away with me. (22) Obtaining help, therefore, from God, until this day I have stood testifying both to small and great, saying nothing beyond what the prophets said, and Moses, would come to pass, (23) that Christ should suffer and as the first that should rise from the dead He should announce light to both the people and the Gentiles.'

(24) And while he was making this defence, Festus said in a loud voice, 'You are mad, Paul. Much learning is driving you to madness.' (25) And Paul said, 'I am not mad, most excellent Festus, but I am uttering words of truth and soberness. (26) For the king knows about these

matters, to whom I speak, addressing him freely; for I am persuaded that none of these things has escaped his notice, for this was not done in a corner. (27) Do you believe, king Agrippa, in the prophets? I know that you believe.' (28) But king Agrippa said to him, 'In short you persuade me to play the Christian'. (29) But Paul said, 'Both in short and at length I would to God that not only you but all that listen to me to-day also would become as I am—apart from these bonds'.

(30) And the king stood up and the governor and Bernice and those sitting with them; (31) and after withdrawing, they spoke with each other, saying, 'This man is doing nothing worthy of death or bonds'. (32) And Agrippa said to Festus, 'This man could have been set free, if he had not appealed to Caesar'.

(1) The Syriac Harklean margin, which often supports a Western reading, adds after 'Paul', 'confident and comforted by the Holy Spirit'. For Paul's gesture cf. xiii. 16, xxi. 40. (2) Paul could win the good-will of his audience as well as any rhetor; and it is true that Agrippa did his utmost to save his people from war with Rome, till it proved inevitable. This speech is marked by its 'good' (classical) Greek prose, and the care bestowed on the speech suggests that Luke heard the original or received an account of it from Paul or some other good source. It is probably nearer the truth about Paul's conversion than either of the other two accounts in ix and xxii. (4) **Manner of life**; this Greek word occurs in the Preface to Ecclesiasticus and in the inscription put up to Jews in Phrygia honoured by their synagogue, c. A.D. 60–80, cf. *I.G. Rom.* 4, 655. **Know**; the classical form of the Greek is used; all the Jews would be those of Cilicia presumably. (5) **Religious cult**; the word is used of outward observance especially, cf. James i. 27; cf. Phil. iii. 5 for Paul's early adherence to the Phariseees. (6) For the Western text of P^{29} cf. *B.C.* iv. 316 and Lagrange, *Critique textuelle*, 409. A 'Western' text of Acts was known in Egypt probably as early as the second century. (7) **Strenuously**, cf. xii. 5, Luke xxii. 44, in which the reference is to prayer on both occasions; behind the use of this word may lie here the

Pauline thought that the Jew hoped to be saved by works. (8) **You;** plural. Paul now addresses the Jews present as well as Agrippa. (9) **The name;** cf. ii. 38, iii. 6, and *B.C.* v, n. xi. Many others besides Stephen seem from this section to have suffered persecution and death. (11) **I used to compel;** the imperfect may mean, 'I tried to compel'; *B.C.* iv. 317 refer to Pliny's famous *Ep.* x. 96, which says that while lapsed Christians and pagans offered wine and incense with supplication to the statues of the gods and reviled Christ, those who were truly Christians could be compelled to do none of those things. (12) **So;** or 'at this time' (lit. 'in which (things)'). It has been suggested that before his conversion Saul had been an official *shaliach* or representative or 'apostle' of the Sanhedrin; but it seems that we cannot be sure that *shaliach* was used before A.D. 70; and after that date it was used by Jews of those sent with Temple dues. But neither this verse nor the reference to the 'vote' in vs. 10 can be taken to point to Saul having been a member of the Sanhedrin. (14) In the other two accounts of the conversion we read that only Paul fell to the ground. **Hebrew;** or Aramaic; the form, 'Saoul' literally, indicates Semitic speech. **It is hard . . . goads;** a Greek proverb, cf. Euripides, *Bacchae*, 795; Aeschylus, *Agamemnon*, 1624; Terence, *Phormio*, i. 2. 27. It is not yet known to have been current in Aramaic as a proverb. This does not prove that the speech was Luke's composition. (16) The narrative of xxii. 14 f. and 17 and ix. 5 is 'telescoped' here, where Luke omits any reference to Ananias, probably intentionally, for the sake of variation; this is more likely than to suppose that he has interpolated the story of Ananias in chs. ix and xxii, having made them 'out of nothing'. **Minister;** cf. on xiii. 5; Witness; cf. i. 8, 22, etc., Paul is to bear his share in the apostolic 'witness', having seen the Lord. (17 f.) Both *B.C.* iv. 319 and Bruce, 444, rightly point out Luke's O.T. style consciously adopted (alongside his good Greek!) here, which is shown in his use of the infinitive with the article in the genitive, to express purpose. (18) Cf. Isa. xlii. 7, 16 and Col. i. 12 ff. (20) Once again the Greek is difficult and points to a lack of final revision. For the text cf. my *Alterations*, 71. (21) **Do away with;** kill, cf. Polyb. i. 21. 8 for this verb. (22) **Obtain help;** a good classical expression. (23) Some scholars have maintained that the doctrine of the Suffering Messiah was held by a section of the Jews before and in our Lord's day; the Christian identification of Jesus with the Suffering Servant may have led the Jewish commentators to avoid it themselves. This view may have some support from the Qumran Scrolls, if Prof. W. H. Brownlee is right in his interpretation of I Q S^a at Isa. lii. 14, 'So have I *anointed* his visage more than any man' (B.A.S.O.R. 132, Dec., 1953, 8 ff.). That Christ should suffer; or lit. 'whether . . .'. Early Christians almost certainly drew up lists of O.T. Proof-texts or Testimonies taken to point to Christ; they may have headed them with short titles, e.g. 'whether Christ should suffer', 'whether He should be the first to rise from the dead', 'whether He should be a light to lighten the Gentiles', as J. Rendel Harris suggested, *Testimonies*, i. 19 f. Cf. the leaf from Qumran Cave 4 of a Testimony list citing Deut. xviii. 15 (cf. Acts iii. 22 f., vii. 37) with Num. xxiv. 17 and Deut. xxiv. 17 (cf. J. T. Milik, *Discoveries in the Judaean Desert*, i, 1955, 121); cf. also the probably Christian fourth-century papyrus giving similar testimonia (C. H. Roberts, *Catalogue of the Greek and Latin Papyri in the John Rylands Library*, iii. 10-10). Christ was the 'first-fruits' of them that slept, as Paul said, 1 Cor. xv. 20, the B^ereshith which could include in its many meanings 'first-fruits', cf. C. F. Burney, *J.T.S.* xxvii, 1926, 160 ff. (24) **Learning**; lit. letters, but with this sense as early as Plato, *Apol.* 26, cf. John vii. 24. Paul's opponents at Corinth said that his letters were weighty and strong but his bodily presence weak and his speech of no account and that he was a 'fool', 2 Cor. x. (25) R.S.V. translates 'I am speaking the sober truth'. (26) Paul could appeal to Agrippa to bear out that the Jewish doctrine of eschatology was a valid one, but the king would not consider the claim that Jesus brought the *eschaton* and that the New Age had arrived with Him. **Done in a corner**; a classical tag, cf. Plato, *Gorgias* 485. (28) Agrippa avoids the dilemma either of saying that he disbelieves the prophets or that Paul's arguments are convincing. **In short**; this may mean 'in brief', and his words are picked up by Paul, possibly in another sense. **To play the Christian**, lit. to make a Christian, but 1 Kings xxi. 7 suggests the meaning 'to play the part of', cf. A. Nairne, *J.T.S.* xxi, 1920, 171 f.

(29) **In short and at length;** probably means 'with few or many words'. **Apart from these bonds;** a grim jest accompanied no doubt by Paul's gesture of extending his hands. (31) As Herod and Pilate had declared Jesus to be innocent, so now the authorities declare the innocence of Paul. (32) The unofficial inquiry is over; the appeal made to Rome had to stand.

xxvii. THE VOYAGE AND SHIPWRECK

(1) And when it was decided that we should sail to Italy, they handed over both Paul and some other prisoners to a centurion, named Julius, of the Augustan cohort. (2) And embarking on a ship of Adramyttium, which was on the point of sailing to places on the coast of Asia, we put out, Aristarchus a Macedonian of Thessalonica being with us. (3) And on the next day we put in at Sidon; and Julius treated Paul in a friendly way and allowed him to go to his friends and have attention paid to him. (4) And putting out from there we sailed under the lee of Cyprus, because the winds were contrary. (5) And after sailing across the sea which is off Cilicia and Pamphylia, we came to Myra in Lycia. (6) And there the centurion, finding a ship of Alexandria sailing to Italy, made us embark on it. (7) And we sailed slowly for many days and came with difficulty over against Cnidus and as the wind did not allow us to go further, we sailed under the lee of Crete over against Salmone. (8) And coasting along it with difficulty, we came to a place called Fair Havens, near which was a city, Lasea.

(9) And when a long time passed and the voyage was now dangerous because the Fast was now gone by, Paul recommended them, saying, (10) 'Gentlemen, I perceive that it will be with much injury and loss not only of the cargo and the ship but also of our lives that the voyage is about to be made'. (11) But the centurion was persuaded rather by the captain and ship-owner than by Paul's words. (12) And as the harbour was unsuitable to winter

in, the majority advised to put out from there in the hope
of being able to reach Phoenix and winter there, it being
a harbour of Crete looking north-east and south-east. (13)
And when the south wind blew gently, thinking that they
had obtained their purpose, they weighed anchor and
coasted along Crete. (14) But shortly a tempestuous wind
called Euraquilo beat down from the land. (15) And when
the ship was caught and could not face into the wind, we
gave way to it and were carried along. (16) And running
under a small island, called Kauda, we were able with
difficulty to make the dinghy secure. (17) They hoisted it
up and used props, trussing the ship; and fearing that
they would be cast on the Syrtis, they lowered the gear
and so were carried along. (18) And as we were exceedingly tempest-tossed, the next day they began to throw
cargo overboard; (19) and on the third day they threw
out with their own hands the ship's tackle. (20) And when
neither sun nor stars appeared for many days and no
small tempest lay on us, all hope of being saved was at
length removed. (21) And as they had long been without
food, Paul stood in the midst of them and said, 'Gentlemen, you should have obeyed me and not put out from
Crete and incurred this injury and loss. (22) And now I
advise you to be of good courage; for there will be no
loss of life among you, but only of the ship. (23) For there
stood by me this night an angel of the Lord, whose I am
and whom I serve; (24) saying, "Fear not, Paul, you
must stand before Caesar; and behold, God has granted
you as a gift all those that sail with you". (25) So be of
good courage, gentlemen, for I trust God that it shall be
so, as it has been told me. (26) But we must be cast upon
some island.'

(27) And when it was the fourteenth night, as we were
carried to and fro in the Adriatic, about midnight the
sailors conjectured that they were nearing land. (28) So
they took soundings and found twenty fathoms; and after
a short distance they took soundings again and found
fifteen fathoms. (29) And fearing that we might be cast
onto rocky places, they threw out four anchors from the

stern and prayed for day to come. (30) And when the sailors sought to escape from the ship and lowered the dinghy into the sea under the pretext of stretching out anchors from the prow, (31) Paul said to the centurion and to the soldiers, 'If these men do not stay in the ship, you cannot be saved'. (32) Then the soldiers cut the rope from the dinghy and let it fall away. (33) And when day was about to dawn, Paul exhorted them all to partake of nourishment and said, 'To-day is the fourteenth day that you have waited without food, having taken nothing. (34) Therefore I beg you to partake of nourishment; for this is for your own safety; for not a hair shall perish from the head of any of you.' (35) And after saying this, and after taking bread, he gave thanks before them all to God and he broke it and began to eat. (36) And they were all of good courage and took nourishment themselves. (37) And we were in all two hundred and seventy-six souls in the boat. (38) And when they had eaten enough, they lightened the ship, casting the wheat out into the sea. (39) And when it was day, they did not recognize the land but they noticed a bay that had a beach onto which they planned, if possible, to drive the ship. (40) And they slipped the anchors and let them go into the sea, at the same time loosening the bands of the rudders; and hoisting the foresail to the wind, they made for the beach. (41) But striking a place where two seas met, they ran the vessel aground; and the prow stuck fast and remained immovable; but the stern began to break up because of the force (of the waves). (42) And it was a plan of the soldiers to kill the prisoners that none should swim off and escape. (43) But the centurion wishing to keep Paul safe prevented them from carrying out their plan; and he ordered those that could swim to throw themselves overboard first and to go to land, (44) and the rest, some on planks and others on other things from the ship; and so it came about that all escaped safely to the land.

(xxvii) The best discussion of this chapter is by James Smith of Jordanhill, *The Voyage and Shipwreck of St. Paul*, 4th ed.,

1880. The vivid narrative as well as the first person plural demands an eye-witness as the source and to say that Luke's account is based on literary sources alone, e.g. Josephus, *Vita*, iii, is most unconvincing, *pace* Dibelius.

(1) **They handed over;** an impersonal plural more frequent in Mark than Luke; partly perhaps because 'they' is not defined, the Western text has rewritten the whole verse without adding to our knowledge, 'And so the governor decided to send him to Caesar and the next day he called a centurion named Julius of the cohort Augusta and handed over Paul and the other prisoners to him'. **The Augustan cohort;** it has been suggested that the *Speira Sebaste* was one of the *Cohortes Sebastenorum* or auxiliary cohorts of Samaritans which were on garrison duty in Jerusalem in Herod's day (Josephus, *B.J.* ii. 3, 4 and 4, 2). But *Sebaste* here must mean 'of Augustus', and it is a fact that a *Cohors Augusta* was in Syria during the first century A.D., cf. *B.C.* v. 443, and it was probably *Cohors Augusta I* of which Julius was centurion. Cf. also on xxviii. 16. (2) **Adramyttium,** in Mysia, north of Pergamos and south-east of Troas. Aristarchus, cf. xix. 29, xx. 4, Philem. 24, Col. iv. 10; from the last reference it seems that he was with Paul in prison, and this points to Rome rather than Ephesus, *pace* Duncan; Luke would hardly have mentioned Thessalonica here again, cf. xix. 29, if that was his home and he were going no farther than it. (3) **Sidon.** 'This stopping at Sidon . . . probably was for the purposes of trade' (Smith, *op. cit.* 64). **His friends;** lit. the friends. Is 'Friends' a name for Christians? Cf. 3 John 15, Luke xii. 4, John xv. 14, and the group around Abercius according to his inscription (English translation in B. J. Kidd, *Documents illustrative of the History of the Church*, i. 111). But later the term is found only in Gnostic circles until modern times. **Attention,** a classical word, but a N.T. *hapax legomenon.* (4) **Under the lee of Cyprus;** this probably means north of the island, the prevailing winds being west or north-west, cf. Smith, *op. cit.* 68. (5) **Sailing across;** this would imply that they did not hug the coast; if they had done the latter, the Western text 'for fifteen days' would have been more plausible than it is. Lucian (*Navigium*, 7) mentions that a crossing took ten days from Sidon to Lycia. **Myra,** though north of Alexandria, was a

natural port of call for grain ships on the way to Rome, owing
to the prevailing westerly winds. Of this place Smith says, 'The
stupendous magnitude of its theatre attests the extent of its
former population; the splendour of its tombs, its wealth' (*op.
cit.* 70); in Appian's day Myra was on a navigable river, but
according to Strabo it lay 20 stadia from the sea, the river
presumably having silted up. (6) **Ship of Alexandria;** the
Egyptian corn-ships were of great size, cf. vs. 37 (Smith, *op.
cit.* 71), and if they were on Government service they could be
used, as here, to transport prisoners. (7) Smith compares Cicero,
ad Fam. xiv. 5, 'Having met with contrary winds and sailed
slowly and with difficulty. . . .' **Cnidus** lay on the Carian headland of Triopium; Luke does not say that they landed there,
though it had two large harbours. Salmone, the headland on the
east of Crete; the ship sailed east and south of Crete to reach
smooth water. Smith thinks that the wind was between N.N.W.
and W.N.W. (*op. cit.* 76). (8) He says that **Fair Havens** is the
last harbour before arriving at Cape Matala, the farthest point
to which an ancient ship could have attained with north-
westerly winds. The ancient name survives in 'Kalolomonia'.
The probable site of **Lasea** was identified a century ago from
ruins; the textual variants Alai and Halassa gave rise to Thalassa
or 'sea', cf. the Vulgate. **The Fast** or Day of Atonement on the
10th of Tishri fell in September-October. A voyage after the
middle of September was thought risky and after November 11th
dangerous; cf. Vegetius, *De re militari*, iv. 39. As Smith says
(*op. cit.* 85), 'It became a question whether they should winter
in Fair Havens or move the ship to Port Phenice, a harbour on
the same side of Crete, about forty miles farther to the west-
ward'. Paul stands out here, as in vs. 31, as a natural leader of
men. It is unnecessary to suppose, with some critics, that these
passages were interpolations, Luke's purpose being to bring
out the force of Paul's personality. The advice of the others
was to make use of the unexpected wind from the south either
to reach Phoenix or even possibly to attempt to get to Italy.
(10) **Injury**, a word used in Pindar of a loss at sea. (11 f.) **The
captain** was ship's master, responsible for choosing and commanding the crew; as Plutarch observes, he was himself chosen
by the ship-owner; on a voyage that was state-organized the

centurion probably had a vote too, hence the word 'majority' in vs. 12. (12) **Looking north-east and south-east;** this translation would be in line with Smith's identification of the harbour with Lutro, one of the best harbours on the south coast, cf. his map, *op. cit.* 96; but, if the Greek is taken quite literally, the meaning may be 'down the south-west and the north-west wind', which would suggest identifying Phoenix with Smith's neighbouring harbour of Phenike to the west of the same squat, pear-shaped promontory. Lack of certainty may be due to Luke not having touched at either place. (14) **Tempestuous,** or more lit. 'typhonic'. The hybrid word Euraquilo denotes a nor'easter. 'The sudden change from a south wind to a violent northerly wind is a common occurrence in these seas' (Smith, *op. cit.* 102). Such a nor'easter could not have driven the ship to Meleda off the Dalmatian coast which, before Smith wrote, was considered sometimes as the scene of the shipwreck. (15) **Face into;** Smith suggests, *op. cit.* 98 n., that the origin of the phrase lay in the custom of putting an eye on each side of the bow of a ship. Smith reckons that the gale struck the boat when it was near a small group of islands, the Paximades, Kauda lying about twenty-three miles to leeward. (16) **Kauda,** B $\aleph^c$ Lat.^{vg}· Syr.^{vg} gave rise to modern Gavdho, Ital. Gozzo; it was known to Pliny as Gaudus (*Nat. Hist.* iv. 12, 61); $\aleph$ 81 read Clauda, which may have been the Alexandrian as opposed to the Latin form. The dinghy had to be hauled on deck as it was probably water-logged. (17) The next task was to frap or truss the boat, or technically to 'hog it' probably, i.e. to stretch a rope not entirely under the boat but above decks from stem to stern to stop it breaking its back by holding stem and stern tight together. See Cadbury, *B.C.* v, note xxviii, esp. p. 351 with its illustration of an Egyptian ship. The props would form a hogging truss, raising the rope above the deck and holding it taut. This illustration, taken from an Egyptian drawing of an expedition of Queen Hatseput some eighteen and a half centuries before Luke, makes it clear, cf. Cadbury, *B.A.H.* 10. **Syrtis** major was the shoal west of Cyrene. **Gear,** a general word for vessel or instrument would cover 'appurtenances of every kind, such as spars, rigging, anchors and cable' (Smith, *op. cit.* 111). (18) **To throw cargo overboard,** cf. Jonah i. 4 LXX, which was probably in Luke's mind as he wrote; some wheat, however, was kept, cf. vs. 38. (19) **Tackle;** Smith suggests that this would include the main-yard. (20) **Sun, stars;** without compass or sextant, the sailors in Paul's day had no other guide. (21) Smith points to the many possible causes in a storm at sea for going without food, including 'the impossibility of cooking or the destruction of provisions from leakage' (*op. cit.* 117 f.); there are other causes too; ancient writers did not refer much to sea-sickness. If Paul used the argument, 'I told you so!' (cf. Bruce, 461), it is strange that he did not meet the fate of Jonah. (27) Smith reckons that it would take about a fortnight for the ship to drift helplessly from Cauda to Malta. The Adriatic covered not only what it means to-day but the eastern Mediterranean waters from Venice to N. Africa. Nearing land; lit. land was approaching; was this a nautical expression? But B with support from *g* and *s* suggests that the original was 'land was re-echoing', i.e. they heard breakers or the echo of their shouts. (28) Smith, *op. cit.* 128, works out that, under the conditions described, a ship starting late in the evening from Kauda would by midnight, fourteen days afterwards, be less than three miles from the entrance to 'St. Paul's bay' at Malta. (29) **Anchors from the stern;** usually anchors are let down from the prow; but as Smith says, both ends of an ancient ship were alike (*op. cit.* 134). **Prayed for day to come;** to see if the shore was 'iron-bound' (Smith) or if it offered a good landing beach. (30) The wind had dropped apparently enough for the dinghy to be lowered with some prospect of it being used as a means of escape. (32) Luke does not record the captain's comments when the soldiers cast off the dinghy. (34) **Safety;** or salvation. **Not a hair shall perish,** cf. Luke xxi. 18; this was a Hebrew proverb. (35) The Eucharistic-sounding language is probably used unconsciously; every meal to a Jew has some religious meaning. (37) Were there 276 on board or only 76? In uncial Greek letters with the numerals contracted, the difference between '276' and 'about 76' is slight; the smaller figure is attested by the Alexandrian B Cop.sa. Eth. Cf. vs. 6 for the size of the ship; Smith thinks that this vessel could have been large enough to hold over 200 souls, cf. Josephus, *Vita*, iii, according to which Josephus sailed from Rome with over 600 on board. It may be a coincidence that 276 is a 'triangular' number, the sum of all numbers from 1-23 inclusive. It is true that Luke liked to qualify numerals with 'about', which favours the smaller figure; but with a figure as small as 76 'about' is hardly in place. (38) **Lightened the ship;** cf. Jonah i. 5 LXX and a similar phrase in Julius Pollux (Smith, *op. cit.* 139); there is no need to accept Naber's emendation *iston*, mast, for *siton*, wheat. (39) The description here, cf. vss. 29, 41, makes the identification with 'St. Paul's bay' certain. **To drive,** *exōsai*, is better than 'to save', *eksōsai*, which is supported by B C Cop. Arm. (40) **Bands of the rudders;** two oars were commonly used as rudders, and ropes or lashings operated and held the rudder. **Foresail;** the Greek *artemon*, found here for the first time, was a borrowing from the Latin word describing a small sail on the foremast which could be used to guide a ship limping into harbour, cf. Smith, *op. cit. Dissertation*, iii. (41) A place of two seas probably means a bar or a shoal; Smith identifies it with a narrow channel between Malta and the island of Salmonetta which 'shelters St. Paul's bay on the N.W.'. **Stuck fast;** the verb means 'to press hard'; here it means struck and stuck. (44) **Planks;** commentators refer to the suggestion of Breusing and Blass that planks had been used to keep the cargo in place; other things could be 'other persons', and *B.C.* iv. 339 f. accepts the suggestion that some were carried ashore (Paul among them?) on the backs of the crew; if Luke got ashore thus, it would explain how he was able to save his notes perhaps, though it is on record that Julius Caesar preserved his papers while swimming 200 paces (Suet. *Jul.* 64). Dibelius' suggestion that 'all' does not include Paul is fantastic.

xxviii. 1-15. FROM MALTA TO ROME

(1) And when we had escaped safely, then we recognized that the island was called Malta. (2) And the natives showed us no ordinary hospitality; for they kindled a fire and welcomed us all to it because of the rain that had set in and because of the cold. (3) And when Paul

gathered a number of sticks and put them onto the fire, a viper came out of the heat and fastened onto his hand. (4) And when the natives saw the creature hanging on his hand, they said to each other, 'This man is surely a murderer, and though he has escaped safely from the sea, Justice has not allowed him to live'. (5) Now he shook off the animal into the fire and suffered no harm. (6) But they expected him to be about to swell up or to fall dead suddenly; and when they expected it for a long time and saw nothing amiss happen to him, they changed their minds and said that he was a god.

(7) And in the parts about that place was a holding belonging to the chief man of the island, Publius, who received us and for three days entertained us hospitably. (8) And it happened that Publius' father lay in the grip of a fever and of dysentery. Paul went in to him and prayed and put his hands on him and healed him. (9) And when this happened, the rest also who were ill in the island came forward and were cured. (10) They loaded us too with many honours and when we put out they placed on board what we needed.

(11) And after three months we put out to sea in a boat that had wintered at the island, an Alexandrian boat with the Twin Brothers as a figure-head. (12) And when we put in to Syracuse, we stayed there for three days. (13) Making a detour from there, we arrived at Rhegium and after one day, when a south wind sprang up, we came in two days to Puteoli; (14) and we found brethren there and were begged by them to remain among them for seven days; and so we came to Rome. (15) And the brethren heard news of us and came to meet us from there as far as Appii Forum and Three Taverns; and when Paul saw them, he gave thanks to God and took courage.

(1) Malta, not Meleda, cf. on xxvii. 14; the Phoenician name Melita meant 'refuge' or 'escape', and Luke may be playing here on the meaning, cf. J. Rendel Harris, *E.T.* xxi, 1909–10, 18. (2) **The natives** (not 'barbarians') spoke a Punic or

Phoenician dialect which would be 'barbarian' to a Greek. **Welcomed;** a variant reading would mean 'refreshed'. **Had set in,** cf. Bruce, 470. (3) **Gathered;** twisted together. **Viper;** there may have been poisonous snakes in Malta then, as there are not now, or Luke may have thought such a snake as the *Coronella Austriaca* to be poisonous. An exactly similar incident happened in recent years to Bishop Philip Strong in New Guinea, cf. Luke x. 19, Mark xvi. 18. **Fastened;** in the sense of bit. (4) **Creature;** the word is still used in Greek, especially of a snake. Cadbury (*B.A.H.* 26 f.) illustrates 'the ineluctable character of justice', i.e. the goddess *Dike* (Justice), from a Greek schoolboy's writing exercise *c.* A.D. 450–550 ending, 'The divine always brings the wicked unto *Dike*'. (6) **Swell up,** cf. i. 18, a word used by Hippocrates. **Amiss,** cf. Luke xxiii. 41; was this a medical word (Bruce, 471)? Harnack thought this whole section to be medical in tone. (7) **Chief man;** inscriptions show that prōtos was the correct local nomenclature, *I.G.* xiv. 601; *C.I.L.* 7495. **Poplius,** i.e. Publius would be merely he *praenomen.* (8) Cf. the medical language of Luke iv. 38. **Fever;** lit. fevers; Maltese fever has become notorious. **Put . . . hands on,** cf. Luke iv. 40, 'Mark' xvi. 18. (10) **Honours;** or gifts? *B.C.* iv. 343 refers to Eccles. xxxviii. 1 and 1 Tim. v. 17 and to Cicero's use of *honos* for a doctor's fee. (11) **Navigation** began after the winter, probably about February to March, cf. on xxvii. 9, when the west winds began to blow. The Twins Castor and Pollux were considered by sailors to be favourable, the sight of the constellation in rough weather being a good omen. It would be natural to 'dedicate' a ship in this way and she would be called by the name of the figure-head. (See thereon the interesting note by F. J. Dölger in *Antike und Christentum* vi, 1950, 276.) (12) **Syracuse,** the famous port on the east coast of Sicily. (13) **Making a detour;** *perielthontes;* the same meaning can be given to *perielontes,* but cf. xxvii. 40 where it meant 'slip', 'cast off'. **Rhegium;** on the west toe of Italy, mod. Reggio di Calabria. **Puteoli,** near Naples, mod. Pozzuoli, was the site of the first Augusteum or shrine to the cult of the Emperor, cf. *B.C.* iv. 344; this port, like Ostia, received the Alexandrian grain-ships. (14) **Brethren;** it is to be noted that Christians had arrived, probably in the course of trading, in

Italy, including Rome, before Peter or Paul did, cf. the Sator inscription, McNeile, *I.S.N.T.*, 2nd ed., 235, which may well point to the existence of Latin-speaking Christians at Pompeii before A.D. 79. **Rome;** Luke anticipates the two stopping-places mentioned in the next verse before Rome is mentioned again. There is no need with Ramsay to suppose that here the district around Rome is meant. **Appii Forum** is forty-three miles southeast of Rome, cf. Horace, *Sat.* i. 5. 3, and **Three Taverns** is ten miles nearer Rome, both on the Appian way.

xxviii. 16-end. THE FINAL SCENE AT ROME

(16) And when we came to Rome, Paul was allowed to stay by himself with the soldier who guarded him.

(17) And it happened that after three days he called together the local leaders of the Jews and when they came together he said to them, 'Brethren, though I have done nothing against the people or the customs of the fathers, I was handed over as a prisoner from Jerusalem into the hands of the Romans. (18) They examined me and wanted to let me go because there was no cause of death in me. (19) And when the Jews opposed it, I was compelled to appeal to Caesar but not as though I had anything of which to accuse my nation. (20) For this reason therefore I asked to see you and to address you. It is for the sake of Israel's hope that I wear this chain.' (21) And they said to him, 'Neither have we received letters about you from Judaea, nor has any one of the brethren come and reported or spoken any ill of you. (22) But we think it right to hear your views from you. For as for this party, it is known to us that it is spoken against everywhere.'

(23) And when they had appointed a day for him, many of them came to his lodging and he expounded to them, testifying to the kingdom of God, and persuading them about Jesus both from the law of Moses and from the prophets from morning till evening. (24) And some be-

lieved the things that were spoken, and some disbelieved. (25) And not being in harmony with one another, they dissolved, Paul speaking one word, 'Well spoke the Holy Spirit through Isaiah the prophet to your fathers saying, (26) "Go to this people and say, 'Hearing you will hear and not understand, and seeing you will see and not perceive; (27) for the heart of this people is grown stupid and the hearing of their ears is made dull and their eyes they have closed; lest they should see with their eyes and hear with their ears and understand with their heart, and turn, and I should heal them '." (28) So let it be known to you that it is to the Gentiles that the salvation of God has been sent; even they shall hear.' (30) And he remained for the space of two whole years in his own hired house and received all who came in to him, (31) preaching the kingdom of God and teaching about the Lord Jesus Christ with all boldness, without hindrance.

(16) The Western text runs, 'The centurion handed over the prisoners to the *stratopedarch* but he allowed Paul . . .'; cf. my *Alterations*, 65-7. It is possible that already in Paul's day the *princeps peregrinorum*, as *g* translates *stratopedarch*, was in charge of troops detailed for special foreign service and may have been already in command of the *frumentarii* in the *castra peregrinorum* on the Coelian hill. The *frumentarii* had as special duty to guard the corn-ships. But the reading of *g* may be due to a scribe's knowledge of the title current in his day, and there is no evidence that a *princeps peregrinorum* existed during the first century A.D. The *stratopedarch* may have been the Praetorian prefect, cf. *C.I.L.* 3.13648, 14187,[5] to whom provincial prisoners were handed or he may have been simply the senior officer or 'military commander', cf. *B.G.U.* 1822.13 (probably of the first century B.C.). In any case Paul was kept under loose 'house-arrest'. Some Western MSS. have 'outside the camp' after 'himself', cf. my *Alterations*, 67.

(21) Paul is said by Luke not to have been delated by the Jews in Jerusalem to the Jews in Rome; to some critics this seems as unlikely as Paul's tactless alienation of Jewish sympathies in vss. 25 ff. But this section cannot be explained away

as propaganda to show that Paul invariably preached first to the Jews and only then to the Gentiles or that the Jews met with rejection by God because they rejected the Gospel themselves. As under Roman law a prosecution which failed was liable to go hard against the prosecutor, the Jews in Rome may have let the matter rest. (22) Even the Jews recognize the Christians as a Jewish party! (23) **Lodging;** hospitality is the usual rendering, though it can mean 'guest-chamber' (*P.S.I.* 1, 50, 16, fourth-fifth century A.D.). The Gospel of the Kingdom is that of the saving acts of God done through Christ. To speak, as *B.C.* iv. 348 does, of the 'transition of the teaching of Jesus into the teaching about Jesus', is to miss the whole point. (25) Isa. vi. 9-10 is cited probably from a list of O.T. Testimonies; as C. H. Dodd says (*According to the Scriptures*, 38), '. . . It seems highly probable Isa. vi. 10 was widely accepted at an early period as a testimonium to the situation which arose when the Jews rejected the Gospel and were found to be excluded from the new people of God, and that it was employed as such in more versions than one, the most influential being a non-Septuagintal version known to Paul and John and possibly to Mark'. Mark iv. 11 f. cites it, implying that Jesus spoke in parables which were intended to be difficult and not to illustrate His teaching. Cf. J. Jeremias, *The Parables of Jesus*, 1954, 13. After 28, the Western and Byzantine texts have 29. 'And when he had said these words, the Jews departed, holding much dispute among themselves.' (30) **In his own hired house;** or 'at his own expense'. The suggestion has been made that the readers of Acts would know that after eighteen months at least in prison any legal proceedings would automatically lapse, if no accusers came forward to present the charges, cf. *B.C.* v. 330 f. (31) Cf. on vs. 23 above. The Western text, probably in order to soften the 'abrupt ending', adds 'because this is the Lord Jesus Christ, the Son of God, through whom the whole world will begin to be judged'. With this may be compared the end of the *Apology* of Aristides. But B. S. Easton (*Purpose*, 10) defends the very last word of all, 'the crisp adverb that points the moral unmistakably'. For the ending, see Introduction, 6.

THE APOSTLES

(See K. H. Rengstorf, *Apostleship*, in Kittel, *T.W.N.T.*, trans. by J. R. Coates, 1952, and the latter's bibliography, p. ix, to which should be added H. Mosbech, *Studia Theologica* ii, 1948, 166-200, H. J. Carpenter, *Minister, Ministry*, in Richardson's *T.W.B.B.* and J. Y. Campbell, *Apostle, ibid.*; W. L. Knox, *Jerusalem*, 363-71; V. Taylor, *The Gospel according to St. Mark*, 619-27; for articles on the word *shaliaḥ* by Dom G. Dix, following up his essay in K. E. Kirk's *The Apostolic Ministry*, ed. 1946, see *Theology*, li. 166-70, 249-56, 341-3 and lii. 385 f. with the objections raised by J. W. Hunkin and H. St. J. Hart.)

RENGSTORF *op. cit.* 4 ff., shows that in the realm of Cynic-Stoic philosophy *kataskopos* (rather than *episkopos*, the Christian term for overseer or bishop) meant an inspector, though the Cynic was *episkopōn*, the examiner of all human behaviour. It may be no accident that the word used in 1 Pet. iv. 15, *allotri(o)episkopos*, 'meddler', 'busybody', lit. 'overseer of other men's business', has two parts, each of which is used by Epictetus, iii. 22, 97, when he is concerned to defend the Cynics on a charge of interfering in the affairs of others. As Rengstorf says, 'We may say that the Cynico-Stoic philosopher in his role as *kataskopos* is the contemporary figure which stands nearest to that of the New Testament apostle'. When Paul spoke in Athens, Acts xvii, he must have resembled such a peripatetic philosopher. The Greek root of *Apostolos* denotes, of course, one who is sent; in classical Greek it could mean a naval expedition, and it often had, as an undercurrent, a connexion with naval matters. But the Jews, who had no love of the sea, rarely used the word. Josephus, *Ant.* xvii. 300, does use it of a despatch of envoys. The word also occurs in 1 Kings xiv. 6 (LXX) where Ahijah the prophet speaks to Jeroboam's wife, 'I am an apostle (*apostolos*)' where the Hebrew is strictly a passive participle, 'sent', cf. also Isa. xviii. 2 (Symmachus, Heb. *çir*); the Rabbis were to use *Shaliᵃḥ* (Aram. *Sheliḥa'*) as a noun with the root meaning 'sent'. *Sheluchin*, or authorized agents, were common in religious and legal circles from the time of the Chronicler onwards, the agent acting with full authority for his principal on the often quoted grounds that 'the

279

one whom a man sends is the equivalent of himself' (*Ber.* 5, 5). An ambassador was as his king. A *shali^aḥ* could also represent a body of people (Rengstorf, 16), ecclesiastical or otherwise. After A.D. 70 the envoys taking money to support poor Jewish scholars in Palestine were *sheluchin*, but there is no evidence that there were authorized Jewish missionaries or agents called thus before that date. The Rabbis also applied the term *shali^aḥ* to the priesthood as a whole and to notable priests or prophets, or both, e.g. Moses, Elijah, Elisha, and Ezekiel (Rengstorf, 21 f.), but not to every prophet.

In the New Testament Christ is called an *Apostolos* only once (Heb. iii. 1) in the phrase, 'Apostle and High Priest of our confession', but the significance of Christ's mission as that of God's unique agent sent from Him is brought out repeatedly in the Gospels, especially the Fourth Gospel, cf. John xiii. 16 (nor is an *apostolos* greater than he that sent him); see Rengstorf, *op. cit.* 26. In turn the Holy Spirit is Christ's *alter ego* and agent, cf. John xvi. 13. Typical of the Fourth Gospel is the utterance, 'As the Father hath sent me, even so send I you', xx. 21, where *pempo* is a mere synonym for *apostello*, cf. Matt. x. 40, 'He that receiveth you, receiveth me and he that receiveth me, receiveth him that sent (*apostello*) me'.

Luke and Paul account for four-fifths of the instances of the use in the New Testament of *apostolos* between them. Luke vi. 13 ascribes not only the choice of the Twelve to Jesus but also their description by the title '*apostolos*' to Him, whereas the parallel passage in Mark iii. 14 uses simply the verb, *apostello*, 'And he appointed twelve that they might be with him and that he might send them forth'; Matt. x. 2 also has this title. This may be a 'reading-back' by Luke and Matthew of a title current in the early Church. Luke seems to wish to confine the title of apostle almost exclusively to the Twelve, perhaps because he owed his ecclesiastical beliefs to a form of Jewish-Christianity adopted before he met Paul, cf. Acts i. 2 ff., xii. 17, but he allows the title to be given to Paul and Barnabas as well, Acts xiv. 14; he may have thought that these two owed their title to the rite which preceded their missionary journey; this rite included prayer, fasting, and the imposition of hands, xiii. 3; but even if these details are correct for the age earlier than Luke's date of writing, they may have been part of a special commission. Paul himself would have denied emphatically that he owed his call to be an apostle to men; for Christ had so called him on the Damascus road. It should be observed that Luke does not ascribe this title to Silas.

APPENDIX 1

On the other hand, Paul uses the term *apostolos* in a wider sense than Luke, perhaps because he was conscious that the Eleven with Matthias were not the only apostles commissioned by divine authority and sent out as apostles, cf. Rom. xvi. 7 where Andronicus and Junias are said to be 'of note among the apostles', which probably means that they were reckoned as apostles and not that they were famous in apostolic eyes. But Paul does not use the title indiscriminately. Titus is not called an apostle, though the same verse, 2 Cor. viii. 23, mentions 'apostles of the churches' with reference to others. This phrase probably points to a distinction in Paul's mind between the original Twelve and those appointed as apostles by the community. Though Paul must have seemed to others to belong to the latter and wider class, he insisted that he was on a level with the former, cf. Gal. i. 1, 1 Cor. iv. 9, ix. 1 f., xv. 9, 2 Cor. xi. 5. In 1 Cor. xv. 5-7 he makes a distinction apparently between the Twelve —they were, in fact, the Eleven, but 'the Twelve' was already a semi-technical term—and 'all the apostles' to whom the Risen Lord appeared, cf. 2 Cor. xi. 5, xii. 11, where the language, albeit sarcastic, points to such a distinction.

Paul's sufferings for Christ were inevitably the basis for his claim to be on a par with the Twelve since his call on the road to Damascus. 'False apostles' from Jerusalem could claim that they were apostles in the wider sense and could maintain that Paul was in the same category and as such owed obedience to the Jerusalem authorities. Though the latter had recognized Paul to be the apostle to the Gentiles, Gal. ii. 9, their recognition meant nothing to him compared with God's separation of him for his work, as God had separated Jeremiah, from his mother's womb, Gal. i. 15, Jer. i. 5.

There can be no reasonable doubt, despite Loisy and other Modernist writers, that Jesus chose the Twelve originally that they might be with Him and that He might send them forth to preach and to have authority to cast out devils, Mark iii. 14 f., cf. Gal. i. 16, 1 Cor. i. 17. The term *sheliḥa'* goes back almost certainly to Jesus Himself (Rengstorf, *op. cit.* 38); even if their mission was at first an *ad hoc* one, the Twelve were the ones chosen for the 'putting in' (lit. 'sending forth', *apostello*) of the sickle into the harvest, Mark iv. 29, and they became heirs of the promise to sit on twelve thrones, judging the twelve tribes of Israel, Matt. xix. 28, Luke xxii. 30. After the Resurrection their previous proximity to Jesus guaranteed also a central place for the Twelve among the apostles, just as James' relationship to Jesus eventually guaranteed him the leadership of the mother-church after Peter's departure from Jerusalem, cf. Gal. i. 19, which can be taken to imply that James also was an 'apostle'.

The apostles, the nucleus of which were the Twelve, had a position of supreme authority in the Church, part of which they found it necessary to delegate to the Seven, vi. 2 ff. It was to their teaching and fellowship and the breaking of the bread and the prayers that early believers adhered. At the same time it is true that the lists of the names of the Twelve show a slight divergence, cf. Mark iii. 16 ff., Matt. x. 2 ff., Luke vi. 13 ff., and Acts i. 13 ff. Luke has in both his lists Judas of James instead of Thaddaeus; it seems that during the second half of the first century those remaining of the original Twelve had passed so far beyond the horizon of the evangelists that the exact composition of the apostolic college was forgotten. The localized ministry inevitably took over in course of time the work which the apostles had done. The latter were itinerant and in some cases their sphere of work and their very names were unrecorded.

Where the apostles went and preached with success, they probably left a body of elders to organize the life of the Church, while they themselves moved on, cf. Acts xiv. 23. Paul's words to the elders of Ephesus at Miletus, xx. 17 ff., show that he had delegated to them the task of shepherding the flock over which the Holy Spirit had made them overseers or bishops, *episkopoi*. It may be that this word, *episkopos*, was chosen to denote one side of an apostle's work, viz. the pastoral oversight of a particular flock, cf. xx. 28, 1 Pet. v. 2 ff., ii. 25, and the choice of this term may have been influenced by the Cynic term *episkopōn*, which denoted one function of the *kataskopos* (see above). The word was also used fourteen times in the LXX, usually to translate from the Heb. root *paqad*, to visit, muster, attend to, appoint; cf. notes on xx. 28. While the usual interpretation of Acts xx. 17, 28 is that elders or *presbuteroi* were more or less synonymous with *episcopoi*, it seems that the evidence of 1 Clement is best taken to point to a contrast between the two; at the end of the first century, at Rome at least, Clement seems to distinguish between the *presbuteroi* and the *episcopos* taken from their number; while they were administrative officers, he controlled worship in the Church (J. H. Bernard, *Studia Sacra*, 1917, 285-97). Luke seems to have written before this distinction was clear.

APPENDIX 2

THE CHURCH

(See K. L. Schmidt, *The Church*, trans. by J. R. Coates from *T.W.N.T.* 1938, and his bibliography on pp. xi. f.; to which may be added H. L. Goudge, *The Church of England and Reunion*, 1938; Sir Edwyn Hoskyns and N. Davey, *The Riddle of the N.T.*, 1931, 27-35; E. L. Mascall, *Corpus Christi: Essays on the Church and the Eucharist*, 1953; K. M. Carey, ed., *The Historic Episcopate in the Fullness of the Church*, 1954; H. Riesenfeld, *The Ministry in the N.T.*, in A. Fridrichsen, *The Root of the Vine*, 1953, 96-127.)

FIFTY years ago the book by A. Schweitzer, the English title of which was *The Quest of the Historical Jesus*, 1910, had a wide influence which is still felt, although his main position has been abandoned. To the earlier 'liberal' theologians who believed in evolution and progress and in the slow and gradual growth of the Kingdom of God on earth by the efforts of men, Schweitzer gave a salutary reminder that such was not the N.T. view. Jesus believed in a Kingdom coming in the immediate future. He was Messiah-designate during His ministry and expected the Parousia to come before He died. The disciples were sent out in urgent haste because the Kingdom was just over the horizon. All that He taught was an ethical code for the interval before the Parousia. He went up to die, to force, as it were, the Father's hand that He might bring in the Kingdom—but 'the wheel of Fate would not turn, so Jesus flung Himself upon it and is left there hanging still'. In going to the opposite extreme from the 'liberal' theologians, Schweitzer fastened attention only on the sayings about a future Kingdom, which appear in Matthew's rather than Luke's Gospel and the absurdities of the lengths to which he went are shown by C. W. Emmet's *The Eschatological Question in the Gospels*, 1911. Yet Schweitzer left the impression on the minds of many that Jesus never intended to found a Church and that a doctrine of the Church of God is no part of the original Gospel.

Since Schweitzer wrote his book, two other outstanding works have appeared with the result that the pendulum has swung back. There has been the partly futurist, partly realized eschatology of R. Otto (*The Kingdom of God and the Son of Man*, Eng. Tr., 1938),

283

according to whom Jesus as Son of Man was a Messianic figure present before His future power; as before a thunderstorm the clouds gather and the atmosphere becomes charged with electricity, so the Ministry of Jesus was big with the power (*dunamis*) before it was to break. There has also been the work of C. H. Dodd, especially in his *Apostolic Preaching and its Developments*, 1936, who places all the emphasis on the 'realized eschatology' of the Gospels. The King has come and the Kingdom is over the threshold. The *Eschaton* has been brought within human experience because the Kingdom has in a real sense arrived.

More recently J. Jeremias (*The Parables of Jesus*, Eng. tr., 1954) has developed and yet modified Dodd's theory. Eschatology is in process of realization. The Parables reveal not only great moral and religious truths but also what is happening, so that they compel His hearers to come to a decision about His person and mission. 'The strong man is disarmed, the forces of evil are in retreat, the physician has come to the sick, the lepers are cleansed, the heavy burden of guilt is removed, the lost sheep has been brought home, the door of the Father's House stands open, the poor and the beggars are summoned to the banquet, a master whose grace is undeserved pays his wages in full, a great joy fills all hearts. For He has been manifested whose veiled kingliness shines through every word and through every parable—the Saviour' (*op. cit.* 159).

The mystery, the secret presence of the Kingdom, embodied in Jesus was not discerned by those who saw in Him and His disciples simply a Rabbi who had been a carpenter's son and His followers. Yet there it was. To the Jew, moreover, the new *Qahal* or *ekklesia* or church, the assembled Israel of the coming Age, would be revealed with the Kingdom of God. Granted the presence of the Kingdom, the eschatological assembly follows. The Kingdom of God is not to be identified simply with the Church of God which is a 'sacrament' of the Kingdom, an outward sign and effective symbol of it. It is probably true that the Galilean mind of the first century never envisaged the conception of evolution, and yet it is equally true that in a peasant community all were aware of the organic unity between seed and fruit or harvest. There is an organic connexion between Jesus with His disciples or Jesus and His Church with the Kingdom. As E. Brunner has said, though Jesus did not 'found' the Church in the sense that any part of the 'Church' to-day can claim exclusively the title of being His Church, Jesus did unquestionably gather around Him a circle of disciples 'of such as were specially related to Him and whom He specially equipped and sent out in His service' (*The Misunderstanding of the Church*, Eng. tr. 1952, 22 f.). It speaks volumes for the careful preservation of the Lord's actual words that *ekklesia* is found only twice in the Gospels and there only in Matthew's, xvi. 18 and xviii. 16, in both of which passages there are considerable difficulties, cf. Schmidt, *op. cit.* 35 ff., though the word occurs constantly in Paul's epistles and in Acts. But the idea is there, as in 1 Peter and in Hebrews, though the word is not used with those two exceptions. The King and His Kingdom, the Builder and the building, the Shepherd and His flock, the Gardener and His vineyard, the Bridegroom and His bride are all images which express the same fundamental conception (cf. Riesenfeld, *op. cit.* 106). It may be that Dr. T. W. Manson is right in giving to the phrase 'Son of Man' a corporate meaning (*The Teaching of Jesus*, 1931, 211-36); Dan. vii had used 'one like unto a Son of Man' to mean the kingdom of the saints of the Most High. Jesus may have passed from the thought of Himself as Son of Man to the group around Him with a 'fluidity of reference' to an individual or a community in rapid alternation which is a mark of the Hebrew mind. Much the same may be true also of the conception of the Suffering Servant, unless He left it to His disciples to make that identification of Himself with Deutero-Isaiah's Servant of the Lord. Quite apart from the meaning of these two titles, it can no longer be said that a doctrine of the Church is not an integral part of the Gospel. By choosing and commissioning the Twelve, by bidding His disciples to share in His suffering in order to enter into His glory, by the common meals, especially by the Last Supper, He made the Church proleptically present just as by His saving acts He made the Kingdom of God proleptically present in 'this Age' as opposed to the 'coming Age'.

The 'ends of the world' were come upon the Church, at the end of one Age and also at the beginning of the next, and whatever date for the Parousia is envisaged, the community of the called of the Messiah is there, continuous with the old Israel but different from it. Brunner (*op. cit.* 20 f.) rightly points to the chief differences. The new community was open to all believers, not to members of one race or nation; the ceremonial and cultic laws of ancient Israel and of Judaism were no longer valid, and the civil laws of the O.T. for Israel as a political and national entity were irrelevant. Yet the Church started as a body within Judaism, claiming to know who the Messiah was and that He was risen from the dead, worshipping in the Temple and continuing steadfastly in the breaking of bread, the fellowship, and the prayers.

Although the plural, *ekklesiai*, is used as well as the singular, *ekklesia*, 'mere localisation is not the main point in these cases' (Schmidt, *op. cit.* 6). Acts ix. 31 can refer to an *ekklesia* throughout all Judaea and Galilee and Samaria. 'The relation of the Churches to the Church is like the relation of our local post-offices to the G.P.O. in London', wrote Goudge (*op. cit.* 168). 'There is only one Post Office, private enterprise not being here permitted. But the G.P.O. has its local representatives in the towns and villages, and in dealing with them we are dealing with the department itself.'

The authority and power of the ministry of the Church were the Spirit and the living Word from the first. Both Protestant and Catholic would agree on that. The latter, as Brunner says, would maintain also not merely the word of Christ but the will of Christ and its unifying function in the Church. He sums up (*op. cit.* 31) the 'Catholic' position: 'Jesus sent out His apostles as His personal plenipotentiaries and equipped them not only with the Word but also with personal authority by their direction to give shape and coherence to the growing Church'. (Cf. Appendix 1 and the references to the '*shali*ᵃ*h*' controversy.) So long as a Church observes Brunner's caveats, it can be both Catholic and Protestant, i.e. so long as any claim to 'Apostolic rule' is interpreted solely in terms of service and not of lordship over the flock and so long as *kybernesis* or government is treated, as by Paul, as one of many *charismata* or grace-gifts of the Spirit and not given predominance; and so long as the recognition of the more rigid claims (like those of the Jerusalem apostolate in Paul's day) remains quite voluntary.

THE GIVING OF THE SPIRIT

(See G. W. H. Lampe, *The Seal of the Spirit*, 1951, esp. chs. iv and v; also C. K. Barrett, *The Holy Spirit and the Gospel Tradition*, 1947; W. Bousset, *Kyrios-Christos*, 1913; F. Büchsel, *Der Geist Gottes im N.T.*, 1926; G. Dix, *Theology Occasional Papers* 5, 1936, and *The Theology of Confirmation in relation to Baptism*, 1946; W. F. Flemington, *The N.T. Doctrine of Baptism*, 1948; J. Jeremias, *Z.N.T.W.* xxviii, 1929, 312 ff. (on Jewish proselyte Baptism); H. Leisegang, *Pneuma Hagion*, 1922; T. W. Manson, *J.T.S.* xlviii, 1947, 25 ff.; H. G. Marsh, *The Origin and Significance of N.T. Baptism*, 1941; S. New, *B.C.* v, note xi, cf. K. Lake, note ix and note x; J. E. L. Oulton, *E.T.* lxvi, 1955, 236-40; A. E. J. Rawlinson, *Christian Initiation*, 1947; H. H. Rowley, *Hebrew Union College Annual*, xv, 1940, 313-34 (on Jewish proselyte Baptism); J. C. Sladden, *C.Q.R.* 146, 1948, 220-45; R. R. Williams in Richardson's *T.W.B.B.* 28 f.)

IN *The History of Primitive Christianity* (Eng. tr. i. 50 f.) J. Weiss summarizes the references in Acts to Baptism and adds, 'These isolated narratives clearly show that baptism was not from the outset a necessary mark of the disciples of Jesus. We must infer then that the author has antedated the situation when he introduces baptism as early as the first Pentecost. *When* baptism was introduced, we have no means of knowing. At any rate it marked a step in the direction of a stable organization, which had been lacking at the beginning of the movement. And we cannot fail to note that the author has followed a very natural inclination to date back the later institutions of the church into its period of origin.' Similarly (vol. ii. 623), he questions the assumption that the conferring of the Spirit was regularly connected with baptism and he presses the question which is primary, baptism or the reception of the Spirit (1 Cor. vi. 11, xii. 13). 'Is it perhaps the descent of the Spirit, as in the case of Cornelius (Acts x. 44, 47), or the baptism itself, as in Jerusalem (*ibid.* ii. 38) and in Samaria (*ibid.* viii. 12, 15)? Here is presented a problem which has not been sufficiently studied' (*sic*). He thought that the passages in Acts reflected the development of an idea. (a) The 'oldest' was the enthusiastic and supernatural conception. By sending down His Spirit, God shows His choice of them, Rom. v. 5, Gal. iv. 6, iii. 2. 'Here baptism must follow this heavenly indication'. (b) Acts ii. 38 shows the second step. While it is firmly hoped that he who has been baptized will also receive the Spirit, it is very striking that in a following verse, ii. 41, although it is recorded that three thousand souls were 'added', no further mention is made of the reception of the Spirit. On the other hand, in xix. 5 ff. we see that after Paul laid his hands on the converts, the Holy Spirit came on them and they spoke with tongues. Weiss took this to serve as a transition to the third step. (c) Acts viii. 12, 15 ff., 'according to which baptism which is performed by one of the Seven does not of itself mediate the reception of the Spirit, which is accomplished only by prayer and the laying on of the hands of *the Apostles*'.

This Teutonic and somewhat doctrinaire approach has been rightly criticized. The silence about the baptism of the 120 persons, i. 14-15, was interpreted to fit his point (a). But not only is an argument from silence precarious generally but here particularly so. S. New could sum up her findings, 'Belief in Jesus (or in His Name), baptism, the remission of sins, the laying on of Apostolic hands, and the reception of the Spirit seem to have formed a single complex of associated ideas, any one of which might in any single narrative be either omitted or emphasized' (*B.C.* v. 134). Even granting that they were not baptized, most if not all of them may well have been disciples of the Baptist before becoming Christians and his water-baptism was thought to be completed by the Spirit-baptism of Pentecost for them. His second point (b) is also based on the argument from silence. Did Luke have to repeat each time all the elements in the 'complex'? However, in *B.C.* i. 340, Lake and F. Jackson thought that the reference to baptism in ii. 38 was an interpolation by a redactor familiar with the customs of a later age; but such an alleged redactor would have introduced other elements of the 'complex' also, e.g. the laying on of hands, cf. Flemington, *op. cit.* 43 f.

There is no doubt that the evidence about Baptism given in Acts seems confusing. An older generation of interpreters who found traces of 'written sources' in Acts could ascribe to them the divergent traditions; any 'discrepancies' would be due to Luke's (unintelligent) use of sources. With the reluctance now to accept any theory of written sources for Acts there has come a stress on the single authorship of Luke and on the saying which occurs frequently and which suggests consistency on his part, 'John indeed baptized with water; but you shall be baptized with the Holy Spirit', i. 5, xi. 16, xix. 2-6, cf. xviii. 25 (cf. Oulton, art. cit., 236, and Marsh, *op. cit.* 159-62).

APPENDIX 3

The questions that are asked about this subject are:

(i) Was Jewish proselyte Baptism practised in the first century A.D. and, if so, did it influence John's Baptism?

(ii) Was Christian Baptism a baptism with the Spirit as opposed to John's baptism with water?

(iii) Even if John's disciples were loosely called 'disciples' sometimes, did his baptism fail to convey the Spirit, which was given normally after Baptism in the name of Jesus and the laying-on of hands?

(iv) Were prayer and the laying-on of hands by apostles or those representing them, rather than Baptism itself, the means through which the Spirit was conferred?

(i) A. The evidence for Jewish proselyte baptism early in the first century A.D. is slight but probably sufficient.

(a) *Pesahim*, viii. 8 (H. Danby, *The Mishnah*, 1933, 148 and 431) relates the controversy between the schools of Hillel and Shammai whether proselytes should be baptized at once after circumcision or after waiting for seven days if they were converted on the eve of the Passover.

(b) *Yebamoth*, 46a, refers to a controversy between Rabbi Jehoshua of the school of Hillel and Rabbi Eliezer of the school of Shammai. The former maintained that one who had undergone the bath even if he was not circumcised was a proselyte; the latter maintained that a circumcised man even if he had not undergone the bath was a proselyte. The date of these Rabbis is c. A.D. 90 and like (a), which in its present form belongs to the second century A.D., probably reflects practice current in the middle of the first century.

(c) Epictetus (Arrian, *Dissert. Epict.* ii. 9, 20) contrasts the full Jewish proselyte with the waverer; the former is one who has been baptized or dipped and has made his choice. The date of this passage is c. A.D. 94, but it suggests again that the distinction made was well established by that date.

(d) According to Jeremias (art. cit.) Paul in 1 Cor. x. 1-5 witnesses to proselyte baptism c. A.D. 55. Why did Paul think of the Israelites as baptized in the cloud and sea? It is the Tannaitic Midrash, not the O.T. itself, which taught this. Why? Because it was providing a theological basis for a custom already established of baptizing proselytes. This may then be the earliest reference to this practice.

(e) In the *Sibylline Oracles*, Book iv, dated c. A.D. 80, lines 165 ff. warns pagans in view of the approaching End to bathe the whole body in continually flowing streams and to stretch hands out to heaven and to ask pardon for former deeds. There is no reference here to circumcision.

One may agree then with Rowley (art. cit.) that while it cannot be definitely established by specific evidence, it is probable that a baptismal rite was practised in the case of proselytes to Judaism in the period preceding the destruction of the Temple, and that presumably it was of earlier origin.

B. It is unlikely, however, that Jewish proselyte baptism influenced John. Both baptisms, indeed, were alike in being administered once, as opposed to the constant ceremonial lustrations of the Jews and especially of the Essenes. Again both were by total immersion and in flowing water. Non-Jews could take part in both, even in John's if the implication of Luke iii. 14 is correct. Both involved a new start in a new community in a sense, though John does not seem to have formed an organized community about him. But the differences are more striking than the resemblances; proselyte baptism was apparently a means of ceremonial purification to make a Gentile ritually clean, but John's baptism was marked by a stress on moral reformation. In proselyte baptism the convert baptized himself in front of witnesses; in the Baptist's, John was the minister as the herald of the Messiah. There is a strong eschatological note in his preaching notably absent from proselyte baptism.

(ii) A contrast between John's water-baptism and Christian Spirit-baptism can be inferred from Mark i. 8, Acts i. 5 and xi. 15-16, cf. the accounts of Cornelius' reception of the Spirit in x. 44-8 and xi. 15-18. However, in x. 47 f. Peter's words refer explicitly to water-baptism, and the illapse of the Spirit before baptism in the case of Cornelius is regarded as exceptional. While *B.C.* i. 340 f. suggests that this reference to water-baptism is an interpolation by a redactor in x. 47 f., it is more probable that Cornelius was treated as an adherent of the Jewish synagogue before his conversion and therefore in a sense as a proselyte already, cf. the notes on x. 2 and 4 and van Unnik's theory. The contrast sometimes inferred from the Dominical saying about John's Baptism probably goes back to Jesus Himself and to a time when those who were later to take their part in the New Israel had already undergone John's Baptism and had not yet been baptized with the Spirit at Pentecost. As Oulton puts it (art. cit. 237), 'Since normally in Acts there is the closest connexion between baptism in water and the gift of the Spirit, it is in the highest degree unlikely that in this saying the one is set in opposition to the other'.

APPENDIX 3

The influence of the example of Jesus in being baptized with water can hardly be exaggerated. It was then that God 'anointed Him with Holy Spirit and with power', Acts x. 38, cf. Ignatius, *ad. Eph.* 18, 2 and *ad Smyrn.* 1, 1. The contrast, then, is not between John's water-baptism and Christian Spirit-baptism but between John's water-baptism and Christian water-and-Spirit baptism.

(iii) The word 'disciple' occurs twenty-eight times in the N.T., and the assumption is that it means a Christian disciple each time, cf. *B.C.* v. 376 ff. But one is apt to be misled by Acts into thinking that all early disciples started from Jerusalem and conformed to the ways of the mother-church. Some of the original disciples of the Lord in Galilee, after being perhaps disciples of the Baptist, may well have gone as far afield as Cyprus, Antioch, or even Ephesus. The word 'disciple' may have been used in some primitive circles rather more loosely than in later days. This may account for the use of the word in Acts xix. 1 in a passage where it is clear that John's baptism did not convey the Spirit and that after baptism and the laying-on of hands, the Spirit came on them and they prophesied. It may also help to account for the wording of the curious passage in xviii. 24-8 where the learned Jew, Apollos, mighty in the scriptures and fervent in spirit (or in the Spirit) was converted but where no mention of his baptism occurs. This, however, may be implied by the words, 'But when Priscilla and Aquila heard him, they took him unto them and expounded unto him the way of God more carefully'. In xix. 2 Paul's question, 'Did you receive the Holy Spirit when you made your act of faith?' implies that, as so often, a definite single act of faith like being baptized was performed after 'hearing and believing'. To 'hear the word' and to 'believe', especially where 'believe' is in the aorist tense, may well imply baptism, cf. ii. 37 f., 41, viii. 12 f., 35 f., xvi. 14-16, 32 f., xviii. 8. The whole gist of the passage xix. 1 ff. demands an affirmative answer to (iii).

(iv) The answer to the fourth question is in the negative, despite the pleas of Dix and others. In view of Dr. Lampe's definitive treatment, one is compelled to accept his conclusion that 'we find there is no precedent in the N.T., nor any clear testimony in the early Fathers, for the view that in the Christian dispensation God's people are sealed as His own possession by undergoing an outward and visible ceremony, other than Baptism in water'. He rejects as unscriptural the view advanced by Fr. L. S. Thornton (*Confirmation to-day*, p. 9) that 'the promise of the Spirit, which according to St. Peter's Pentecostal sermon the ascended Christ "received from the

Father", is implanted for us only when through the apostolic ministry (i.e. through the Bishop in confirmation) we are sealed by the same Spirit "unto the day of redemption", and he adds that such a theory implies that no unconfirmed person is a true Christian. On the contrary, in the N.T. the "seal" is the inward mark or stamp of the indwelling Spirit of God which is received by the convert who is justified by faith in Christ and through Baptism is sacramentally made a partaker of Him in His death and Resurrection' (Lampe, *op. cit.* 306 f.) Incorporation into Christ or His Church was by baptism in(to) His name, the name denoting His possession, cf. Jer. viii. 10. For those who stood outside the apostolic ranks and who could not claim to have seen the Lord, Baptism was an effective piece of 'realised eschatology', when they were confronted by the Lord and made one with Him in His dying and rising again as they descended into the waters and rose from them, cf. Rom. vi. (Cf. Flemington, *op. cit.* 46 f.) To be incorporated thus into Christ meant to be made partaker of His Spirit, the pledge or first-instalment of all that would be given in the future Kingdom or Church triumphant.

At the same time the laying-on of hands was a natural symbol to use in appointing anyone to office, as in the consecration of kings in ancient Rome or in the appointment by Rabbis of other Rabbis or indeed in appointing to any office, cf. Num. xxvii. 18, 23 and Deut. xxxiv. 9, Acts vi. 6 (of the Seven); or in the offering of a sacrifice, e.g. Exod. xxix. 10, whether the 'purity' of the victim cleansed the offerer or the impurity of the latter was borne away by the victim; or in conferring a blessing, cf. Gen. xlviii. 13 f., or in handing on a portion of what was conceived in primitive thought as a tenuous fluid, the Spirit, cf. Deut. xxxiv. 9, again where Moses gave Joshua the spirit of wisdom. In the N.T. it was a symbol used fittingly by Jesus when He healed the sick, Mark v. 23, or blessed children, Mark x. 13 ff. In the Bible this symbol denotes the incorporation of the person on whom the hands are laid into the community or into office in the community or the imparting by the Spirit-filled community of the power to undertake a special task, cf. on xiii. 3. Both Lampe and Oulton rightly emphasize that Luke's purpose is to delineate the progress of a *missionary* Church. As the former says (*op. cit.* 69 f.) of the imposition of hands on the Samaritan converts, 'An unprecedented situation demanded quite exceptional methods', and he maintains that this symbol here was a token of fellowship and solidarity of the converts with the Church; and only in the second place was it an effective symbol of the gift of the Spirit. The evangelization of

APPENDIX 3

Samaria was a turning-point in the Church's march; here a new base camp was to be set up from which the Church could advance again upon the world. What could be more fitting than for the apostles themselves to use this symbol as a confirmation of the baptisms in Samaria rather than of the baptized? Cf. Hort, *The Christian Ecclesia*, 54 f., cited by Oulton, art. cit., 238.

Though it is true to say, as Lampe does (*op. cit.* 65), that Luke has an insufficient appreciation of the Spirit as the inner principle of the ordinary believer's life in Christ and that for Luke the Spirit is essentially the power of guiding the missionary expansion of the Church and assisting the progress of the Gospel by signs, prophesyings, and speaking with tongues, yet it is easy to exaggerate the primitive, almost Old Testament, conception of the Spirit in Acts and to imagine that Luke thought of the Spirit's coming on the Church simply as a series of illapses on special occasions or with Bousset to suggest that the idea of the Spirit in Acts is of an impersonal power or force working apart from Christ, it being left to Paul to achieve a synthesis between the traditional O.T. and early Jewish-Christian belief and his own Christ-mysticism, which resulted in the Spirit being recognized as the all-important principle of life 'in Christ'. For from the first the Church is a Spirit-filled body, the unity of which rested on something deeper than sporadic illapses, and the love, peace, and joy of which were the harvest of Spirit. Without the Spirit, the fellowship and common life in the Body of Christ would have been an impossibility, cf. Acts vi. 5, 8, vii. 55 xi. 24, and xiii. 52.

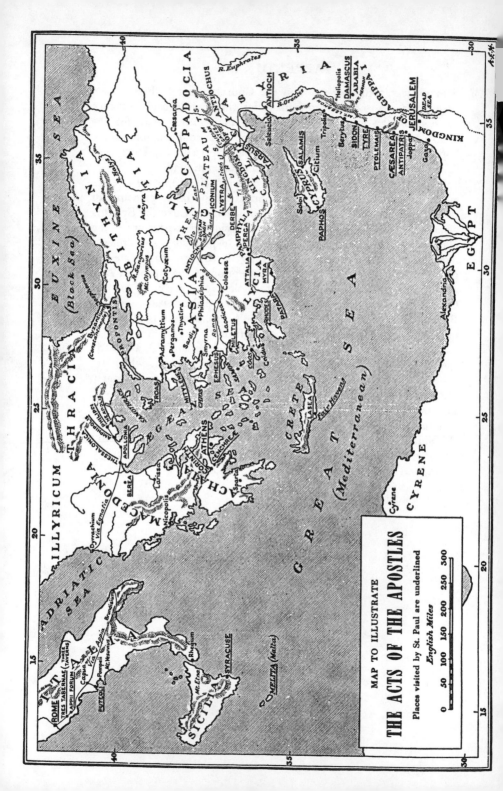

MAP TO ILLUSTRATE

THE ACTS OF THE APOSTLES

Places visited by St. Paul are underlined

English Miles

0   50   100 150 200 250 300

INDEX OF SUBJECTS

INDEX OF PROPER NAMES

INDEX OF PROPER NAMES